Catullus
The Poems

Catullus
The Poems

EDITED WITH
INTRODUCTION, REVISED TEXT
AND COMMENTARY

by

KENNETH QUINN

Professor of Classics
University College Toronto

Second Edition

ST MARTIN'S PRESS

First edition 1970
Second edition 1973
Reprinted 1976, 1979, 1980, 1981, 1982, 1985
1987, 1988

Published by
MACMILLAN EDUCATION LTD
Houndmills, Basingstoke, Hampshire RG21 2XS
and London
Companies and representatives
throughout the world

Printed in Hong Kong

Library of Congress Catalog Card No. 7694751

ISBN 0—333—01787—0

TO GAMBY

Contents

Preface

THIS edition is intended to provide a complete text of Catullus and a complete commentary of a size and along lines suited to the needs of sixth-formers and university students.

A list is given in the Introduction, Section 5, of some sixty cases where the text differs significantly from Sir Roger Mynors's Oxford text (revised impression, 1967). In about half of these I have returned to the reading of the primary MSS. (e.g. 62. 9 *uisere*, 64. 14 *feri*). The rest are readings or conjectures not accepted by Mynors (e.g. 14. 16 *salse*, 63. 54 *opaca*, 64. 148 *meminere*), or proposed since Mynors's text was first published in 1958 (e.g. 64. 254 *cui Thyades*); some (e.g. 6. 12 *nam nil stupra ualet* or 29. 23 *urbis o piissimi*) have been adopted very much as a pis-aller, preferable only to nonsense. Once or twice a change in punctuation has meant a significant change in the syntactical structure (e.g. 43. 5). Notes on the text are limited to important points and are mostly printed in square brackets, so that those who choose can steer clear of them; for the rest the student of Catullus is well served by Mynors's *apparatus* and the excellent facsimile of the Oxford manuscript published in the series *Codices Graeci et Latini* by Messrs A. W. Sijthoff of Leyden in 1966.

The commentary is aimed at a fairly broad spectrum of consultants. I have not hesitated to explain simple points where they might trip up the less experienced. Nor have I been held back from going into some things more fully by the thought that what I said might be beyond the needs or over the heads of some who would use the book. On all matters of detail I have tried to be brief, in order to concentrate on what I took to be the main task of a commentator on Catullus with 500 years of printed texts and commentaries behind him: to reconstruct, by piecing together the data provided by the text or deducible from the text as a plausible, necessary deduction, the hypothesis upon which each poem rests. My object has been to discuss each poem as a structural and poetic whole that made the kind of sense a poem can be expected to make to the attentive, responsive reader. Bibliographies listing important articles, etc., follow the commentaries on individual poems.

I should like to express my thanks to Nan Michels, who first put the idea in my head that I might write a commentary on Catullus; to Ernst Badian, Frank Copley, George Goold, John Sharwood Smith and Ronald Syme, who in various ways helped to make it better; above all to Guy Lee for advice, assistance and encouragement throughout.

Toronto, Easter, 1970   K.Q.

In this second edition the bibliographies have been revised and brought up to date and an Index has been added.

Toronto, January, 1973   K.Q.

Introduction

THE modern world might easily have had to content itself with one poem of Catullus and a score or so of fragments (mostly single lines or couplets) quoted by other writers.[1] The poem numbered 62 in our texts (the second marriage hymn) is preserved in a ninth-century anthology of Latin poetry, the manuscript of which subsequently came into the possession of the French historian and politician Jacques de Thou (1553–1617), whence its modern name, the *codex Thuaneus* (**T**). The rest we owe to a single manuscript (**V**). It came to light in Verona towards the end of the thirteenth century — and then disappeared again during the following century. Fortunately it had been copied at least twice. One copy (**O**) has survived and is now in the Bodleian Library at Oxford. The second (usually referred to as **X**) has disappeared, but we possess two copies made from it. One (**G**) is dated 1375; it was once in the Abbey of St-Germain-des-Prés (whence its name, the *Sangermanensis*), and is now in the Bibliothèque nationale. The other (**R**) can hardly be much later; it also disappeared (as the result of a cataloguer's mistake in the Vatican library), but was found again in 1896 by the American scholar W. G. Hale. From these three copies of the Verona manuscript (**O**, **G** and **R**) all other manuscripts of Catullus (some hundred and twenty) and all printed editions are believed to derive.[2]

Yet in antiquity Catullus was among the most read
and the most talked about of Roman poets. That
Virgil had studied the poems as one craftsman studies
the work of another is clear from the frequent echoes
in his own poetry, and from the fact that they are
often far from obvious echoes (e.g. the echo of 66. 39
in *Aeneid* 6. 460, or the echo of 68. 107–8 in *Aeneid* 3.
421–2). Horace also knew Catullus well, despite the
disparaging tone of his one reference to him (*S.* 1. 10.
19): his Europa, for example, (*Carm.* 3. 27) owes much
to Catullus' Ariadne. Propertius refers to Catullus
with the respect one owes a master: his poetry has
made Lesbia better known, he says, than Helen herself
(2. 34. 88 *Lesbia quis ipsa notior est Helena*). Ovid speaks
of him in the same breath as Virgil (*Am.* 3. 15. 7
Mantua Vergilio gaudet, Verona Catullo). Pliny the
Younger and Martial imitated him.

1 *CATULLUS* ... *the life and writings of Catullus,*
that imbroglio of problems where dogma
and ingenuity have their habitation,
where argument moves in circles, and no
new passage in or out. — Ronald
Syme, *Classica et Mediaevalia* 17
(1956) 131.

WHAT do we know about the author of these poems?
Very little. His full name, pretty certainly, was *Gaius*
Valerius Catullus — the praenomen Quintus found in
some MSS. can be safely rejected; the cognomen is
possibly a diminutive of Cato. His father seems to have

been an important citizen of Verona (then part of Cisalpine Gaul), and still alive in the time of Caesar's proconsulship (see Suetonius, *Jul.* 73, quoted on Poem 57; cf. Poems 43; 67; 68. 27–35; and 100). Catullus himself lived in Rome (see especially 68. 34–5), though he seems to have returned to Verona more than once. Poems 67 and 68 seem to have been written in Verona before the year in Bithynia; Poem 31 suggests he returned there after the year in Bithynia; cf. Poem 35. The reconciliation with Caesar (see on Poem 57) presumably took place in Verona — either before or after Bithynia.[3]

In Rome Catullus became one of a group of poets, often referred to in modern times as the *neoteroi* or the *poetae noui*. Both terms are taken from Cicero (*Att.* 7. 2. 1 and *Orat.* 161). The former passage can perhaps count as evidence for the existence of a school, the latter scarcely. But if there was not a school, there was at any rate a group of friends who shared ideas about poetry and about life. Its other prominent members were the orator Licinius Calvus (see on Poem 50) and the minor politician Helvius Cinna (see on Poem 95), and perhaps the poetaster Furius Bibaculus, though it is by no means certain that he is the Furius we meet in Catullus (see on Poem 23). Only small crumbs of their verse survive, preserved by later writers, usually grammarians, but this might easily have happened with Catullus himself.

About Catullus' *writing-life* three reasonably safe assumptions can be drawn.

(1) Four poems (Poems 11, 29, 55, and 113), possibly Poems 45 and 53, can be assigned, on the

basis of references in the text, to the period 55–54 B.C.
Since one of these (Poem 11) is pretty clearly a final
poem to Lesbia (a dismissal, intended to recall Poem
51, though not *necessarily* of course the last poem
Catullus wrote to her), we can probably fix 54 B.C.
as the *terminus ad quem* for some collection made
by Catullus himself — possibly that introduced by
Poem 1. Certainly no poem can be dated later than
54 B.C.

(2) Assuming Lesbia was Clodia (see next Section),
the *terminus a quo* is fixed by Poem 83, which requires
Lesbia to have a husband; Clodia's husband, Metellus,
is probably also the *ille* of Poem 51 (cf. 68. 143–8 and
see on 68. 29). We know that Metellus was dead by
about March 59 B.C.

(3) It seems clear from Poems 10 and 28 that
Catullus went to Bithynia as a member of the *cohors
praetoria* of C. Memmius. Memmius' term as governor
probably ran from the spring of 57 B.C. to the spring of
56 B.C. Poem 46 suggests that Catullus travelled out to
Bithynia with the rest of the *cohors* and makes it fairly
certain that he returned at the same time as the rest
the following spring.

These facts, and the assumptions which can be
based on them when they are examined along with
the poems quoted above, suggest a writing-life extend-
ing from about 61–60 B.C. to about 54 B.C., and
divided into two parts by the year spent in Bithynia.
Catullus is unlikely to have been less than twenty-one
when he went to Bithynia;[4] as far as service with the
cohors was concerned he could easily have been ten
years older than that, but it seems a reasonable

inference from 68. 15–20 (written, probably, just
before Bithynia) that he was still quite a young man.
If he were twenty-five when he left for Bithynia, that
would make him about twenty-one or twenty-two
when the affair with Lesbia began; if he died in 54 B.C.
(as is commonly assumed, since no poem can be dated
later than that year), he would then have been in his
twenty-eighth or twenty-ninth year at the time of his
death. He is usually assumed to have been a year or
two older, but the grounds for the assumption are
shaky.[5]

2 *LESBIA*   *sic sua lasciuo cantata est saepe Catullo*
                   femina, cui falsum Lesbia nomen erat.
                   OVID, *Tr.* 2. 427–8.

SOME twenty-six poems arise more or less directly out
of the poet's liaison with the woman he called Lesbia.
Catullus' contemporaries seem to have taken it for
granted that the poems reflected an actual affair.
Most likely, he chose the name Lesbia as an innocent-
sounding substitute for his mistress's real name in the
first poem he addressed to her — a version of Sappho:
she could read between the lines and substitute her
own name if she chose (see on Poem 51). The name
occurs in only thirteen poems, but we are clearly
expected to take along with these at least another
dozen poems, in which the poet's mistress is referred
to as *mea puella* (in Poem 8 simply *puella*) or *mulier mea*
(Poem 70), or merely as *illa* (Poem 76). One poem
(Poem 85) seems to avoid reference to her altogether.

When we talk about the Lesbia poems, then, we mean the following (poems in which the name Lesbia occurs are marked with an asterisk):

2	3	5*	7*	8	11	13
36	37	43*	51*	58*	68	70
72*	75*	76	79*	83*	85	86*
87*	92*	104	107*	109		

Some might reject the inclusion of one or two of these (e.g. Poems 13 and 36), or make additions to the list (e.g. Poems 42, 82, 91). On the other hand Poems 43 and 86, though they name Lesbia, name her only in passing.

The fact is, the Lesbia poems cannot be isolated from the rest. The majority of the Lesbia poems form none the less a tightly coherent group: they create the illusion, as has been well said, of fragments in a dramatic continuum;[6] though separated by poems often on quite dissimilar themes, they represent a monologue, repeatedly resumed, in which the poet is always the speaker — and the addressee his mistress, a friend or friends, the world at large, or himself — and in which the same themes keep recurring with an insistence that sometimes approaches obsession. Nothing, for example, that we can point to in the text connects Poem 85 with the Lesbia affair. Yet who can doubt that it belongs — or deny that it gains in strength and poignancy from our recognition of this? The order of the poems is clearly not chronological (so that we can never do more than guess the actual circumstances) but it is almost certainly not accidental.

Lesbia is thought to be one of the best known of all Roman women, the infamous Clodia, elder sister of

P. Clodius Pulcher, and wife of Q. Caecilius Metellus
Celer (governor of Cisalpine Gaul in 62–61 B.C. and
consul in 60 B.C.) — the woman Cicero calls βοῶπις
(= 'Juno') in his letters to Atticus (2. 9. 1; 12. 2; 14.
1; 22. 5; 23. 3), and whom he made the butt of his
biting ridicule when he defended her ex-lover, M.
Caelius Rufus, in April 56 B.C., accused (among other
charges) of attempting to poison her. In modern times
the identification has often been made the basis of
quite irresponsible fantasies on the part of Catullus'
Romantic biographers.[7] It remains none the less
extremely probable. The evidence is as follows:

(1) Apuleius (*Apology* 10), defending his own use of
·pseudonyms, cites a list of famous cases from literature:

> eadem igitur opera accusent C. Catullum, quod
> Lesbiam pro Clodia nominarit, et Ticidam similiter,
> quod quae Metella erat Perillam scripserit, et
> Propertium, qui Cunthiam dicat, Hostiam dis-
> simulet, et Tibullum, quod ei sit Plania in animo,
> Delia in uorsu.

Apuleius, who is clearly familiar with Catullus' poetry
(he quotes him a couple of times in the course of his
defence), talks as though the real identity of Lesbia
were common knowledge in his day (the trial took
place about 158 A.D.); he does not say *which* Clodia
(the identification with Clodia Metelli seems to have
been first made by the Italian humanist Petrus
Victorius, in the sixteenth century); nor can we tell
whether the identification rested on any continuous
tradition, or was just a shrewd guess based on the
poems themselves.

(2) The strongest evidence is provided by Poem 79.
Almost certainly the reference is to the incestuous
relationship — common gossip at the time — between
Clodia and her brother. (See on Poem 79.) Indeed it
seems not unlikely that one purpose of these lines was
to put the name Lesbia in a context that left no doubt
who she was. Poem 79 also makes very improbable the
suggestion sometimes advanced that the Clodia
meant by Apuleius was a sister of Clodia Metelli.

(3) In the absence of other evidence nothing of
course could be argued from the fact that Metellus had
been governor of Cisalpine Gaul. The picture of the
young Catullus, fresh in Rome from Verona (possibly
Metellus' headquarters in Cisalpine Gaul), seeking
out the hospitality of the former governor, has proved
irresistible to many biographers. But it is not wholly
devoid of plausibility.

If Lesbia was Clodia, the wife of Metellus, it follows
that Catullus was supplanted as Clodia's *amant en titre*
by Caelius Rufus, probably in 59 B.C. — perhaps
when Catullus returned to Verona following the death
of his brother (Poem 68. 19–35). Clodia, freshly
widowed (Metellus had died suddenly early the same
year) and then about thirty-six, was leading, even if
we believe only the half of what Cicero says, a very gay
life indeed. When Catullus returned from Bithynia the
two had already parted; indeed Catullus must have
returned not long after Cicero had successfully defend-
ed Caelius against the prosecution of which he insists
Clodia was the prime instigator. That a resumption of
the affair was talked of, or actually took place, seems a
reasonable construction to put upon Poems 109 and

107 respectively, but there is no way of dating these poems. Poem 11 must be assigned to late 55 or early 54 B.C. But Poem 11 is an *open* dismissal, written as a counterpart to Poem 51. It represents the last word spoken publicly. The actual affair could easily have petered out long before.

3 THE CAELIUS AND
THE RUFUS POEMS

IF LESBIA was Clodia, it is tempting to assume that Poem 58, addressed to a man called Caelius, is Catullus' bitterly ironical public statement to Caelius Rufus of what Catullus and he knew to be the sordid truth about the woman who had discarded them both. It seems only natural that the Caelius of Poem 100 should be the same man, though Catullus speaks of him as if he were a fellow Veronese (nothing we know of the historical Caelius connects him with Verona).[8] Whether the Rufus of Poems 69 (and presumably 71) and 77 is Clodia's lover we cannot tell.

If the rollicking persiflage of Poems 69, 71, and 100 seems remote from both the anguished reproaches of Poem 77 and the bitter irony of Poem 58, that need not mean more than that the five poems were written at different times under very different circumstances.

To add to our exasperation, only one of the five (Poem 77) makes any reference to a betrayal of Catullus by his friend — unless we are to read this into Poem 71 (the text of which is almost certainly corrupt). On the other hand Poem 91 plainly accuses

Gellius, one of Catullus' two principal *bêtes noires* (the other is Mamurra) of stealing Lesbia from Catullus.

4 *THE COLLECTION*

As USUALLY printed, the collection comprises 113 poems[9]; 2b, 14b, 58b, 78b, and 95b are so designated in order to preserve the traditional numbering, though some, if not all of these, are better taken as separate fragments. The poems fall easily into three groups.

(1) The first group (Poems 1–60), usually referred to as *the polymetric poems*, comprises some 57–60 separate poems or fragments.[10] Forty of these, if we adopt the traditional numbering, are written in hendecasyllabics, 8 in limping iambics, 2 in sapphic stanzas, the remainder (Poems 4, 17, 25, 29, 30, 34, and 52) in a variety of metres.

(2) The second group (Poems 61–8), usually referred to as *the long poems*, comprises 7 poems of varying length (the longest has 408 lines, the shortest 48 lines) and a short introduction (24 lines) to Poem 66 (numbered separately as Poem 65). Poem 61 is in glyconic stanzas, Poems 62 and 64 in dactylic hexameters, Poem 63 in galliambics, and Poems 65–8 in elegiac couplets.

(3)· The third group (Poems 69–116), usually referred to as *the elegiac fragments*, is made up, like the first group, of short poems; the longest (Poem 76) has 26 lines, the majority are less than 10 lines in length. They represent an extraordinarily interesting experiment: traditional qualities of epigram, such as ingenuity and precision of statement and ironical juxtaposition of opposed statements, are employed in the expression of complex ideas and feelings quite beyond the traditional range of epigram.

The first poem in the collection is an introductory poem, but it can hardly have been written to introduce the collection as it now stands. Poem 1 speaks of a single volume whose slick appearance we are clearly intended to regard as betokening its contents. But the poems make up something like 2300 lines — nearly half as long again as the longest ancient *liber* known to us. Moreover Poem 14b looks rather like a fragment from a separate introduction.

To suppose the original collection did not include the long poems, as some suggest, on the grounds that they are not *nugae*, is pretty surely to take too literally the ironical self-depreciation which Catullus considered appropriate to an introductory poem and a dedication. In any case, that would still leave two groups (the polymetric poems, and the elegiac fragments), not one. On internal grounds only, the most likely (but quite unprovable) hypothesis is that Poems 1–60 were published by Catullus, whereas Poems 69–116 (a scrappier and shorter collection) are the work of somebody who gathered together complete poems and fragments. There can be no question that Poems 1–60 represent a haphazard collection of all the short poems — except for those in elegiacs — that Catullus was known to have written: if the arrangement is the work of a later editor, he was an intelligent and sophisticated one. The curious impression of unity given by 69–116 could perhaps be the result of Catullus' continuing passionate, almost obsessive, concern with a dominant theme — what went wrong between him and Lesbia? As for the long poems, which, if any, were published in Catullus' lifetime seems anybody's guess.

The fact that the arrangement in both 1–60 and 69–116 is clearly not chronological need not mean more than that Catullus went to some pains to jumble chronology — perhaps hoping that we would read his poems as poetry rather than autobiography.[11] But whether Catullus wished it or not, the collection records a way of life: the details may be missing or confused, but the picture is clear. The words Cicero used of Philodemus' poems about Piso could, with very little adaptation, be applied to the poems of Catullus (*Pis.* 70–1):

> poema porro facit ita festiuum, ita concinnum, ita elegans, nihil ut fieri possit argutius. . . . ita multa ad istum de isto quoque scripsit ut omnis hominis libidines, omnia stupra, omnia cenarum genera conuiuiorumque, adulteria denique eius delicatissimis uersibus expresserit, in quibus si qui uelit possit istius tamquam in speculo uitam intueri.

5 *TEXT*[12]

THE PAST hundred and fifty years have witnessed a fundamental reappraisal of the manuscript tradition.

Karl Lachmann, the first modern editor to deal systematically with textual problems, had at his disposal only MSS. dating from the fifteenth century. During the seventy years following the publication of

Lachmann's edition in 1829, these were displaced from their position of authority by three fourteenth-century MSS. Attention was first drawn to the importance of **G** by L. Schwabe (*Quaestiones catullianae* [1862]); this was followed by Baehrens's recognition (in his *Analecta Catulliana* [1874]) of the value of **O** (acquired by the Bodleian Library in 1817, but first brought to the attention of scholars by Ellis in 1867), and then by Hale's rediscovery of **R** in 1896. A heated and protracted controversy ensued regarding the relative importance of the fifteenth-century MSS., especially the weight to be attached to **M** (= Mynors's m) and **D**;[13] barring fresh discoveries, the controversy seems to have been settled by Mynors's edition of 1958, which attributes primary importance to **O**, and places **R** ('Parisini frater, ut ita dicam') equal to **G** and before **M** or **D**.[14]

The resultant gains have been modest. **O**, **G** and **R** abound in trivial errors. They frequently offer a reading that is unmetrical or meaningless, or both; whole lines (34. 3, 51. 8, 61. 91, 65. 9, and 68. 47), even groups of lines (after 61. 78 and 107) are occasionally omitted, and there are probably other lacunae whose presence cannot be demonstrated objectively by breaks in the metrical structure. In addition, the division between individual poems is indicated only in haphazard fashion. All that can be said by way of consolation is that the scribes at any rate took pains to stick to what they had before them – as the writer of **G** says in self-defence:

   tu lector quicumque ad cuius manus hic libellus

obuenerit, scriptori da ueniam si tibi corruptus
uidebitur, quoniam a corruptissimo exemplari
transcripsit; non enim quodpiam aliud extabat,
unde posset libelli huius habere copiam exemplandi.

Modern editors depart from the reading of the
primary MSS., and the alternative readings recorded
in these by the original scribes, in something like 800
cases. More than a hundred of these are corrections
added by a later hand, or hands, in **R** and **G**
(= Mynors's r and g), or contained in a fifteenth-
century copy of **R** (= Mynors's m); these are usually
classified as emendations, though it is possible that
some derive from MSS. older than, or independent of,
V but now lost. About 300 more are found in various
fifteenth-century MSS. (Mynors's α to θ) and a
further 200 or more are due to Renaissance editors.
The remainder are corrections proposed by scholars
since the sixteenth century.

Naturally the more trivial errors tended to be the
first to be removed, while the most desperate textual
surgery was left in the main to nineteenth-century
hands (e.g. 63. 5, though even here the first step had
been taken by Avanzi at the beginning of the sixteenth
century). A glance, however, at an *apparatus criticus*
shows how heavy our debt is to the ingenuity and
feeling for Latin of Renaissance humanists. A few
passages remain where we must apparently despair of
recovering what Catullus wrote (e.g. 55. 9–12, 68.
155–8) and some others where the received text is at
best suspect (e.g. 1. 9), as well as a much larger
number of cases (between fifty and a hundred) where

editors continue to be divided on the need to emend
(e.g. 11. 11), or on the choice between variant read-
ings or rival conjectures (e.g. 64. 11).

The following is a list of passages where the text
printed differs from that of Mynors's Oxford text
(revised edition 1967). Changes involving only
punctuation or minor changes in spelling are not
included.

		Mynors OCT	*This edition*	*Source*
5.	12	†nam inista preualet†	nam nil stupra ualet	Scaliger & Haupt
11.	11	horrible aequor	horribilesque	V
14.	16	false	salse	G
.	11	me me†	meus iam	Parma edition
2.	5	palimpseston	palimpsesto	— o in V
9.	5	†mulier aries†	Murcia arbitros	Putnam & MacKay
9.	23	†urbis opulentissime†	urbis o piissimi	Lachmann & Haupt
5.	10	iocose	iocosis	Riese
9.	11	pinguis	parcus	V
2.	4	nostra	uestra	V
2.	14	potes	potest	Late MS.
4.	17	ulta	ultu'	Muret
4.	2	†et erit†	Hirri	Hermes
		rustice	rustica	Turnebus
4.	5	Sufficio	Fufidio	Bickel
5.	8	sereno	serenas	Late MS.
7.	9	socii	socii et	V
8b.	2-3	(Transposed in Mynors; printed here as in MSS.)		
1.	215-16	insciis . . . omnibus	insciens . . . obuiis	V & Pleitner

62. 9	uincere	uisere	TV
62. 58b	(This line, not found in MSS., is omitted here.)		
63. 54	omnia	opaca	Müller
64. 11	prima ... Amphitriten	proram ... Amphitrite	O & correctio in O
64. 14	freti	feri	V
64. 23b	iter ⟨um ...	iter ⟨um, saluete, bonarum⟩	Peerlkamp
64. 37	Pharsalum	Pharsaliam	V
64. 89	praecingunt	progignunt	Late MS.
64. 148	metuere	meminere	Czwalina
64. 174	Cretam	Creta	O
64. 184	colitur sola insula	litus, sola insula,	V
64. 243	infecti	inflati	V
64. 254	quae tum alacres	cui Thyades	O. Skutsch
64. 273	leuiterque	lenique	Late MS.
64. 395	Amarunsia	Ramnusia	Veneta editio
66. 7	lumine	limine	Baehrens
66. 21	et	at	GR
66. 58	Canopitis	Canopeis	Fordyce
66. 59	†hi dii uen ibi†	inde Venus	Postgate
	lumine	limine	Late MS.
66. 78	uilia	milia	V
66. 93	corruerint	cur iterent	V
67. 20	attigerit	attigerat	Late MS.
68. 11	Mani	Malli	Late MS. (mali V)
68. 27	Catullo	Catulle	V
68. 29	tepefactet	tepefactat	Correction in R
68. 30	Mani	Malli	See on 68. 11
68. 63	ac	hic	GR
68. 156	⟨ipsa⟩ in qua	in qua ⟨nos⟩	Late MS.
68. 158	bona	bono	V
76. 10	iam te cur	cur te iam	V

90. 5	gratus	gnatus	V
97. 5	hoc	os	Late MS. &
			Froehlich
99. 8	abstersisti omnibus	abstersti mollibus	O & A. G. Lee
00. 6	ex igni est	est igni tum	Palmer
12. 1	quin	qui	Scaliger
12. 2	te scindat	descendit	V
15. 5	saltusque paludesque	altasque paludes	Late MS.
16. 7	†amitha	acta	Baehrens

6 *STYLE*

THE LATIN of Catullus' short poems stands halfway
between that of Plautus and that of the *Satires* of
Horace. This is the Latin of conversation, improved
upon: a literary idiom that preserves the illusion of the
poet's ordinary speaking voice. As a distinct poetic
language it has not fully assumed its final shape in
Catullus: words, forms and constructions which the
written Latin of the Augustan age was to discard still
survive, usually as alternatives to their more familiar
classical counterparts. Full maturity and precision of
expression in this style is not reached till we come to
Horace's *Epistles*. The Latin of the long poems
naturally stands closer to the traditional high style of
epic and tragedy, but colloquialism and verbal irony
find their place here, too.

The extent to which Catullus was able to achieve
mastery of his chosen style varies. The polymetric
poems are characterized by the same nonchalant
elegance which we find in Cicero's letters to his more
intimate friends. Structurally they are a good deal

more tightly organized. Balanced understatement is the keynote, passing easily from colloquialism to angry insult with devastating directness, or to the obsessive repetition of phrases which seem to change in meaning each time they recur; or sliding off with equal assurance into succinctly evocative imagery. The style of the elegiac fragments is drier: the main tool here is logic rather than imagery; the dominant mood, a characteristically Roman determination to get things straight — or, on less important occasions, to expose a fool to ridicule by the ironic use of antithesis and juxtaposition. In the long poems, the range is from the extraordinarily poignant virtuosity of Poem 63 to that strange mixture of styles, Poem 68, where the most exciting imagery of the whole collection is embedded in a structure that seems at times almost perversely prosaic.

7 *MORPHOLOGY*

THE FOLLOWING are the more notable non-classical forms:

Verbs Short perfects: 99. 8 *abstersti*, 91. 9 *duxti*, 66. 21 *luxti*, 14. 14 *misti*, 110. 3 *promisti*, 77. 3 *subrepsti*, and 66. 30 *tristi*. Passive infinitives in -*ier*: 61. 42 *citarier*, 61. 65 etc. *compararier*, 68. 141 *componier*, and 61. 68 *nitier*. Imperfects without -*e*-: 84. 8 *audibant*, 64. 319 *custodibant*, and 68. 85 *scibant*. Miscellaneous by-forms such as 34. 8 *deposiuit*, 63. 5 *deuolsit*, 36. 16 etc. *face*, 17. 24 etc. *pote* and 65. 3 etc. *potis*, 44. 19 *recepso*, 61. 53 *solŭunt* (cf. 95. 6 *peruolŭent* and probably 64. 350 *solŭent*), 63. 47 *tetulit*, 8. 9 etc. *uolt*.

Nouns   A few old-fashioned forms are found: 55. 13 *labōs*, 64. 394 *Mauors*, 66. 91 *unguinis*. Words like 1. 6 *aeuum*, 3. 3 *mortuus* etc. should perhaps be written *aeuom*, *mortuos* etc., even where the MSS. give the usual forms in -*u*- (cf. 53. 3 *Caluos*, 66. 54 *equos*).

Adverbs   64. 265 *amplifice*, 63. 49 *miseriter*, 39. 14 etc. *puriter*.

Pronouns   29. 15 *alid*, 66. 28 *alis*, 63. 46 etc. *quis* (= *quibus*), 17. 17 *uni* (genitive; cf. 5. 3 *unius*).

Adjectives   Forms like 44. 10 *Sestianus* and 14. 3 *Vatiniano* (in place of the genitive 44. 19 *Sesti* etc.) are fairly common; see on 64. 1 *Peliaco*.

Probably some of these forms are conscious archaisms, used for literary effect; the majority, however, seem to be colloquial by-forms, or simply old-fashioned forms which the literary language of the next generation discarded. No doubt here and there a by-form which was metrically convenient has been preferred to the more common form.[15]

8 *VOCABULARY*

IN HIS choice of words Catullus follows chiefly the everyday written Latin of his time, a fairly complete picture of which can be obtained from Cicero's letters to his friends and their letters to him. We find in Catullus a few old-fashioned words, such as 67. 2 *auctet*, 44. 2 *autumant*, 4. 26 *senet* and 78b. 2 *suauia* — mostly used, it seems, for mock-solemn effect — and a few picturesque words such as 25. 1 *cuniculi*, 97. 6 *ploxeni*, and 53. 5 *salaputium*. Words normally ranked as obscene are used pretty freely; sometimes they are words that have passed into colloquial usage and changed their meaning as a result (see introductory note on Poem 15); sometimes Catullus means more what he says, planting the obscene word or expression (e.g. 29. 13 *diffututa mentula*) in an elegantly worded context for its abusive force — or simply in order to shock the squeamish by the urbanely casual use of words which do not normally find their way into literature (e.g. 6. 13 or 32. 8). Neologisms — words made up for the occasion for comic effect (e.g. 6. 11 *argutatio*, or 7. 1 *basiationes*) or experiments for literary effect with compound adjectives (e.g. 7. 4 *lasarpiciferis*, 11. 6 *sagittiferosue*, and 11. 7 *septemgeminus*) — are not uncommon; see on 63. 23 *hederigerae*. Greek words are fairly frequent; they are mostly the names of particular objects — e.g. 98. 4 *carpatinas*, 25. 7 *catagraphos*, 98. 4 *crepidas*, 12. 13 *mnemosynum*, 22. 5 *palimpsesto*, 63. 60 *palaestra*, and 64. 65 *strophi*.

Two groups of words call for special comment.

The first, mostly adjectives, are used by Catullus to embody key concepts of the smart set to which he belonged — words like *bellus*, *dicax*, *delicatus*, *doctus*, *facetus*, *formosus*, *iucundus*, *lepidus*, *miser*, *urbanus*, and *uenustus*. Most are words in common use, but in Catullus they come to acquire very complex patterns of overtones; see, e.g., on 50. 3 *delicatos*, 8. 1 *miser*, and 3. 2 *uenustiorum*. A number of nouns belong to the same category; see on 6. 16 *amores* and 2. 1 *deliciae*.

The other group consists of diminutives. These are very numerous, many of them pretty clearly coined for their context. Some of the more striking are: 30. 2

amiculi, 64. 316 *aridulis . . . labellis*, 57. 7 *erudituli*, 64.
131 *frigidulos*, 15. 4 *integellum*, 55. 17 *lacteolae*, 64. 331
languidulos, 63. 35 *lassulae*, 25. 2 *medullula*, 64. 103
munuscula, 65. 6 *pallidulum*, 4. 4 *palmulis*, 28. 2 *sarcinulis*
10. 3 *scortillum*, 2. 7 *solaciolum*, 99. 2 and 14 *suauiolum*,
3. 18 *turgiduli . . . ocelli*, 16. 6 and 50. 4 *uersiculos* (16. 3
uersiculis). Both nouns and adjectives occur. The poly-
syllabic diminutive specially coined for its context is
also a feature of Cicero's letters (e.g. *Att.* 16. 11. 8
hilarula, *Fam.* 7. 5. 3 *putidiusculi*, and *Att.* 4. 5. 1
subturpicula), as it is of the language of Plautus: it adds
vivacity to the description of everyday events, and
provides an outlet for a pleasure in the manipulation
of words generally considered too subjective for the
high style. Catullus' use of diminutives in the long
poems is all the more striking therefore.

These diminutives seldom have much to do with
size. They express an attitude, often a complex
attitude, to the object named or described, ranging
between the two extremes of irony and pathos. Some-
times the diminutive mocks; sometimes it expresses
affection; sometimes it claims sympathy for the poet
or his mistress or a dramatic character such as Attis;
sometimes it is part of a process of realistic, 'modern'
description of scenes or characters from legend.[16]

9 *SYNTAX*

THE BASIS is a crisp, vigorous simplicity enlivened by
a turn of phrase that is often proverbial or colloquial
(e.g. 3. 2 *quantum est hominum uenustiorum*, or 5. 2–3

B

rumoresque senum seueriorum | omnes unius aestimemus assis)
or picturesque (e.g. 23. 3–4 *quorum | dentes uel silicem
comesse possunt*) — and is occasionally provocative or
outrageous. Common features are the jingle (e.g. 8. 2
quod uides perisse perditum ducas, or 31. 12–13 *ero gaude |
gaudente*) and, in more emotionally charged contexts,
a use of repetition that becomes at times almost
obsessive in intensity, as in 107. 1–6:

> Si quicquam *cupido* optantique optigit umquam
>   *insperanti*, hoc est *gratum* animo proprie.
> quare hoc est *gratum*, *nobis* quoque, carius auro,
>   quod te *restituis*, Lesbia, mi *cupido*.
> *restituis cupido* atque *insperanti*, ipsa refers te
>   *nobis* . . .

The typical Catullan sentence is no more than a
few lines long, but there are frequent exceptions. A
rise in the emotional pressure can result in an elabor-
ately balanced sentence that makes up a whole poem
by itself (e.g. Poems 48, 49, 58, 75, 81, or 96). Rarer
are more ramblingly prosaic structures such as Poem
65 or 68. 1–14. Poems 63 and 64 contain some interest-
ing experiments with sentence structure (see on 63.
27–38 and 39–43, and Poem 64, *Structure*). For the use
of parallel juxtaposed couplets see on Poem 78.

10 IMAGERY

SOME striking imagery occurs in the formal similes, of
which the most important are 11. 22–4; 17. 18–20;
25. 12–13; 61. 21–5 and 87–9; 62. 39–45 and 49–56;
63. 33; 64. 105–10, 269–77 and 353–5; 65. 19–24; 68.

57–62, 63–6 and 108–16. Other notable uses of imagery are 7. 3–8; 11. 3–4; 17. 14–15; 25. 1–4; 48. 5–6; 63. 39–43; 64. 12–18 and 330–2; 68. 133–4; 70. 4; and 97. 5–8.

11 *METRE*

(a) *Hendecasyllabics* (also called 'phalaeceans'). The commonest metre in Catullus, used in some 40 poems. The usual pattern is:

$$-\,-\,-\,\cup\,\cup\,-\,\cup\,-\,\cup\,-\,\smile$$
$$-\,\cup$$
$$\cup\,-$$

A spondaic opening is the most frequent. A special variation occurs in Poems 55 and 58b (see on these poems). The metre is found only occasionally in Greek in choral odes and scolia.

(b) *Limping iambics* (also called 'choliambics' and 'scazons'). Used in 8 poems (Poems 8, 22, 31, 37, 39, 44, 59, and 60):

$$\smile\,-\,\cup\,-\,|\,\smile\,-\,\cup\,-\,|\,\cup\,-\,-\,\smile$$

The 1st and 3rd feet may be spondaic, but the 5th foot is always an iamb. This metre, regarded by the Greeks as a deformed or mutilated version of the ordinary iambic line (hence its Greek names), seems to have been devised by Hipponax, to suggest by his halting lines the distorted subjects with which they dealt – the vices and perversions of humanity. (See on Poem 8, *Metre*.)

(c) *Glyconic combinations*. See the introductory notes to Poems 17, 34, and 61.

(d) *Sapphics*. Used in Poems 11 and 51:

$$- \cup - \underline{\cup} \mid - \cup \cup - \mid \cup - - \text{ (ter)}$$
$$- \cup \cup - \mid \underline{\cup}$$

(e) *Greater asclepiad*. Only in Poem 30:

$$- - - \cup \cup - \parallel - \cup \cup - \parallel - \cup \cup - \cup \underline{\cup}$$

(f) *Iambic trimeters*. The normal line as used by Archilochus (6 iambs, but spondees permitted in place of the 1st and 3rd iamb) is found only in Poem 52:

$$\underline{\cup} - \cup - \underline{\cup} \parallel - \cup \blacksquare \cup - \cup \underline{\cup}$$

Poems 4 and 29 are written in pure iambic trimeters.

$$\cup - \cup - \cup \parallel - \cup \parallel - \cup - \cup \underline{\cup}$$

(g) *Iambic tetrameter catalectic*. Only in Poem 25:

$$\overline{\cup} - \cup - \cup - \cup - \parallel \overline{\cup} - \cup - \overline{\cup} - \overline{\cup}$$

(h) *Galliambics*. See introductory note on Poem 63.

(i) *Dactylic hexameters*. Poems 62 and 64:

$$- \overline{\cup\cup} - \overline{\cup\cup} - \parallel \overline{\cup\cup} - \parallel \overline{\cup\cup} - \overline{\cup\cup} - \underline{\cup}$$

For 5th-foot spondees see on 64. 3.

(j) *Elegiac couplets*. Dactylic hexameters as in (i) alternating with pentameters:

$$- \overline{\cup\cup} - \overline{\cup\cup} - \parallel - \cup \cup - \cup \cup \underline{\cup}$$

Poems 65–116 are all in this metre.

12 *BIBLIOGRAPHY*

Editions and commentaries

The following list will be found helpful in identifying the principal editions and commentaries which have appeared in the 500 years since the text of Catullus was first printed.

1472   'Veneta' edition.

1502 'Aldina' edition, with notes by Hier. Avantius (= Avanzi).

1521 'Guarini' edition, with text and notes by Alessandro Guarino; these incorporate many emendations previously suggested by his father, Battista Guarino.

1554 M. Ant. Muretus (= Muret).

1566 Achilles Statius (= Estaço).

1577 Ios. Scaliger (= Della Scala).

1684 Is. Vossius (= Voss).

1710 Io. Ant. Vulpius (= Volpi).

1829 Karl Lachmann (reprinted 1861 and 1874).

1876 Emil Baehrens (text only, revised by K. P. Schulze 1893; Latin commentary 1885).

1867 Robinson Ellis (*editio maior*; reprinted 1878; English commentary 1876, 2nd edition 1889; *editio minor* [= Oxford Classical text] 1904, reprinted 1910).

1893 E. T. Merrill, with English commentary; reprinted 1951.

1908 Gustav Friedrich, with German commentary.

1923 Wilhelm Kroll, with German commentary; 2nd edition 1929, 5th edition 1968.

1928 M. Lenchantin De Gubernatis, with Italian commentary; reprinted 1933, 1953.

1949 M. Schuster (Teubner text; revised by W. Eisenhut 1958).

1958 R. A. B. Mynors (Oxford Classical Text, replacing that by Robinson Ellis; reprinted with corrections 1960, 1967).

1961   C. J. Fordyce (Mynors's text with English commentary, omitting 32 poems; reprinted with corrections 1965).

The most helpful commentaries are those by Fordyce and Merrill — the latter especially for the poems omitted by Fordyce. On difficult or doubtful points students will often find it worth while to consult as well the commentaries by Kroll (in German) and Lenchantin (in Italian). Robinson Ellis's very full commentary is still interesting; one of its particular merits is the wide range of parallel passages cited. Baehrens's Latin commentary is often excellent.

Other standard reference books

Neudling, Chester Louis, *A Prosopography to Catullus* (1955). Attempts to identify all persons named in the poems. Full references.

Wetmore, Munroe Nichols, *Index Verborum Catullianus* (1912, reprinted 1961). Lists each occurrence of all words used by Catullus.

Books about Catullus

Ferrero, Leonardo, *Un' introduzione a Catullo* (1955).

Havelock, E. A. *The Lyric Genius of Catullus* (1939).

Quinn, Kenneth, *The Catullan Revolution* (1959, revised edition 1969).

Wheeler, A. L., *Catullus and the Traditions of Ancient Poetry* (1934, reprinted 1964).

Special studies

Alfonsi, Luigi, *Poetae novi: storia di un movimento poetico* (1945).

Granarolo, Jean, *L'oeuvre de Catulle* (1967). Detailed study of religious, moral and stylistic aspects.

Heusch, Heinrich. *Das Archaische in der Sprache Catulls* (1954).

Ronconi, Alessandro, *Studi Catulliani* (1953). Chapters on Catullus' use of alliteration, diminutives, grecisms, and irony.

Ross, David O., Jr, *Style and Tradition in Catullus* (1969).

Svennung, J. von, *Catulls Bildersprache* (1945). Detailed study of metaphor and simile in Catullus.

Weinreich, Otto, *Die Distichen des Catull* (1926, reprinted 1964). Detailed studies of Poems 85, 93, 94, 105, 106, and 112.

Williams, Gordon, *Tradition and Originality in Roman Poetry* (1968).

Published since first edition of Commentary

Bardon, Henry, *Catulli Carmina* (1970). New edition of text with French translation.

Bardon, Henry, *Propositions sur Catulle* (1970). Critical interpretation.

Granarolo, J., *D'Ennius à Catulle* (1971). Catullus' Roman predecessors.

Loomis, Julia W., *Studies in Catullan Verse* (1972). Analysis of metrical patterns in Poems 1–60.

Quinn, Kenneth (ed.), *Approaches to Catullus* (1972). Articles on Catullus by various hands.

Quinn, Kenneth, *Catullus: an Interpretation* (1972).

Wiseman, T. P., *Catullan Questions* (1969). Deals with arrangement of the collection and the problem of the historical Lesbia.

NOTES ON THE INTRODUCTION

1. The longest is 27. 1–4, quoted by Gellius, 6. 20. 6.

2. See Section 5 ('Text') below.

3. It seems from Poem 44 that he also had an estate near Tibur.

4. Caelius Rufus seems to have been twenty-one when he went to Africa as a *contubernalis* of Q. Pompeius in 61 B.C.: one gathers from Cicero (*Cael.* 72–3) that the accepted practice was for a young man to continue his education in Rome until he was old enough to look after himself and then look for an opportunity of service abroad, *cum paulum iam roboris accessisset aetati*, thus gaining that *usus prouincialis non sine causa a maioribus huic aetati tributus.*

5. The only evidence is that provided by two entries in Jerome's *Chronicle*: *An. Abr.* 1930 (=87 B.C.), *C. Valerius Catullus scriptor lyricus Veronae nascitur*; and *An. Abr.* 1959 (=58 B.C.), *Catullus XXX aetatis anno Romae moritur*. The second date is clearly wrong. The first, if right, would make Catullus a good deal older than seems likely. Jerome may have been right none the less about Catullus' age at death. One possibility is that he confused the first consulship of L. Cornelius Cinna (87 B.C.) with the fourth (84 B.C.).

6. See on Poem 70.

7. Dealt with with vigorous good sense by R. G. C. Levens in *Fifty Years of Classical Scholarship* (1955) 288–92.

8. See R. G. Austin's Appendix III, 'Caelius and Catullus' in his edition of Cicero's *Pro Caelio*.

9. Excluding, i.e., 18–20 (see note on these) and two short fragments (one, a complete hendecasyllabic line, *at non effugies meos iambos*, the other an incomplete line, *de meo ligurrire libido est*, in the same metre as Poem 17) attributed to Catullus by ancient grammarians etc., but not found in the MSS.

10. Poems 18–20 are probably not by Catullus; 14b is pretty clearly a separate fragment and so, probably, are 2b and 58b.

11. It is interesting to compare what the younger Pliny says in his opening letter: 'The arrangement', he says, 'is not chronological' (*non seruato temporis ordine* –– he maintains he just took the letters as they came to hand) — 'after all I was not writing a history' (*neque enim historiam componebam*).

12. See opening para.

13. See Levens *op. cit.* 294–300 (written prior to Mynors's edition).

14. See G. P. Goold, 'A new text of Catullus', *Phoenix* 12 (1958) 93–116.

15. On archaisms in Catullus the standard work is Heinrich Heusch, *Das Archaische in der Sprache Catulls* (1954).

16. On diminutives in Catullus see A. Ronconi, 'Del diminutivo' in *Studi Catulliani* (1953) 107–50.

Abbreviations

AP	*Anthologia Palatina*
Cat. Rev.	Kenneth Quinn, *The Catullan Revolution* (repr. 1969)
CIL	*Corpus Inscriptionum Latinarum*
Critical Essays	*Critical Essays on Roman Literature,* ed. J. P. Sullivan (vol. i, 1962)
FPL	*Fragmenta Poetarum Latinorum,* ed. W. Morel (repr. 1963)
GP	*The Greek Anthology, Hellenistic Epigrams,* ed. A. S. F. Gow and D. L. Page (1965)
Latin Explorations	Kenneth Quinn, *Latin Explorations* (1963)
L & S	Lewis and Short, *Latin Dictionary*
LGS	*Lyrica Graeca Selecta,* ed. D. L. Page (1968)
OCD	*Oxford Classical Dictionary*
OLD	*Oxford Latin Dictionary*

Works of Latin authors are abbreviated as in the *Oxford Latin Dictionary*; periodicals as in the *Année philologique*; names of editors etc. as in Sandys (the unlatinized form being used for preference). Standard commentaries (on Catullus and other classical authors) and other works listed in the Bibliography are referred to simply by names of editors

(Fordyce, Lenchantin, Austin etc.) or authors
(Wheeler, Havelock etc.). References in block letters
(FRAENKEL etc.) refer the reader to the bibliography
following the commentary on poem concerned.

The Poems

1

Cui dono lepidum nouum libellum
arida modo pumice expolitum?
Corneli, tibi: namque tu solebas
meas esse aliquid putare nugas
iam tum, cum ausus es unus Italorum   5
omne aeuum tribus explicare cartis
doctis, Iuppiter, et laboriosis.
quare habe tibi quidquid hoc libelli
qualecumque; quod, ⟨o⟩ patrona uirgo,
plus uno maneat perenne saeclo.   10

2

Passer, deliciae meae puellae,
quicum ludere, quem in sinu tenere,
cui primum digitum dare appetenti
et acris solet incitare morsus,
cum desiderio meo nitenti   5
carum nescio quid lubet iocari,
et solaciolum sui doloris,
credo, ut tum grauis acquiescat ardor:
tecum ludere sicut ipsa possem
et tristis animi leuare curas! . . .   10

1

tam gratum est mihi quam ferunt puellae
pernici aureolum fuisse malum,
quod zonam soluit diu ligatam.

3

Lugete, o Veneres Cupidinesque,
et quantum est hominum uenustiorum:
passer mortuus est meae puellae,
passer, deliciae meae puellae,
quem plus illa oculis suis amabat —   5
nam mellitus erat suamque norat
ipsam tam bene quam puella matrem,
nec sese a gremio illius mouebat,
sed circumsiliens modo huc modo illuc
ad solam dominam usque pipiabat: 10
qui nunc it per iter tenebricosum
illud, unde negant redire quemquam.
at uobis male sit, malae tenebrae
Orci, quae omnia bella deuoratis:
tam bellum mihi passerem abstulistis.   15
o factum male! o miselle passer!
tua nunc opera meae puellae
flendo turgiduli rubent ocelli.

4

Phaselus ille quem uidetis, hospites,
ait fuisse nauium celerrimus,
neque ullius natantis impetum trabis
nequisse praeterire, siue palmulis
opus foret uolare siue linteo.   5
et hoc negat minacis Hadriatici

negare litus insulasue Cycladas
Rhodumque nobilem horridamque Thraciam
Propontida trucemue Ponticum sinum
(ubi iste post phaselus antea fuit   10
comata silua — nam Cytorio in iugo
loquente saepe sibilum edidit coma.)
Amastri Pontica et Cytore buxifer,
tibi haec fuisse et esse cognitissima
ait phaselus, ultima ex origine   15
tuo stetisse dicit in cacumine,
tuo imbuisse palmulas in aequore;
et inde tot per impotentia freta
erum tulisse, laeua siue dextera
uocaret aura, siue utrumque Iuppiter   20
simul secundus incidisset in pedem;
neque ulla uota litoralibus deis
sibi esse facta, cum ueniret a mari
nouissimo hunc ad usque limpidum lacum.
sed haec prius fuere; nunc recondita   25
senet quiete seque dedicat tibi,
gemelle Castor et gemelle Castoris.

5

Viuamus, mea Lesbia, atque amemus,
rumoresque senum seueriorum
omnes unius aestimemus assis!
soles occidere et redire possunt;
nobis cum semel occidit breuis lux,   5
nox est perpetua una dormienda.
da mi basia mille, deinde centum;
dein mille altera, dein secunda centum;

deinde usque altera mille, deinde centum.
dein, cum milia multa fecerimus —   10
conturbabimus illa, ne sciamus,
aut ne quis malus inuidere possit,
cum tantum sciat esse basiorum.

6

Flaui, delicias tuas Catullo,
ni sint illepidae atque inelegantes,
uelles dicere nec tacere posses.
uerum nescio quid febriculosi
scorti diligis: hoc pudet fateri.   5
nam te non uiduas iacere noctes
nequiquam tacitum cubile clamat
sertis ac Syrio fragrans oliuo,
puluinusque peraeque et hic et ille
attritus, tremulique quassa lecti   10
argutatio inambulatioque.
nam nil stupra ualet, nihil tacere.
cur? non tam latera ecfututa pandas,
ni tu quid facias ineptiarum.
quare, quidquid habes boni malique,   15
dic nobis. uolo te ac tuos amores
ad caelum lepido uocare uersu.

7

Quaeris, quot mihi basiationes
tuae, Lesbia, sint satis superque?
quam magnus numerus Libyssae harenae
lasarpiciferis iacet Cyrenis

oraclum Iouis inter aestuosi 5
et Batti ueteris sacrum sepulcrum;
aut quam sidera multa, cum tacet nox,
furtiuos hominum uident amores:
tam te basia multa basiare
uesano satis et super Catullo est, 10
quae nec pernumerare curiosi
possint nec mala fascinare lingua.

8

Miser Catulle, desinas ineptire,
et quod uides perisse perditum ducas.
fulsere quondam candidi tibi soles,
cum uentitabas quo puella ducebat
amata nobis quantum amabitur nulla; 5
ibi illa multa cum iocosa fiebant
quae tu uolebas nec puella nolebat,
fulsere uere candidi tibi soles.
nunc iam illa non uolt: tu quoque impote⟨ns noli⟩,
nec quae fugit sectare, nec miser uiue, 10
sed obstinata mente perfer, obdura.
uale, puella. iam Catullus obdurat,
nec te requiret nec rogabit inuitam.
at tu dolebis, cum rogaberis nulla.
scelesta, uae te, quae tibi manet uita? 15
quis nunc te adibit? cui uideberis bella?
quem nunc amabis? cuius esse diceris?
quem basiabis? cui labella mordebis?
at tu, Catulle, destinatus obdura.

9

Verani, omnibus e meis amicis
antistans mihi milibus trecentis,
uenistine domum ad tuos penates
fratresque unanimos anumque matrem?
uenisti. o mihi nuntii beati!   5
uisam te incolumem audiamque Hiberum
narrantem loca, facta, nationes,
ut mos est tuus, applicansque collum
iucundum os oculosque suauiabor?
o quantum est hominum beatiorum,   10
quid me laetius est beatiusue?

10

Varus me meus ad suos amores
uisum duxerat e foro otiosum —
scortillum (ut mihi tum repente uisum est)
non sane illepidum neque inuenustum;
huc ut uenimus, incidere nobis   5
sermones uarii, in quibus, quid esset
iam Bithynia, quo modo se haberet,
et quonam mihi profuisset aere.
respondi id quod erat — nihil neque ipsis
nec praetoribus esse nec cohorti,   10
cur quisquam caput unctius referret —
praesertim quibus esset irrumator
praetor, nec faceret pili cohortem.
'at certe tamen,' inquiunt 'quod illic
natum dicitur esse, comparasti   15
ad lecticam homines.' ego (ut puellae
unum me facerem beatiorem)

'non' inquam 'mihi tam fuit maligne,
ut, prouincia quod mala incidisset,
non possem octo homines parare rectos.'   20
(at mi nullus erat nec hic neque illic,
fractum qui ueteris pedem grabati
in collo sibi collocare posset.)
hic illa, ut decuit cinaediorem,
'quaeso', inquit 'mihi, mi Catulle, paulum   25
istos commoda: nam uolo ad Serapim
deferri.' 'mane,' inquii puellae,
'istud quod modo dixeram me habere . . .
fugit me ratio: meus sodalis —
Cinna est Gaius — is sibi parauit;   30
uerum utrum illius an mei, quid ad me?
utor tam bene quam mihi pararim —
sed tu insulsa male et molesta uiuis,
per quam non licet esse neglegentem!'

11

Furi et Aureli, comites Catulli —
siue in extremos penetrabit Indos,
litus ut longe resonante Eoa
      tunditur unda,
siue in Hyrcanos Arabasue molles,   5
seu Sagas sagittiferosue Parthos,
siue quae septemgeminus colorat
      aequora Nilus,
siue trans altas gradietur Alpes,
Caesaris uisens monimenta magni,   10
Gallicum Rhenum horribilesque ulti-
      mosque Britannos —

omnia haec, quaecumque feret uoluntas
caelitum, temptare simul parati,
pauca nuntiate meae puellae   15
    non bona dicta:
cum suis uiuat ualeatque moechis,
quos simul complexa tenet trecentos,
nullum amans uere, sed identidem omnium
    ilia rumpens;   20
nec meum respectet, ut ante, amorem,
qui illius culpa cecidit uelut prati
ultimi flos, praetereunte postquam
    tactus aratro est.

12

Marrucine Asini, manu sinistra
non belle uteris, in ioco atque uino,
tollis lintea neglegentiorum.
hoc salsum esse putas? fugit te, inepte:
quamuis sordida res et inuenusta est.   5
non credis mihi? crede Pollioni
fratri, qui tua furta uel talento
mutari uelit — est enim leporum
differtus puer ac facetiarum.
quare aut hendecasyllabos trecentos   10
exspecta, aut mihi linteum remitte,
quod me non mouet aestimatione,
uerum est mnemosynum mei sodalis.
nam sudaria Saetaba ex Hiberis
miserunt mihi muneri Fabullus   15
et Veranius; haec amem necesse est
ut Veraniolum meum et Fabullum.

13

Cenabis bene, mi Fabulle, apud me
paucis, si tibi di fauent, diebus —
si tecum attuleris bonam atque magnam
cenam, non sine candida puella
et uino et sale et omnibus cachinnis;   5
haec si, inquam, attuleris, uenuste noster,
cenabis bene; nam tui Catulli
plenus sacculus est aranearum.
sed contra accipies meros amores,
seu quid suauius elegantiusue est: 10
nam unguentum dabo, quod meae puellae
donarunt Veneres Cupidinesque;
quod tu cum olfacies, deos rogabis,
totum ut te faciant, Fabulle, nasum.

14

Ni te plus oculis meis amarem,
iucundissime Calue, munere isto
odissem te odio Vatiniano:
nam quid feci ego quidue sum locutus,
cur me tot male perderes poetis?   5
isti di mala multa dent clienti,
qui tantum tibi misit impiorum.
quod si, ut suspicor, hoc nouum ac repertum
munus dat tibi Sulla litterator,
non est mi male, sed bene ac beate,   10
quod non dispereunt tui labores.
di magni, horribilem et sacrum libellum!
quem tu scilicet ad tuum Catullum

misti, continuo ut die periret,
Saturnalibus, optimo dierum!   15
non non hoc tibi, salse, sic abibit.
nam, si luxerit, ad librariorum
curram scrinia, Caesios, Aquinos,
Suffenum, omnia colligam uenena,
ac te his suppliciis remunerabor.   20
·uos hinc interea ualete abite
illuc, unde malum pedem attulistis,
saecli incommoda, pessimi poetae.

14b

Si qui forte mearum ineptiarum
lectores eritis manusque uestras
non horrebitis admouere nobis. . . .

15

Commendo tibi me ac meos amores,
Aureli. ueniam peto pudentem,
ut, si quicquam animo tuo cupisti,
quod castum expeteres et integellum,
conserues puerum mihi pudice,   5
non dico a populo — nihil ueremur
istos, qui in platea modo huc modo illuc
in re praetereunt sua occupati —
uerum a te metuo tuoque pene
infesto pueris bonis malisque.   10
quem tu qua lubet, ut lubet, moueto
quantum uis, ubi erit foris paratum:
hunc unum excipio, ut puto, pudenter.

quod si te mala mens furorque uecors
in tantam impulerit, sceleste, culpam, 15
ut nostrum insidiis caput lacessas,
a tum te miserum malique fati!
quem attractis pedibus patente porta
percurrent raphanique mugilesque.

16

Pedicabo ego uos et irrumabo,
Aureli pathice et cinaede Furi,
qui me ex uersiculis meis putastis,
quod sunt molliculi, parum pudicum.
nam castum esse decet pium poetam 5
ipsum, uersiculos nihil necesse est;
qui tum denique habent salem ac leporem,
si sunt molliculi ac parum pudici,
et quod pruriat incitare possunt,
non dico pueris, sed his pilosis 10
qui duros nequeunt mouere lumbos.
uos, quod milia multa basiorum
legistis, male me marem putatis?
pedicabo ego uos et irrumabo.

17

O Colonia, quae cupis ponte ludere longo,
et salire paratum habes, sed uereris inepta
crura ponticuli axulis stantis in rediuiuis,
ne supinus eat cauaque in palude recumbat:
sic tibi bonus ex tua pons libidine fiat, 5
in quo uel Salisubsali sacra suscipiantur,

munus hoc mihi maximi da, Colonia, risus.
quendam municipem meum de tuo uolo ponte
ire praecipitem in lutum per caputque pedesque,
uerum totius ut lacus putidaeque paludis   10
liuidissima maximeque est profunda uorago.
insulsissimus est homo, nec sapit pueri instar
bimuli tremula patris dormientis in ulna.
cui cum sit uiridissimo nupta flore puella
et puella tenellulo delicatior haedo,   15
adseruanda nigerrimis diligentius uuis,
ludere hanc sinit ut lubet, nec pili facit uni,
nec se subleuat ex sua parte; sed uelut alnus
in fossa Liguri iacet suppernata securi,   19
tantundem omnia sentiens quam si nulla sit usquam,
talis iste meus stupor nil uidet, nihil audit,
ipse qui sit, utrum sit an non sit — id quoque nescit.
nunc eum uolo de tuo ponte mittere pronum,
si pote stolidum repente excitare ueternum,
et supinum animum in graui derelinquere caeno,   25
ferream ut soleam tenaci in uoragine mula.

21

Aureli, pater esuritionum,
non harum modo, sed quot aut fuerunt
aut sunt aut aliis erunt in annis,
pedicare cupis meos amores.
nec clam: nam simul es, iocaris una,   5
haerens ad latus omnia experiris.
frustra: nam insidias mihi instruentem
tangam te prior irrumatione.
atque id si faceres satur, tacerem:

nunc ipsum id doleo, quod esurire   10
meus iam puer et sitire discet.
quare desine, dum licet pudico,
ne finem facias, sed irrumatus.

22

Suffenus iste, Vare, quem probe nosti,
homo est uenustus et dicax et urbanus,
idemque longe plurimos facit uersus.
puto esse ego illi milia aut decem aut plura
perscripta, nec sic ut fit in palimpsesto   5
relata: cartae regiae, noui libri,
noui umbilici, lora rubra, membranae,
derecta plumbo et pumice omnia aequata.
haec cum legas tu, bellus ille et urbanus
Suffenus unus caprimulgus aut fossor   10
rursus uidetur: tantum abhorret ac mutat.
hoc quid putemus esse? qui modo scurra
aut si quid hac re scitius uidebatur,
idem infaceto est infacetior rure,
simul poemata attigit, neque idem umquam   15
aeque est beatus ac poema cum scribit:
tam gaudet in se tamque se ipse miratur.
nimirum idem omnes fallimur, neque est quisquam
quem non in aliqua re uidere Suffenum
possis. suus cuique attributus est error;   20
sed non uidemus manticae quod in tergo est.

23

Furi, cui neque seruus est neque arca
nec cimex neque araneus neque ignis,
uerum est et pater et nouerca, quorum
dentes uel silicem comesse possunt:
est pulcre tibi cum tuo parente   5
et cum coniuge lignea parentis —
nec mirum; bene nam ualetis omnes,
pulcre concoquitis, nihil timetis,
non incendia, non graues ruinas,
non facta impia, non dolos ueneni,   10
non casus alios periculorum.
atqui corpora sicciora cornu
aut siquid magis aridum est habetis
sole et frigore et esuritione?
quare non tibi sit bene ac beate?   15
a te sudor abest, abest saliua,
mucusque et mala pituita nasi.
hanc ad munditiem adde mundiorem,
quod culus tibi purior salillo est,
nec toto decies cacas in anno —   20
atque id durius est faba et lapillis,
quod tu si manibus teras fricesque,
non umquam digitum inquinare posses.
haec tu commoda tam beata, Furi,
noli spernere nec putare parui,   25
et sestertia quae soles precari
centum desine: nam sat es beatus.

24

O qui flosculus es Iuuentiorum,
non horum modo, sed quot aut fuerunt
aut posthac aliis erunt in annis,
mallem diuitias Midae dedisses
isti, cui neque seruus est neque arca, 5
quam sic te sineres ab illo amari.
'qui? non est homo bellus?' inquies. est:
sed bello huic neque seruus est neque arca.
hoc tu quam lubet abice eleuaque:
nec seruum tamen ille habet neque arcam. 10

25

Cinaede Thalle, mollior cuniculi capillo
uel anseris medullula uel imula oricilla
uel pene languido senis situque araneoso,
idemque, Thalle, turbida rapacior procella,
cum diua Murcia arbitros ostendit oscitantes, 5
remitte pallium mihi meum, quod inuolasti,
sudariumque Saetabum catagraphosque Thynos,
inepte, quae palam soles habere tamquam auita.
quae nunc tuis ab unguibus reglutina et remitte,
ne laneum latusculum manusque mollicellas 10
inusta turpiter tibi flagella conscribillent,
et insolenter aestues, uelut minuta magno
deprensa nauis in mari, uesaniente uento.

26

Furi, uillula uestra non ad Austri
flatus opposita est neque ad Fauoni
nec saeui Boreae aut Apheliotae,
uerum ad milia quindecim et ducentos.
o uentum horribilem atque pestilentem!   5

27

Minister uetuli puer Falerni
inger mi calices amariores,
ut lex Postumiae iubet magistrae
ebrioso acino ebriosioris.
at uos quo lubet hinc abite, lymphae,   5
uini pernicies, et ad seueros
migrate. hic merus est Thyonianus.

28

Pisonis comites, cohors inanis,
aptis sarcinulis et expeditis,
Verani optime tuque mi Fabulle,
quid rerum geritis? satisne cum isto
uappa frigoraque et famem tulistis?   5
ecquidnam in tabulis patet lucelli
expensum, ut mihi, qui meum secutus
praetorem refero datum lucello?
o Memmi, bene me ac diu supinum
tota ista trabe lentus irrumasti.   10
sed, quantum uideo, pari fuistis
casu: nam nihilo minore uerpa
farti estis. pete nobiles amicos!
at uobis mala multa di deaeque
dent, opprobria Romuli Remique.   15

29

Quis hoc potest uidere, quis potest pati,
nisi impudicus et uorax et aleo,
Mamurram habere quod Comata Gallia
habebat uncti et ultima Britannia?
cinaede Romule, haec uidebis et feres? 5
et ille nunc superbus et superfluens
perambulabit omnium cubilia,
ut albulus columbus aut Adoneus?
cinaede Romule, haec uidebis et feres?
es impudicus et uorax et aleo. 10
eone nomine, imperator unice,
fuisti in ultima occidentis insula,
ut ista uestra diffututa mentula
ducenties comesset aut trecenties?
quid est alid sinistra liberalitas? 15
parum expatrauit an parum elluatus est?
paterna prima lancinata sunt bona,
secunda praeda Pontica, inde tertia
Hibera, quam scit amnis aurifer Tagus:
nunc Galliae timetur et Britanniae. 20
quid hunc, malum, fouetis? aut quid hic potest
nisi uncta deuorare patrimonia?
eone nomine urbis o piissimi
socer generque, perdidistis omnia?

30

Alfene immemor atque unanimis false sodalibus,
iam te nil miseret, dure, tui dulcis amiculi?
iam me prodere, iam non dubitas fallere, perfide?
nec facta impia fallacum hominum caelicolis placent.
quae tu neglegis ac me miserum deseris in malis.   5
eheu quid faciant, dic, homines cuiue habeant fidem?
certe tute iubebas animam tradere, inique, ⟨me⟩
inducens in amorem, quasi tuta omnia mi forent.
idem nunc retrahis te ac tua dicta omnia factaque
uentos irrita ferre ac nebulas aereas sinis.   10
si tu oblitus es, at di meminerunt, meminit Fides,
quae te ut paeniteat postmodo facti faciet tui.

31

Paene insularum, Sirmio, insularumque
ocelle, quascumque in liquentibus stagnis
marique uasto fert uterque Neptunus,
quam te libenter quamque laetus inuiso,
uix mi ipse credens Thyniam atque Bithynos   5
liquisse campos et uidere te in tuto.
o quid solutis est beatius curis,
cum mens onus reponit, ac peregrino
labore fessi uenimus larem ad nostrum,
desideratoque acquiescimus lecto?   10
hoc est quod unum est pro laboribus tantis.
salue, o uenusta Sirmio, atque ero gaude
gaudente; uosque, o Lydiae lacus undae,
ridete quidquid est domi cachinnorum.

32

Amabo, mea dulcis Ipsitilla,
meae deliciae, mei lepores,
iube ad te ueniam meridiatum.
et si iusseris, illud adiuuato,
ne quis liminis obseret tabellam,   5
neu tibi lubeat foras abire,
sed domi maneas paresque nobis
nouem continuas fututiones.
uerum si quid ages, statim iubeto:
nam pransus iaceo et satur supinus   10
pertundo tunicamque palliumque.

33

O furum optime balneariorum
Vibenni pater et cinaede fili
(nam dextra pater inquinatiore,
culo filius est uoraciore),
cur non exilium malasque in oras   5
itis, quandoquidem patris rapinae
notae sunt populo, et natis pilosas,
fili, non potes asse uenditare?

34

Dianae sumus in fide
puellae et pueri integri:
⟨Dianam pueri integri⟩
puellaeque canamus.

o Latonia, maximi   5
magna progenies Iouis,
quam mater prope Deliam
    deposiuit oliuam,

montium domina ut fores
siluarumque uirentium   10
saltuumque reconditorum
    amniumque sonantum:

tu Lucina dolentibus
Iuno dicta puerperis,
tu potens Triuia et notho es   15
    dicta lumine Luna.

tu cursu, dea, menstruo
metiens iter annuum,
rustica agricolae bonis
    tecta frugibus exples.   20

sis quocumque tibi placet
sancta nomine, Romulique,
antique ut solita es, bona
    sospites ope gentem.

35

Poetae tenero, meo sodali,
uelim Caecilio, papyre, dicas
Veronam ueniat, Noui relinquens
Comi moenia Lariumque litus.
nam quasdam uolo cogitationes   5
amici accipiat sui meique.

quare, si sapiet, uiam uorabit,
quamuis candida milies puella
euntem reuocet, manusque collo
ambas iniciens roget morari.   10
quae nunc, si mihi uera nuntiantur,
illum deperit impotente amore.
nam quo tempore legit incohatam
Dindymi dominam, ex eo misellae
ignes interiorem edunt medullam.   15
ignosco tibi, Sapphica puella
musa doctior; est enim uenuste
Magna Caecilio incohata Mater.

36

Annales Volusi, cacata carta,
uotum soluite pro mea puella.
(nam sanctae Veneri Cupidinique
uouit, si sibi restitutus essem
desissemque truces uibrare iambos,   5
electissima pessimi poetae
scripta tardipedi deo daturam
infelicibus ustulanda lignis.
et hoc pessima se puella uidit
iocosis lepide uouere diuis.)   10
nunc o caeruleo creata ponto,
quae sanctum Idalium Vriosque apertos
quaeque Ancona Cnidumque harundinosam
colis quaeque Amathunta quaeque Golgos
quaeque Durrachium Hadriae tabernam,   15
acceptum face redditumque uotum,
si non illepidum neque inuenustum est.

c

at uos interea uenite in ignem,
pleni ruris et infacetiarum
annales Volusi, cacata carta.   20

37

Salax taberna uosque contubernales,
a pilleatis nona fratribus pila,
solis putatis esse mentulas uobis,
solis licere, quidquid est puellarum,
confutuere et putare ceteros hircos?   5
an, continenter quod sedetis insulsi
centum (an ducenti?) non putatis ausurum
me una ducentos irrumare sessores?
atqui putate: namque totius uobis
frontem tabernae sopionibus scribam.   10
puella nam mi, quae meo sinu fugit,
amata tantum quantum amabitur nulla,
pro qua mihi sunt magna bella pugnata,
consedit istic. hanc boni beatique
omnes amatis, et quidem, quod indignum est, 15
omnes pusilli et semitarii moechi;
tu praeter omnes une de capillatis,
cuniculosae Celtiberiae fili,
Egnati, opaca quem bonum facit barba
et dens Hibera defricatus urina.   20

38

Malest, Cornifici, tuo Catullo,
malest, me hercule, et laboriose,

et magis magis in dies et horas.
quem tu, quod minimum facillimumque est,
qua solatus es allocutione?   5
irascor tibi. sic meos amores?
paulum quid lubet allocutionis,
maestius lacrimis Simonideis.

39

Egnatius, quod candidos habet dentes,
renidet usquequaque. si ad rei uentum est
subsellium, cum orator excitat fletum,
renidet ille; si ad pii rogum fili
lugetur, orba cum flet unicum mater,   5
renidet ille. quidquid est, ubicumque est,
quodcumque agit, renidet: hunc habet morbum,
neque elegantem, ut arbitror, neque urbanum.
quare monendum est ⟨te⟩ mihi, bone Egnati.
si urbanus esses aut Sabinus aut Tiburs   10
aut parcus Vmber aut obesus Etruscus
aut Lanuuinus ater atque dentatus
aut Transpadanus, ut meos quoque attingam,
aut quilubet, qui puriter lauit dentes,
tamen renidere usquequaque te nollem: 15
nam risu inepto res ineptior nulla est.
nunc Celtiber ⟨es⟩: Celtiberia in terra,
quod quisque minxit, hoc sibi solet mane
dentem atque russam defricare gingiuam,
ut, quo iste uester expolitior dens est,   20
hoc te amplius bibisse praedicet loti.

40

Quaenam te mala mens, miselle Rauide,
agit praecipitem in meos iambos?
quis deus tibi non bene aduocatus
uecordem parat excitare rixam?
an ut peruenias in ora uulgi?   5
quid uis? qualubet esse notus optas?
eris, quandoquidem meos amores
cum longa uoluisti amare poena.

41

Ameana puella defututa
tota milia me decem poposcit,
ista turpiculo puella naso,
decoctoris amica Formiani.
propinqui, quibus est puella curae,   5
amicos medicosque conuocate:
non est sana puella, nec rogare
qualis sit solet aes imaginosum.

42

Adeste, hendecasyllabi, quot estis
omnes undique, quotquot estis omnes.
iocum me putat esse moecha turpis,
et negat mihi uestra reddituram
pugillaria, si pati potestis.   5
persequamur eam et reflagitemus.
quae sit, quaeritis? illa, quam uidetis
turpe incedere, mimice ac moleste
ridentem catuli ore Gallicani.

circumsistite eam, et reflagitate, 10
'moecha putida, redde codicillos,
redde, putida moecha, codicillos!'
non assis facis? o lutum, lupanar,
aut si perditius potest quid esse.
sed non est tamen hoc satis putandum. 15
quod si non aliud potest, ruborem
ferreo canis exprimamus ore.
conclamate iterum altiore uoce
'moecha putida, redde codicillos,
redde, putida moecha, codicillos!' 20
sed nil proficimus, nihil mouetur.
mutanda est ratio modusque uobis,
siquid proficere amplius potestis:
'pudica et proba, redde codicillos.'

43

Salue, nec minimo puella naso
nec bello pede nec nigris ocellis
nec longis digitis nec ore sicco
nec sane nimis elegante lingua.
decoctoris amica Formiani, 5
ten prouincia narrat esse bellam?
tecum Lesbia nostra comparatur?
o saeclum insapiens et infacetum!

44

O funde noster — seu Sabine seu Tiburs —
nam te esse Tiburtem autumant, quibus non est
cordi Catullum laedere; at quibus cordi est,

quouis Sabinum pignore esse contendunt —
sed seu Sabine siue uerius Tiburs,   5
fui libenter in tua suburbana
uilla, malamque pectore expuli tussim,
non inmerenti quam mihi meus uenter,
dum sumptuosas appeto, dedit, cenas.
(nam, Sestianus dum uolo esse conuiua,   10
orationem in Antium petitorem
plenam ueneni et pestilentiae legi.
hic me grauedo frigida et frequens tussis
quassauit usque, dum in tuum sinum fugi,
et me recuraui otioque et urtica.)   15
quare refectus maximas tibi grates
ago, meum quod non es ultu' peccatum.
nec deprecor iam, si nefaria scripta
Sesti recepso, quin grauedinem et tussim
non mi, sed ipsi Sestio ferat frigus,   20
qui tunc uocat me, cum malum librum legi.

45

Acmen Septimius suos amores
tenens in gremio 'mea' inquit 'Acme,
ni te perdite amo atque amare porro
omnes sum assidue paratus annos,
quantum qui pote plurimum perire,   5
solus in Libya Indiaque tosta
caesio ueniam obuius leoni.'
hoc ut dixit, Amor sinistra ut ante
dextra sternuit approbationem.
   at Acme leuiter caput reflectens   10
et dulcis pueri ebrios ocellos

illo purpureo ore suauiata,
'sic', inquit 'mea uita Septimille,
huic uni domino usque seruiamus,
ut multo mihi maior acriorque   15
ignis mollibus ardet in medullis.'
hoc ut dixit, Amor sinistra ut ante
dextra sternuit approbationem.
    nunc ab auspicio bono profecti
mutuis animis amant amantur.   20
unam Septimius misellus Acmen
mauult quam Syrias Britanniasque:
uno in Septimio fidelis Acme
facit delicias libidinesque.
quis ullos homines beatiores   25
uidit, quis Venerem auspicatiorem?

46

Iam uer egelidos refert tepores,
iam caeli furor aequinoctialis
iucundis Zephyri silescit aureis.
linquantur Phrygii, Catulle, campi
Nicaeaeque ager uber aestuosae: 5
ad claras Asiae uolemus urbes.
iam mens praetrepidans auet uagari,
iam laeti studio pedes uigescunt.
o dulces comitum ualete coetus,
longe quos simul a domo profectos   10
diuersae uarie uiae reportant.

47

Porci et Socration, duae sinistrae
Pisonis, scabies famesque mundi,

uos Veraniolo meo et Fabullo
uerpus praeposuit Priapus ille?
uos conuiuia lauta sumptuose 5
de die facitis, mei sodales
quaerunt in triuio uocationes?

48

Mellitos oculos tuos, Iuuenti,
si quis me sinat usque basiare,
usque ad milia basiem trecenta
nec numquam uidear satur futurus,
non si densior aridis aristis 5
sit nostrae seges osculationis.

49

Disertissime Romuli nepotum,
quot sunt quotque fuere, Marce Tulli,
quotque post aliis erunt in annis,
gratias tibi maximas Catullus
agit pessimus omnium poeta, 5
tanto pessimus omnium poeta,
quanto tu optimus omnium patronus.

50

Hesterno, Licini, die otiosi
multum lusimus in meis tabellis,
ut conuenerat esse delicatos:
scribens uersiculos uterque nostrum

ludebat numero modo hoc modo illoc, 5
reddens mutua per iocum atque uinum.
atque illinc abii tuo lepore
incensus, Licini, facetiisque,
ut nec me miserum cibus iuuaret
nec somnus tegeret quiete ocellos, 10
sed toto indomitus furore lecto
uersarer, cupiens uidere lucem,
ut tecum loquerer simulque ut essem.
at defessa labore membra postquam
semimortua lectulo iacebant, 15
hoc, iucunde, tibi poema feci,
ex quo perspiceres meum dolorem.
nunc audax caue sis, precesque nostras,
oramus, caue despuas, ocelle,
ne poenas Nemesis reposcat a te; 20
est uemens dea: laedere hanc caueto.

51

Ille mi par esse deo uidetur,
ille, si fas est, superare diuos,
qui sedens aduersus identidem te
    spectat et audit
dulce ridentem, misero quod omnis 5
eripit sensus mihi: nam simul te,
Lesbia, aspexi, nihil est super mi . . .

.   .   .

lingua sed torpet, tenuis sub artus
flamma demanat, sonitu suopte 10
tintinant aures, gemina teguntur
    lumina nocte.

otium, Catulle, tibi molestum est:
otio exsultas nimiumque gestis:
otium et reges prius et beatas   15
    perdidit urbes.

52

Quid est, Catulle? quid moraris emori?
sella in curuli struma Nonius sedet,
per consulatum peierat Vatinius:
quid est, Catulle? quid moraris emori?

53

Risi nescio quem modo e corona,
qui, cum mirifice Vatiniana
meus crimina Caluos explicasset,
admirans ait haec manusque tollens,
'di magni, salaputium disertum!'   5

54

Othonis caput oppido est pusillum;
Hirri rustica, semilauta crura,
subtile et leue peditum Libonis,
si non omnia, displicere uellem
tibi et Fufidio seni recocto . . .   5
irascere iterum meis iambis
inmerentibus, unice imperator.

55

Oramus, si forte non molestum est,
demonstres ubi sint tuae tenebrae.

te Campo quaesiuimus minore,
te in Circo, te in omnibus libellis,
te in templo summi Iouis sacrato.   5
in Magni simul ambulatione
femellas omnes, amice, prendi,
quas uultu uidi tamen serenas.
†auelte†, sic ipse flagitabam,
Camerium mihi pessimae puellae.   10
quaedam inquit, nudum reduc . . .
'en hic in roseis latet papillis.'
sed te iam ferre Herculi labos est:
tanto te in fastu negas, amice.
dic nobis ubi sis futurus, ede   15
audacter, committe, crede luci.
nunc te lacteolae tenent puellae?
si linguam clauso tenes in ore,
fructus proicies amoris omnes.
uerbosa gaudet Venus loquella.   20
uel, si uis, licet obseres palatum,
dum uestri sim particeps amoris.

56

O rem ridiculam, Cato, et iocosam,
dignamque auribus et tuo cachinno!
ride quidquid amas, Cato, Catullum:
res est ridicula et nimis iocosa.
deprendi modo pupulum puellae   5
trusantem; hunc ego, si placet Dionae,
pro telo rigida mea cecidi.

57

Pulcre conuenit improbis cinaedis,
Mamurrae pathicoque Caesarique.
nec mirum: maculae pares utrisque,
urbana altera et illa Formiana,
impressae resident nec eluentur: 5
morbosi pariter, gemelli utrique,
uno in lecticulo erudituli ambo,
non hic quam ille magis uorax adulter,
riuales socii et puellularum.
pulcre conuenit improbis cinaedis.   10

58

Caeli, Lesbia nostra, Lesbia illa,
illa Lesbia, quam Catullus unam
plus quam se atque suos amauit omnes,
nunc in quadriuiis et angiportis
glubit magnanimi Remi nepotes.   5

58b

Non custos si fingar ille Cretum,
non si Pegaseo ferar uolatu;
non Ladas ego pinnipesue Perseus,
non Rhesi niueae citaeque bigae;
adde huc plumipedas uolatilesque,   5
uentorumque simul require cursum,
quos iunctos, Cameri, mihi dicares:
defessus tamen omnibus medullis
et multis languoribus peresus
essem te mihi, amice, quaeritando.   10

59

Bononiensis Rufa Rufulum fellat,
uxor Meneni, saepe quam in sepulcretis
uidistis ipso rapere de rogo cenam,
cum deuolutum ex igne prosequens panem
ab semiraso tunderetur ustore.   5

60

Num te leaena montibus Libystinis
aut Scylla latrans infima inguinum parte
tam mente dura procreauit ac taetra,
ut supplicis uocem in nouissimo casu
contemptam haberes, a nimis fero corde?   5

61

Collis o Heliconii
cultor, Vraniae genus,
qui rapis teneram ad uirum
uirginem, o Hymenaee Hymen,
    o Hymen Hymenaee: 5

cinge tempora floribus
suaue olentis amaraci,
flammeum cape laetus, huc
huc ueni, niueo gerens
    luteum pede soccum;   10

excitusque hilari die,
nuptialia concinens
uoce carmina tinnula,

pelle humum pedibus, manu
   pineam quate taedam.   15

namque Iunia Manlio,
qualis Idalium colens
uenit ad Phrygium Venus
iudicem, bona cum bona
   nubet alite uirgo.   20

floridis uelut enitens
myrtus Asia ramulis
quos Hamadryades deae
ludicrum sibi roscido
   nutriunt umore.   25

quare age, huc aditum ferens,
perge linquere Thespiae
rupis Aonios specus,
nympha quos super irrigat
   frigerans Aganippe.   30

ac domum dominam uoca
coniugis cupidam noui,
mentem amore reuinciens,
ut tenax hedera huc et huc
   arborem implicat errans.   35

uosque item simul, integrae
uirgines, quibus aduenit
par dies, agite in modum
dicite, o Hymenaee Hymen,
   o Hymen Hymenaee.   40

ut lubentius, audiens
se citarier ad suum
munus, huc aditum ferat
dux bonae Veneris, boni
   coniugator amoris.   45

quis deus magis est ama-
tis petendus amantibus?
quem colent homines magis
caelitum, o Hymenaee Hymen,
   o Hymen Hymenaee?   50

te suis tremulus parens
inuocat, tibi uirgines
zonula soluunt sinus,
te timens cupida nouus
   captat aure maritus.   55

tu fero iuueni in manus
floridam ipse puellulam
dedis a gremio suae
matris, o Hymenaee Hymen,
   o Hymen Hymenaee.   60

nil potest sine te Venus
fama quod bona comprobet
commodi capere, at potest
te uolente. quis huic deo
   compararier ausit?   65

nulla quit sine te domus
liberos dare, nec parens

stirpe nitier; at potest
te uolente. quis huic deo
    compararier ausit?   70

quae tuis careat sacris,
non queat dare praesides
terra finibus: at queat
te uolente. quis huic deo
    compararier ausit?   75

claustra pandite ianuae.
uirgo adest. uiden ut faces
splendidas quatiunt comas?

    .   .   .   .   .   .

    .   .   .   .   .   .

    .   .   .   .   .

    .   .   .   .   .

tardet ingeпuus pudor.
quem tamen magis audiens,   80
    flet quod ire necesse est.

flere desine. non tibi, Au-
runculeia, periculum est,
ne qua femina pulcrior
clarum ab Oceano diem   85
    uiderit uenientem.

talis in uario solet
diuitis domini hortulo
stare flos hyacinthinus.
sed moraris, abit dies.   90
    ⟨prodeas noua nupta.⟩

prodeas noua nupta, si
iam uidetur, et audias
nostra uerba. uiden? faces
aureas quatiunt comas: 95
    prodeas noua nupta.

non tuus leuis in mala
deditus uir adultera,
probra turpia persequens,
a tuis teneris uolet   100
    secubare papillis,

lenta sed uelut adsitas
uitis implicat arbores,
implicabitur in tuum
complexum. sed abit dies: 105
    prodeas noua nupta.

o cubile, quod omnibus
.   .   .   .   .   .
.   .   .   .   .   .
.   .   .   .   .   .
    candido pede lecti,

quae tuo ueniunt ero,
quanta gaudia, quae uaga   110
nocte, quae medio die
gaudeat! sed abit dies:
    prodeas noua nupta.

tollite, ⟨o⟩ pueri, faces:
flammeum uideo uenire.   115

ite concinite in modum
'io Hymen Hymenaee io,
  io Hymen Hymenaee.'

ne diu taceat procax
Fescennina iocatio,   120
nec nuces pueris neget
desertum domini audiens
  concubinus amorem.

'da nuces pueris, iners
concubine! satis diu   125
lusisti nucibus: lubet
iam seruire Talasio.
  concubine, nuces da.

sordebant tibi uilicae,
concubine, hodie atque heri: 130
nunc tuum cinerarius
tondet os. miser a miser
  concubine, nuces da.

diceris male te a tuis
unguentate glabris marite   135
abstinere, sed abstine.
io Hymen Hymenaee io,
  ⟨io Hymen Hymenaee.⟩

scimus haec tibi quae licent
sola cognita, sed marito   140
ista non eadem licent.
io Hymen Hymenaee io,
  io Hymen Hymenaee.'

nupta, tu quoque quae tuus
uir petet caue ne neges,   145
ni petitum aliunde eat.
io Hymen Hymenaee io,
    io Hymen Hymenaee.

en tibi domus ut potens
et beata uiri tui!   150
quae tibi sine seruiat
(io Hymen Hymenaee io,
    io Hymen Hymenaee)

usque dum tremulum mouens
cana tempus anilitas   155
omnia omnibus annuit.
io Hymen Hymenaee io,
    io Hymen Hymenaee.

transfer omine cum bono
limen aureolos pedes,   160
rasilemque subi forem.
io Hymen Hymenaee io,
    io Hymen Hymenaee.

aspice intus ut accubans
uir tuus Tyrio in toro   165
totus immineat tibi.
io Hymen Hymenaee io,
    io Hymen Hymenaee.

illi non minus ac tibi
pectore uritur intimo   170
flamma, sed penite magis.

io Hymen Hymenaee io,
   io Hymen Hymenaee.

mitte brachiolum teres,
praetextate, puellulae: 175
iam cubile adeat uiri.
io Hymen Hymenaee io,
   io Hymen Hymenaee.

⟨uos⟩ bonae senibus uiris
cognitae bene feminae,   180
collocate puellulam.
io Hymen Hymenaee io,
   io Hymen Hymenaee.

iam licet uenias, marite:
uxor in thalamo tibi est,   185
ore floridulo nitens,
alba parthenice uelut
   luteumue papauer.

at, marite, ita me iuuent
caelites, nihilo minus   190
pulcer es, neque te Venus
neglegit. sed abit dies:
   perge, ne remorare.

non diu remoratus es:
iam uenis. bona te Venus   195
iuuerit, quoniam palam
quod cupis cupis, et bonum
   non abscondis amorem.

ille pulueris Africi
siderumque micantium   200
subducat numerum prius,
qui uestri numerare uolt
    multa milia ludi.

ludite ut lubet, et breui
liberos date. non decet   205
tam uetus sine liberis
nomen esse, sed indidem
    semper ingenerari.

Torquatus uolo paruulus
matris e gremio suae   210
porrigens teneras manus
dulce rideat ad patrem
    semihiante labello.

sit suo similis patri
Manlio et facile insciens   215
noscitetur ab obuiis,
et pudicitiam suae
    matris indicet ore.

talis illius a bona
matre laus genus approbet,   220
qualis unica ab optima
matre Telemacho manet
    fama Penelopeo.

claudite ostia, uirgines:
lusimus satis. at boni   225
coniuges, bene uiuite et

　　　munere assiduo ualentem
　　　exercete iuuentam.

62

Vesper adest, iuuenes, consurgite: Vesper Olympo
exspectata diu uix tandem lumina tollit.
surgere iam tempus, iam pinguis linquere mensas,
iam ueniet uirgo, iam dicetur hymenaeus.
Hymen o Hymenaee, Hymen ades o Hymenaee!　　5

Cernitis, innuptae, iuuenes? consurgite contra;
nimirum Oetaeos ostendit Noctifer ignes.
sic certest; uiden ut perniciter exsiluere?
non temere exsiluere: canent quod uisere par est.
Hymen o Hymenaee, Hymen ades o Hymenaee!　　10

Non facilis nobis, aequales, palma parata est;
aspicite, innuptae secum ut meditata requirunt.
non frustra meditantur: habent memorabile quod sit;
nec mirum, penitus quae tota mente laborant.
nos alio mentes, alio diuisimus aures:　　　　　15
iure igitur uincemur: amat uictoria curam.
quare nunc animos saltem conuertite uestros;
dicere iam incipient, iam respondere decebit.
Hymen o Hymenaee, Hymen ades o Hymenaee!

Hespere, quis caelo fertur crudelior ignis?　　20
qui natam possis complexu auellere matris,

complexu matris retinentem auellere natam,
et iuueni ardenti castam donare puellam.
quid faciunt hostes capta crudelius urbe?
Hymen o Hymenaee, Hymen ades o Hymenaee! 25

Hespere, quis caelo lucet iucundior ignis?
qui desponsa tua firmes conubia flamma,
quae pepigere uiri, pepigerunt ante parentes,
nec iunxere prius quam se tuus extulit ardor.
quid datur a diuis felici optatius hora? 30
Hymen o Hymenaee, Hymen ades o Hymenaee!

Hesperus e nobis, aequales, abstulit unam. . . .

namque tuo aduentu uigilat custodia semper,
nocte latent fures, quos idem saepe reuertens,
Hespere, mutato comprendis nomine Eous. 35
at lubet innuptis ficto te carpere questu.
quid tum, si carpunt, tacita quem mente requirunt?
Hymen o Hymenaee, Hymen ades o Hymenaee!

Vt flos in saeptis secretus nascitur hortis,
ignotus pecori, nullo conuolsus aratro, 40
quem mulcent aurae, firmat sol, educat imber;
multi illum pueri, multae optauere puellae:
idem cum tenui carptus defloruit ungui,
nulli illum pueri, nullae optauere puellae:

sic uirgo, dum intacta manet, dum cara suis est;   45
cum castum amisit polluto corpore florem,
nec pueris iucunda manet, nec cara puellis.
Hymen o Hymenaee, Hymen ades o Hymenaee!

Vt uidua in nudo uitis quae nascitur aruo,   49
numquam se extollit, numquam mitem educat uuam,
sed tenerum prono deflectens pondere corpus
iam iam contingit summum radice flagellum;
hanc nulli agricolae, nulli coluere iuuenci:
at si forte eadem est ulmo coniuncta marito,
multi illam agricolae, multi coluere iuuenci: 55
sic uirgo dum intacta manet, dum inculta senescit;
cum par conubium maturo tempore adepta est,
cara uiro magis et minus est inuisa parenti.
et tu ne pugna cum tali coniuge, uirgo.
non aequom est pugnare, pater cui tradidit ipse,   60
ipse pater cum matre, quibus parere necesse est.
uirginitas non tota tua est, ex parte parentum est,
tertia pars patrist, pars est data tertia matri,
tertia sola tua est: noli pugnare duobus,
qui genero sua iura simul cum dote dederunt.   65
Hymen o Hymenaee, Hymen ades o Hymenaee!

63

Super alta uectus Attis celeri rate maria,
Phrygium ut nemus citato cupide pede tetigit
adiitque opaca siluis redimita loca deae,
stimulatus ibi furenti rabie, uagus animis,
deuolsit ilei acuto sibi pondera silice.   5
itaque, ut relicta sensit sibi membra sine uiro,
etiam recente terrae sola sanguine maculans,
niueis citata cepit manibus leue typanum,
typanum tuum, Cybebe, tua, mater, initia,
quatiensque terga tauri teneris caua digitis   10
canere haec suis adorta est tremebunda comitibus.
   'agite ite ad alta, Gallae, Cybeles nemora simul,
simul ite, Dindymenae dominae uaga pecora,
aliena quae petentes uelut exules loca
sectam meam exsecutae duce me mihi comites   15
rapidum salum tulistis truculentaque pelagi,
et corpus euirastis Veneris nimio odio;
hilarate erae citatis erroribus animum.
mora tarda mente cedat: simul ite, sequimini
Phrygiam ad domum Cybebes, Phrygia ad
                                           nemora deae,   20
ubi cymbalum sonat uox, ubi tympana reboant,
tibicen ubi canit Phryx curuo graue calamo,
ubi capita Maenades ui iaciunt hederigerae,
ubi sacra sancta acutis ululatibus agitant,
ubi sueuit illa diuae uolitare uaga cohors,   25
quo nos decet citatis celerare tripudiis.'
   simul haec comitibus Attis cecinit notha mulier,
thiasus repente linguis trepidantibus ululat,
leue tympanum remugit, caua cymbala recrepant,

uiridem citus adit Idam properante pede chorus.   ?
furibunda simul anhelans uaga uadit animam agens
comitata tympano Attis per opaca nemora dux,
ueluti iuuenca uitans onus indomita iugi,
rapidae ducem sequuntur Gallae properipedem.
itaque, ut domum Cybebes tetigere lassulae,   ?
nimio e labore somnum capiunt sine Cerere,
piger his labante languore oculos sopor operit,
abit in quiete molli rabidus furor animi.

   sed ubi oris aurei Sol radiantibus oculis
lustrauit aethera album, sola dura, mare ferum,   4
pepulitque noctis umbras uegetis sonipedibus,
ibi Somnus excitam Attin fugiens citus abiit;
trepidante eum recepit dea Pasithea sinu.
ita de quiete molli rapida sine rabie,
simul ipsa pectore Attis sua facta recoluit,   4
liquidaque mente uidit sine quis ubique foret,
animo aestuante rusum reditum ad uada tetulit.
ibi maria uasta uisens lacrimantibus oculis,
patriam allocuta maestast ita uoce miseriter.

   'patria o mei creatrix, patria o mea genetrix,   5
ego quam miser relinquens, dominos ut erifugae
famuli solent, ad Idae tetuli nemora pedem,
ut aput niuem et ferarum gelida stabula forem,
et earum opaca adirem furibunda latibula,
ubinam aut quibus locis te positam, patria, reor?   5
cupit ipsa pupula ad te sibi derigere aciem,
rabie fera carens dum breue tempus animus est.
egone a mea remota haec ferar in nemora domo?
patria, bonis, amicis, genitoribus abero?
abero foro, palaestra, stadio et gyminasiis?   6
miser a miser, querendum est etiam atque etiam, anime

uod enim genus figuraest, ego non quod obierim?
ço mulier, ego adolescens, ego ephebus, ego puer;
ço gymnasi fui flos; ego eram decus olei;
ihi ianuae frequentes, mihi limina tepida, 65
ihi floridis corollis redimita domus erat,
nquendum ubi esset orto mihi sole cubiculum.
ço nunc deum ministra et Cybeles famula ferar?
ço Maenas, ego mei pars, ego uir sterilis ero?
ço uiridis algida Idae niue amicta loca colam? 70
ço uitam agam sub altis Phrygiae columinibus,
bi cerua siluicultrix, ubi aper nemoriuagus?
m iam dolet quod egi, iam iamque paenitet.'
roseis ut huic labellis sonitus ⟨citus⟩ abiit,
eminas deorum ad aures noua nuntia referens, 75
i iuncta iuga resoluens Cybele leonibus
euumque pecoris hostem stimulans ita loquitur.
gedum', inquit 'age ferox ⟨i⟩, fac ut hunc furor ⟨agitet⟩,
c uti furoris ictu reditum in nemora ferat,
ea libere nimis qui fugere imperia cupit, 80
ge caede terga cauda, tua uerbera patere,
c cuncta mugienti fremitu loca retonent,
tilam ferox torosa ceruice quate iubam.'
t haec minax Cybebe religatque iuga manu:
rus ipse sese adhortans rapidum incitat animo, 85
adit, fremit, refringit uirgulta pede uago.
ubi umida albicantis loca litoris adiit,
neramque uidit Attin prope marmora pelagi,
cit impetum. illa demens fugit in nemora fera;
i semper omne uitae spatium famula fuit. 90
dea, magna dea, Cybebe, dea domina Dindymi,
rocul a mea tuos sit furor omnis, era, domo:
ios age incitatos, alios age rabidos.

64

Peliaco quondam prognatae uertice pinus
dicuntur liquidas Neptuni nasse per undas
Phasidos ad fluctus et fines Aeeteos,
cum lecti iuuenes, Argiuae robora pubis,
auratam optantes Colchis auertere pellem   5
ausi sunt uada salsa cita decurrere puppi,
caerula uerrentes abiegnis aequora palmis.
diua quibus retinens in summis urbibus arces
ipsa leui fecit uolitantem flamine currum,
pinea coniungens inflexae texta carinae;   10
illa rudem cursu proram imbuit Amphitrite.
quae simul ac rostro uentosum proscidit aequor
tortaque remigio spumis incanuit unda,
emersere feri candenti e gurgite uultus,
aequoreae monstrum Nereides admirantes.   15
illa, atque ⟨haud⟩ alia, uiderunt luce marinas
mortales oculis nudato corpore Nymphas
nutricum tenus exstantes e gurgite cano.
tum Thetidis Peleus incensus fertur amore,
tum Thetis humanos non despexit hymenaeos,   20
tum Thetidi pater ipse iugandum Pelea sensit.
o nimis optato saeclorum tempore nati
heroes, saluete, deum genus! o bona matrum
progenies, saluete iter⟨um, saluete bonarum!⟩   23b
uos ego saepe, meo uos carmine compellabo.
teque adeo eximie taedis felicibus aucte,   25
Thessaliae columen Peleu, cui Iuppiter ipse,
ipse suos diuum genitor concessit amores —
tene Thetis tenuit pulcerrima Nereine?

tene suam Tethys concessit ducere neptem,
Oceanusque, mari totum qui amplectitur orbem? 30
    quae simul optatae finito tempore luces
aduenere, domum conuentu tota frequentat
Thessalia, oppletur laetanti regia coetu:
dona ferunt prae se, declarant gaudia uultu.
deseritur Cieros, linquunt Pthiotica Tempe   35
Crannonisque domos ac moenia Larisaea,
Pharsaliam coeunt, Pharsalia tecta frequentant.
rura colit nemo, mollescunt colla iuuencis,
non humilis curuis purgatur uinea rastris,
non glebam prono conuellit uomere taurus,   40
non falx attenuat frondatorum arboris umbram,
squalida desertis rubigo infertur aratris.
    ipsius at sedes, quacumque opulenta recessit
regia, fulgenti splendent auro atque argento.
candet ebur soliis, collucent pocula mensae,   45
tota domus gaudet regali splendida gaza.
puluinar uero diuae geniale locatur
sedibus in mediis, Indo quod dente politum
tincta tegit roseo conchyli purpura fuco.
haec uestis priscis hominum uariata figuris   50
heroum mira uirtutes indicat arte.
namque fluentisono prospectans litore Diae,
Thesea cedentem celeri cum classe tuetur
indomitos in corde gerens Ariadna furores,
necdum etiam sese quae uisit uisere credit,   55
utpote fallaci quae tum primum excita somno
desertam in sola miseram se cernat harena.
immemor at iuuenis fugiens pellit uada remis,
irrita uentosae linquens promissa procellae.
quem procul ex alga maestis Minois ocellis,   60

saxea ut effigies bacchantis, prospicit, eheu,
prospicit et magnis curarum fluctuat undis,
non flauo retinens subtilem uertice mitram,
non contecta leui uelatum pectus amictu,
non tereti strophio lactentis uincta papillas,   65
omnia quae toto delapsa e corpore passim
ipsius ante pedes fluctus salis alludebant.
sed neque tum mitrae neque tum fluitantis amictus
illa uicem curans toto ex te pectore, Theseu,
toto animo, tota pendebat perdita mente.   70
a misera, assiduis quam luctibus externauit
spinosas Erycina serens in pectore curas,
illa tempestate, ferox quo ex tempore Theseus
egressus curuis e litoribus Piraei
attigit iniusti regis Gortynia templa.   75
    nam perhibent olim crudeli peste coactam
Androgeoneae poenas exsoluere caedis
electos iuuenes simul et decus innuptarum
Cecropiam solitam esse dapem dare Minotauro.
quis angusta malis cum moenia uexarentur,   80
ipse suum Theseus pro caris corpus Athenis
proicere optauit potius quam talia Cretam
funera Cecropiae nec funera portarentur.
atque ita naue leui nitens ac lenibus auris
magnanimum ad Minoa uenit sedesque superbas. 85
hunc simul ac cupido conspexit lumine uirgo
regia, quam suauis exspirans castus odores
lectulus in molli complexu matris alebat,
quales Eurotae progignunt flumina myrtus
auraue distinctos educit uerna colores,   90
non prius ex illo flagrantia declinauit
lumina, quam cuncto concepit corpore flammam

funditus atque imis exarsit tota medullis.
heu misere exagitans immiti corde furores
sancte puer, curis hominum qui gaudia misces,   95
quaeque regis Golgos quaeque Idalium frondosum,
qualibus incensam iactastis mente puellam
fluctibus, in flauo saepe hospite suspirantem!
quantos illa tulit languenti corde timores!
quanto saepe magis fulgore expalluit auri,   100
cum saeuum cupiens contra contendere monstrum
aut mortem appeteret Theseus aut praemia laudis!
non ingrata tamen frustra munuscula diuis
promittens tacito succepit uota labello.
nam uelut in summo quatientem brachia Tauro   105
quercum aut conigeram sudanti cortice pinum
indomitus turbo contorquens flamine robur
eruit (illa procul radicitus exturbata
prona cadit, late quaeuis cumque obuia frangens),
sic domito saeuum prostrauit corpore Theseus   110
nequiquam uanis iactantem cornua uentis.
inde pedem sospes multa cum laude reflexit
errabunda regens tenui uestigia filo,
ne labyrintheis e flexibus egredientem
tecti frustraretur inobseruabilis error.   115
  sed quid ego a primo digressus carmine plura
commemorem, ut linquens genitoris filia uultum,
ut consanguineae complexum, ut denique matris,
quae misera in gnata deperdita laeta⟨batur⟩,
omnibus his Thesei dulcem praeoptarit amorem: 120
aut ut uecta rati spumosa ad litora Diae
⟨uenerit,⟩ aut ut eam deuinctam lumina somno
liquerit immemori discedens pectore coniunx?
saepe illam perhibent ardenti corde furentem

clarisonas imo fudisse e pectore uoces,   125
ac tum praeruptos tristem conscendere montes,
unde aciem ⟨in⟩ pelagi uastos protenderet aestus,
tum tremuli salis aduersas procurrere in undas
mollia nudatae tollentem tegmina surae,
atque haec extremis maestam dixisse querellis,   130
frigidulos udo singultus ore cientem:
'sicine me patriis auectam, perfide, ab aris,
perfide, deserto liquisti in litore, Theseu?
sicine discedens neglecto numine diuum,
immemor a! deuota domum periuria portas?   135
nullane res potuit crudelis flectere mentis
consilium? tibi nulla fuit clementia praesto,
immite ut nostri uellet miserescere pectus?
at non haec quondam blanda promissa dedisti
uoce mihi, non haec miserae sperare iubebas,   140
sed conubia laeta, sed optatos hymenaeos,
quae cuncta aerii discerpunt irrita uenti.
nunc iam nulla uiro iuranti femina credat,
nulla uiri speret sermones esse fideles;   144
quis dum aliquid cupiens animus praegestit apisci,
nihil metuunt iurare, nihil promittere parcunt:
sed simul ac cupidae mentis satiata libido est,
dicta nihil meminere, nihil periuria curant.
certe ego te in medio uersantem turbine leti
eripui, et potius germanum amittere creui,   150
quam tibi fallaci supremo in tempore dessem.
pro quo dilaceranda feris dabor alitibusque
praeda, neque iniacta tumulabor mortua terra.
quaenam te genuit sola sub rupe leaena,   154
quod mare conceptum spumantibus exspuit undis,
quae Syrtis, quae Scylla rapax, quae uasta Carybdis,

talia qui reddis pro dulci praemia uita?
si tibi non cordi fuerant conubia nostra,
saeua quod horrebas prisci praecepta parentis,
attamen in uestras potuisti ducere sedes,   160
quae tibi iucundo famularer serua labore,
candida permulcens liquidis uestigia lymphis,
purpureaue tuum consternens ueste cubile.
sed quid ego ignaris nequiquam conquerar auris,
externata malo, quae nullis sensibus auctae   165
nec missas audire queunt nec reddere uoces?
ille autem prope iam mediis uersatur in undis,
nec quisquam apparet uacua mortalis in alga.
sic nimis insultans extremo tempore saeua
fors etiam nostris inuidit questibus auris.   170
Iuppiter omnipotens, utinam ne tempore primo
Cnosia Cecropiae tetigissent litora puppes,
indomito nec dira ferens stipendia tauro
perfidus in Creta religasset nauita funem,
nec malus hic celans dulci crudelia forma   175
consilia in nostris requiesset sedibus hospes!
nam quo me referam? quali spe perdita nitor?
Idaeosne petam montes? at gurgite lato
discernens ponti truculentum diuidit aequor.   179
an patris auxilium sperem? quemne ipsa reliqui
respersum iuuenem fraterna caede secuta?
coniugis an fido consoler memet amore?
quine fugit lentos incuruans gurgite remos?
praeterea nullo litus, sola insula, tecto,
nec patet egressus pelagi cingentibus undis.   185
nulla fugae ratio, nulla spes: omnia muta,
omnia sunt deserta, ostentant omnia letum.
non tamen ante mihi languescent lumina morte,

D

nec prius a fesso secedent corpore sensus,
quam iustam a diuis exposcam prodita multam   190
caelestumque fidem postrema comprecer hora.
quare facta uirum multantes uindice poena
Eumenides, quibus anguino redimita capillo
frons exspirantis praeportat pectoris iras,
huc huc aduentate, meas audite querellas,   195
quas ego, uae misera, extremis proferre medullis
cogor inops, ardens, amenti caeca furore.
quae quoniam uerae nascuntur pectore ab imo,
uos nolite pati nostrum uanescere luctum,
sed quali solam Theseus me mente reliquit,   200
tali mente, deae, funestet seque suosque!'

   has postquam maesto profudit pectore uoces,
supplicium saeuis exposcens anxia factis,
annuit inuicto caelestum numine rector;
quo motu tellus atque horrida contremuerunt   205
aequora concussitque micantia sidera mundus.
ipse autem caeca mentem caligine Theseus
consitus oblito dimisit pectore cuncta,
quae mandata prius constanti mente tenebat,
dulcia nec maesto sustollens signa parenti   210
sospitem Erectheum se ostendit uisere portum.
namque ferunt olim, classi cum moenia diuae
linquentem gnatum uentis concrederet Aegeus,
talia complexum iuueni mandata dedisse:
'gnate mihi longa iucundior unice uita,   215
gnate, ego quem in dubios cogor dimittere casus,
reddite in extrema nuper mihi fine senectae,
quandoquidem fortuna mea ac tua feruida uirtus
eripit inuito mihi te, cui languida nondum
lumina sunt gnati cara saturata figura,   220

non ego te gaudens laetanti pectore mittam,
nec te ferre sinam fortunae signa secundae,
sed primum multas expromam mente querellas,
canitiem terra atque infuso puluere foedans,
inde infecta uago suspendam lintea malo,   225
nostros ut luctus nostraeque incendia mentis
carbasus obscurata dicet ferrugine Hibera.
quod tibi si sancti concesserit incola Itoni,
quae nostrum genus ac sedes defendere Erecthei
annuit, ut tauri respergas sanguine dextram,   230
tum uero facito ut memori tibi condita corde
haec uigeant mandata, nec ulla oblitteret aetas;
ut simul ac nostros inuisent lumina collis,
funestam antennae deponant undique uestem,
candidaque intorti sustollant uela rudentes,   235
quam primum cernens ut laeta gaudia mente
agnoscam, cum te reducem aetas prospera sistet.'
haec mandata prius constanti mente tenentem
Thesea ceu pulsae uentorum flamine nubes
aereum niuei montis liquere cacumen.   240
at pater, ut summa prospectum ex arce petebat,
anxia in assiduos absumens lumina fletus,
cum primum inflati conspexit lintea ueli,
praecipitem sese scopulorum e uertice iecit,
amissum credens immiti Thesea fato.   245
sic funesta domus ingressus tecta paterna
morte ferox Theseus, qualem Minoidi luctum
obtulerat mente immemori, talem ipse recepit.

   quae tum prospectans cedentem maesta carinam
multiplices animo uoluebat saucia curas.   250
at parte ex alia florens uolitabat Iacchus
cum thiaso Satyrorum et Nysigenis Silenis,

te quaerens, Ariadna, tuoque incensus amore.
cui Thyades passim lymphata mente furebant,
euhoe bacchantes, euhoe capita inflectentes.   255
harum pars tecta quatiebant cuspide thyrsos,
pars e diuolso iactabant membra iuuenco,
pars sese tortis serpentibus incingebant,
pars obscura cauis celebrabant orgia cistis,
orgia quae frustra cupiunt audire profani;   260
plangebant aliae proceris tympana palmis,
aut tereti tenuis tinnitus aere ciebant;
multis raucisonos efflabant cornua bombos
barbaraque horribili stridebat tibia cantu.

talibus amplifice uestis decorata figuris   265
puluinar complexa suo uelabat amictu.
quae postquam cupide spectando Thessala pubes
expleta est, sanctis coepit decedere diuis.
hic, qualis flatu placidum mare matutino
horrificans Zephyrus procliuas incitat undas,   270
Aurora exoriente uagi sub limina Solis,
quae tarde primum clementi flamine pulsae
procedunt lenique sonant plangore cachinni,
post uento crescente magis magis increbrescunt,
purpureaque procul nantes ab luce refulgent: 275
sic tum uestibuli linquentes regia tecta
ad se quisque uago passim pede discedebant.
quorum post abitum princeps e uertice Pelei
aduenit Chiron portans siluestria dona: 279
nam quoscumque ferunt campi, quos Thessala magnis
montibus ora creat, quos propter fluminis undas
aura parit flores tepidi fecunda Fauoni,
hos indistinctis plexos tulit ipse corollis,
quo permulsa domus iucundo risit odore.

confestim Penios adest, uiridantia Tempe,   285
Tempe, quae siluae cingunt super impendentes,
†Minosim linquens †doris celebranda choreis,
non uacuos: namque ille tulit radicitus altas
fagos ac recto proceras stipite laurus,
non sine nutanti platano lentaque sorore   290
flammati Phaethontis et aerea cupressu.
haec circum sedes late contexta locauit,
uestibulum ut molli uelatum fronde uireret.
post hunc consequitur sollerti corde Prometheus,
extenuata gerens ueteris uestigia poenae,   295
quam quondam silici restrictus membra catena
persoluit pendens e uerticibus praeruptis.
inde pater diuum sancta cum coniuge natisque
aduenit, caelo te solum, Phoebe, relinquens
unigenamque simul cultricem montibus Idri: 300
Pelea nam tecum pariter soror aspernata est,
nec Thetidis taedas uoluit celebrare iugalis.

    qui postquam niueis flexerunt sedibus artus,
large multiplici constructae sunt dape mensae,
cum interea infirmo quatientes corpora motu   305
ueridicos Parcae coeperunt edere cantus.
his corpus tremulum complectens undique uestis
candida purpurea talos incinxerat ora,
at roseae niueo residebant uertice uittae,
aeternumque manus carpebant rite laborem.   310
laeua colum molli lana retinebat amictum,
dextera tum leuiter deducens fila supinis
formabat digitis, tum prono in pollice torquens
libratum tereti uersabat turbine fusum,
atque ita decerpens aequabat semper opus dens,   315
laneaque aridulis haerebant morsa labellis,

quae prius in leui fuerant exstantia filo:
ante pedes autem candentis mollia lanae
uellera uirgati custodibant calathisci.
haec tum clarisona pellentes uellera uoce   320
talia diuino fuderunt carmine fata,
carmine, perfidiae quod post nulla arguet aetas.

   o decus eximium magnis uirtutibus augens,
Emathiae tutamen, Opis carissime nato,
accipe, quod laeta tibi pandunt luce sorores,   325
ueridicum oraclum: sed uos, quae fata sequuntur,
   currite ducentes subtegmina, currite, fusi.
adueniet tibi iam portans optata maritis
Hesperus, adueniet fausto cum sidere coniunx,
quae tibi flexanimo mentem perfundat amore,   330
languidulosque paret tecum coniungere somnos,
leuia substernens robusto brachia collo.
   currite ducentes subtegmina, currite, fusi.
nulla domus tales umquam contexit amores,
nullus amor tali coniunxit foedere amantes,   335
qualis adest Thetidi, qualis concordia Peleo.
   currite ducentes subtegmina, currite, fusi.
nascetur uobis expers terroris Achilles,
hostibus haud tergo, sed forti pectore notus,
qui persaepe uago uictor certamine cursus   340
flammea praeuertet celeris uestigia ceruae.
   currite ducentes subtegmina, currite, fusi.
non illi quisquam bello se conferet heros,
cum Phrygii Teucro manabunt sanguine ⟨campi⟩,
Troicaque obsidens longinquo moenia bello   345
periuri Pelopis uastabit tertius heres.
   currite ducentes subtegmina, currite, fusi.
illius egregias uirtutes claraque facta

saepe fatebuntur gnatorum in funere matres,
cum incultum cano soluent a uertice crinem,   350
putridaque infirmis uariabunt pectora palmis.
    currite ducentes subtegmina, currite, fusi.
namque uelut densas praecerpens messor aristas
sole sub ardenti flauentia demetit arua,
Troiugenum infesto prosternet corpora ferro.   355
    currite ducentes subtegmina, currite, fusi.
testis erit magnis uirtutibus unda Scamandri
quae passim rapido diffunditur Hellesponto,
cuius iter caesis angustans corporum aceruis
alta tepefaciet permixta flumina caede.   360
    currite ducentes subtegmina, currite, fusi.
denique testis erit morti quoque reddita praeda,
cum teres excelso coaceruatum aggere bustum
excipiet niueos perculsae uirginis artus.
    currite ducentes subtegmina, currite, fusi.   365
nam simul ac fessis dederit fors copiam Achiuis
urbis Dardaniae Neptunia soluere uincla,
alta Polyxenia madefient caede sepulcra;
quae, uelut ancipiti succumbens uictima ferro,
proiciet truncum summisso poplite corpus.   370
    currite ducentes subtegmina, currite, fusi.
quare agite optatos animi coniungite amores.
accipiat coniunx felici foedere diuam,
dedatur cupido iam dudum nupta marito.
    currite ducentes subtegmina, currite, fusi.   375
non illam nutrix orienti luce reuisens
hesterno collum poterit circumdare filo,   377
anxia nec mater discordis maesta puellae   379
secubitu caros mittet sperare nepotes.   380
    currite ducentes subtegmina, currite, fusi.

talia praefantes quondam felicia Pelei
carmina diuino cecinerunt pectore Parcae.
   praesentes namque ante domos inuisere castas
heroum, et sese mortali ostendere coetu,   385
caelicolae nondum spreta pietate solebant.
saepe pater diuum templo in fulgente reuisens,
annua cum festis uenissent sacra diebus,
conspexit terra centum procumbere tauros.
saepe uagus Liber Parnasi uertice summo   390
Thyadas effusis euantis crinibus egit,
cum Delphi tota certatim ex urbe ruentes
acciperent laeti diuum fumantibus aris.
saepe in letifero belli certamine Mauors
aut rapidi Tritonis era aut Ramnusia uirgo   395
armatas hominum est praesens hortata cateruas.
sed postquam tellus scelere est imbuta nefando
iustitiamque omnes cupida de mente fugarunt,
perfudere manus fraterno sanguine fratres,
destitit extinctos gnatus lugere parentes,   400
optauit genitor primaeui funera nati,
liber ut innuptae poteretur flore nouercae,
ignaro mater substernens se impia nato
impia non uerita est diuos scelerare penates —
omnia fanda nefanda malo permixta furore   405
iustificam nobis mentem auertere deorum.
quare nec talis dignantur uisere coetus,
nec se contingi patiuntur lumine claro.

65

Etsi me assiduo confectum cura dolore
  seuocat a doctis, Hortale, uirginibus,
nec potis est dulcis Musarum expromere fetus
  mens animi, tantis fluctuat ipsa malis —
namque mei nuper Lethaeo gurgite fratris   5
  pallidulum manans alluit unda pedem,
Troia Rhoeteo quem subter litore tellus
  ereptum nostris obterit ex oculis . . .

. . . .

  numquam ego te, uita frater amabilior,   10
aspiciam posthac? at certe semper amabo,
  semper maesta tua carmina morte canam,
qualia sub densis ramorum concinit umbris
  Daulias, absumpti fata gemens Ityli —
sed tamen in tantis maeroribus, Hortale, mitto   15
  haec expressa tibi carmina Battiadae
(ne tua dicta uagis nequiquam credita uentis
  effluxisse meo forte putes animo),
ut missum sponsi furtiuo munere malum
  procurrit casto uirginis e gremio,   20
quod miserae oblitae molli sub ueste locatum,
  dum aduentu matris prosilit, excutitur,
atque illud prono praeceps agitur decursu,
  huic manat tristi conscius ore rubor.

66

Omnia qui magni dispexit lumina mundi,
   qui stellarum ortus comperit atque obitus,
flammeus ut rapidi solis nitor obscuretur,
   ut cedant certis sidera temporibus,
ut Triuiam furtim sub Latmia saxa relegans   5
   dulcis amor gyro deuocet aereo:
idem me ille Conon caelesti in limine uidit,
   e Bereniceo uertice caesariem,
fulgentem clare, quam multis illa dearum
   leuia protendens brachia pollicita est,   10
qua rex tempestate nouo auctus hymenaeo
   uastatum finis iuerat Assyrios,
dulcia nocturnae portans uestigia rixae,
   quam de uirgineis gesserat exuuiis.
estne nouis nuptis odio Venus? anne parentum 15
   frustrantur falsis gaudia lacrimulis,
ubertim thalami quas intra limina fundunt?
   non, ita me diui, uera gemunt, iuerint.
id mea me multis docuit regina querellis
   inuisente nouo proelia torua uiro.   20
at tu non orbum luxti deserta cubile,
   sed fratris cari flebile discidium?
quam penitus maestas exedit cura medullas!
   ut tibi tunc toto pectore sollicitae
sensibus ereptis mens excidit! at ⟨te⟩ ego certe 25
   cognoram a parua uirgine magnanimam.
anne bonum oblita es facinus, quo regium adepta es
   coniugium, quod non fortior ausit alis?
sed tum maesta uirum mittens quae uerba locuta es!
   Iuppiter, ut tristi lumina saepe manu!   30

quis te mutauit tantus deus? an quod amantes
   non longe a caro corpore abesse uolunt?
atque ibi me cunctis pro dulci coniuge diuis
   non sine taurino sanguine pollicita es,
si reditum tetulisset. is haut in tempore longo   35
   captam Asiam Aegypti finibus addiderat.
quis ego pro factis caelesti reddita coetu
   pristina uota nouo munere dissoluo.
inuita, o regina, tuo de uertice cessi,
   inuita: adiuro teque tuumque caput,   40
digna ferat quod si quis inaniter adiurarit:
   sed qui se ferro postulet esse parem?
ille quoque euersus mons est, quem maximum in oris
   progenies Thiae clara superuehitur,   44
cum Medi peperere nouum mare, cumque iuuentus
   per medium classi barbara nauit Athon.
quid facient crines, cum ferro talia cedant?
   Iuppiter, ut Chalybon omne genus pereat,
et qui principio sub terra quaerere uenas
   institit ac ferri stringere duritiem!   50
abiunctae paulo ante comae mea fata sorores
   lugebant, cum se Memnonis Aethiopis
unigena impellens nutantibus aera pennis
   obtulit Arsinoes Locridos ales equos,
isque per aetherias me tollens auolat umbras   55
   et Veneris casto collocat in gremio:
ipsa suum Zephyritis eo famulum legarat,
   Graiia Canopeis incola litoribus.
inde Venus uario ne solum in limine caeli
   ex Ariadnaeis aurea temporibus   60
fixa corona foret, sed nos quoque fulgeremus
   deuotae flaui uerticis exuuiae,

uuidulam a fluctu cedentem ad templa deum me
    sidus in antiquis diua nouum posuit.
Virginis et saeui contingens namque Leonis   65
    lumina, Callisto iuncta Lycaoniae,
uertor in occasum, tardum dux ante Booten,
    qui uix sero alto mergitur Oceano;
sed quamquam me nocte premunt uestigia diuum,
    lux autem canae Tethyi restituit.   70
pace tua fari hic liceat, Ramnusia uirgo,
    namque ego non ullo uera timore tegam —
nec si me infestis discerpent sidera dictis —
    condita quin ueri pectoris euoluam: 74
non his tam laetor rebus, quam me afore semper,
    afore me a dominae uertice discrucior.
quicum ego, dum uirgo quondam fuit, omnibus expers
    unguentis, una milia multa bibi.
nunc uos, optato quas iunxit lumine taeda,
    non prius unanimis corpora coniugibus   80
tradite nudantes reiecta ueste papillas,
    quam iucunda mihi munera libet onyx —
uester onyx, casto colitis quae iura cubili.
    (sed quae se impuro dedit adulterio,
illius a! mala dona leuis bibat irrita puluis: 85
    namque ego ab indignis praemia nulla peto;
sed magis, o nuptae, semper concordia uestras,
    semper amor sedes incolat assiduus.)
tu uero, regina, tuens cum sidera diuam
    placabis festis luminibus Venerem,   90
unguinis expertem non siris esse tuam me,
    sed potius largis affice muneribus,
sidera cur iterent 'utinam coma regia fiam!
    proximus Hydrochoi fulgeret Oarion!'

67

O dulci iucunda uiro, iucunda parenti,
   salue, teque bona Iuppiter auctet ope,
ianua, quam Balbo dicunt seruisse benigne
   olim, cum sedes ipse senex tenuit,
quamque ferunt rursus gnato seruisse maligne,   5
   postquam es porrecto facta marita sene.
dic agedum nobis, quare mutata feraris
   in dominum ueterem deseruisse fidem.
'Non (ita Caecilio placeam, cui tradita nunc sum)
   culpa mea est, quamquam dicitur esse mea,   10
nec peccatum a me quisquam pote dicere quicquam:
   uerum †istius populi ianua qui te† facit,
qui, quacumque aliquid reperitur non bene factum,
   ad me omnes clamant: ianua, culpa tua est.'
Non istuc satis est uno te dicere uerbo,   15
   sed facere ut quiuis sentiat et, uideat.
'Qui possum? nemo quaerit nec scire laborat.'
   Nos uolumus: nobis dicere ne dubita.
'Primum igitur, uirgo quod fertur tradita nobis,
   falsum est. non illam uir prior attigerat,   20
languidior tenera cui pendens sicula beta
   numquam se mediam sustulit ad tunicam;
sed pater illius gnati uiolasse cubile
   dicitur et miseram conscelerasse domum,
siue quod impia mens caeco flagrabat amore,   25
   seu quod iners sterili semine natus erat,
ut quaerendum unde ⟨unde⟩ foret neruosius illud,
   quod posset zonam soluere uirgineam.'

Egregium narras mira pietate parentem,
   qui ipse sui gnati minxerit in gremium.   30
'Atqui non solum hoc dicit se cognitum habere
   Brixia Cycneae supposita speculae,
flauus quam molli praecurrit flumine Mella,
   Brixia Veronae mater amata meae,
sed de Postumio et Corneli narrat amore,   35
   cum quibus illa malum fecit adulterium.
dixerit hic aliquis: quid? tu istaec, ianua, nosti,
   cui numquam domini limine abesse licet,
nec populum auscultare, sed hic suffixa tigillo
   tantum operire soles aut aperire domum?   40
saepe illam audiui furtiua uoce loquentem
   solam cum ancillis haec sua flagitia,
nomine dicentem quos diximus, utpote quae mi
   speraret nec linguam esse nec auriculam.
praeterea addebat quendam, quem dicere nolo   45
   nomine, ne tollat rubra supercilia.
longus homo est, magnas cui lites intulit olim
   falsum mendaci uentre puerperium.'

68

Quod mihi fortuna casuque oppressus acerbo
   conscriptum hoc lacrimis mittis epistolium,
naufragum ut eiectum spumantibus aequoris undis
   subleuem et a mortis limine restituam,
quem neque sancta Venus molli requiescere somno 5
   desertum in lecto caelibe perpetitur,
nec ueterum dulci scriptorum carmine Musae
   oblectant, cum mens anxia peruigilat:

id gratum est mihi, me quoniam tibi dicis amicum,
   muneraque et Musarum hinc petis et Veneris. 10
sed tibi ne mea sint ignota incommoda, Malli,
   neu me odisse putes hospitis officium,
accipe, quis merser fortunae fluctibus ipse,
   ne amplius a misero dona beata petas.   14
tempore quo primum uestis mihi tradita pura est,
   iucundum cum aetas florida uer ageret,
multa satis lusi: non est dea nescia nostri,
   quae dulcem curis miscet amaritiem.
sed totum hoc studium luctu fraterna mihi mors
   abstulit. o misero frater adempte mihi,   20
tu mea tu moriens fregisti commoda, frater,
   tecum una tota est nostra sepulta domus,
omnia tecum una perierunt gaudia nostra,
   quae tuus in uita dulcis alebat amor.
cuius ego interitu tota de mente fugaui   25
   haec studia atque omnes delicias animi.
quare, quod scribis, 'Veronae turpe, Catulle,
   esse, quod hic quisquis de meliore nota
frigida deserto tepefactat membra cubili,'
   id, Malli, non est turpe, magis miserum est. 30
ignosces igitur si, quae mihi luctus ademit,
   haec tibi non tribuo munera, cum nequeo.
nam, quod scriptorum non magna est copia apud me,
   hoc fit, quod Romae uiuimus: illa domus,
illa mihi sedes, illic mea carpitur aetas;   35
   huc una ex multis capsula me sequitur.
quod cum ita sit, nolim statuas nos mente maligna
   id facere aut animo non satis ingenuo,
quod tibi non utriusque petenti copia posta est:
   ultro ego deferrem, copia siqua foret.   40

Non possum reticere, deae, qua me Allius in re
    iuuerit aut quantis iuuerit officiis,
ne fugiens saeclis obliuiscentibus aetas
    illius hoc caeca nocte tegat studium:
sed dicam uobis, uos porro dicite multis   45
    milibus et facite haec carta loquatur anus.

    .   .   .   .

    notescatque magis mortuus atque magis,
nec tenuem texens sublimis aranea telam
    in deserto Alli nomine opus faciat.   50
nam, mihi quam dederit duplex Amathusia curam,
    scitis, et in quo me torruerit genere,
cum tantum arderem quantum Trinacria rupes
    lymphaque in Oetaeis Malia Thermopylis,
maesta neque assiduo tabescere lumina fletu   55
    cessarent tristique imbre madere genae,
qualis in aerii perlucens uertice montis
    riuus muscoso prosilit e lapide
(qui cum de prona praeceps est ualle uolutus,
    per medium densi transit iter populi,   60
dulce uiatori lasso in sudore leuamen,
    cum grauis exustos aestus hiulcat agros).
hic uelut in nigro iactatis turbine nautis
    lenius aspirans aura secunda uenit
iam prece Pollucis, iam Castoris implorata,   65
    tale fuit nobis Allius auxilium.
is clausum lato patefecit limite campum,
    isque domum nobis isque dedit dominae,
ad quam communes exerceremus amores.
    quo mea se molli candida diua pede   70

intulit et trito fulgentem in limine plantam
  innixa arguta constituit solea,
coniugis ut quondam flagrans aduenit amore
  Protesilaeam Laudamia domum
inceptam frustra, nondum cum sanguine sacro   75
  hostia caelestis pacificasset eros.
nil mihi tam ualde placeat, Ramnusia uirgo,
  quod temere inuitis suscipiatur eris.
quam ieiuna pium desideret ara cruorem,
  docta est amisso Laudamia uiro,   80
coniugis ante coacta noui dimittere collum,
  quam ueniens una atque altera rursus hiems
noctibus in longis auidum saturasset amorem,
  posset ut abrupto uiuere coniugio,
quod scibant Parcae non longo tempore abesse,   85
  si miles muros isset ad Iliacos.
nam tum Helenae raptu primores Argiuorum
  coeperat ad sese Troia ciere uiros,
Troia (nefas!) commune sepulcrum Asiae Europaeque,
  Troia uirum et uirtutum omnium acerba cinis,   90
quaene etiam nostro letum miserabile fratri
  attulit? ei misero frater adempte mihi,
ei misero fratri iucundum lumen ademptum,
  tecum una tota est nostra sepulta domus,
omnia tecum una perierunt gaudia nostra,   95
  quae tuus in uita dulcis alebat amor.
quem nunc tam longe non inter nota sepulcra
  nec prope cognatos compositum cineres,
sed Troia obscena, Troia infelice sepultum
  detinet extremo terra aliena solo.   100
ad quam tum properans fertur ⟨lecta⟩ undique pubes
    Graeca penetralis deseruisse focos,

ne Paris abducta gauisus libera moecha
   otia pacato degeret in thalamo.
quo tibi tum casu, pulcerrima Laudamia,   105
   ereptum est uita dulcius atque anima
coniugium: tanto te absorbens uertice amoris
   aestus in abruptum detulerat barathrum,
quale ferunt Grai Pheneum prope Cyllenaeum
   siccare emulsa pingue palude solum,   110
quod quondam caesis montis fodisse medullis
   audit falsiparens Amphitryoniades,
tempore quo certa Stymphalia monstra sagitta
   perculit imperio deterioris eri,
pluribus ut caeli tereretur ianua diuis,   115
   Hebe nec longa uirginitate foret.
sed tuus altus amor barathro fuit altior illo,
   qui tamen indomitam ferre iugum docuit.
nam nec tam carum confecto aetate parenti
   una caput seri nata nepotis alit,   120
qui, cum diuitiis uix tandem inuentus auitis
   nomen testatas intulit in tabulas,
impia derisi gentilis gaudia tollens,
   suscitat a cano uolturium capiti;
nec tantum niueo gauisa est ulla columbo   125
   compar (quae multo dicitur improbius
oscula mordenti semper decerpere rostro,
   quam quae praecipue multiuola est mulier).
sed tu horum magnos uicisti sola furores,
   ut semel es flauo conciliata uiro.   130
aut nihil aut paulo cui tum concedere digna
   lux mea se nostrum contulit in gremium,
quam circumcursans hinc illinc saepe Cupido
   fulgebat crocina candidus in tunica.

quae tamen etsi uno non est contenta Catullo, 135
  rara uerecundae furta feremus erae,
ne nimium simus stultorum more molesti.
  saepe etiam Iuno, maxima caelicolum,
coniugis in culpa flagrantem concoquit iram,
  noscens omniuoli plurima furta Iouis.   140
atqui nec diuis homines componier aequum est —
  ingratum tremuli tolle parentis onus;
nec tamen illa mihi dextra deducta paterna
  fragrantem Assyrio uenit odore domum,
sed furtiua dedit mira munuscula nocte,   145
  ipsius ex ipso dempta uiri gremio.
quare illud satis est, si nobis is datur unis
  quem lapide illa dies candidiore notat.
hoc tibi, quod potui, confectum carmine munus
  pro multis, Alli, redditur officiis,   150
ne uestrum scabra tangat rubigine nomen
  haec atque illa dies atque alia atque alia.
huc addent diui quam plurima, quae Themis olim
  antiquis solita est munera ferre piis.
sitis felices et tu simul et tua uita,   155
  et domus in qua ⟨nos⟩ lusimus et domina,
et qui principio nobis †terram dedit aufert†,
  a quo sunt primo omnia nata bono,
et longe ante omnes mihi quae me carior ipso est,
  lux mea, qua uiua uiuere dulce mihi est.   160

69

Noli admirari, quare tibi femina nulla,
    Rufe, uelit tenerum supposuisse femur,
non si illam rarae labefactes munere uestis
    aut perluciduli deliciis lapidis.
laedit te quaedam mala fabula, qua tibi fertur
    ualle sub alarum trux habitare caper.
hunc metuunt omnes, neque mirum: nam mala ualde e
    bestia, nec quicum bella puella cubet.
quare aut crudelem nasorum interfice pestem,
    aut admirari desine cur fugiunt.

70

Nulli se dicit mulier mea nubere malle
    quam mihi, non si se Iuppiter ipse petat.
dicit: sed mulier cupido quod dicit amanti,
    in uento et rapida scribere oportet aqua.

71

Si cui iure bono sacer alarum obstitit hircus,
    aut si quem merito tarda podagra secat,
aemulus iste tuus, qui uestrum exercet amorem,
    mirifice est †a te nactus utrumque malum.
nam quotiens futuit, totiens ulciscitur ambos:
    illam affligit odore, ipse perit podagra.

72

cebas quondam solum te nosse Catullum,
Lesbia, nec prae me uelle tenere Iouem.
exi tum te non tantum ut uulgus amicam,
sed pater ut gnatos diligit et generos.
nc te cognoui: quare etsi impensius uror,   5
multo mi tamen es uilior et leuior.
.i potis est, inquis? quod amantem iniuria talis
cogit amare magis, sed bene uelle minus.

73

·sine de quoquam quicquam bene uelle mereri
aut aliquem fieri posse putare pium.
·nia sunt ingrata, nihil fecisse benigne
⟨prodest,⟩ immo etiam taedet obestque magis;
mihi, quem nemo grauius nec acerbius urget,   5
quam modo qui me unum atque unicum amicum habuit.

74

·llius audierat patruum obiurgare solere,
·si quis delicias diceret aut faceret.
·c ne ipsi accideret, patrui perdepsuit ipsam
·uxorem et patruum reddidit Arpocratem.
.od uoluit fecit: nam, quamuis irrumet ipsum
·nunc patruum, uerbum non faciet patruus.

75

Huc est mens deducta tua mea, Lesbia, culpa
  atque ita se officio perdidit ipsa suo,
ut iam nec bene uelle queat tibi, si optima fias,
  nec desistere amare, omnia si facias.

76

Siqua recordanti benefacta priora uoluptas
  est homini, cum se cogitat esse pium,
nec sanctam uiolasse fidem, nec foedere nullo
  diuum ad fallendos numine abusum homines,
multa parata manent in longa aetate, Catulle,
  ex hoc ingrato gaudia amore tibi.
nam quaecumque homines bene cuiquam aut dicere possi
  aut facere, haec a te dictaque factaque sunt.
omnia quae ingratae perierunt credita menti.
  quare cur te iam amplius excrucies?
quin tu animo offirmas atque istinc teque reducis,
  et dis inuitis desinis esse miser?
difficile est longum subito deponere amorem?
  difficile est, uerum hoc qualubet efficias:
una salus haec est, hoc est tibi peruincendum,
  hoc facias, siue id non pote siue pote.
o di, si uestrum est misereri, aut si quibus umquam
  extremam iam ipsa in morte tulistis opem,
me miserum aspicite et, si uitam puriter egi,
  eripite hanc pestem perniciemque mihi,
quae mihi subrepens imos ut torpor in artus
  expulit ex omni pectore laetitias.

non iam illud quaero, contra me ut diligat illa,
    aut, quod non potis est, esse pudica uelit: 24
ipse ualere opto et taetrum hunc deponere morbum.
    o di, reddite mi hoc pro pietate mea.

77

Rufe mihi frustra ac nequiquam credite amice
    (frustra? immo magno cum pretio atque malo),
sicine subrepsti mi, atque intestina perurens
    ei misero eripuisti omnia nostra bona?
eripuisti, heu heu nostrae crudele uenenum   5
    uitae, heu heu nostrae pestis amicitiae.

78

Gallus habet fratres, quorum est lepidissima coniunx
    alterius, lepidus filius alterius.
Gallus homo est bellus: nam dulces iungit amores,
    cum puero ut bello bella puella cubet.   4
Gallus homo est stultus, nec se uidet esse maritum,
    qui patruus patrui monstret adulterium.

78b

sed nunc id doleo, quod purae pura puellae
    suauia comminxit spurca saliua tua.
uerum id non impune feres: nam te omnia saecla
    noscent et, qui sis, fama loquetur anus.

79

Lesbius est pulcer. quid ni? quem Lesbia malit
    quam te cum tota gente, Catulle, tua.
sed tamen hic pulcer uendat cum gente Catullum,
    si tria notorum suauia reppererit.

80

Quid dicam, Gelli, quare rosea ista labella
    hiberna fiant candidiora niue,
mane domo cum exis et cum te octaua quiete
    e molli longo suscitat hora die?
nescio quid certe est: an uere fama susurrat   5
    grandia te medii tenta uorare uiri?
sic certe est: clamant Victoris rupta miselli
    ilia, et emulso labra notata sero.

81

Nemone in tanto potuit populo esse, Iuuenti,
    bellus homo quem tu diligere inciperes
praeter quam iste tuus moribunda ab sede Pisauri
    hospes inaurata pallidior statua,
qui tibi nunc cordi est, quem tu praeponere nobis   5
    audes, et nescis quod facinus facias?

82

Quinti, si tibi uis oculos debere Catullum
  aut aliud si quid carius est oculis,
eripere ei noli, multo quod carius illi
  est oculis seu quid carius est oculis.

83

Lesbia mi praesente uiro mala plurima dicit:
  haec illi fatuo maxima laetitia est.
mule, nihil sentis? si nostri oblita taceret,
  sana esset: nunc quod gannit et obloquitur,   4
non solum meminit, sed, quae multo acrior est res,
  irata est. hoc est, uritur et loquitur.

84

Chommoda dicebat, si quando commoda uellet
  dicere, et insidias Arrius hinsidias,
et tum mirifice sperabat se esse locutum,
  cum quantum poterat dixerat hinsidias.
credo, sic mater, sic liber auunculus eius,   5
  sic maternus auus dixerat atque auia.
hoc misso in Syriam requierant omnibus aures:
  audibant eadem haec leniter et leuiter,
nec sibi postilla metuebant talia uerba,
  cum subito affertur nuntius horribilis: 10
Ionios fluctus, postquam illuc Arrius isset,
  iam non Ionios esse sed Hionios.

85

Odi et amo. quare id faciam, fortasse requiris?
nescio, sed fieri sentio et excrucior.

86

Quintia formosa est multis. mihi candida, longa,
   recta est: haec ego sic singula confiteor.
totum illud formosa nego: nam nulla uenustas,
   nulla in tam magno est corpore mica salis.   4
Lesbia formosa est, quae cum pulcerrima tota est,
   tum omnibus una omnis surripuit Veneres.

87

Nulla potest mulier tantum se dicere amatam
   uere, quantum a me Lesbia amata mea est.
nulla fides ullo fuit umquam foedere tanta,
   quanta in amore tuo ex parte reperta mea est.

88

Quid facit is, Gelli, qui cum matre atque sorore
   prurit et abiectis peruigilat tunicis?
quid facit is, patruum qui non sinit esse maritum?
   ecquid scis quantum suscipiat sceleris?
suscipit, o Gelli, quantum non ultima Tethys   5
   nec genitor Nympharum abluit Oceanus:
nam nihil est quicquam sceleris, quo prodeat ultra,
   non si demisso se ipse uoret capite.

89

Gellius est tenuis: quid ni? cui tam bona mater
  tamque ualens uiuat tamque uenusta soror
tamque bonus patruus tamque omnia plena puellis
  cognatis, quare is desinat esse macer?   4
qui ut nihil attingat, nisi quod fas tangere non est,
  quantumuis quare sit macer inuenies.

90

Nascatur magus ex Gelli matrisque nefando
  coniugio et discat Persicum aruspicium
(nam magus ex matre et gnato gignatur oportet,
  si uera est Persarum impia religio)
gnatus ut accepto ueneretur carmine diuos,   5
  omentum in flamma pingue liquefaciens.

91

Non ideo, Gelli, sperabam te mihi fidum
  in misero hoc nostro, hoc perdito amore, fore,
quod te cognossem bene constantemue putarem
  aut posse a turpi mentem inhibere probro;   4
sed neque quod matrem nec germanam esse uidebam
  hanc tibi, cuius me magnus edebat amor.
et quamuis tecum multo coniungerer usu,
  non satis id causae credideram esse tibi.
tu satis id duxti: tantum tibi gaudium in omni
  culpa est, in quacumque est aliquid sceleris.   10

92

Lesbia mi dicit semper male nec tacet umquam
    de me: Lesbia me dispeream nisi amat.
quo signo? quia sunt totidem mea: deprecor illam
    assidue, uerum dispeream nisi amo.

93

Nil nimium studeo, Caesar, tibi uelle placere,
    nec scire utrum sis albus an ater homo.

94

Mentula moechatur. moechatur mentula? certe.
    hoc est quod dicunt: ipsa olera olla legit.

95

Zmyrna mei Cinnae nonam post denique messem
    quam coepta est nonamque edita post hiemem,
milia cum interea quingenta Hortensius uno
     4
Zmyrna cauas Satrachi penitus mittetur ad undas,
    Zmyrnam cana diu saecula peruoluent.
at Volusi annales Paduam morientur ad ipsam
    et laxas scombris saepe dabunt tunicas.

95b

Parua mei mihi sint cordi monimenta . . .,
    at populus tumido gaudeat Antimacho.

96

Si quicquam mutis gratum acceptumue sepulcris
    accidere a nostro, Calue, dolore potest,
quo desiderio ueteres renouamus amores
    atque olim missas flemus amicitias,
certe non tanto mors immatura dolori est   5
    Quintiliae, quantum gaudet amore tuo.

97

Non (ita me di ament) quicquam referre putaui,
    utrumne os an culum olfacerem Aemilio.
nilo mundius hoc, nihiloque immundius illud,
    uerum etiam culus mundior et melior:
nam sine dentibus est. os dentis sesquipedalis,   5
    gingiuas uero ploxeni habet ueteris,
praeterea rictum qualem diffissus in aestu
    meientis mulae cunnus habere solet.
hic futuit multas et se facit esse uenustum,
    et non pistrino traditur atque asino?   10
quem siqua attingit, non illam posse putemus
    aegroti culum lingere carnificis?

98

In te, si in quemquam, dici pote, putide Victi,
    id quod uerbosis dicitur et fatuis.
ista cum lingua, si usus ueniat tibi, possis
    culos et crepidas lingere carpatinas.
si nos omnino uis omnes perdere, Victi,   5
    hiscas: omnino quod cupis efficies.

99

Surripui tibi, dum ludis, mellite Iuuenti,
    suauiolum dulci dulcius ambrosia.
uerum id non impune tuli: namque amplius horam
    suffixum in summa me memini esse cruce,
dum tibi me purgo nec possum fletibus ullis   5
    tantillum uestrae demere saeuitiae.
nam simul id factum est, multis diluta labella
    guttis abstersti mollibus articulis,
ne quicquam nostro contractum ex ore maneret,
    tamquam commictae spurca saliua lupae.   10
praeterea infesto miserum me tradere Amori
    non cessasti omnique excruciare modo,
ut mi ex ambrosia mutatum iam foret illud
    suauiolum tristi tristius elleboro.
quam quoniam poenam misero proponis amori, 15
    numquam iam posthac basia surripiam.

100

Caelius Aufillenum et Quintius Aufillenam
    flos Veronensum depereunt iuuenum,
hic fratrem, ille sororem. hoc est, quod dicitur, illud
    fraternum uere dulce sodalicium.
cui faueam potius? Caeli, tibi: nam tua nobis   5
    perspecta est igni tum unica amicitia,
cum uesana meas torreret flamma medullas.
    sis felix, Caeli, sis in amore potens.

101

Multas per gentes et multa per aequora uectus
   aduenio has miseras, frater, ad inferias,
ut te postremo donarem munere mortis
   et mutam nequiquam alloquerer cinerem.
quandoquidem fortuna mihi tete abstulit ipsum,   5
   heu miser indigne frater adempte mihi,
nunc tamen interea haec, prisco quae more parentum
   tradita sunt tristi munere ad inferias,
accipe fraterno multum manantia fletu,
   atque in perpetuum, frater, aue atque uale.   10

102

Si quicquam tacito commissum est fido ab amico,
   cuius sit penitus nota fides animi,
meque esse inuenies illorum iure sacratum,
   Corneli, et factum me esse puta Arpocratem.

103

Aut sodes mihi redde decem sestertia, Silo,
   deinde esto quamuis saeuus et indomitus:
aut, si te nummi delectant, desine quaeso
   leno esse atque idem saeuus et indomitus.

104

Credis me potuisse meae maledicere uitae,
  ambobus mihi quae carior est oculis?
non potui, nec, si possem, tam perdite amarem:
  sed tu cum Tappone omnia monstra facis.

105

Mentula conatur Pipleium scandere montem:
  Musae furcillis praecipitem eiciunt.

106

Cum puero bello praeconem qui uidet esse,
  quid credat, nisi se uendere discupere?

107

Si quicquam cupido optantique optigit umquam
  insperanti, hoc est gratum animo proprie.
quare hoc est gratum, nobis quoque, carius auro,
  quod te restituis, Lesbia, mi cupido.
restituis cupido atque insperanti, ipsa refers te   5
  nobis. o lucem candidiore nota!
quis me uno uiuit felicior, aut magis †hac est
  †optandus uita dicere quis poterit?

108

Si, Comini, populi arbitrio tua cana senectus
   spurcata impuris moribus intereat,
non equidem dubito quin primum inimica bonorum
   lingua exsecta auido sit data uulturio,
effossos oculos uoret atro gutture coruus,   5
   intestina canes, cetera membra lupi.

109

Iucundum, mea uita, mihi proponis amorem
   hunc nostrum inter nos perpetuumque fore.
di magni, facite ut uere promittere possit,
   atque id sincere dicat et ex animo,
ut liceat nobis tota perducere uita   5
   aeternum hoc sanctae foedus amicitiae.

110

Aufillena, bonae semper laudantur amicae:
   accipiunt pretium, quae facere instituunt.
tu, quod promisti mihi quod mentita inimica es,
   quod nec das et fers saepe, facis facinus.
aut facere ingenuae est, aut non promisse pudicae, 5
   Aufillena, fuit: sed data corripere
fraudando officiis, plus quam meretricis auarae ⟨est⟩,
   quae sese toto corpore prostituit.

111

Aufillena, uiro contentam uiuere solo,
    nuptarum laus ex laudibus eximiis:
sed cuiuis quamuis potius succumbere par est,
    quam matrem fratres ex patruo . . .

112

Multus homo es, Naso, neque tecum multus homo ⟨est qu
    descendit: Naso, multus es et pathicus.

113

Consule Pompeio primum duo, Cinna, solebant
    Maeciliam: facto consule nunc iterum
manserunt duo, sed creuerunt milia in unum
    singula. fecundum semen adulterio.

114

Firmano saltu non falso Mentula diues
    fertur, qui tot res in se habet egregias,
aucupium omne genus, piscis, prata, arua ferasque.
    nequiquam: fructus sumptibus exsuperat.
quare concedo sit diues, dum omnia desint.
    saltum laudemus, dum †modo ipse egeat.

115

Mentula habet instar triginta iugera prati,
 quadraginta arui: cetera sunt maria.
cur non diuitiis Croesum superare potis sit,
 uno qui in saltu tot bona possideat,
prata arua ingentes siluas altasque paludes   5
 usque ad Hyperboreos et mare ad Oceanum?
omnia magna haec sunt, tamen ipsest maximus ultro,
 non homo, sed uero mentula magna minax.

116

Saepe tibi studioso animo uenante requirens
 carmina uti possem mittere Battiadae,
qui te lenirem nobis, neu conarere
 tela infesta ⟨meum⟩ mittere in usque caput,   4
hunc uideo mihi nunc frustra sumptum esse laborem,
 Gelli, nec nostras hic ualuisse preces.
contra nos tela ista tua euitabimus acta
 at fixus nostris tu dabi' supplicium.

COMMENTARY

A preface to a collection of short poems, offering C.'s fresh, smart volume to Cornelius Nepos, the historian and biographer.

Poem 1 dramatizes the act of dedication: Cornelius gets the presentation copy, but there will be other copies, of course, which will circulate in the normal way — a repetition on a larger scale of the process through which many of the individual poems, if not all, have already passed.

What did the volume contain? The collection introduced by Poem 1 certainly included poems originally sent to various addressees, but now gathered together (and perhaps revised) for formal publication. But the Catullan *corpus*, as we have it, though fragmentary, is too big for a single papyrus roll, and it comprises poems (61–8) hardly to be described as *nugae*. Did Poem 1 introduce a 'first collected edition' along the lines of the present 1–60 but shorter — Poem 14b looks like a fragment from another preface? How many (if any) of 69–116 were included? On these difficult questions see Wheeler 1–32.

Metre: hendecasyllabics (the metre of about two thirds of 1–60).

1. An echo of the question with which Meleager began a longer, more artificial introduction to his famous *Garland* (*AP* 4. 1. 1): Μοῦσα φίλα, τίνι τάνδε φέρεις πάγκαρπον ἀοιδάν;

dono: note the mood (indicative) and the tense (present). The act of dedication stands outside time; cf. 4. 26 *dedicat*. But the present also anticipates our curiosity about the recipient, and justifies the description *lepidum nouum libellum* — Cornelius' copy awaits inspection. Ostensibly the adjectives describe its appearance ('smart', 'fresh') (cf. Suffenus' *noui libri*, 22. 6–8); at the same time they imply an apt description of the contents; cf. 6. 17 *lepido uersu*, 14. 8–9 *nouum munus* ('novel', 'unprecedented'); *libellum*, a colloquial or 'affective' diminutive (the roll need not have been a small one), introduces connotations ('modest', 'unpretentious') appropriate to 4 *nugas*. Cf. the ambiguities in Horace, *Ep*. 1. 20.

2. Also ambiguous. Strictly appropriate to the primary meaning only of *expolitum*, as *modo* indicates; i.e. 'freshly polished up'; pumice was used to smooth the ends of the roll of papyrus. But *arida pumice* also draws out transferred meanings of *expolitum* as ironical overtones ('smooth', 'slick'), while the connotations of *aridus* as a description of style ('dull', 'lifeless') suggest the paradox 'dull grind produces bright verse'. For the process of smoothing the ends of the roll see 22. 8; for this style Propertius 3. 1. 8 *exactus tenui pumice uersus eat*. [*arido* V; but Servius remarks on Verg. *A*. 12. 587 that C. made *pumex* feminine; modern editors accordingly print *arida* here.]

3. *Corneli, tibi*: for the pattern of question and answer see 100. 5.

3–4. The imperfect *solebas* (= 'you *are* always saying you think ...') adopts the point of view of the recipient of the dedication, a usage common in the opening words of a letter, but seldom maintained throughout (contrast 5 *ausus es*, not *ausus eras*).

4. *nugas*: COPLEY 203 argues for the usual colloquial meaning, 'rubbish', 'junk' — i.e. *nugae* does not yet designate a recognized literary genre ('scraps of verse'); contrast on 50. 4 *uersiculos*.

5–7. Cornelius has 'only this very moment had the courage to tackle' (*iam tum, cum ausus es ... explicare*) a formidable work; the fact adds weight to his opinion of C.'s *nugae*, and makes him the obvious person to receive the presentation copy.

A 3-volume history was not long by contemporary standards — Cornelius' own *De uiris illustribus* was to run into 16 at least: what called for courage was the arduous research involved. On Cornelius Nepos and his *Chronica*, now lost, a kind of chronological survey, see J. C. Rolfe in *OCD* — his strictures ('colloquial features and many archaisms, not used for artistic effect, but from indifference') perhaps misconstrue an affectation of conversational nonchalance not unlike C.'s; Cornelius is also said to have written love poetry; he makes only one brief passing reference to C., in his life of Atticus (12. 4). A Cornelius is the addressee of Poem 102 and the name occurs again in 67. 35.

Unqualified admiration was not the done thing in the Catullan circle: *cartae* (cf. 22. 6 *cartae regiae*) is hardly a grand synonym for *uolumina* (though it is used by Lucretius 3. 10); *explicare* similarly undercuts the grandiloquence of *omne aeuum*, soliciting a visual image of 'the whole of time' laid out on three sheets of papyrus; the *cartae* are *doctae, Iuppiter* ('damned sound scholarship' — though *doctus* implies taste as well as learning; see on 35. 17), but they are also *laboriosae* (a word that suggests going out of one's way to make work for oneself — cf. Cic. *Cael.* 1 *uos laboriosos existumet*).

5. *unus Italorum*: i.e. Greeks had perhaps done this, but Cornelius was the only man in the whole country with the courage to attempt it.

6. *explicare*: 'expound'; primarily of the labour of composition; but also of the finished work, in which the author expounds his subject to the reader.

9–10. The casual colloquialism of *quidquid hoc libelli qualecumque* ('my little book, such as it is, for what it's worth') offsets the earnestness of the final prayer. *patrona uirgo* gives the cliché of the poet's muse a characteristically Roman twist, that of the *patronus-cliens* relationship — she becomes his protectress, not his source of inspiration; C. unlike Horace does not specify which muse he means, but then neither does Homer — or Meleager; to do so here might overdo the mock solemnity which invests the genuine feeling latent in this prayer. [Line 9, metrically a syllable short, is usually repaired by the insertion of *o*, but objections have been raised to both text and syntax — see Fordyce.]

10. *saeclo*: 'generation'; cf. 43. 8 and 95. 6. With the final prayer cf. that in Poem 50.

See:

Francis Cairns, 'Catullus I', *Mnemosyne* 22 (1969), 153–8.

Frank O. Copley, 'Catullus, *c.* 1', *TAPhA* 82 (1951), 200–6.

J. P. Elder, 'Catullus I, his poetic creed, and Nepos', *HSPh* 71 (1966), 143–9.

P. Levine, *California St. Class. Ant.* 2 (1969) 209–16.

D. Singleton, *CPh* 67 (1972) 192–6.

Marcello Zicàri, 'Sul primo carme di Catullo', *Maia* 17 (1965), 232–40.

2

Poem 2 parodies the formal layout of a hymn to a god or goddess; for Hellenistic precedents see Meleager, *AP* 7. 195–6 (= 4058–73 *GP*), the first to a locust, the second to a cicada. Working in an essentially frivolous tradition, C. has written a serious poem about himself and Lesbia, in which he contrasts, with exquisite wry irony, his mistress's melancholy and his own: hers seems easily assuaged; he knows that his is not. Unfortunately, despite the fascination these lines possess for all who read them, there are difficulties of interpretation to which no wholly satisfactory solution has been found. The text and interpretation adopted here give a 10-line poem of almost mathematical precision in its structure, followed by a 3-line fragment. Eight out of the 10 lines depend grammatically on the first word. The first 8 lines lead up to the last 2, and in these the focus of attention is transferred from the sparrow and its mistress to the poet; at the same time, the mood changes: the poem takes on a seriousness that thrusts formal banter aside; the last word is *curas*. Is Poem 2, like Poem 51, a declaration and a challenge? Does C. suspect Lesbia loves him, but hesitate like her to take the irrevocable step?

Metre: hendecasyllabics.

1–4. No difficulty. As in the two Meleager epigrams, the first word of the poem names an addressee; the *passer* is identified by an appositional expansion (*deliciae meae puellae*), then described in a series of relative clauses, arranged in an increasing triad (a short half-line; a longer half-line; a complete line flowing over into a second complete line). This is how one goes about stating the attributes of the divinity in a hymn to a god or goddess; cf. Poem 34 and Lucretius' opening address to Venus.

1. *passer*: vocative; the traditional translation, 'sparrow'

suggests a slightly improbable pet; various alternative identifications ('chaffinch', etc.) have been proposed. Aphrodite is represented, however, by Sappho (Fr. 1 LP = *LGS* 191, lines 9–12) as riding in a chariot drawn by sparrows (στροῦθοι).

deliciae meae puellae: 'my mistress's darling'. The phrase is repeated at 3. 4 (*meae puellae* also 3. 3 and 17) — a series of verbal echoes binding the two poems together. The plural *deliciae* has three distinguishable meanings in Cicero: (1) 'pet', 'darling', often coupled with *amores*; e.g. *Att.* 1. 5. 8 (Cicero is referring to his daughter) *Tulliola, deliciae nostrae*; *Att.* 16. 6. 4 *salutem dices et Atticae, deliciis atque amoribus meis*; *Diu.* 1. 79 *amores et deliciae tuae*, Roscius; cf. *Phil.* 13. 26 *deliciae atque amores populi Romani*, *L. Antonius*; (2) any display of over-fastidiousness or self-indulgence, normally in a pejorative sense: e.g. *Att.* 1. 17. 9 *ecce aliae deliciae equitum, uix ferendae!* (3) 'love-making'; Cicero implies this use of *deliciae* belonged to the jargon of the smart set (*Cael.* 44 *amores . . . et deliciae quae uocantur*).

C. uses the word 4 times (2. 1; 3. 4; 6. 1; 32. 2) in sense (1), twice in sense (3) in the phrase *delicias facere* (45. 24; 74. 2); the meaning of the word in 68. 26 and 69. 4 is less easily fixed.

For *deliciae* of an animal cf. Petronius 137 *occidisti Priapi delicias, anserem omnibus matronis acceptissimum* and Martial 1. 109. 5 (a reminiscence of C.); in the phrase *in deliciis habere*, Cicero, *Diu.* 1. 76 (of a monkey) and Valerius Maximus 1. 5. 3 (of a puppy).

For the corresponding adjective *delicatus* see on 50. 3.

For *puella* = C.'s mistress see on 51. 7.

2. *ludere*: picked up by *ludere* in line 9; dependent here, like *tenere* and 4 *incitare*, on 4 *solet*.

in sinu: *sinus* denotes a fold or curve, in the body or in one's dress. Here 'in her lap' rather than 'to her breast' in view of 3. 8 *nec sese a gremio illius mouebat*.

3. *primum digitum*: = 'finger tip'.

4. An example of (1) '*appositional syntax*', a feature of archaic style (especially frequent in similes), common in place of a second relative clause (as here); often a different case of the relative (here

probably *cuius*) would be required; (2) '*superflux*', a flowing-on of
the sense, when the statement appears complete, into a fresh line
of verse; a feature of Virgil's style in the *Aeneid*.

5–13. These lines raise almost as many separate problems as
they contain groups of words. For the text and interpretation
adopted see Appendix following commentary on line 13. This
interpretation assumes that 1–8 lead up to the wish expressed in
9–10.

5–6. *cum desiderio meo nitenti . . . lubet*: take *cum* as the conjunc-
tion, *desiderio meo nitenti* as dative with *lubet*. BAKER's suggestion
that we are meant to assume that *cum* is the preposition and then
reject the assumption merits consideration.

5. *desiderio*: 'the object of my affection'; cf. Cicero, *Fam.* 14. 2.
2 (addressing his wife) *hem, mea lux, meum desiderium . . . te nunc,
mea Terentia, sic uexari!* Cf. *Rep.* 1. 4. 7 *maioremque laetitiam ex
desiderio bonorum percepimus.*

nitenti: 'radiant'; cf. 61. 21 *enitens* and 186 *nitens*; Horace,
Carm. 1. 5. 13 *intemptata nites*.

6. *carum nescio quid . . . iocari*: = *nescio quid cari iocari*, 'to play
some sweet game'. For *nesciŏ* ('iambic shortening') see on 6. 16.

7. *et solaciolum sui doloris*: take as an expansion of 6 *carum nescio
quid*; *solaciolum*, 'some small comfort', a diminutive pretty certain-
ly constructed for this context — it is not found elsewhere in
classical Latin. For *dolor* of the 'pain' of love see on 50. 17. In
AP 7. 195. 1 Meleager calls his locust ἐμῶν ἀπάτημα πόθων.

8. *credo*: take equally with what precedes and with what
follows; the affirmation implies, as often, a trace of irony — he
would like her *ardor* to be *grauis*, but is it really?

ut tum grauis acquiescat ardor: take as final, dependent on 6
lubet iocari.

9–10. The address to the *passer* is now complete. C.'s prayer
follows. Take *possem*, 'if only I could' (unrealizable wish), with
sicut ipsa: C. can play with the sparrow, but he can't, like Lesbia,
relieve his passion thereby — i.e. her passion (he fears) is more
easily relieved than his.

9. *ipsa*: = 'your mistress'. A slave refers to his master as *ipse*.

10. *tristis*: accusative plural.

curas: 'tortures' — a strong word.

11–13. Take as a separate fragment. (Often printed as 2b. 1–3.)

11. *tam gratum est*: either 'it gives me as much pleasure' or 'it would give me as much pleasure'; cf. *longum est*, 'it would be a long story'.

12. *pernici*: 'swift'.

aureolum: a diminutive found in Plautus.

13. *quod*: the relative pronoun rather than the conjunction.

ligatum: [*negatam* V.]

APPENDIX ON 5–13

The chief problems are (1) the sense of lines 5–10; (2) the relationship of lines 11–13. In dealing with (1) nearly all editors resort to textual repair. Most solve (2) by assuming that 11–13 belong to a separate poem, or are at any rate separated from 1–10 by a lacuna.

After a few minor corrections lines 1–10 may be taken to have stood in V as follows:

> Passer deliciae meae puellae
> quicum ludere quem in sinu tenere
> cui primum digitum dare adpetenti
> et acris solet incitare morsus
> cum desiderio meo nitenti   5
> carum nescio quid lubet iocari
> et solaciolum sui doloris
> credo ut cum grauis acquiescet ardor
> tecum ludere sicut ipsa possem
> et tristis animi leuare curas   10

The interpretation adopted here depends, i.e., on changing 8 *cum . . . acquiescet* to *tum . . . acquiescat*.

The main alternatives rejected are —

5. Older editors favoured taking *cum* as the preposition and *desiderio* etc. as ablative. This makes 6 *carum nescio quid lubet iocari*

the principal clause round which the remainder of 1–10 has to be built. Lines 5–6 in that case = 'I want with my shining love to play some sweet game', and lines 9–10 have to be taken as final or consecutive with 8 *ut*.

7. Some regard *et solaciolum sui doloris* as a second vocative, parallel to 1 *deliciae*. This will not work if line 6 is taken as the principal clause; with the interpretation of 1–6 adopted here it seems an unnecessary break in the unity of structure of 1–10.

All interpretations of 1–7 except that adopted here involve a use of *sui* (instead of the more normal *eius*) which is doubtful Latin. Garrod's *simul*, described as 'neat' by Fordyce, is hardly convincing.

8–9. All interpretations based on the inherited text involve taking 8 *ut* with 9 *possem*. Those who take line 6 as the principal clause are almost forced to read *possim* (final or consecutive). Those who take *ut . . . possem* as expressing a wish are left with an unsatisfactory rhythm in line 8. Some therefore change *ut* to *et*, or transpose 7 *et* and 8 *ut* (with minor consequent changes in interpretation). Vossius' *posse*, a brilliant effort to weld 1–10 to 11–13, is rather too good to be true.

11–13. These lines were pronounced a separate fragment by the Renaissance editor B. Guarino (to whom the conjecture *ut tum . . . acquiescat* is also due). The only thing certain about the lines is that they allude to the story of how Atalanta lost a race in pursuit of an apple (and a husband).

There are three main possibilities. The first is to make 11–13 follow without a break, as in the MSS, capping somehow the pattern of syntax and sense built up in 1–10. The difficulty lies in choosing between the different interpretations of the complete poem thus constituted. Moreover lines 1–8 seem to lead up to a climax in 9–10, so that a second climax seems uncalled for. Another possibility is to assume a lacuna: 1–13 still belong to a single poem, but something has dropped out. The third possibility (that assumed here) is that 11–13 are a fragment of another poem; this raises the question, why should the fragment have become attached to a poem with which it has nothing to do? but Poem 14b shows that this can occur; some would point to the final stanza of Poem 51 as evidence that editors can be over-zealous in detaching fragments (or in detecting lacunae).

See:

Sheridan Baker, 'Catullus' *cum desiderio meo*', *CPh* 53 (1958), 243–4.

J. David Bishop, 'Catullus 2 and its hellenistic antecedents', *CPh* 61 (1966), 158–67.

C. O. Brink, *Latin Studies and the Humanities*, Cambridge Inaugural Lecture (1957), 9–13.

Werner Eisenhut, 'Zu Catull *c.* 2A und der Trennung der Gedichte in den Handschriften', *Philologus* 109 (1965), 301–5.

H. Gugel, *Latomus* 27 (1968) 810–22.

Godo Lieberg, *Puella divina* (1962), 99–110 (in favour of taking 11–13 with 1–10).

3

If Poem 2 is a mock hymn, Poem 3 follows closely the traditional pattern of a dirge. The mockery implicit in the choice of subject is made explicit in the irony of the opening two lines and by the change of focus in the concluding couplet. Poem 3 is also related to another traditional genre, that of poems about pet animals. Ovid made use of the same traditional material when he wrote an elegy on the death of Corinna's parrot (*Am.* 2. 6). But whereas Ovid's poem is burlesque, Poem 3 is a delicately ironical, graceful love poem, wary of any surrender to sentimentality, its claim on our emotions all the surer because the claim is not overpitched.

A 2nd century A.D. marble plaque found at Auch in France preserves a charming parody (in hendecasyllabics) of C.; the subject is a lap-dog called 'Flea' (*Anthologia Latina* II. 2. 1512):

> Quam dulcis fuit ista, quam benigna,
> quae cum uiueret, in sinu iacebat

somni conscia semper et cubilis.
o factum male, Myia, quod peristi.
latrares modo, si quis adcubaret
riualis dominae, licentiosa.
o factum male, Myia, quod peristi.
altum iam tenet insciam sepulcrum,
nec seuire potes nec insilire,
nec blandis mihi morsibus renides.

Structure: 1–3 — an appropriately solemn statement of the data passing into 4–10 — a *laudatio* of the deceased, concluding (after a long descriptive aside) with 11–12 — an appropriately dignified and lugubrious statement of the commonplace 'gone, never to return'; 13–16 — an outburst of indignation, concluding with 17–18 — a surprise shift of focus from the sparrow to Lesbia.

Metre: hendecasyllabics.

1–3. The first word is an imperative *lugete*; the appropriate circle of mourners is set out in an increasing triad.

1. *Veneres Cupidinesque*: Perhaps a proverbial expression or traditional jingle — the phrase recurs at 13. 12 (and in the singular at 36. 3, where the plural might have been extremely clumsy). The idea that there was more than one Aphrodite seems to have become a commonplace of Alexandrian mythology — cf. Callimachus, Fr. 200a P. But possibly an allusion to Plato's *Symposium* (180d–182a), where Pausanias defends, with the gravity appropriate to that occasion, the thesis that there are two Aphrodites (=*Veneres*), each with her own Eros (=*Cupido*). One is Aphrodite Pandemos, the ordinary sort; the other is an older, more respectable divinity, Aphrodite Uranios.

2. *quantum est hominum uenustiorum*: an ambiguity playing on the two meanings of *Venus* (the name of the goddess and the abstraction 'charm', 'attractiveness'). In comedy *uenustus* (and *inuenustus*) are used only of women (and of Venus). In C. *uenustus* becomes one of the key-words associated with the ideal of *urbanitas*; in 4 of the 6 contexts in which the word occurs it is used of men. Here, the primary meaning is 'all who are especially men of *uenus*', i.e.

endowed with charm, refinement, sensibility; but inevitably *Veneres* in the preceding line elicits a secondary meaning, 'all who are especially men of Venus'. Cf. the play on *uenustas* in 36. 17 and in Poem 86.

3. *passer mortuus est meae puellae*: the basic datum, plainly stated.

4–5. The key-word *passer* now becomes the basis of an expanding triad, in which the second member is *deliciae meae puellae* and the third member line 5. At the same time line 4 repeats 2. 1 (now nominative, instead of vocative). For *puella* of C.'s mistress see on 51. 7. For the idiom *plus . . . oculis suis* cf. 14. 1 and Poem 87.

6–10. Explain why Lesbia loved the sparrow so much.

6. *mellitus erat*: almost = 'he was her honey'; for the colloquialism cf. 48. 1 and 99. 1. Cicero, *Att.* 1. 18. 1, refers to his son as *mellitus Cicero*.

6–7. *suam . . . ipsam*: = 'his own mistress'; *ipse* and *ipsa* are the slave's words for 'master' and 'mistress'; cf. 2. 9.

6. *norat*: 'had got to know', and therefore = 'knew'. See KHAN.

7. *puella matrem*: 'as well as a little girl knows her own mother' seems the natural interpretation, rather than taking *puella* as = *mea puella*; so Kroll and Lenchantin; the idea is then developed in the image of lines 8–10.

8–10. For the imagery cf. 61. 209–12:

> Torquatus uolo paruulus
> matris e gremio suae
> porrigens teneras manus
> dulce rideat ad patrem.

8. *illius*: the middle syllable is short.

10. *ad*: cf. 61. 212 *dulce rideat ad patrem*.

    usque: 'continually'.

    pipiabat: Only here in Classical Latin; Columella 8. 5. 14 of unhatched chickens, Tertullian, *Monogamia* 16 of children; possibly both associations are intended here, the word being chosen to tie together the imagery of 6–10. Observe that the form and sound of *pipiabat* pick up *amabat* at the end of line 5.

11–12. A commonplace, of course, effectively expressed. C. was not the first to elaborate this conceit of a household pet. (For examples from the Greek Anthology see Fordyce.) Naturally, the ancients did not seriously suppose that animals went down to Hades. *tenebricosum* seems hardly a more solemn word than *pipiabat* — Varro uses it of a henhouse (*R.* 3. 9. 19) and Cicero of a tavern (*Pis.* 18).

13. *uobis . . . malae tenebrae*: these words mark more plainly the assumption of mock serious style.

male . . . malae: the jingle for emphasis. For the idiom (= 'may it go ill with you') *male sit* cf. 14. 10.

14. *Orci*: an old, solemn word; usually a person, as in Horace, *Carm.* 2. 3. 24 *uictima nil miserantis Orci*.

bella: C. prefers the colloquial *bellus* to *pulcher*; see on 86. 5. But *bellus* 'smart' is, like *uenustus*, a key concept of the *urbani*, often linked idiomatically with *homo* (*homo bellus* = 'smart chap', 'clever fellow' in 24. 7, 78. 3 and 81. 2); like *uenustus*, a description of character or behaviour rather than appearance.

16. [V is corrupt: *bonum factum male bonus ille passer*; *o factum male* is restored from the epitaph on a lap-dog quoted in the introduction; *o miselle*, a conjecture first found in the Parma edition of 1473 (the second printed edition of C.), convincingly prepares for the diminutives in the last line of the poem.] Attempts to move the hiatus after *male* are probably needless; cf. 38. 2 and 76. 10. GOOLD's *quod, miselle passer*, (*factum male* anticipating *tua opera*) is tempting.

18. *turgiduli*: 'a little swollen'; cf. 41. 3 *turpiculo*, 'rather nasty'. The diminutive expresses a complex range of overtones of emotional involvement (affection, compassion etc.) with the person or thing described, not necessarily any objective denotation of size or degree.

ocelli: the diminutive form occurs also at 31. 2, 43. 2, 45. 11, 50. 10 and 19, and 64. 60.

See:

G. P. Goold, 'Catullus 3. 16', *Phoenix* 23 (1969), 186–203.

N. I. Herescu, 'Catulle 3: un écho des nénies dans la littérature, *REL* 25 (1947), 74–6.

H. Akbar Khan, 'A note on the expression *solum . . . nosse* in Catullus', *CPh* 62 (1967), 34–7.

4

Autobiographical reminiscences of a yacht: a fine, fast ship in its day, it has seen a lot of the world since it left its home on the shores of the Black Sea, and never been in trouble; now it has retired from the sea.

Though timorous sailors, the Romans were not insensible to the aesthetic appeal of a well-built ship; see e.g. Cicero, *de Orat.* 3. 180:

> quid tam in nauigio necessarium quam latera, quam cauernae, quam prora, quam puppis, quam antennae, quam uela, quam mali? quae tamen hanc habent in specie uenustatem, ut non solum salutis, sed etiam uoluptatis causa inuenta esse uideantur.

The starting-point of Poem 4, however, is more the warm, sentimental affection we feel for an object that has served us well.

Did C. own the yacht? He could have done, many have therefore supposed he did. What is more important is that the *speaker* in Poem 4 talks as though he had no personal knowledge of the facts, but insists he is reporting the yacht's own statements (2 *ait*, 6 *negat*, 15 *ait*, 16 *dicit* — 9 dependent infinitives). Until we accept this basic hypothesis we have not tuned in to the poem.

There is a fragment of Alcaeus (*LGS* 119) in which a 'ship, decayed and ancient, weary after many voyages, unfit for further use, is described in terms applicable to a courtesan, grown old and diseased, at the end of a long and exacting career' (Denys Page, *Sappho and Alcaeus* [1955], 195). We find in the Greek Anthology short epigrams (e.g. *AP* 6. 69 and 70, a variation on the ex-voto inscription — cf. Horace, *Carm.* 3. 26) dedicating to Poseidon ships that have outlived their usefulness, and others (e.g. *AP* 9. 34 and 36 — a variation on the grave-inscription) setting out briefly the life-story of a ship. Roman grave-epigrams, too, commonly tabulate the deceased's biography for the information of the passer-by; e.g. the epitaph of Claudia (ascribed to the period of the Gracchi), in which, as in Poem 4, the passer-by is addressed by the speaker (*CIL* I² 1211 = *Anthologia Latina* II. 1. 52):

> Hospes quod deico paullum est: asta ac pellege.
> heic est sepulcrum hau pulcrum pulcrai feminae.
> nomen parentes nominarunt Claudiam.
> suom mareitum corde deilexit souo.
> gnatos duos creauit. horunc alterum
> in terra linquit, alium sub terra locat.
> sermone lepido, tum autem incessu commodo.
> domum seruauit, lanam fecit. dixi. abei.

The form of C.'s poem is closer to the epitaph of Claudia. It has the same metre, iambic trimeters, though in C. the metre is strictly iambic, giving the poem a buoyant vitality of which there is little trace in the heavily spondaic *senarii* of the epitaph. At the same time, the adumbration of a dramatic context is made more definite. Instead of laconic brevity, we have a conversational discursiveness that (a) suggests an actual speaker in a setting (C. himself, if we like, showing some friends round his estate), (b) suggests a personality for the yacht itself.

Poem 4, in short, is a monologue, more or less dramatic, based on a formal, impersonal verse-pattern designed for an actual occasion — expanded and made more varied in content, to fit an informal, personal but very possibly fictitious occasion. The yacht becomes an old, garrulous slave (see on 19 *erum*), proud of a successful career of faithful service. Naturally in retrospect that career assumes a pattern, which the speaker follows — familiar places through which the yacht moves back in memory from Italy and the present to the shores of the Black Sea where it was born. After a central section devoted to the yacht's beginnings in life, the second half of the poem (lines 18–24) moves forward again in time and space and this time the yacht's career is spoken of in

terms of things experienced rather than places visited. In each
case it is the travels of a lifetime which we seem invited to imagine,
not a particular journey.

An amusing parody of the poem has come down to us among
the minor pieces ascribed to Virgil (*Cat.* 10), extolling the exploits
of a muleteer called Sabinus.

> Sabinus ille, quem uidetis, hospites,
> ait fuisse mulio celerrimus,
> neque ullius uolantis impetum cisi
> nequisse praeterire, siue Mantuam
> opus foret uolare, siue Brixiam.
> et hoc negat Tryphonis aemuli domum
> negare nobilem insulamue Ceryli
> (ubi iste post Sabinus, ante Quinctio,
> bidente dicit attodisse forcipe
> comata colla, ne Cytorio iugo
> premente dura uulnus ederet iuba).
> Cremona frigida et lutosa Gallia,
> tibi haec fuisse et esse cognitissima
> ait Sabinus, ultima ex origine
> tua stetisse dicit in uoragine,
> tua in palude deposisse sarcinas,
> et inde tot per orbitosa milia
> iugum tulisse, laeua siue dextera
> strigare mula siue utrumque ceperat. . . .
> neque ulla uota semitalibus deis
> sibi esse facta praeter hoc nouissimum,
> paterna lora proximumque pectinem.
> sed haec prius fuere; nunc eburnea
> sedetque sede seque dedicat tibi,
> gemelle Castor et gemelle Castoris.

Structure: The layout is A (5, opening boast, +4, appeal to
witnesses, +3, explanatory parenthesis) +B (5, beginnings in
life, +4, the yacht's travels, +3, a final boast) + C (3, tailpiece).

Metre: Each line is composed of 6 iambs — the same metre as

29; purely iambic *senarii* are found only in these two poems. In 9
Propontida and 18 *impotentia* a final short vowel is lengthened
before two consonants in the following **syllable**.

1–5. The rhetorical structure of the yacht's opening boast
(flat assertion, 'I was the fastest ship there was', +the elaborate
amplification *neque ... nequisse ... siue ... siue*, 'no ship could
touch me either under sail or when they rowed') and the tone of
confident, proud reminiscence are tensioned to the level of poetic
statement by the syntactical Graecism *ait ... celerrimus*, the
imagery of lines 3–5, and a vivid, characteristically poetic diction
(see on 3 *natantis impetum trabis*, 4 *palmulis*, 5 *linteo*). Cf. the
dialogue of tragedy, in which the characters ring true psycho-
logically, but their talk is poetry.

1. *phaselus*: (Greek for 'bean-pod'), a small ocean-going vessel;
Cicero's friend Atticus travelled from Italy to Greece on one (*Att.*
1. 13. 1), Propertius (3. 21) thought of doing the same.

hospites: The addressee of a grave-epigram, including literary
amplifications of the form (e.g. Propertius 4. 1), is normally
singular; the plural here is a hint of an actual dramatic setting.

2. *celerrimus*: The nominative, restored against the reading of
the MSS on the authority of the corresponding phrase in *Cat.* 10
(where the adjective agrees with the adjacent nominative noun,
mulio), though normal Greek syntax when verb of saying and
dependent infinitive have a common subject, is rare in Latin (a
few examples in the Augustan poets); on the stylistic possibilities
of distinctively Greek syntax see *Cat. Rev.* 66–7. The agreement in
gender with *phaselus* instead of with *nauium* is normal Latin syntax.

3. *trabis*, 'beam', i.e. 'ship'; poetic from Ennius onwards, but
the tensioned structure of *ullius natantis trabis* re-elicits the basic
statement, 'headless rush of any spar afloat' (*natare* = both 'float'
and 'swim' and is used of both objects and persons, though more
commonly of persons).

4. *palmulis*: 'with its little palms'; cf. 17 *palmulas* and 64. 7
palmis. The dictionary translation 'oar blade' obscures the capacity
of the Latin word to contribute to a personification.

5. *linteo*: 'canvas', more vivid than *uelum*. Ocean-going craft normally travelled under sail, using oars in clearing harbour or in an emergency. Cf. Propertius giving instructions (in his imagination) to the crew of his *phaselus*, 3. 21. 11–14.

6–9. A rattle of place names leads us back to the shipyard on the Black Sea where the yacht was built. The sound of 6–7 (particularly the long a's) reinforces the sense, by inviting a change of tone in passing from 1–5 to line 6; *negat ... negare* introduces a hint of banter, suggesting the old yacht is not to be taken too seriously.

8. *Thraciam*: adjectival with *Propontida*.

9. *trucemue Ponticum sinum*: 'the savage recess of Pontus'; as a geographical name *sinus* normally = 'bay' or 'gulf'; the word denotes, however, a variety of curved structures; here overtones suggesting seclusion and remoteness (see *L & S*) are perhaps appropriate to the Black Sea, secluded from the Mediterranean by the Bosporus. The Black Sea was traditionally inhospitable (*trucem*) to sailors.

10–12. The parenthesis (1) slows down the tempo at the conclusion of the first half of the poem; (2) reinforces the reader's feeling that he is listening to an actual speaker.

10. *iste post phaselus*: 'your yacht to be'; the adjectival use of an adverb (common in Greek) occurs mainly in Latin in colloquial or technical language; with *iste* cf. 17. 21 *iste meus stupor*.

11. *comata*: The collective *coma* is used particularly of long hair. Poets since Homer (*Od.* 23. 195) have spoken of a tree's foliage as its 'hair'; the rare form *comata* and its combination with *silua* ('long-haired forest') revive a jaded metaphor; cf. 29. 3 *Comata Gallia*.

Cytorio in iugo: the hills behind Cytorus, on the Black Sea.

12. *loquente*: the forest's hair can also speak when the wind whistles (*sibilum edidit*) through it. Note the highly tensioned, artificial verbal structure of the concluding line of the first section, and also the appropriateness of the s-sounds in *saepe sibilum*.

13–17. Amastris is another port near Cytorus. The region was famous for its boxwood (*buxifer*), a finely grained timber, apparently used more for making musical instruments than in shipbuilding. The appeal to Amastris-Cytorus to bear out the yacht's statements reinforces the personification implicit in 6–9.

Some editors print a colon after *phaselus* in 15, making Amastris-Cytorus the authority for everything asserted in 15–24. A poem moves of course within an area of fantasy of its own choosing. Even so, intimate knowledge (14 *cognitissima*) of what happened after the yacht left home waters is not easily ascribed to Amastris-Cytoris. It seems better to take *haec . . . cognitissima* as summing up 10–12 (for this use of *haec* cf. line 25 and 13. 6) and *ultima . . . cacumine* and *tuo . . . aequore* as variations on the same general idea — that the region where the yacht came from must know about its beginnings in life; 18–24 then carry the narrative of the ship's career forward again.

14. *tibi*: though two vocatives precede (a variation on the common rule of agreement with the nearer); cf. 26 *tibi*.

16. *stetisse*: while still a clump of trees (*silua*).

17. *palmulas*: the same ambiguity as in 4.

18–21. The general parallelism of structure between 1–12 and 13–24 suggests a break after 17 *aequore* (19 *tulisse* must still depend of course on 16 *dicit*), and this removes the awkwardness of assuming that Amastris and Cytorus are asked to confirm facts of which they cannot have personal knowledge. The travels referred to in 18–21 are those retraced in 6–9.

18. *inde*: both spatial ('from there') and temporal ('after that').

impotentia: of persons 'lacking self-control' (cf. 8. 9), 'raging', used metaphorically of the sea.

19. *erum*: the slave's word for his master; cf. 31. 12. Not necessarily a single owner throughout of course.

19–20. *laeua siue dextera . . . aura*: tacking was naturally an important part of ancient navigation under sail.

20. *Iuppiter*: primarily the weather god and *secundus* (line 21) primarily therefore in a technical sense, = a following wind. But

the sense 'well disposed' is also present as an overtone; i.e. if you got a wind dead astern and did not have to tack, it meant Jove was in a good mood.

21. *pedem*: 'sheet' — the rope attached to each lower corner of the square sail, used to set the sail at the appropriate angle to the wind. The wind 'fell equally on each sheet' when it was dead astern, filling the sail equally on either side of the mast.

22–4. *nouissimus* is used normally of a series as viewed by the speaker, 'the last of all'; so *nouissimum* in the parody, *Cat.* 10. 21; cf. 60. 4 *in nouissimo casu. mare nouissimum* should be therefore the last sea the yacht sailed on, the one now nearest at hand, i.e. the Adriatic. (The traditional view that *nouissimo* here means 'the most remote', i.e. the Black Sea, the starting-point of the yacht's journeys, can hardly be sustained; see Fordyce, who favours *nouissime*, the reading of V.) KHAN's suggestion that *nouissimo* has also an epitaphic ring (cf. Verg., *A.* 4. 650 *nouissima uerba* — Dido's self-epitaph) is attractive.

It follows that 23 *cum ueniret* should designate the moment when the yacht was about to retire from its career on the open sea, to come 24 *hunc ad usque limpidum lacum* (*usque* implying the *lacus* was some distance inland from the open sea). (With the traditional interpretation of *nouissimo*, the *cum*-clause would more naturally apply to the whole of the ship's working life, *usque* emphasizing that the life had been a long one.)

It follows that 21–2 *neque ulla uota* etc. should mean that, at the moment of its quitting the sea, the yacht made no vows. A departure from normal is implied, but what was it? A ship which ends its days away from the sea — either beached, or (like our yacht, apparently) tied up in a quiet backwater — might well have had its career terminated by a storm, and been only saved from total destruction by *uota litoralibus deis facta*. Not so our ship: it retired voluntarily, perhaps continued to ply for a time on the *lacus*, and has only now withdrawn from service (see lines 25–7). The polysyllable *litoralibus*, as often in C., carries with it a hint of irony, a suggestion perhaps of the ship's pride in its own self-sufficiency. 24 *lacum* can denote any confined area of calm water, not necessarily a lake (see, e.g., Verg., *A.* 8. 66); to assume the *lacus* meant is that of 31. 13, though tempting, is neither necessary nor plausible.

25–7. A dramatic restatement perhaps of a dedicatory plaque.

25. *sed haec prius fuere*: a transition from biography to tailpiece. But also a clue to interpretation.

26. *senet*: an archaism.

dedicat: a present outside time, like 1. 1 *dono*.

27. *gemelle Castoris*: Pollux. The Dioscuri, as the twins were called, were frequently invoked by sailors; cf. 68. 65. The phenomenon of St. Elmo's fire during an electrical storm was taken as a sign of their presence. Cf. Horace, *Carm.* 1. 3. 2.

See:

On Poem 4 as autobiography, F. O. Copley, 'Catullus *c.* 4: the world of the poem', *TAPhA* 89 (1958), 9–13; an opposing view in M. C. J. Putnam, 'Catullus' journey', *CPh* 57 (1962), 10–19; cf. Wheeler 98–102.

On the structure, R. A. Hornsby, 'The craft of Catullus (*Carm.* 4)', *AJPh* 84 (1963), 256–65.

On the metre, U. von Wilamowitz-Moellendorf, *Hellenistische Dichtung* (1924) ii 295–8 (the rapid movement of the verse suggests the patter of a professional guide).

Other discussions: H. Akbar Khan, 'The humor of Catullus, *Carm.* 4, and the theme of Virgil, *Catalepton* 10', *AJPh* 88 (1967), 163–72; H. J. Mette, 'Catull *Carm.* 4', *RhM* 105 (1962), 153–7 (on the form); M. Schmidt, '*Phaselus ille*: zu Catull 4', *Gymnasium* 62 (1955), 43–9 (on the dramatic setting).

5

'Let us live and love — and let those too old to understand mind their own business!'

Already in line 2 the simple, direct lyricism of the opening line gives way to a deftly manipulated irony. The following lines develop each of the ideas in the opening triad: 4–6 = *uiuamus* — thoughts of death urge us to make the most of life; 7–9 = *amemus*; in 10–13 (the longest of these three sections, just as the third member of the opening triad is the longest) we return to the *senes seueriores* — steps will be taken to confound their curiosity.

Compare Poem 7 and contrast Poem 48. The common supposition that Poem 16 refers to Poem 5 cannot be upheld (see on Poem 16).

Metre: hendecasyllabics.

1. *uiuamus . . . amemus*: emphatic: 'let us *live* . . .!' Cf. 68. 160.

Lesbia: for the name (first occurrence here) see on 51. 7.

2. *rumores*: the jealous mutterings of those too old to have fun themselves. Cf. Propertius 2. 30. 13 *ista senes licet accusent conuiuia duri*.

seueriorum: either (1) 'more critical than they used to be'; or (2) 'more critical than some', i.e. unusually critical.

3. *omnes unius*: emphatic juxtaposition.

assis: 'let us put the lot at a single *as*' (genitive of price); idiomatic (cf. 42. 13); also prepares the way for the juggling with figures in 7–13.

4. *soles*: = 'the light of the sun', or 'the sun each day'; for examples of this plural see Fordyce on 8. 3.

5. *nobis*: with *dormienda*. The tense of *occidit* makes it clear that *nobis* = 'by us mortals'.

cum . . . occidit: frequentative. If C. and Lesbia were meant, *occiderit* (future perfect) would be required. The shortness of life is a cliché, as is the light of the sun as a symbol of human life. But the traditional ideas are freshened by (1) crisp restatement; (2) the irony of a personal reference implied in line 6.

semel: a colloquial reinforcing of *cum* = 'once and for all'.

breuis lux: 'our brief light'. Note the contrast between the singular here and the plural *soles*. The Greeks regularly called man 'ephemeral' — the creature of one day.

7–9. A thousand kisses should be plenty, but it is not enough for C.; so he adds a modest supplementary order ('a further hundred'), then throws restraint to the winds and repeats the order for a thousand. And so it goes on. The reader is tempted to keep a tally — then C. says *conturbabimus illa!*

7. *da mi*: = 'supply'. No suggestion that Lesbia should assume the initiative; *da mi* + name of article + quantity was perhaps the formula for placing an order with a merchant (hence *basia mille*, not *mille basia*).

10-13. Difficult. After the elaborate show of passion kept under rational control, *conturbabimus* plainly symbolizes the flurry of surrender to passion. Take *illa* with *conturbabimus*, not with *sciamus*. We are invited perhaps to imagine the kisses stacked in rows (like sacks of grain, say) as the quantities specified are delivered — and then jumbled up in a single pile. But in this context of figures, the meaning of *conturbare* as a technical term of bookkeeping, 'to throw accounts into confusion', cannot be excluded. Accounts are muddled (among other reasons) to conceal assets. C. suggests Lesbia and he should do this (1) so that they shouldn't know themselves (*ne sciamus*) what the figure was; accurate records might act as a deterrent; or perhaps some proverb like our 'counting your chickens' lies behind C.'s words; (2) to keep information out of the hands of anybody whose ill will had been aroused by such heavy transacting in kisses (*cum tantum sciat esse basiorum*); knowledge of the actual figures could put the lovers in his power.

10. *fecerimus*: future perfect indicative. The penultimate i is long.

11. *conturbabimus*: the future indicative amounts to an invitation to Lesbia to join in C.'s plan.

12. *inuidere*: 'cast spells', 'get us in his power'; cf. 7. 11-12.

13. *esse*: not *fuisse* — as though kisses were a commodity that remained stored up.

sciat: better taken as temporal than as causal; subjunctive by attraction.

See:

S. Commager, 'The structure of Catullus 5', *CJ* 59 (1964), 361-4.

E. A. Fredricksmeyer, *AJPh* 91 (1970) 431–45.

Charles Segal, 'Catullus 5 and 7', *AJPh* 89 (1968), 284–301.

On the commercial imagery, H. J. Levy, *AJPh* 62 (1941), 222–4 — his suggestion that the reference is to an abacus is rejected by R. Pack, *AJPh* 77 (1956), 47–51; cf. N. T. Pratt, *CPh* 51 (1956), 99–100; R. E. Grimm, *CJ* 59 (1963), 15–22; J. H. Turner, *CJ* 47 (1951), 63–74.

Modern imitations: Ronsard, 'A sa maistresse' ('La Lune est coustumiere...'), Pléiade edition i 439–40; Jonson, 'Kisse me, sweet...' (a fusion of themes from Poems 5 and 7), Stuart edition 92; Crashaw, 'Come let us live my Deare...', Oxford edition 194.

6

Flavius has a girl-friend — the facts speak for themselves; if he won't make her available for inspection (like Varus in Poem 10) it must be because he is ashamed of her. C. demands details, with a view to celebrating the affair appropriately in verse.

No doubt Poem 6 was aimed less at eliciting the information asked for than at pulling a friend's leg. Cf. Poems 55 and 58b — Camerius has disappeared from circulation — and Poem 80. Horace, *Carm.* 2. 4 and 1. 27 represent the exploitation of the same theme at a strictly literary level. Nothing is known of Flavius.

Structure: 1–5 accuse. 6–14 offer proof. 15–17 appeal for a confession.

Metre: hendecasyllabics.

1. *delicias*: 'darling'. See on 2. 1; stronger (a touch of mockery therefore) than 16 *amores*.

2. *illepidae . . . inelegantes*: according to the standards of C.'s circle, a girl had to be sophisticated too. In 10. 4 C. approves of Varus' find on these grounds. Cf. C.'s case for preferring Lesbia to Quintia in Poem 86.

2–3. *sint . . . uelles*: often in earlier Latin (and occasionally in classical prose) the present subjunctive in conditional sentences refers to present, not future, time; the imperfect subjunctive later becomes normal. Here we have both tenses; another example of the present subjunctive in lines 13–14.

3. *dicere*: 'describe', 'talk about' — a sense of *dicere* common in verse; the sense 'mention', 'name' is common in prose.

4. *febriculosi*: 'feverish'; probably vaguely pejorative.

5. *scorti diligis*: the blunt *scorti* sharpens the oxymoron; *diligis* = 'are fond of'; cf. 72. 3–4. For *nesciŏ* see on 16 *uolo*.

6. *uiduas*: 'celibate'; cf. 68. 6 *in lecto caelibe*.

7–13. Circumstantial evidence. For the mock gravity of the long technical-sounding words see on 7. 1 *basiationes*.

12. *nam nil stupra ualet*: [The first half of this line is both meaningless and unmetrical in the MSS. Haupt's version of syllables 2–6 (based on Scaliger) is commonly accepted, though not by Mynors.]

15–17. C. coaxes Flavius, tongue in cheek: there are the makings of a poem here; C.'s verses (if not Flavius' girl) can be relied on to be *lepidi*.

16. *uolŏ*: 'iambic shortening', as in 17. 8 and 23, 35. 5 and 61. 209; cf. 24. 7 and 115. 8 *homŏ* (not 17. 12 or 81. 2); also 50. 18 and 19 and 61. 145 *cauĕ* and 2. 6 etc. *nesciŏ* (= *ne sciŏ*). See Austin on Virg., *A.* 2. 735.

   amores: 'girl-friend'; cf. 10. 1, 15. 1, 21. 4, 40. 7, 45. 1.

See:

S. V. Tracy, *CPh* 64 (1969) 234–5.

7

Poem 7 picks up Poem 5; together they form two fragments in a dramatic continuum. The mathematics of Poem 5 drew perhaps the response from Lesbia, 'Just how many kisses *do* you want?' C.'s answer is, 'no limit'. To express the concept 'no limit' he has recourse to two traditional images of infinity, one (the sands of the desert) hot and exotic, the other (the stars in the sky) serene and cool (cf. 61. 199–203). Infinity is safer too.

'The poem, like No. 51, is a poem of courtship, but the technique of courtship in this society is a delicate and sophisticated affair. The Lesbias were not only beautiful; they were intelligent, well-read, and witty, and one courted them on all counts. Hence the form of this poem and its symbolism, are all-important. The very question itself — "How many kisses?" — has a slightly intellectual twist, and the poet can play with it and can... be learned, too, if only his learning is never paraded for its own sake but sits lightly and is used with graceful humor.' ELDER 108.

Structure: 1–2 — hypothesis; 3–6 — first image of infinity; 7–8 — second image of infinity; 9–12 — justification of infinity.

Metre: hendecasyllabics; in line 2 the first syllable is short.

1. *quaeris*: question and answer get the poem under way. But the question can easily be felt as one Lesbia might put, to tease C., after reading Poem 5.

basiationes: the learned-sounding polysyllable ('kissifications') lends the question an ironical inflexion. (Coined no doubt for the occasion; imitated by Martial 2. 23. 4 and 7. 95. 17.) Cf. 4 *lasarpiciferis*, 6. 11 *argutatio inambulatioque*, 12. 12 *aestimatione*, 21. 1 *esuritionum*, 32. 8 *fututiones*, 47. 7 *uocationes*, 48. 6 *osculationis*. See on 46. 1 *egelidos*.

2. *tuae*: are the kisses Lesbia's because she was asked in 5. 7 to provide them?

satis superque: 'enough and to spare'; a common idiom.

3–6. Already in Homer (*Il.* 9. 385) Achilles speaks of 'gifts as numerous as sand'; Horace's Archytas (*Carm.* 1. 28. 1–2) was said to have solved the problem of measuring the sands of the sea-shore. But the sands of the Libyan desert are an excuse for launching the poem upon its imaginative course. 'How can one reasonably make love by at once dragging in the Libyan desert, the asafoetida-bearing district of Cyrene (with its association of foul odor), the oracle of sweating Jove and, worst, old Battus' tomb? The learning is perfectly correct. Cyrene did export asafoetida, and near by lay the shrine of Juppiter Ammon (and even a god might sweat in the desert's heat). Battus founded Cyrene. All this, then, appears to center around Cyrene. But why? One immediate answer, and the obvious

and usual one, is that Callimachus not only came from
Cyrene but claimed to be descended from Battus.' ELDER 108.

3. *Libyssae*: a Greek form, feminine of *Libys*, found in this
context in *AP* 12. 145. 3.

4. *lasarpiciferis*: (The first a is wrongly given as short in *L & S*.)
'rich in silphium'; if the plant, the main export of Cyrene, *was*
asafoetida (the identification is doubtful), then perhaps C.
devised his learned polysyllable as an ironic corrective to the
literary associations of the name Cyrene. Silphium was employed
in medicine, apparently for a variety of purposes. See PAOLI and
Fordyce. There is a magnificent 6th century Laconian cup
thought to show King Arkesilas of Cyrene supervising the weigh-
ing of silphium; see, e.g., Pierre Devambez, *Greek Painting* (1962),
plate 59.

    Cyrenis: the plural denotes the territory (Cyrenaica) of
which Cyrene was the main town. The y, short here, is more often
long.

5. *oraclum Iouis*: the temple of Ammon (the Egyptian counter-
part of Jupiter) situated on the southern tip of the border of
Egypt and Cyrenaica.

    aestuosi: (1) 'sweltering' — as Jove would be, if he visited his
temple deep in the desert; cf. 46. 5; probably also (2) 'lusty' — a
not inapposite reference to Jove's amorous reputation (see
MOORHOUSE and cf. Plautus, *Bacch.* 470–1 and *Truc.* 350).

6. *Batti*: Battus, the first king of Cyrene; his tomb, worshipped
as a shrine (*sacrum sepulcrum*), stood in the centre of Cyrene (the
site is described by Pindar, *P.* 5. 125–6). Callimachus, a native of
Cyrene, calls himself Battiades in Epigram 35, in which he refers
to his own tomb; C. calls Callimachus *Battiades* in 65. 16 and
116. 2.

7–8. Second image of infinity, the stars in the night sky; a
veiled self-reference, for while *furtiuos amores* leans on a literary
tradition that goes back to Mimnermus (Fragment 1 lists 'stolen
love' [κρυπταδίη φιλότης — the phrase is from Homer, *Il.* 6.
161] among the pleasures that make life worth while), C. plainly

alludes to his liaison with Lesbia. For *furtiuus amor* = 'liaison' cf.
Verg., *A.* 4. 171 *nec iam furtiuum Dido meditatur amorem.* The stars
look on (*uident* — like watchful eyes) while night enters into the
conspiracy of silence (*tacet nox*).

Cf. the *mira nox* of 68. 145, when G. received from his mistress
her *furtiua munuscula, ipsius ex ipso dempta uiri gremio.*

9. *basia . . . basiare*: The repetition appropriately recalls
basiationes at the moment of summing up.

10. *uesano*: 'crazy'; the unexpectedly strong word momentarily
cuts through the persiflage. Love was of course traditionally a
form of madness (C. uses the word again in 100. 7).

satis et super: picks up 2 *satis superque.*

Catullo: not *mihi* — a detached judgment.

11. *pernumerare*: note the preverb: infinity would be too much
for the *curiosi*, whatever pains they took.

12. *possint*: potential subjunctive — 'couldn't even if they tried'.

mala . . . lingua: nominative (a second subject of *possint*), as
the metre shows (wrongly given as ablative in *L & S*, s.v. *fascino*).

fascinare: 'weave spells around'.

See:

Steele Commager, 'Notes on some poems of Catullus', *HSPh* 70
(1965), 84–6.

J. P. Elder, 'Notes on some conscious and subconscious elements
in Catullus' poetry', *HSPh* 60 (1951), 101–36.

A. C. Moorhouse, 'Two adjectives in Catullus 7', *AJPh* 84 (1963),
417–18 (on *lasarpiciferis* and *aestuosi*).

Brooks Otis, *Virgil* (1964), 102–5 (on C.'s poems as fragments in
a dramatic continuum).

Charles Segal, 'Catullus 5 and 7', *AJPh* 89 (1968), 284–301.

U. E. Paoli, *Rome, its People, Life and Customs* (1958), 210–11 (on
silphium).

8

Poem 8 gives dramatic form to a struggle in the poet's mind
(which the poem records — or rather reconstructs) between

ntellectual rejection of an impossible situation and emotional
reluctance to face the inevitable squarely, and 'write off as lost
what is plainly lost'.

Elegance of form, crisp matter-of-factness of statement, a
restraint that does no more than threaten to get out of control, the
hints even of self-mockery — all these strike a note very different
from the anguished tone of Poem 76, leading many to assume a
more trivial occasion; e.g. Wheeler 230: 'He takes a typical
situation from Greek erotic and applies it with imagination and
with humor to his own case. . . . Who can say whether the idea of
writing such a poem first came to him from some experience of his
own — some insignificant tiff with Lesbia — or from his reading?'
Fordyce rejects such evident misreadings ('the utter simplicity of
the words, only a hairsbreadth removed from conversational
prose, is a guarantee of their sincerity') but underrates the com-
plexity of feeling and structure. Contrast FRAENKEL 53: 'The
truly wonderful thing about the poem . . . is the complete absence
of self-pity. The poet describes a most crushing humiliation,
describes it with minute precision, but at the same time he accepts
it, without whining, as inevitable, as if it were an act of Nature.
This supreme detachment in the midst of profound passion is due
to the artistic discretion and maturity of the young poet.'

Structure: 1–2 — self-admonition. 3–11 — past happiness (3
quondam), contrasted with present misery (9 *nunc*), leading to self-
exhortation (5 imperatives *noli, sectare, uiue, perfer, obdura*).
12–14 — farewell; a series of affirmations — to convince himself.
15–18 — 'A storm of passion, sweeping away the affirmative clauses,
brings in a rush of tempestuous questions.' (FRAENKEL 53).
19 — C. pulls himself up short: future and past have become
confused.

Note the mosaic pattern of repetitions: *miser* (1 and 10);
puella (4, 7, 12); *uolebas* (7), *nolebat* (7), *non uolt* (9), *noli* (9);
obstinata (11), *destinatus* (19); *obdura* (11), *obdurat* (12), *obdura* (19);
at tu (14), *at tu* (19). Line 8 practically repeats line 3.

Metre: Variously called *choliambics* (= 'limping iambics') or *scazons*, a form associated with Hipponax of Ephesus and with abusive or satirical verse generally. Of the other seven poems by C. in this metre, 22, 37, 39, 44, 59 and probably 60 are attacks on contemporaries; 31 seems the exception.

Pointing out that the lines are all end-stopped (contrary to C.'s usual practice), FRAENKEL 52 remarks: 'The sustained staccato will not have been lost on the ear of an ancient reader.... The hard rhythm, produced by the incision at the end of every single line, is in keeping with the hard tone of the whole poem.'

1. *miser*: a word C. is fond of (he uses it 31 times) and the stock description of the unhappy lover. In addition to denoting the lover's dejected state of mind, the word implies that the lover is hard done by; frequent in this sense in elegy. See ALLEN. The first word of the poem, therefore, suggests the theme.

Catulle: C. addresses himself again in Poems 46, 51, 52, 76 and 79; see Fordyce on 68. 135. A common device for getting a poem under way; here also an effective dramatization of the poet's awareness of a conflict within himself.

desinas: = *desine*. The subjunctive is characteristic of colloquial style (and also of the style of serious poetry); uncommon in classical prose.

ineptire: the *ineptus* is the man who misjudges the realities of of the situation; Cicero, *de Orat.* 2. 17 *quid tempus postulet non uidet, aut plura loquitur.* . . . But the word, like *illepidus* and *inuenustus*, belongs to C.'s technique of condemnation by understatement; the verb *ineptire* occurs twice in Terence.

2. *quod uides perisse perditum ducas*: apparently proverbial (cf. Plautus, *Trin.* 1026 *quin tu quod periit periisse ducis?*). Perhaps from bookkeeping (cf. Poem 5). *perire* serves as the passive of *perdere*; cf. 45. 5.

3. *fulsere*: the 'over-and-done-with' force of the perfect; cf. Virgil, *A.* 2. 325 *fuimus Troes*, etc.; *quondam* reinforces the idea.

candidi: 'bright and shining'. An emotionally charged word (see e.g. 68. 70). It occurs 15 times in C.

soles: = 'the light of the sun'; see on 5. 4.

4. *cum*: the *cum*-clause states what regularly took place during the period summed up by the perfect *fulsere*; the imperfect indicative is normal syntax in such cases.

uentitabas . . . ducebat: perhaps of actual meetings by arrangement, dictated by Lesbia; cf. the rendezvous at the house lent by Allius, 68. 67–72, and the stress there on bright and shining in the imagery.

5. *nobis*: dative of agent. The transition from first person singular to first person plural is common; it adds perhaps a trace of grandiloquence to the line, but hardly implies recognition by C. of an *alter ego*.

quantum amabitur nulla: 'as none will be loved'; cf. 87. 1–2. There is an echo of this line in 37. 12, and a more distant echo in 58. 1–3.

6–8. Take 6 *ibi* as local, 'there' — i.e. the meeting place implied by 4 *quo*. Many take *ibi* as temporal, 'then', but this is clumsy. FRAENKEL, arguing that the late position of *cum* is unparalleled in C., adopts *tum*, the reading of R, also read by Kroll and Lenchantin. But objection to the position of *cum* carries less weight if the clause is regarded as parallel to the *cum*-clause in 4; 3–8 thus assume a chiastic structure: 3–5 build up to the emphatic *nulla*; in 6–8 the mood becomes increasingly nostalgic as C. detaches himself from a past that is gone for ever.

6–7. Cf. 61. 144–6.

6. *iocosa*: the plaintive whimsy of understatement.

fiebant: passive, as if love had nothing to do with the will; cf. 85. 2 *fieri*.

8. On repetition for rhythmical or incantatory effect see on 79. 3 *cum gente Catullum*; cf. the refrains in 61. 5 etc. and 64. 326–7 etc.

9–11. A cruel monosyllabic present (9 *non uolt*) followed by 5 imperatives underlines the transition from reminiscence (3 *quondam*) and the langorous imperfects of 4–7 to present reality (9 *nunc iam*).

9. *noli*: The end of the line is missing; *noli* (conjectured by the

F

Renaissance editor Avanzi) picks up and continues 7 *nolebat* and 9 *non uolt*. With *impotens* cf. 4. 18 *impotentia*.

   10. *sectare*: imperative.

      miser uiue: cf. 10. 33 *molesta uiuis*.

   11. *obstinata*: a fragment of Accius *obstinato animo*, and Livy 6. 3. 9 *animi obstinati ad decertandum* suggest that *mente* is not just half-adverbial but carries its full weight of meaning. The basic force of *ob-* ('in the way of') is repeated in *obdura*. The function of the will is to bar C. from surrender to his emotions.

   12–18. One way of committing oneself to a decision is to announce it to the person most concerned; C. follows the announcement by a threat of the consequences, expressed as a series of questions. 13–16 form a chiasmus: 13 *requiret* ('seek you out') is picked up by 16 *adibit*; 13 *rogabit* by 14 *rogaberis*. An alternating pattern is imposed on the 7 questions by the 3rd-foot caesura. The questions are rhetorical in the sense that they do not expect the answer 'nobody' or 'half of Rome'; still less 'a rival', who could be named; their purpose is to challenge Lesbia to admit that the answer is 'not Catullus'.

   13. *rogabit*: 'invite'. Ovid, *Am.* 1. 8. 43 (*casta est, quam nemo rogauit*) provides the best commentary on this use of *rogare*.

   14. *nulla*: equivalent to an emphatic negative. Cf. Plautus, *Asin.* 408 *is nullus uenit*. So 17. 20 *si nulla sit*. For other examples of this colloquialism see Fordyce on 17. 20. Contrast 5 *amabitur nulla*.

   15. *scelesta*: 'wretched', a common imprecation in comedy, implying bad luck as often as bad morals; cf. Plautus, *Asin.* 475–6 *age. impudice, | sceleste, non audes mihi scelesto subuenire?*

      uae te: [Balthasar Venator thus emended *ne te*, the reading of V, following Plautus, *Asin.* 481.]

   16. *nunc*: i.e. 'now that I have made up my mind to leave you'; but the notion that the future is already upon Lesbia is helped by the present tense of *manet* just preceding.

   17. *cuius esse diceris?*: 'whose will they say you are?'

   18. The questions almost get out of hand — C. is not so much threatening as recalling the past.

19. *at tu*: cf. *at tu* in 14.

    destinatus: *obstinatus* stresses the beginning of the process, *destinatus* its continuance; cf. *oppressus* ('struck down') and *depressus* ('held down').

See:

A. W. Allen, 'Elegy and the classical attitude toward love', *YClS* 11 (1950), 255–77 (on *miser*).

Steele Commager, 'Notes on some poems of Catullus', *HSPh* 70 (1965), 90–2.

Eduard Fraenkel, 'Two poems of Catullus', *JRS* 51 (1961), 51–3.

H. A. Kahn, *Latomus* 27 (1968) 355–74.

L. A. Moritz, '*Miser Catulle*: a postscript', *G & R* 13 (1966), 155–7.

R. L. Rowland, '*Miser Catulle*: an interpretation of the eighth poem of Catullus', *G & R* 13 (1966), 15–21.

R. A. Swanson. *CJ* 58 (1963) 193–6.

9

A poem to welcome a friend back from Spain.

Structure: Two rhetorical questions, and the poet's reaction to each. 1–4 — first question: 'Are you home again?' 5 — 'Yes, you are. Oh, happy news!' 6–9 — second question: 'Shall we be together again?' 10–11 — 'Oh, how happy I am!'

But these joyful, apparently spontaneous lines are a good example of lyric form under conscious intellectual control. Lines 1–4 get the poem going: (1) they put the reader in the picture by summarizing the basic data; (2) they provide the emotional context which makes the data meaningful. Lines 6–9 continue the process. By the time we reach the end of this ebullient, light-hearted trifle we know all we need to know about Veranius and what he meant to C.

Metre: hendecasyllabics.

    1. *Verani*: For Veranius see on Poem 28; he crops up again in Poems 12 and 47; most probably he had in Spain the kind of job C. had in Bithynia under Memmius (see on Poem 10).

    2. *antistans mihi milibus trecentis*: 'worth more to me than three

hundred thousand friends'. Cf. Cicero, *Att.* 2. 5. 1 *Cato ille noster qui mihi unus est pro centum milibus*, and *Brut.* 191 *Plato enim mihi unus instar est centum milium.* Either 'three hundred' or 'a thousand' would have done; the two numerals reinforce the note of extravagant enthusiasm; Veranius is (a) C.'s best friend, (b) worth all the friends in the world; but lines 1–2 are not seriously concerned with precise, logical statement.

3–5. *uenistine . . .? uenisti*: for the pattern of question and answer cf. 12. 6, 77. 3–5 and 88. 4–5.

4. *fratresque unanimos*: cf. Virgil, *A.* 7. 335 *tu potes unanimos armare in proelia fratres*; *A.* 4. 8 *unanimam sororem.*

anumque: [Restored by Faerno.] For the adjectival use cf. 68. 46, 78b. 4.

5. *nuntii beati*: either (1) exclamatory genitive (common in Greek, rare in Latin), or (2) nominative plural. C. uses the exclamatory accusative in 14. 12, 26. 5, 56. 1 and 107. 6.

6. *uisam*: = both 'watch' and 'visit'.

Hiberum: genitive plural of *Hiber*, or the short form of the genitive plural of *Hiberus.*

7. *narrantem loca, facta, nationes*: a neat summary of the contents of travellers' tales.

8–11. C. has heard Veranius before (8 *ut mos est tuus*); Veranius' mother and brother (line 4) remain in the background — C. counts on being a privileged listener.

9. *iucundum . . . suauiabor*: cf. Horace's friend (likewise back from Spain), *Carm.* 1. 36. 4–7: *qui nunc Hesperia sospes ab ultima / caris multa sodalibus, / nulli plura tamen diuidit oscula / quam dulci Lamiae.*

10. *quantum est hominum beatiorum*: amounts to a partitive genitive; cf. 3. 2 *quantum est hominum uenustiorum.* The turn of phrase in lines 10–11 is plainly colloquial.

10

A poem in the Roman satiric tradition of relaxed, urbane personal reminiscence. Everything partakes of the laconic spirit of the occasion. At the same time this is more than anecdote, and more than narrative. As in Horace, *S.* 1. 9, the irony is double-edged: ostensibly, the subject is Varus' girl-friend (C. was obliged to revise his opinion of her — to begin with she was *non sane illepidum neque inuenustum*; two thirds of the way through she becomes *cinaediorem*; by the end she is *insulsa male et molesta*); the petulance of C.'s reaction is offset, however, by a wry, detached self-observation.

Structure: A matter of mood more than syntax. 1–8 — conversational. 9–13 — C. gets worked up. 14–23 — they calm him down; he starts to preen himself. 24–34 — the girl catches him out; C. ticks her off.

Metre: hendecasyllabics.

1–2. Take *ad suos amores* with *duxerat*, and *uisum* (=supine of *uidere*) as an explanatory expansion, 'had taken me to his girl-friend's place, to have a look' (it is clear from line 3 that C. is meeting the girl for the first time); cf. 32. 3 *ad te ueniam meridiatum*; with *uisum* used absolutely cf. 61. 146 *ni petitum aliunde eat*. The supine is colloquial: see Austin on Virgil, *A.* 2. 786. (Many take *ad suos amores* with *uisum* [=supine of *uisere*]; *ad* with *uisere* is used of visiting the sick; some therefore assume that Varus' girl-friend is sick and that this is the reason for the visit to Serapis proposed in line 26.) For *suos amores* = 'girl-friend' see on 6. 16. The pluperfect *duxerat* gets the explanatory recapitulation out of the way quickly, in order to concentrate on the main scene.

1. *Varus*: The addressee of 22. 1; we know of a lawyer Alfenus Varus (perhaps the Alfenus of Poem 30) and a Quintilius Varus, friend of Horace and Virgil (cf. *Carm.* 1. 24).

3. *scortillum*: 'little wench'. A diminutive, found only here; *scortum*, though scarcely complimentary (cf. 6. 5), can have (like 'wench') overtones of tolerant approval; cf. Horace, *Carm.* 2. 11. 21. The tone is not that suggested by the translations in *L & S* but that, say, of Sheridan's *Rivals* or Mozart's *Don Giovanni*; *scortillum*, like *otiosum* ('having nothing better to do'), probably belongs to the jargon of C.'s set, the *urbani*.

tum repente: i.e. C.'s first impression on arrival.

4. *illepidum neque inuenustum*: =36. 17; *lepos* and *uenus* are the key concepts of the *urbani*. It is clear from what follows that the approval expressed is not of the girl's appearance but of the impression she gave (to begin with) of knowing how to conduct herself in the presence of sophisticated young men. Cf. Poem 86.

5. *huc ut uenimus*: after a brief indication of scene and persons the narrative proper begins here.

incidere: perfect indicative; = 'we fell to talking'.

6–8. Their talk naturally turned to Bithynia, where C. had just been. Note the easy progression from (1) 'what is the place like and how is it doing nowadays?' (C. can speak with the authority of the man recently back) to (2) 'what did you make out of the trip?' Cf. Poem 46.

6. *sermones uarii*: 'one subject after another' (*sermones diuersi* would = 'unrelated subjects').

7. *se haberet*: cf. Sulpicius Rufus in Cicero, *Fam.* 4. 5. 6 *de iis rebus quae hic geruntur, quemadmodumque se prouincia habeat, certiorem faciam.*

8. *et quonam mihi profuisset aere*: The *nam* adds emphasis to the final question — as though they were getting round to the real point. It was taken for granted that a reasonable governor would let his staff make something on the side. [Estaço's *ecquonam* is perhaps the right reading. Cf. Cicero, *Att.* 9. 9. 1. No real doubt implied of course.]

9. *id quod erat*: 'the facts'.

ipsis: 'the natives'; if *they* were penniless, it followed there was nothing for governors or their entourage; for the generalizing plural *praetoribus* see on 63. 68. (Kroll, following Löfstedt, takes *ipsis* as 'the bosses', anticipating *praetoribus*, and regards the first *nec* in line 10 as a colloquial pleonasm.) There is some doubt about the text.

11. *cur . . . unctius referret*: the construction develops into a loosely formulated indirect question (in place of the more regular *quo unctius referret*).

caput unctius: the sense is fixed by the comparative *unctius* — what a man had made out of his time in Bithynia wouldn't even contribute significantly to keeping him in hair oil. We hear a lot about Roman hair oil.

12. *praesertim*, etc.: = 'particularly if people had a bastard for a governor'. C.'s *praetor* was C. Memmius, husband of Sulla's daughter (the notorious Fausta), governor of Bithynia-Pontus in 57–56. He was also the patron of Lucretius — hence perhaps his interest in C.; he may still have been as mean as C. implies here — and states with some emphasis in 28. 7–10. But cf. Wheeler 103: 'Perhaps the motive which led Memmius . . . to prevent the members of his suite from enriching themselves . . . was not wholly selfish. Perhaps the poor provincials were grateful. At any rate we should bear in mind that abuse from the mouth of a hot-tempered poet . . . should be heavily discounted.'

quibus esset: = 'if as in our case'; plural because C. is thinking of himself and his friends; *esset* is generic subjunctive.

irrumator: = 'bastard', one who doesn't give a damn for others; the charge is repeated, with lurid exploitation of the latent imagery, 28. 9–10. On *irrumare* see on 16. 1. Lenchantin suggests that *irrumator*, etc., belonged to the *sermo castrensis*. Note the jingle *irrumator praetor*.

13. *faceret pili*: genitive of price. Cf. 5. 3 *omnes unius aestimemus assis*.

cohortem: see on 28. 1–5.

14. *inquiunt*: the plural invites us to take the direct speech as the gist of the several remarks of the two speakers organized into a single coherent statement.

14–15. *quod illic natum*: 'the local product' (i.e. bearers); the eight-men litter (20 *octo homines*) seems to have been associated with Bithynia; cf. Cicero, *Ver*. 5. 27.

17. *unum me . . . beatiorem*: 'to pass myself off as exceptionally lucky'. Emphatic *unus* also in 107. 7 *me uno* and 31. 11 *hoc est quod unum est*.

19. *quod . . . incidisset*: Rejected reason: C. *had* been allotted a rotten province, but that didn't mean. . . .

20. *parare*: picks up 15 *comparasti*; a compound verb is often repeated without the preverb. Cf. 62. 3 *surgere* and 89. 5 *tangere*.

rectos: 'holding themselves straight'; cf. 86. 2 *recta*.

21. *nec hic neque illic*: i.e. neither in Rome nor in Bithynia; a way of making the denial more emphatic.

22. *fractum . . . ueteris pedem grabati*: i.e. a fragment of a bed, just as one bearer would be a fragment of a team, and equally useless. For *grabatus*, a cheap bed, cf. Furius Bibaculus *FPL* p. 81, Lucilius 284 W *tres a Deucalione grabati* and *Mor.* 5. Observe the note of sophisticated poverty.

23. *collo . . . collocare*: note the assonance and alliteration.

24. *cinaediorem*: 'a particularly shameless hussy'; for *cinaedus* (a term of abuse C. uses fairly freely) see on 16. 2.

25. *quaeso*: = 'please'.

26. *istos*: the eight men C. has not got.

commoda: the final a is short, a colloquial pronunciation.

ad Serapim: i.e. to the temple of Serapis, an Egyptian divinity. Repeated attempts were made about this time to suppress the cult, which continued to gain in popularity.

27. For *manĕ* ('prosodic hiatus') see on 55. 4 *tĕ in omnibus* also 97. 1 and 114. 6. Distinguish from 'iambic shortening' (see on 6. 16 *uolŏ*). For other cases of hiatus see on 3. 16, 11. 11, 38. 2, 66. 11, 68. 158, 76. 10 and 107. 1. The form *inquii*, which does not occur elsewhere, was restored by Scaliger. [*me inquit* V.]

28. *istud quod . . .*: a colloquial formula for getting the sentence going while C. thinks of something to say.

29. *fugit me ratio*: 'I didn't think' (i.e. 'the proper way of it escaped me').

30. *Cinna est Gaius*: The order and the disjointed syntax represent C. still struggling to find a respectable white lie. For C.'s friend the orator and poet Gaius Cinna see on Poem 95. Did he serve with C. in Bithynia? A fragment of a verse-letter, apparently written from Bithynia to accompany a poem (*FPL* p. 89), suggests the possibility.

31. *uerum utrum illius an mei*: the double elision suggests the rush of words now that the white lie has been found.

  quid ad me?: sc. *attinet*: 'what's it matter to me?'

32. *tam . . . quam mihi pararim*: *tamquam* without *si* commonly introduces a comparative clause; the perfect subjunctive is normal.

33. *insulsa male*: = 'a silly bore' (lit. 'inopportunely lacking in taste'); the girl shows her lack of breeding by failing to appreciate that a man is entitled to boast a bit, without being embarrassed by boring people who take his words literally.

  molesta: cf. 68. 137 *molesti*.

  uiuis: in comedy *uiuo* is an emphatic substitute for *sum*.

34. *neglegentem*: 'careless', i.e. about facts.

See:

W. B. Sedgwick, 'Catullus X: a rambling commentary', *G & R* 16 (1947), 108–14; on the social background see *Cat. Rev.* Chapter 5.

11

Poem 11 marks the end of the affair, no less plainly than Poem 51 marks the beginning. The Sapphic stanza is used in both poems, and in these two only (unless we regard 51. 13–16 as a separate fragment); moreover 11. 19 *identidem* is clearly a cross-reference to 51. 3 — the word is too unusual for the repetition to be fortuitous. Only the order is wrong — why 11 before 51? Accident? Or a device, on the part of the poet or his editor, aimed at heightening the illusion of fragments gathered at random of a dramatic continuum? The date seems fixed by the reference in 10–12 to Caesar's campaigns of 55 B.C. (well after C.'s *return* from Bithynia) — another reason for supposing the dismissal literary and public (written or rewritten for a collected edition), rather than a personal letter which has fallen into our hands.

But what has the romantic travelogue of lines 2–14 to do with the 'brief, harsh' message Furius and Aurelius are asked to take to C.'s mistress? Doesn't the first half awkwardly overshadow the second? And how can C. address the Furius of Poems 16, 23 and 26 and the Aurelius of Poems 15, 16 and 21 as though they were trusted friends? The key seems to lie in the antithesis 13 *omnia haec* and 15–16 *pauca . . . non bona dicta.*

Does C. dismiss, then, the big, false talk of Furius and Aurelius? Are they included in the contempt C. expresses for his mistress? Are they asked to deliver the message because 'they belong to the circle to which Lesbia has now sunk' (WILAMOWITZ 307)? It is hard to accept the violence done to lines 2–14, the evocative imagery in particular of 3–4 and 7–8, by this reading. The obvious reminiscence of 2–14 in the opening lines of Horace, *Carm.* 2. 6 is in favour of regarding 2–14 as seriously poetic. (To assume that Horace does not intend *his* lines as seriously poetic is to miss their delicate irony — *Carm.* 2. 6 rejects the romantic appeal of distant places and the adventurous life in favour of a life of quiet, hedonist retirement.)

If anything, the tone of Horace's poem authorizes the assumption, which we might well make anyway, that 2–14 are not so much derisive of Furius and Aurelius, or a contemptuous rejection of their friendship, as a wrily ironical answer to their offer to stand by C. under any circumstances (for the idea 'under any circumstances' translated in a series of evocative images and place names, cf. Horace, *Carm.* 1. 22). They are perhaps as anxious to help as Quintius in Poem 82; perhaps they still have hopes of a reconciliation. 'Thank you,' says C. in effect, 'but here is something much simpler which you can do for me: tell her to go to hell.' Poem 11, i.e., puts *'finis'* both to the affair and to the group of poems which record it.

Structure: The 24 lines form a single sentence. 1 — Furius and Aurelius addressed. 2–12 — a parenthesis formed by a string of alternatives, each introduced by *siue* or *seu*; the arrangement is geographical (India, the Middle East, the far North) rather than logical or rhetorical. 13–16 — résumé of parenthesis, followed by request. 17–24 — C.'s message.

Metre: Sapphic stanzas (as in Poem 51); there is no running over of the sense between stanzas. The fourth syllable is short in lines 6 and 15, a licence admitted by Sappho but avoided by Horace.

1. *comites*: the word used of one another by the members of a *cohors* (cf. 46. 9). Did Furius and Aurelius suggest that all three might get a staff job with Crassus in the East, or with Caesar (on his second expedition to Britain)?

2. *extremos . . . Indos*: For Horace, too, (*Ep.* 1. 1. 45, 1. 6. 6) India marks the eastern extremity of the world.

3. *litus*: Beyond India naturally lay Oceanus, whose waters according to ancient belief ran right round the plain of the earth; *Eoa unda* = that part of Oceanus which lay to the east of India.

   ut: 'where' as in 17. 10; an archaism, supported by the spatial use of ὡς in Hellenistic Greek.

   longe resonante: = πολυφλοίσβῳ a contribution to the epic flavour of the clause.

4. *tunditur unda*: note the sound.

5-8. A series of names evoking the area we should now call the Middle East. The Hyrcani and the Arabes stand for oriental effeminacy (5 *molles*); the Sagae and Parthi are represented in terms closer to the reality of Rome's recent military adventures in the Middle East; each time the epithet applies equally to the two proper names. Finally Egypt is represented by its most famous geographical feature, the river Nile.

7. *septemgeminus*: the seven mouths of the Nile are meant.

   colorat: the Nile silt discolours the Mediterranean. So Baehrens, Kroll, Lenchantin. Others take C. to mean the flooding of the flat land through which the Nile flows.

9-12. Provided we do not push the details of 5-8 too far, we can feel that we have moved steadily closer to home — away from India, the edge of the world, to the Nile. Now we launch out in a fresh direction to the edge of the world again — across the Alps, to Germany and Britain.

10. *Caesaris . . . monimenta magni*: 'testimonials to Caesar's greatness', rather than 'memorials' — Caesar was not yet dead; *monimentum* = anything which reminds us of a person or a fact; cf. Horace, *Carm.* 3. 30. 1 *exegi monumentum aere perennius.*

11. *Rhenum*: the reference is to Caesar's summer campaign of 55 B.C. when he threw a temporary bridge across the Rhine and made an expedition into Germany.

11–12. *horribilesque ulti-mosque*: an unusually marked hiatus, if not an impossible one: see on 3. 16 and 10. 27. But appropriate, whether we regard it as underpinning a feeling of revulsion inspired by the sight of the Britons, or a feeling of breathlessness at the end of the long journey from India to Britain. Most modern editors (not Lenchantin) adopt Haupt's conjecture *horribile aequor* — i.e. the 'rough expanse' of the English Channel, which caused Caesar so much trouble (*Gal.* 4. 28). Though palaeographically plausible, Haupt's conjecture gives lame sense and introduces an unpleasing repetition (8 *aequora*, 11 *aequor*). With the line division *ulti-mosque* cf. Horace, *Carm.* 1. 2. 19–20 etc. It seems clear that in the original form of the Sapphic stanza the fourth line was continuous with the third. With *ultimos . . . Britannos* cf. 29. 4 *ultima Britannia*; the idea afterwards became a commonplace — e.g. Horace, *Carm.* 1. 35. 29, 4. 14. 48, and Virgil, *Ecl.* 1. 66; a century and a half later Britain was still a strange land at the end of the world — cf. Tacitus' description *Ag.* 10–12.

13. *omnia haec*: take with 14 *temptare.*

quaecumque: neuter plural accusative; i.e. C.'s friends are ready to face not only all those things (*omnia haec*) which have been mentioned, but whatever the gods have in store for C.

14. *temptare*: an echo in Horace, *Carm.* 3. 4. 29–31 *utcumque mecum uos eritis, libens | insanientem nauita Bosphorum | temptabo*, etc.

simul: = *una* — the commonest meaning of *simul* in C.; cf. 21. 5, 46. 10, 50. 13, 63. 12, etc.

15. *meae puellae*: the usual formula (see on 51. 7 *Lesbia*), here ironical.

16. *non bona dicta*: *non* negates a virtual compound; for *bona*

dicta = 'fine words' cf. Plautus, *Am.* 24–5 *uerum profecto hoc petere me precario | a uobis iussit leniter dictis bonis.* For the idea of an un-welcome message cf. Virgil, *A.* 12. 75–6 *nuntius haec, Idmon, Phrygio mea dicta tyranno | haud placitura refer.*

17. *uiuat ualeatque*: a dismissal; cf. Terence, *An.* 889 *ualeat uiuat cum illa*; Horace, *S.* 2. 5. 110 and *Ep.* 1. 6. 67; the other sense of *ualere* ('prosper') is present as an overtone.

moechis: strictly, *moechus* = 'adulterer', the lover of a married woman; cf. 37. 14–16.

18. *trecentos*: for the numeral cf. 9. 2 and 12. 10.

19. *identidem*: 'repeatedly'; again 51. 3.

omnium: the last syllable is elided before *ilia* in the next line. Cf. 22 *prati* and Horace, *Carm.* 2. 2. 18. (For the heavy elision in this line, a characteristic of passages expressing intense personal feeling, see on 73. 6.)

20. *ilia rumpens*: cf. 80. 7–8 *rupta ... ilia* and 63. 5 *ilei ... pondera*.

21. *nec meum respectet* etc.: 'she must not count on my love (i.e. take it for granted), as once she could'.

22. *qui*: i.e. *meus amor*.

culpa: see on 75. 1.

prati: the last syllable is elided; cf. 19 *omnium*.

23. *ultimi*: i.e. at the edge of the field. The flower (a poppy perhaps) is not ploughed under (like the rest), but merely grazed by the plough in passing — and left lying; the two belong, as it were, to different worlds, but a moment's contact suffices to destroy the flower. Did C. consciously end the second and last of his poems in Sapphics (and the affair with Lesbia) with an allusion to a poem of Sappho (Fr. 105c *LP* = *LGS* 225, a hyacinth lies on the ground in the mountains, trampled by herdsmen)? Is the reminiscence in 62. 39–48 earlier, and are the concluding words of Poem 11 an echo of 62. 40 *nullo conuolsus aratro*? Virgil improved on the idea (combining Homer, *Il.* 8. 306–8 — poppies drooping in the rain), *A.* 9. 435–6: his flower is snipped off at the roots (*succisus*), so that it dies slowly (*languescit moriens*).

See:

A. Hudson-Williams, 'Catullus 11, 9–12', *CQ* ns 2 (1952), 186 (he
    suggests *horribilem gelu*).

T. E. Kinsey, 'Catullus 11', *Latomus* 24 (1965), 537–44.

L. Richardson Jr., '*Furi et Aureli, comites Catulli*', *CPh* 58 (1963),
    93–106.

U. von Wilamowitz-Moellendorf, *Hellenistische Dichtung* (1924)
    ii 307–8.

12

'Asinius Marrucinus, please return the table-napkin you have
pinched: it has sentimental value.'

A piece of occasional verse, the outcome of circumstances
beyond our conjecture. But the circumstances are not really so
important; nor need we seek for undercurrents of irony running
counter to what C.'s words assert.

Cf. Poems 25, 33 and 42. Martial has two epigrams (8. 59 and
12. 29) on napkin-thieves. The Romans apparently took their own
napkins to a dinner party; they ate of course with their fingers.

Structure: 1–3 — data. 4–9 — reproach. 10–11 — threat. 12–17
— explanation.

Metre: hendecasyllabics.

1–2. *manu sinistra non belle uteris:* left hands have their legitimate
uses, but Asinius misapplies his (2 *non belle uteris*). Ovid makes
Ajax remark that Ulysses' left hand is *nata ad furta* (*Met.* 13. 111);
see on 47. 1; contrast 33. 3.

1. *Marrucine:* If *Marrucinus* was Asinius' *cognomen* (geographical
cognomina are not uncommon), the order need not be significant —
Cicero in his letters often puts *cognomen* before *nomen*. The word
can only stand at the beginning of the line for metrical reasons;
all the same, a competent poet chooses his opening word —
gauche behaviour was perhaps to be expected of a man connected
with such a remote part of Italy. (The Marrucini lived on the

Adriatic coast close to the river Sangro; for the connexion with
that area of the family of the Asinii see Fordyce.)

2. *in ioco atque uino*: = 'at dinner parties'; cf. 50. 6 *per iocum
atque uinum*. Take equally with 2 *uteris* and 3 *tollis*.

3. *tollis*: 'lift' — a polite euphemism.

lintea neglegentiorum: the plural (see on 63. 68) helps to turn
Asinius into a habitual thief (see on 7–8).

5. *quamuis*: 'to what extent you like', i.e. 'as can be'; this is the
original sense of *quamuis*.

sordida . . . inuenusta: the first adjective expresses C.'s indig-
nation (pinching napkins is a low trick); the second provides
Asinius with a loophole: if he thought the practice smart, his
judgment was at fault.

6–9. The hint in *inuenusta* that Asinius was trying to be smart
and failed is developed by the appeal to the judgment of Asinius'
brother Pollio, who can tell the difference between urbane joke
and vulgar theft.

6. *Pollioni*: almost certainly Gaius Asinius Pollio, the orator
and historian and the friend of Virgil and Horace.

7–8. *qui tua furta . . . uelit*: Note how the hypothesis on which
the poem depends is filled out by the implications of this phrase:
(1) that Asinius, like Martial's napkin-thieves, makes a practice of
pinching napkins — C., in short, is merely the latest victim;
(2) that Pollio knows all about his brother's habit; the plain
words *tua furta* are perhaps to be felt as virtually oblique —
Pollio, i.e., does not mince matters.

7. *talento*: a very large sum of money, of course.

8. *uelit*: potential subjunctive — Pollio, unfortunately, cannot
undo his brother's thefts with money. For the idea cf. Virgil, *A.*
10. 503–4 *Turno tempus erit, magno cum optauerit emptum | intactum
Pallanta.*

9. *differtus*: [Passerat's conjecture; the MSS have *dissertus*, an
appropriate enough description of Pollio (i.e. Pollio is an authority
on witty pranks); but the genitives *leporum* and *facetiarum* are
grammatically difficult. See G. P. Goold, *Phoenix* 12 (1958),

93–4.] If Pollio was 'crammed to overflowing with clever pranks', i.e. hardly able to restrain himself, then his condemnation of his brother's napkin-pinching is naturally more impressive.

  puer: Pollio was born in 76 B.C.

  10–11. *quare aut . . . aut*: for the form of the threat cf. 69. 9–10 and 103. 1–3.

  10. *hendecasyllabos*: see on 42. 1–2.

    trecentos: see on 9. 2.

  12. *quod*: relative pronoun.

  13. *mnemosynum mei sodalis*: 'a souvenir of a friend of mine'. A Greek word, restored by the Renaissance editor Calfurnio, and found only here in Latin; Cicero frequently uses Greek words and expressions in his correspondence.

  14. *Saetaba*: Saetabis in Spain was famous for its linen goods.

    ex Hiberis: [*exhibere* V.]

  15. *miserunt*: i.e. before they returned. Veranius is just back from Spain at the time of Poem 9; for Fabullus see Poem 13. The natural implication of C.'s words is that Veranius and Fabullus both sent C. napkins.

  muneri: final dative.

  16. *amem*: subjunctive without *ut* after *necesse est*.

  17. *Veraniolum*: this diminutive again at 47. 3.

    meum: with both *Veraniolum* and *Fabullum*.

13

'Dear Fabullus: You'll get a fine dinner — any day now — at my place — provided you bring everything (food, wine, girl-friend) yourself. I'm stony broke. All I can supply is scent: it's hers — absolutely divine!'

Poem 13 hardly reads like the light-hearted invitation to dinner most take it to be. An actual invitation should specify time and date; a good contemporary example is Philodemus' verse epistle to his patron Piso (under whom Fabullus served in

Macedonia — see on Poem 28), *AP* 11. 44 ('come tomorrow at
the ninth hour; the food and drink won't be up to much, but the
conversation and the company will be good . . .'); cf. Horace,
Ep. 1. 5 ('come this evening'). Of course in a poem arranged for
publication details can become superfluous: no date or time,
therefore, in Horace, *Carm.* 4. 12 (an echo of Poem 13 in lines
17–24) or in *Carm.* 1. 20 and 3. 29. C.'s opening lines, however,
read more like procrastination than an invitation.

   Fabullus is just back from Spain, perhaps, like his friend
Veranius (Poem 9; for their time in Spain see 12. 14–17). Cf.
Plautus, *Bac.* 186–7 *hospitium et cenam pollicere, ut conuenit | peregre
aduenienti.* In his eagerness for news of C., has he dropped a hint
that an invitation to dinner would be welcome? Perhaps he has
heard rumours and wants to know what C. has been up to (cf.
Poems 6 and 55). He may feel an opportunity to see for himself
is called for (cf. Poem 10). Something of the sort seems the appro-
priate background for Poem 13. C.'s answer seems to be, 'yes,
soon; bring a girl; not much to eat or drink, of course; but you'll
like *her*.'

   For fashionable women at dinner parties see Cicero's account
(*Fam.* 9. 26) of a dinner he attended in 46 B.C. at which the mime-
actress Cytheris, mistress of his host, and later of Mark Antony,
was among those present; cf. *Att.* 2. 14. 1 (59 B.C.) — Atticus has
been at a smart dinner party where Clodia ('Ox-eyes') was
among the guests.

   Metre: hendecasyllabics.

   1. *mi Fabulle*: Again 28. 3. For Fabullus see on Poem 28.

   2. *paucis . . . diebus*: 'pretty soon'.

   si tibi di fauent: 'if you are lucky'. The phrase might be a
mere saving formula, =our 'God willing'; but it is more likely
that it is a valid clue, to be added to *paucis diebus*.

   3–5. Two points to note in these lines: (1) C. is hard up (cf.
the atmosphere of smart poverty in 10. 21–3); (2) food and drink
don't really matter much — C. has something more important
up his sleeve.

4. *non sine*: 'not forgetting'.

candida: strictly of complexion, but with connotations of approval, rather like our 'blonde'; cf. 35. 8 and 86. 1; also 68. 70.

5. *sale*: pun ambiguity: the alignment with *uino* suggests the literal sense, but the following words restore the figurative sense, 'wit'; see on 86. 4.

omnibus cachinnis: =something like 'all the latest stories'. For *cachinnis*, 'ripples of laughter', see 31. 14.

6–8. The point that nothing (except the one thing to be mentioned in a moment) is to be expected of C. is repeated for emphasis; Fabullus of course might be expected to guess that the reason his friend is stony broke is a woman.

8. *plenus . . . aranearum*: proverbial. In Plautus, *Aul.* 84–7, Euclio's old servant complains that the house [*aedes*] *inaniis sunt oppletae atque araneis*. Cf. Homer, *Od.* 16. 35 (of Odysseus' bed), Cratinus 190K, and Afranius 410. See 23. 2, 25. 3 and 68. 49.

9–14. What C. *will* be able to offer in return, he says, is scent; the scent is his mistress's; she got it from the Powers of Desire. Surely a series of statements calculated to intrigue. But if Fabullus is invited to bring a *candida puella*, isn't it likely that the planned party is to be a foursome? (Hence perhaps the present uncertainty about date.) If C. avoids saying in so many words that his mistress will be present, isn't that part of the *urbanitas* which makes the letter into a poem?

9. *sed contra accipies* etc.: cf. the invitation of Philodemus to Piso, line 5: ἀλλ' ἑτάρους ὄψει παναληθέας etc.

meros amores: = 'something you'll absolutely fall in love with'. Though the usual meaning in C. of *amores* is 'girl-friend' (see on 6. 16), it is clear from the echo in Martial (14. 206–7 *collo necte, puer, meros amores, / ceston de Veneris sinu calentem*) that the phrase can denote an object — here the scent. [*meros* X; *meos* O.]

11. *nam unguentum dabo*: scent was *de rigueur* at a Roman dinner party, and that at any rate C. will provide.

11–12. *quod meae puellae* etc.: usually taken as hyperbole; some compare Homer, *Od.* 18. 190–6 (not really a parallel, the talk

there is of goddesses and no gift is mentioned). Propertius 2. 29.
15–18 probably provides the clue we need:

> quae cum Sidoniae nocturna ligamina mitrae
>   soluerit atque oculos mouerit illa graues,
> afflabunt tibi non Arabum de gramine odores,
>   sed quos ipse suis fecit Amor manibus—

a reference to the idea that a lovely woman, like a goddess,
emitted a special characteristic fragrance which was her *aura*; see
Latin Explorations 176, adding Virgil, *A.* 1. 403–4 to the examples
quoted. Cf. Baudelaire, 'Le Chat' (speaking of '*ma femme*'):

> Et des pieds jusques à la tête,
> Un air subtil, un dangereux parfum,
> Nagent autour de son corps brun.

Was the scent, in other words, not one presented to C. by his
mistress, but the alluring fragrance of her person?

13–14. A final extravagance offsets any unseemly over-
commitment in the previous lines. Cf. 86. 6.

See:

M. Schuster, 'Zur Auffassung von Catulls 13. Gedicht', *WS* 43
  (1922–3), 227–34.

D. W. T. C. Vessey, *Latomus* 30 (1971) 45–55.

14

On the eve of the Saturnalia (the traditional time for giving gifts),
Calvus, the orator (cf. Poem 53) and poet (cf. Poems 50 and 96),
has sent his friend an anthology of contemporary verse. C. sends
it back to Calvus with a mock-indignant verse epistle.

Did Calvus think the poems good? Disagreement about
particular poems is not after all uncommon among members of
the same school. C. pretends of course to assume the present was
meant as a joke — Calvus got the book perhaps from the critic
Sulla and was quick to dispose of the gift. Or are BUCHHEIT and
FRAENKEL right in arguing one object of the poem is to pillory
publicly a group of *pessimi poetae*? Observe that Poem 14

implies a closer friendship between C. and Calvus than Poem 50.

Structure: The structure is essentially a logical one. 1–5 — indignation. 6–11 — there must be an explanation. 12–15 — further outburst of indignation, leading to 16–20 — threat of revenge. 21–3 — dismissal.

Metre: hendecasyllabics.

1. *plus oculis meis*: for the idiom cf. 3. 5, 82. 1–4 and 104. 2. The opening lines survive of a parody of Poem 14 by Maecenas addressed to Horace (*FPL* p. 102).

2. *iucundissime*: the superlative implies a consciously conciliatory note in C.'s expression of indignation.

munere isto: 'in view of your present'; cf. 68. 87 *Helenae raptu*. Since Poem 14 accompanies Calvus' book of poems on their return journey, there is no need to define *isto*.

3. *odissem*: =an imperfect subjunctive.

odio Vatiniano: 'a hatred like the one Vatinius has for you'. For the feud between Calvus and Vatinius see on Poem 53.

5. *male perderes*: =*omnino perderes*, 'finish me off'; for the idiom cf. Horace, *S.* 2. 1. 6–7 *peream male, si non | optimum erat*.

6. *isti . . . clienti*: *isti* points to a definite, known antecedent — a *cliens*, i.e., has somehow been referred to; the easiest assumption is that Calvus explained in an accompanying note that he had got the volume from a *cliens*. C. proceeds therefore to conjecture about the identity of this *cliens*. For *iste* = 'the one mentioned in your letter' cf., e.g., Cicero, *Att.* 11. 2. 1 *ex multis meis et miserrimis curis est una leuata, si, ut scribis, ista hereditas fidem et famam meam tueri potest*. The *cliens* was possibly a man Calvus had defended in court, though the Latin word does not mean 'client' of course in our sense.

7. *tantum . . . impiorum*: =*tot impios*.

8–11. A play on the two meanings of *litterator* ('critic' and 'schoolmaster'), supported by a play on the two meanings of *munus* ('gift' and 'task'). The primary statement is: 'Of course, if the critic Sulla has made you this novel gift, one so out of the ordinary . . .'. Behind the surface meaning lurks an alternative statement: 'Of course, if the schoolmaster Sulla has imposed on you this novel task . . .' (i.e. the task of wading through poetry like this). Then at line 10 the primary meaning re-establishes itself: 'At any rate,' says C., 'the gift is a recognition of your efforts on his behalf.'

9. *dat*: the present is the tense regularly used of the donor of a gift; so 1. 1 *dono*, 4. 26 *dedicat*; cf. Virgil, *A.* 9. 266 *cratera antiquum quem dat Sidonia Dido.*

Sulla: The man meant was perhaps Cornelius Epicadus, a freedman of the dictator Sulla, though there is no evidence at all of freedmen taking the *cognomen* of their master; see Suetonius, *Gram.* 12, and Neudling 165.

litterator: The *locus classicus* for this word is Suetonius, *Gram.* 4 *Cornelius quoque Nepos libello quo distinguit litteratum ab erudito, litteratos quidem uulgo appellari ait eos qui aliquid diligenter et acute scienterque possint aut dicere aut scribere, ceterum proprie sic appellandos poetarum interpretes. qui a Graecis grammatici nominentur. Eosdem litteratores uocitatos Messala Coruinus in quadam epistula ostendit, non esse sibi dicens rem cum Furio Bibaculo, ne cum Ticida quidem aut litteratore Catone; significat enim haud dubie Valerium Catonem, poetam simul grammaticumque notissimum.* Suetonius goes on to say that some distinguish *litterator* and *litteratus* (using the former of a schoolmaster and the latter of a scholar or critic). But he implies that this is splitting hairs: clearly in ordinary usage Suetonius admits *litterator* as a word for either a schoolmaster or a critic and authority on literature. (The Suetonius passage has been mis-interpreted: many have taken it as proof that 'schoolmaster' is the normal meaning of *litterator*; some have therefore denied that Cornelius Epicadus, Sulla's freedman, can be meant here since he was an authority on literature of some standing.) Martianus Capella (3. 229), who quotes C.'s line, seems to regard *litterator* as the old-fashioned equivalent of *litteratus*: *itaque assertor nostri nunc litteratus dicitur, litterator antea uocabatur.* He goes on to imply that the distinction between schoolmaster and critic is mainly a matter of the progress of the craft (230): *officium uero meum tunc fuerat docte*

scribere legereque; nunc etiam illud accessit ut meum sit erudite intellegere
probareque.

10. *non est mi male*: = 'I have no complaint'; cf. 3. 13.

bene ac beate: = 'I'm jolly pleased'.

12. *di magni*: cf. 53. 5 and 109. 3.

horribilem . . . libellum: accusative of exclamation. Also 26. 5, 56. 1 and 107. 6.

sacrum: 'blessed'; cf. 71. 1.

14. *misti*: = *misisti*; cf. 15. 3 *cupisti*, 77. 3 *subrepsti*, etc.

continuo: either the adverb = 'on the spot', 'at once'; or an adjective agreeing with *die* ('a whole, long day'). The former involves assuming that *die* is separated from its adjective *optimo* by the appositional *Saturnalibus*. The second fits in better with 17 *si luxerit*, the inference being that C. has spent the whole day — and that day when he should have been enjoying himself — ploughing through the blessed book.

periret: 'suffer agonies'; cf. 5 *perderes*.

15. *Saturnalibus*: The Saturnalia properly speaking fell on 17 December, but the festivities came to be prolonged over several days. Gifts were given at the Saturnalia; indeed Martial's fourteenth book is a collection of couplets to accompany such presents including (14. 195) a copy of C.

optimo dierum: i.e. 'a day when one expects to enjoy oneself'.

16. *salse*: 'wit' — i.e. C. assumes the gift is a joke. [*false* ('traitor') OR; cf. 30. 1.]

17. *si luxerit*: = 'tomorrow', i.e. it is now too late to do anything about it today. The use of *si* (=*ubi*) in such cases (so 68. 86 *si . . . isset*; cf. Virgil, *A.* 5. 64–5, Horace, *Ep.* 1. 7. 10) amounts to a polite saving formula, like our 'God willing'.

18. *Caesios, Aquinos*: = 'poets like Caesius and Aquinus'; generalizing plurals. Caesius is unknown; Aquinus may be the poet mentioned by Cicero, *Tusc.* 5. 63.

19. *Suffenum*: Derided in Poem 22, where C. accuses him of fatuous conceit — the charge laid by Cicero against Aquinus.

There is no evidence that all three poets belonged to the old school; they may have been simply, like those in the volume received from Calvus, at any rate in C.'s judgment, rotten poets (23 *pessimi poetae*).

20. *suppliciis*: the 'tortures' inflicted by all these poisonous poets (19 *omnia . . . uenena*) are those of boredom.

21. *uos*: emphatic — the poets in Calvus' volume as opposed to those whose works C. will collect the next day.

   interea: i.e. until C. gets round to buying the others.

22. *unde malum pedem attulistis*: A play on words: (1) 'whence you set out on your ill-omened journey'; (2) 'whence you limped my way' — implying metrical incompetence. A similar ambiguity in Horace, *Ep.* 2. 2. 37 *i pede fausto*. Both senses are supported by the jerky rhythm of the line.

23. *saecli incommoda*: 'the curse of our day'; the poets in Calvus' volume, i.e. are contemporary poets.

   pessimi poetae: cf. 49. 5 *pessimus omnium poeta* (of himself).

See:

Eduard Fraenkel, 'Catulls Trostgedicht für Calvus', *WS* 69 (1956), 280–1.

Vinzenz Buchheit, 'Catulls Dichterkritik in C. 36', *Hermes* 87 (1959), 312–13.

14b

These lines, which follow in the MSS without a break, seem to be the fragment of a second preface.

Metre: hendecasyllabics.

1. *ineptiarum*: self-disparagement. For the word cf. 6. 14; for the sense cf. 1. 4 *nugas*.

3. *nobis*: the poet identified with his poems — a regular idiom; cf. 14. 21–3.

15

Poem 15 belongs to a largish group (21, 32, 33, 41, the Gellius epigrams are other examples) which raise special problems of interpretation. We can hardly doubt that the persons addressed in these poems exist: if not historically all identifiable, they seem too tightly enmeshed in the known facts of C.'s life to be fictitious. What then about the assertions, often outrageous, explicit or implied in these poems? Two views are possible. We may take the poems at their face value: Poem 15, e.g., is a warning to Aurelius intended to be taken seriously, a verse epistle that happens to have come into our hands; granted some exaggeration, C. means what he says. Or we may take these poems as light-hearted pasquinades directed primarily at a wider audience; C., i.e., does not really mean what he says. The latter seems the right view, and in some cases intrinsically the more probable. After all, it is not so much the subject matter of these poems which challenges acceptance or credulity, as the exuberant, detailed treatment of it. To keep a *puer delicatus* seems to have been hardly more scandalous than to frequent a *scortillum*. But it is hard to imagine circumstances under which Poem 32, e.g., could be sent as an actual message with the statements made intended to be taken, essentially, at their face value; it is much more likely that Ipsitilla is being got at.

One does not of course publicly accuse a friend of promiscuous paederasty in cold blood. A hard word may be flung out in good-humoured abuse. But a sustained circumstantial charge with hair-raising details and threats of revenge is another matter. In part such poems are intended to shock, to scandalize the *senes seueriores* of Poem 5, or the man in the street of Poem 15, by the open, light-hearted discussion of things customarily treated with embarrassed innuendo, and the cheerful nonchalance with which C. calls spades spades.

Poem 15 is less a warning than a warning-off; the penalty

threatened is picturesque and literary (see below) rather than a
measure seriously contemplated. In any case, as in Poem 10, the
irony is directed at C. himself, as much as at the ostensible victim.
One assumes, naturally, a grain of malice in the accusations
levelled. What matters, however, is the *urbanitas* with which the
malice is expressed. Given this, the most conventional standards
of C.'s day allowed liberties we should hesitate to take (e.g., those
taken by Cicero with Clodia's reputation in the *pro Caelio*;
Cicero himself expresses tolerance of *maledictio*, provided it is
wittily expressed, *ibid.* 6 *maledictio autem nihil habet propositi praeter
contumeliam*: *quae, si petulantius iactatur, conuicium, si facetius,
urbanitas nominatur*; cf. *Off.* 1. 29. 104). It is the *urbanitas*, in short, of
the pasquinade that makes it worth publishing. The disclaimer in
Poem 16, whether placed after Poem 15 by C. or by some subse-
quent editor, naturally applies.

C. reverts to the charge in Poem 21, and Aurelius may be the
man referred to in Poem 81. In Poem 11 he is appealed to, along
with Furius, to take 'a brief harsh message' to Lesbia; in Poem 16
the two are upbraided for taking C.'s *uersiculi molliculi ac parum
pudici* too literally. He is unidentifiable.

Structure: 1–13 — a polite request. 14–18 — threat.

Metre: hendecasyllabics.

1. *commendo*: 'place in your hands'; the double object *me ac meos
amores* suggests that Aurelius is being made the recipient of C.'s
confidence rather than that the *puer* is being entrusted to his care.

meos amores: possibly the Juventius of Poems 24, 48, 81 and
99. For the expression see on 6. 16.

2. *Aureli*: see on Poem 11.

ueniam . . . pudentem: 'a modest favour'.

3. *ut*: introduces the favour, which is preceded by a (mock-
solemn) appeal to Aurelius to put himself in C.'s shoes.

cupisti: =*cupiisti*. See on 14. 14 *misti*.

4. *integellum*: the diminutive adds a hint of pathos to the appeal.

6–8. C. means he is not worried about the ordinary run of
people the boy encounters in the street (cf. the *huc et huc euntium* on

the Via Sacra of Horace, *Ep.* 4. 9); *in re sua occupati* means the passers-by have other things to think about.

6. *a populo*: (the word *populus* connotes no social disparagement). For the construction cf. Plautus, *Curc.* 51 *tam a me pudica est quasi soror mea sit.*

7. *istos*: 'your friends'; the word perhaps implies a hint of promiscuity — see lines 10 ff.

9. *uerum*: always a strong 'but'.

a te metuo: cf. Livy 23. 36. 1 *ab Hannibale metuens.*

pene: according to Cicero, *Fam.* 9. 22. 2, the word ranked as obscene.

12. *foris*: 'abroad', i.e. not among those who trust you. (For a different explanation see Lenchantin.)

paratum: neuter; i.e. 'an opportunity'.

13. *ut puto, pudenter*: cf. line 2. But C.'s intentions are of course, *ex hypothesi*, honourable; *ut puto* expresses the reservation which is *de rigueur* when praising oneself.

15. *sceleste*: proleptic; but see on 8. 15.

16. *nostrum . . . caput lacessas*: according to Kroll and Lenchantin = *me*. But the expression, being equivalent to 'my life', is perhaps more likely to refer to the object of C.'s affection; cf. 45. 13 *mea uita*; in that case *lacessas* = 'molest'.

insidiis: 'funny business'; the word is commonly used of all kinds of trickery; for this particular kind cf. 21. 7 *insidias mihi instruentem*, and Plautus, *Curc.* 25 *num tu pudicae quoipiam insidias locas?*

17–19. It seems part of the *urbanitas* of the poem that the penalty should be out of proportion to the offence contemplated — see above on line 16. C. casts himself in the role of the outraged husband: the punishment threatened is a refinement on a penalty for adultery with a literary pedigree, ῥαφανίδωσις — cf. Aristophanes, *Clouds* 1083, and the scholiast thereon; *mugiles* (without *raphani*) are cited by Juvenal 10. 314–17 among punishments exacted by angry husbands, when *dolor exigit plus quam lex ulla dolori concessit* — more than likely (despite the scholiast) a reminiscence of C.

17. *te miserum*: exclamatory accusative.

mali . . . fati: descriptive genitive, or possibly genitive of price.

16

In Poem 16 C. abuses Aurelius and Furius, his friends of Poem 11, for jumping to conclusions. While the dedicated poet must keep clear of indecency, his verse is free from any such obligation. C. will show them whether he is a man or not.

These lines amount to a *prise de position*. The disclaimer, however, is a poetic structure in its own right, a conceit built around the key words *pedicabo* and *irrumabo*. Once again, we may suspect, an addressee is being told something he already knows — for our benefit. The explicit cross-reference in line 12 is probably to Poem 48. But doubtless C. had no less in mind poems such as 15, 21, 24, 25, 97 or 99. It is not likely that there is a reference to Poems 5 and 7 (though many take this for granted).

For Aurelius see on Poem 15; for Furius see Poems 23 and 26.

Metre: hendecasyllabics.

1. *pedicabo . . . irrumabo*: Literally, *pedicare* = *mentulam in podicem inserere* and *irrumare* = *mentulam in os inserere*. Colloquially, *te irrumabo* was perhaps the basic stereotype, with a meaning somewhere between 'I'll treat you with contempt' and 'go to hell!'. In addition to the present passage, the verb is found in 21. 13 *irrumatus*, 28. 10 *irrumasti*, 37. 8 *irrumare*, and 74. 5 *irrumet*; the derivatives used by C. are 10. 12 *irrumator* and 21. 8 *irrumatione*; in all these contexts except 10. 12 a conflict between the literal and the colloquial meanings is exploited. Usually the colloquial meaning is the primary one and the literal meaning a deliberately elicited overtone; the clearest case is 74. 5; see also on 21. 8, 28. 9–12 and 37. 9–10. Possibly *te pedicabo* was also a colloquialism; or the words may acquire colloquial status from association with *irrumabo*; in 21. 4, the only other example of *pedicare* in C., the word has its literal meaning.

We may translate line 1 with Copley, 'Nuts to you, boys, nuts and go to hell'. But the literal, obscene meaning, though submerged, remains available, to add its contribution to the *sal ac lepos* of these *uersiculi molliculi ac parum pudici*. It is drawn a little nearer the surface by line 2, in preparation for full-scale exploitation in lines 12 and 13; so that, when the concluding line of the poem repeats the opening line, the relationship of the two meanings is almost reversed.

2. *pathice . . . cinaede*: Literally, *pathicus = is qui irrumatur*; *cinaedus = is qui pedicatur* — a chiasmus. But both adjectives are terms of abuse in their own right (cf. 10. 24 *cinaediorem*); they are readily drawn, therefore, into the pattern of ambiguity and innuendo which the poem proceeds to weave round the possibilities latent in line 1; *cinaedus* also 10. 24, 25. 1, 29. 5 and 9, 33. 2, 57. 1 and 10; *pathicus* also 57. 2 and 112. 2.

5–6. C.'s disclaimer, by laying down a distinction between the life a poet lives and the things he writes about, is apt to sound odd to us on the lips of a poet often praised for his sincerity. It seems clear from lines 7–11 that C. is not talking about his serious love poetry, but about his *uersiculi*. Cf. Poem 50, where *uersiculos* (line 3) is contrasted with *poema* (line 16). He would not have regarded his liaison with Lesbia as contradicting the principle: *castum esse decet pium poetam ipsum* — as is plain from Poem 76; *castum esse decet* = 'should stay clear of dirty behaviour', not 'should stay chaste'. Many of his *uersiculi*, however, would certainly have contradicted the principle, if the confessions and accusations of gross indecency they contain had been meant seriously; in fact, they are examples of *urbanitas* — outrageous exaggerations, often perhaps with a hint of malice to them — and therefore harmless, whatever their effect on *senes seueriores* with dirty minds. Ovid (*Tr.* 2. 354) and Martial (1. 4. 8) made similar disclaimers. Pliny, *Ep.* 4. 14. 5 quotes lines 5–8 with approval; cf. *Ep.* 5. 3.

8. *molliculi ac parum pudici*: 'a shade suggestive and not quite decent'. Note the echo of line 4. C. is talking of what Cicero, *Att.* 9. 22. 1, calls indecency *in re*. Actually, while his poetry is often wildly indecent in language, gross indecency of the kind

common in Martial (as opposed to light-hearted irreverence for the facts of life) *is* rare in C. (Poem 56 is exceptional.)

9. *possunt*: 'may' — i.e. C.'s *uersiculi* very likely have this effect, but that is not their object.

10-11. Teenagers naturally react this way; but so do shaggy old men. C. expects normal readers to savour the *salem ac leporem* of his *uersiculi*. Hence his indignation when Aurelius and Furius miss the point.

10. *pueris . . . pilosis*: dative of the person interested.

11. *duros*: stiff with age, and therefore sluggish.

12. *quod*: i.e. they have taken verses such as Poem 48 as evidence of effeminacy. [The MSS are corrupt: *quod* is a correction found in R. The conjecture *qui* (adopted by Kroll and Lenchantin) is preferable if we suppose, as some do, that the reference is to Poems 5 and 7: the meaning in that case is: can anyone doubt, after reading Poems 5 and 7, that C. is a man?]

13. *male*: cf. 10. 33 *insulsa male*.

14. The opening line repeated, but with the literal meaning now drawn to the surface. For identical first and last lines cf. Poems 36, 52 and 57.

See:

A. E. Housman, 'Praefanda', *Hermes* 66 (1931), 408 (on the colloquial use of *irrumare* etc. in C.).

T. E. Kinsey, *Latomus* 25 (1966) 101–6.

H. D. Rankin, *Latomus* 29 (1970) 119–21.

G. N. Sandy, *Phoenix* 25 (1971) 51–7.

17

In a country town, probably Verona, preparations are complete for the fun and games of a rustic festival. The rickety old bridge, on which the rude dance is to take place, has been patched up for the occasion; but the town is anxious in case the bridge collapses under the strain into the marsh beneath (1–4). C. proposes a propitiatory victim — he knows a suitable candidate — describing with some gusto how he would like that part of the show to go

(5–11). After a further 11 lines (12–22) setting out C.'s grievance against his fellow-townsman, the last 4 lines revert to the theme of 1–11: C. is willing to undertake the ducking personally — he hopes that the mud bath will have a beneficial effect.

There are intriguing references to an ancient custom at Rome of throwing sexagenarians off a bridge. By C.'s time all that seems to have remained was a proverbial expression (*sexagenarios de ponte* [*deici oportet*], or something of the sort), and a picturesque ceremony in which rush effigies were substituted for living sexagenarians (see Frazer's 35-page excursus on Ovid, *Fast.* 5. 621). A remark by Cicero in his first speech in a criminal case (*S. Rosc.* 100) shows that the proverb, if not the practice, was still sufficiently current to be made the subject of laughter in court. Frazer inclines to the view that the rite was originally a sacrifice to the river-god to ensure his continued toleration of the bridge which spanned his waters; BIRT argues that the dance was a military display of force, since the bridge linked the town with enemy territory. For ancient references (the main one is Festus 450 L, s.v. *sexagenarios* — a series of guesses about the meaning of a proverbial saying) see Klotz in *RE*, s.v. *sexagenarii*; Klotz, like Frazer and BIRT, rejects the innocent explanation adopted by *L & S*. But if the ceremony provides the starting-point, C. is more interested in the victim. The butt of his righteous indignation is that stock character, more often treated by love poets with tolerant ridicule, the deceived husband. The bridge, shaky on its pins, unable to play its part in a life of fun and gaiety, is the symbol of the husband. But it is C.'s anger that he provokes, not his sympathy. Really it is insufferable that the fellow should do so little to protect his pretty, frisky wife. Perhaps a ducking, while magically restoring the bridge to health and strength, will make a new man of the husband too.

Structure: 1–4 — data. 5–11 — C. expresses his goodwill and makes a request. 12–22 — the reason for the request. 23–6 — the request repeated.

Metre: priapeans: each line consists of a glyconic

⏑◡|–◡◡–|◡–) followed by a pherecratean (⏑◡|–◡◡–|–):
cf. Poems 34 and 61. The name priapean comes from the use of
the metre in Hellenistic times for hymns to Priapus.

1. *Colonia*: [V is corrupt; *Colonia* is restored from line 7.] It is pretty
clear from 8 *municipem* that Verona is meant. (For objections
raised on various technical grounds see Fordyce 140.) But does C.
mean to be specific, or is the actual place left as an open secret?

ludere: = 'to have fun and games' — a general word of wide
connotation, limited here by *ponte longo* to the festivities (*ludi
Salisubsali?*) now imminent. But the fun and games of the towns-
people find their counterpart in the fun and games (17 *ludere*) of
the pretty young wife. See below on line 17. Cf. 50. 2 *lusimus* and
5 *ludebat*, 61. 225 *lusimus*, 68. 17 *lusi* and 156 *lusimus*.

2. *salire*: = 'jump around' — also a general word, limited by its
context and by the fact that the word evokes the name of the
ceremony. Cf. 37. 1 *salax taberna*.

paratum habes: a common idiom, more often associated with
a noun (as in 60. 4–5 *supplicis uocem contemptam haberes*) than an
infinitive.

2–4. *inepta crura ... stantis ... supinus ... recumbat*: These words
build up an image of the bridge: clumsy on its feet, liable to fall
flat on its back. The word which elicits the personification is
crura — *pes* is the word for the 'leg' of an inanimate object. The
bridge, i.e., is the one person concerned for whom the fun and
games are likely to prove too much.

3. *ponticuli*: the diminutive ('poor old bridge') suggests the
pathetic infirmity of the *pons longus* rather than its size.

axulis stantis in rediuiuis: [*ac sulcis tantis* V.] The main objec-
tion to the text printed, which has been generally adopted by
modern editors, is that *axula* (a diminutive of *axis* not found else-
where, though *assulas* is restored in an epigram of Furius Bibaculus
on Cato, *FPL* p. 80) should denote the planking of the bridge
rather than any part of the understructure ('piles', 'beams') 'on'
('in') which the bridge could be said to stand; *rediuiuis* (a builder's
term for second-hand material) sounds convincing. The

bridge, i.e., has collapsed before and been patched up again.

4. *caua . . . in palude*: the swamp and its banks form a basin.

5. *sic*: the function of *sic* is to stress that the wish expressed is subject to a condition — the familiar Roman concept of a *quid pro quo*. 'May your bridge prove up to all your requirements, (*tibi bonus ex tua pons libidine fiat*) says C., 'but on the following condition . . .'. For the pattern *sic* + subjunctive, followed by an imperative see Virgil, *Ecl.* 9. 30–2 *sic tua Cyrneas fugiant examina taxos, | sic cytiso pastae distendant ubera uaccae, | incipe, si quid habes* cf. Horace, *Carm.* 1. 3. 1–8, etc.; in 45. 13 *sic* is picked up by the *ut* following.

6. *uel Salisubsali sacra*: most likely *Salisubsali* is genitive, 'even the rites of Salisubsalus' (or -ius); something like the *tripudium* perhaps of the *Salii*; *uel*, 'even', implies that, while the bridge might easily stand up to ordinary use, the rites of Salisubsalus put it to an extreme test. If Salisubsalus is a god, we know nothing about him; possibly the name (which repeats twice over the significant syllable of 2 *salire*; cf. *Marmar* in the Arval Hymn) is made up for the occasion. Note in any case the sound and rhythm of this line.

7. *munus hoc maximi da . . . risus*: a planned ambiguity. The primary meaning is 'give me the following task, it would be a terrific joke'; C., as we see from line 23, is proposing to undertake the task of ducking his suggested victim personally. But a second meaning, 'assign me the task of organizing a terrifically funny spectacle' (for this sense of *munus* see *L & S* IIC 2a), and a third meaning, 'make me the present of a terrific laugh', readily suggest themselves, and are not immediately dispelled by 9 *ire praecipitem*. Whether we take *maximi risus* as defining genitive or descriptive genitive depends on the emphasis we give to *munus mihi da*; *maximi* is the first of seven superlatives which contribute to the note of gay exuberance in the poem.

8. *quendam municipem meum*: i.e. a fellow-Veronese; he doesn't have to be named because C. is proposing to take the matter in hand personally; *meum*, not *tuum*, for the same reason — it does

not imply, as some have supposed, that the town addressed is not C.'s own home town.

9. *per caputque pedesque*: 'head, feet and all'; emphatic rather than idiomatic (the phrase is not found elsewhere); the double *-que* is a mannerism of high-style poetry.

10. *uerum*: 'but where'; *uerum* is always emphatic. Cf. Terence, *Hau.* 598 *dicam, uerum ut aliud ex alio incidit.*

totius: the i is short, as regularly in C. with this and similar genitives; an exception is 67. 23.

ut: 'where'; so 11. 3.

lacus . . . paludis: *lacus* denotes the clear water beneath the bridge, *paludis* the stagnant water of a swamp.

11. *liuidissima*: cf. Virgil, *A.* 6. 320 *uada liuida*; *liuidus* is the colour of ripe grapes (Horace, *Carm.* 2. 5. 10) but the word tends to have less pleasant associations — in Latin spite or envy, not anger, turns you livid.

uorago: 'abyss'; the central feature, i.e., of the basin beneath the bridge is a repulsive-coloured bottomless pit of slime. The word is picked up in the last line.

12. *insulsissimus est homo*: 'the fellow is an absolute boor'; like Varus' girl-friend (10. 33) he makes a nuisance of himself through not knowing how to behave; *homo*, as often, is slightly disparaging (*L & S* II).

12–13. *nec sapit . . . dormientis in ulna*: The point is not so much that the husband is stupid, but that he is innocent (i.e. he fails to notice what is going on under his nose) — as innocent as a child; the imagery of line 13 defines the quality of the husband's insipience, described explicitly in 21 *nil uidet, nihil audit.*

13. *bimuli*: a rare diminutive of *bimus.*

tremula: In 64. 128 *tremuli salis* the adjective denotes the regular up-and-down movement of the waves of the sea; in 61. 51 *tremulus parens* and 154–5 *tremulum tempus*, 64. 307 *corpus tremulum.* and 68. 142 *tremuli parentis* it denotes the tremulousness of old age. The child is not just an imagined two-year-old, but the son of C.'s *municeps* — *ex hypothesi* old and feeble, like the bridge,

G

possibly even a *sexagenarius*, like the old men in the proverb; *nec sapit* etc. = 'he is no more aware of what is going on than his two-year-old son, asleep on his father's trembly arm'.

14–22. C.'s fellow-citizen has a wife who is (1) young and attractive; (2) frisky; (3) the sort of wife, in short, to be treasured. A line is devoted to each point. Notice that nothing is said directly of her appearance. The husband is *insulsissimus* (1) because he is too dull-witted to twig what is going on; and (2) doesn't therefore retaliate. Observe that the basis of C.'s condemnation of the husband is not moral but social.

14. *cui cum sit . . . nupta . . . puella*: = 'though he married a girl'. In Latin (and occasionally in 17th and 18th-century English, but not in modern English) a relative pronoun need not provide a subject or object for the principal clause; cf. Cicero, *Fam.* 6. 6. 5 *quibus ille* [= *Pompeius*] *si paruisset, esset hic* [=*Caesar*] *quidem clarus in toga et princeps.*

uiridissimo . . . flore: = 'in the very tenderest bloom of youth', descriptive ablative with *puella*. A fusion of two idioms: (1) *flos aetatis* = 'youthful innocence', but *flos* often = 'splendour', 'glory', that point in the development of a thing when it is at its best; (2) *uiridis*, 'green', 'fresh', 'vigorous', used of things approaching their perfection; cf. Virgil, *A.* 5. 295 (Euryalus is *forma insignis uiridique iuuenta*). The superlative emphasizes that the girl's *flos aetatis* was at the very moment of perfection when she married. Curtius may have had C. in mind when he wrote of Alexander (10. 5. 10): *tam uiridem et in flore aetatis fortunaeque . . . ereptum.* The semantic clash evident in the English equivalents of *uiridissimo flore* ('greenest flower . . .') was perhaps not perceptible in the Latin words.

15. *puella*: note the repetition and chiastic arrangement of the qualifying phrases.

tenellulo delicatior haedo: Descriptive both of the girl's youthful appearance and her youthful friskiness. Goats were proverbial for their amorousness — cf. Horace's *haedus*, *Carm.* 3. 13. 4–5: *cui frons turgida cornibus | primis et uenerem et proelia destinat.*

For *delicatus* ('naughty', almost 'wanton') see on 50. 3, though the
word pretty certainly denotes a reaction to the girl's appearance
as well as to her personality. Augustus is said to have remarked
that he had two gadabout daughters to put up with, Rome and
Julia (Macrobius 2. 5. 4): *duas se habere filias delicatas, quas necesse
haberet ferre*; cf. Cicero, *Att.* 1. 19. 8 (how he has won over the
younger generation): *odia autem illa libidinosae et delicatae iuuentutis*
etc. Cf. also Virgil, *Priap.* 2. 10 *capella delicata*. See on 2. 1 *deliciae*.
tenellulo may also have erotic overtones; the double diminutive is
found in a fragment of Laevius, *FPL* p. 56;

> Te Andromacha per ludum manu
> lasciuola ac tenellula
> capiti meo, trepidans libens,
> insolita plexit munera.

16. *adseruanda*: 'to be watched over'; the function of the simile
is to indicate the nature of the danger: it lies in the husband's
neighbours and friends, who cannot be relied on to keep their
hands off; no moral condemnation of the girl.

17. *ludere*: The verb (1) carries on the notion of playful
innocence suggested by the simile of the previous line; (2) picks
up *ludere* in line 1 — the girl, like the people of Colonia, likes to
have a good time. But this general connotation is made more
precise by the erotic overtones of *ludere*; cf. 61. 211, 68. 17, 99. 1,
Laevius (*FPL* p. 56) *lasciuiterque ludunt*, and Ovid *Am.* 1. 8. 43
ludunt formosae: *casta est quam nemo rogavit*.

nec pili facit uni: The husband, i.e., though his wife flirts
under his nose, is not in the least concerned — he is so stupid he
does not take in the significance of what he sees and hears (21
talis iste meus stupor nil uidet, nihil audit). *uni*=*unius*, an occasional
by-form. Genitive of price, as in 5. 3 *omnes unius aestimemus assis*.

18. *nec se subleuat ex sua parte*: 'nor does he bestir himself on his
own account'. It is possible that *nec se subleuat* means 'he doesn't
get up and go away' (i.e. he hangs around uncomprehending).
But *ex sua parte* suggests that the meaning is rather that he makes
no effort at retaliatory action — the obvious step to take accord-

ing to the standards of C. and his circle. For *ex sua parte* in this sense ('as far as his side of the matter is concerned') cf. 87. 4; the suggestion of some editors that the phrase = *ex sua parte lecti* is improbable.

19. *Liguri*: more naturally with *securi* than with *fossa*. The highlands of ancient Liguria are said to have been heavily forested.

suppernata: 'hamstrung'. [Estaço's brilliant correction of *superata* V.] Note that the gender of the adjective attaches it formally to *alnus*, not the husband. There is therefore a double metaphor: the husband is like a felled log; the log is like a hamstrung animal.

20. *tantundem*: 'just as much' — ironical precision.

sentiens: 'perceiving'.

quam si nulla sit usquam: 'as if it (the alder) weren't there at all'. Colloquial. Cf. Livy 32. 35. 2 *Philippus nullus usquam*. See on 8. 14 *cum rogaberis nulla*.

21. *talis iste meus stupor*: = 'that's what he is like, this slow-wit I've picked on for you'; *talis* picks up *uelut*; *iste* = 'he is the man you want'; he is called *meus* because he is C.'s candidate for the ducking; *stupor* — the idiomatic use of abstract nouns applying to persons is not uncommon; cf. 29. 13 *ista uestra*, 39. 20 *iste uester*, 71. 3 and 81. 3 *iste tuus*. [Passerat's *iste merus*, favoured by Fordyce, is unnecessary.]

21–2. *nil uidet* etc.: cf. Euripides, *Bacchae* 506 οὐκ οἶσθ' ὅτι ζῆς οὐδ' ὃ δρᾷς, οὐδ' ὅστις εἶ, and Plautus, *Aul.* 714–15 *nescio, nil uideo, caecus eo atque equidem quo eam aut ubi sim aut qui sim | nequeo cum animo certum inuestigare*.

22. *qui*: = *quis* before a word beginning with s; see Löfstedt, *Syntactica* ii (1933), 79–96; cf. 66. 42. Note the sequence of short words, and the s and t sounds in this line.

23. *mittere*: 'hurl' (*L & S* II K); note that C. now makes it plain he wants to do the job himself.

pronum: 'head foremost', i.e. predicative with *mittere*; *mittere pronum*, i.e., = 9 *ire praecipitem*. For this sense of *pronus* cf. Virgil, *A.* 1. 115–16 *excutitur pronusque magister | uoluitur in caput*.

24. *si pote stolidum*: 'in case he can'. [*si potest olidum* V; but *olidum* ('stinking'), though appropriate to the swamp, is inappropriate to the victim.] With the 'long' final syllable of *pote* before the following st, a usage avoided in Augustan verse, cf. 44. 18 *nefaria*, 63. 53 *gelida*, 64. 186 *nulla* and 67. 32 *specula*; a final e is lengthened in Tibullus 1. 5. 28. With *pote* = *potest* cf. 45. 5, 67. 11, 76. 16, and 98. 1.

ueternum: 'lethargy'; a word occasionally used of spineless indifference (cf. Caelius in a letter to Cicero, *Fam.* 8. 6. 4 *ueternus ciuitatem occupasset*), but strictly, it seems, a disease of old people: Celsus 3. 20 on lethargy (*lethargus — inexpugnabilis paene dormiendi necessitas*) recommends, among other remedies, cold showers and offensive odours, so that the therapeutic value of the shock treatment proposed here may have rested on medical authority. BIRT links Varro, *Men.* 487 *sensibus crassis homulli non uidemu'* quid fiat with apparent references to the *sexagenarii*, 493–4 *acciti sumus, ut depontaremur. . . .* '*uix effatus erat*', cum more maiorum ultro carnales arripiunt, de ponte in Tiberim deturbant. *excitare*, the word used here by C., is the term employed by Celsus: *hos aegros quidam subinde excitare nituntur. . . .*

25. *supinum*: A planned ambiguity: (1) attributive, the husband is to shed his 'spineless mind'; (2) predicative, the mind is to be left 'flat on its back' in the mud. In both cases of course the husband is to act as a substitute for the bridge (4 *ne supinus eat*).

derelinquere: 'leave behind'.

26. *soleam*: instead of shoes nailed to the hooves, Roman horses had detachable leather slippers soled with metal; for references see Fordyce.

uoragine: picks up 11 *uorago*.

mula: cf. 83. 3 *mule* (of Lesbia's husband).

See:

Th. Birt, '*Pontifex* und *sexagenarii de ponte*', RhM 75 (1926), 115–27.
J. Glenn, CPh 65 (1970) 256–7.
H. A. Kahn, CPh 64 (1969) 88–97.
R. M. Ogilvie, *The Romans and their Gods* (1969) 87–8.

M. C. J. Putnam, *Hermes* 96 (1968) 552–8.

Kenneth Quinn, 'Practical criticism: a reading of Propertius
    1. 21 and Catullus 17', *G & R* 16 (1969), 19–29.

Niall Rudd, 'Colonia and her bridge', *TAPhA* 90 (1959), 238–42.

J. W. Zarker, *CJ* 64 (1969) 172–7.

Critical Essays 38–40.

18–20

In the MSS Poem 17 is followed by Poem 21. Between them Muret
in his edition of 1554 inserted the fragmentary address to
Priapus beginning *hunc lucum tibi dedico . . .* (= Mynors's Fragment
I) and two monologues by Priapus (*hunc ego . . .*, and *ego haec . . .*).
Modern editors follow Lachmann in removing these three pieces
from the text of C.; *hunc ego . . .* and *ego haec . . .* have been since
ancient times ascribed to Virgil (=*Priap.* 3 and 2 — in antiquity
included in the collection *Catalepton*). For a history of the facts and
a discussion of these pieces see John W. Zarker, 'Catullus 18–20',
TAPhA 93 (1962), 502–22 (arguing Catullan authorship).

21

'Lay off, you Prince of Hungriness, or it will be the worse for you.'

    Ostensibly a warning-off and ostensibly obscene; in reality,
like Poem 15, a pasquinade and a further example of *uersiculi* that
are *molliculi* and *parum pudici*; the *sal ac lepos* lies in the exploitation
of a similar ambiguity.

    Metre: hendecasyllabics.

    1. *Aureli*: for Aurelius see on Poem 15.

    pater esuritionum: A mock honorific title, rather as Herodotus
was called *pater historiae* (Cicero, *Leg.* 1. 1. 5) or Isocrates *pater
eloquentiae* (id. *de Orat.* 2. 3. 10); for the plural cf. Zeno, called by
Cicero (*N.D.* 3. 9. 23) *pater iste Stoicorum*. Aurelius, however, is
called 'the father of appetites' either because he was always
hungry, or because of his recherché tastes.

    2–3. The mock eulogy becomes more and more expansive in
preparation for the *coup de massue* in line 4. For examples of the

rhetorical commonplace see Kroll. There is an echo of these lines in 24. 2–3. Cf. also 58. 2–3.

2. *harum*: i.e. the everyday ones.

4. *pedicare*: see on 16. 1.

meos amores: see on 6. 16.

5–6. Observe that the clear evidence (5 *clam*) cited by C. is not to the unprejudiced eye particularly damning. With line 6 cf. Cicero, *Amic.* 1 *a senis latere numquam discederem*.

7. *frustra*: for the idea cf. 14. 16 and Horace, *Carm.* 3. 7. 21–2 *frustra*: *nam scopulis surdior Icari | uoces audit.*

insidias . . . instruentem: cf. 15. 16.

8. *tangam te . . . irrumatione*: = *te irrumabo* (see on 16. 1). The context forces us to entertain, and then reject, the literal meaning: even as a fantasy along the lines of Poem 56 the literal meaning is hardly a practical possibility. But *tangam te . . . irrumatione* isn't *te irrumabo*; something more precise than 'I'll show my contempt for you' or 'I'll make you look a fool' is obviously needed. The *irrumatio* threatened is easily guessed: C. will forestall Aurelius by publicly ridiculing him and thus spoil his chances (7 *frustra*). The present lines are only a hint of what is to come; Aurelius still has a chance to escape with his reputation (12 *dum licet pudico*).

For similar exploitations of a planned conflict between the colloquial and the literal meanings of *irrumare* see 28. 9–12 and 37. 8–10. For C.'s fondness for learned polysyllables see on 7. 1 *basiationes.*

prior: i.e. 'I shall strike before you can'.

9–11. *urbanitas* requires that C.'s indignation should appear disinterested. Association with Aurelius will make the boy . . . as hungry and as thirsty as Aurelius himself.

9. *id si faceres*: i.e. the behaviour complained of in lines 6–7; unreal present condition.

10. *nunc ipsum id doleo*: 'as it is, this is just what distresses me'.

11. *meus iam*: [*me me* V. The line, obelized by some modern editors, is variously restored; *meus iam* is the conjecture of the Parma edition of 1473.] A short first syllable in hendecasyllabics is not uncommon.

12. *dum licet pudico*: = 'while you can do so and still be *pudicus* —
i.e. before I start on you'.

13. *irrumatus*: the poem ends with a repetition of the ambiguity
built around 8 *irrumatione*.

22

The sad case of the poetaster Suffenus (one of the poisonous poets
with whom C. vowed to plague his friend Calvus in Poem 14).
Though by no means a fool (C. allows him, as a man, qualities
the *poetae noui* prize — see line 2), the moment he turns to poetry
(15 *simul poemata attigit*) you'd think this sophisticated man about
town was a garrulous country yokel; and yet he's so pleased with
himself.

We can treat Poem 22 as a historical document: like Poems 14,
36 and 95 it touches, with the impatient intolerance of one
deeply involved, on questions of critical theory about which the
poetae noui were intransigent. First, Suffenus writes too much;
though one of the smart set, he belongs as a poet to the old school
who wrote without critical restraint (cf. C.'s indictment of
Hortensius in Poem 95 and Horace's criticism of Lucilius, *S.* 1. 4.
9–13). Second, when Suffenus turns to poetry, the critical, ironic
attitude he brings to bear on everyday life disappears. The matter
is lightly put, but seriously meant. Poem 22 amounts in fact to an
assertion of important principles which C. attempted to put into
effect in Poem 64 etc., no less than in his shorter poems.

Poem 22 has also a function as social criticism. Suffenus isn't
merely 'too lazy to write properly', as Horace was to complain
about Lucilius (*piger scribendi ferre laborem, scribendi recte*): he is
fatuously conceited about the merits of his verse. Well, we all
have our blind spots. The wry concession with which the poem
concludes helps to soften its polemical severity.

Structure: 1–3 — Hypothesis: Suffenus (a) is *uenustus et dicax et
urbanus*, (b) *longe plurimos facit uersus.* 4–8 — (b) substantiated.

And Suffenus is proud of what he writes! 9–11 — The curious
gulf between the Suffenus of (a) and the Suffenus of (b). 12–17 —
Whatever the explanation, there is no doubt about the fact
(12–15); what's more, Suffenus thinks he's good! (15–17).
18–21 — Moral: Suffenus is no worse than the rest of us — *non
uidemus manticae quod in tergo est.*

Metre: limping iambics.

1. *Suffenus*: we met Suffenus at 14. 19; he does not appear
again.

Vare: we met Varus in Poem 10 — he took C. to meet his
girl-friend.

quem probe nosti: 'you know the man well'; for this idiomatic
use of *probe* cf. Cicero, *de Orat.* 3. 194 *Antipater ille Sidonius quem
tu . . . probe meministi*; *nosti = nouisti*.

2. *homo*: 'chap'; cf. 17. 12.

uenustus . . . dicax . . . urbanus: three terms of approval in the
jargon of the *poetae noui*. Suffenus has polish, he has a sharp and
witty tongue and he belongs to the smart set — all qualities we
find in the verse of C., but conspicuously lacking, it seems, in that
of Suffenus; *dicax* from *dicare*, not *dicere*.

3. *idemque*: = 'yet he'; excessive output, i.e., is in itself a
contradiction of the qualities attributed to Suffenus in the
previous line.

longe plurimos: probably idiomatic = 'a terrific lot'; Hor-
tensius (95. 3) might have rivalled him.

4–8. Suffenus already has at least 10,000 lines to his credit
(= e.g. one complete epic poem). And these are works published
in *éditions de luxe*, not just stuff jotted down on second-hand
papyri.

4. Five elisions in this line.

5. *perscripta*: 'written out'.

sic ut fit: any practising poet, i.e., is bound to have yards of
stuff in rough draft.

5–6. *in palimpsesto relata*: 'written down on second-hand
papyrus'. Cicero, *Fam.* 7. 18. 2, praises the 'sense of economy'

(*parsimoniam*) shown by his friend Trebatius in writing to him *in palimpsesto*. Normally in this technical sense *referre in* takes the accusative; but *in palimpsesto* was probably a fixed expression — part of the practising writer's jargon. [Mynors in the 1960 reprint of his text prints *in palimpseston*.]

6–8. C. did not object to handsome books; cf. what he says about his own *libellus* in 1. 1–2. His complaint is that, in Suffenus' case, the contents had not had the care expended on them that had been given to the rolls which contained them.

6. *cartae regiae*: perhaps a technical term for paper of the best quality; for *cartae* cf. 1. 6.

libri: 'rolls'.

7. *umbilici*: the projecting knobs used in handling the rolls.

lora rubra, membranae: The *membranae* were parchment jackets enclosing the papyrus rolls; the *lora rubra*, another special touch (perhaps because the *lora* were dyed red), were the leather thongs for tying the jacket, perhaps incorporating a title tag. (Some take *membranae* as dative with *lora*.)

8. *derecta plumbo*: 'ruled with lead' (i.e. in lines to guide the hand of the scribe); neuter plural with *omnia*.

pumice . . . aequata: 'smoothed with pumice'; see on 1. 2.

9. *cum legas tu*: the subjunctive is often used when a second person singular has no definite antecedent; equivalent to our 'one'.

bellus: 'smart'; often coupled idiomatically with *homo* (24. 7, 78. 3 and 81. 2). The emphasis is on behaviour rather than appearance.

10. *unus*: idiomatic = 'any ordinary'; cf. Cicero, *Att.* 9. 10. 2 *me . . . torquet, quod non Pompeium tamquam unus manipularis secutus sim.*

caprimulgus: 'goat-milker'. The unusual, picturesque, specific term is preferred to some such general word as *rusticus*. (No suggestion of course that Suffenus writes pastoral poetry.)

11. *rursus*: 'on the other hand', 'alternatively' (*L & S* II A — a common meaning).

tantum abhorret ac mutat: 'he is so out of place, so changed';

for this sense of *abhorrere* (*L & S* II B 3 β) cf. Cicero, *de Orat.* 2. 20.
85 *plane abhorrebit et erit absurdus*; *mutat* is intransitive.

12. *hoc quid putemus esse?*: 'what are we to make of this?'
Deliberative subjunctive.

   scurra: 'a wit'; the sort of man who always had a quip
ready. We meet the type a number of times in Horace.

13. *scitius*: 'shrewder', 'sharper'. [*tristius* V, *scitius* Müller.]

   uidebatur: C. insists on the impression produced (cf. 11
uidetur) — sharp-witted and deft in the use of words as an
acquaintance; slow-witted and clumsy in the use of words as a
poet.

14. *infaceto . . . infacetior*: With the reproach cf. 36. 19 *pleni
ruris et infacetiarum*; with the syntactical pattern cf. 27. 4, 99. 2 and 14.

15. *simul*: = *simul atque*, as often in C.

   idem: this word keeps recurring; first in line 3, again in
line 14; as though C. could scarcely believe it was the same
person.

16. *aeque . . . ac . . . cum*: 'equally . . . as when'.

17. *gaudet in se*: 'is pleased with himself'.

18. *nimirum*: 'clearly'; cf. 62. 7.

   idem . . . fallimur: 'we make the same mistake'; *idem* here
neuter.

19–20. *quem non . . . uidere Suffenum possis*: = *qui non Suffenus
uideri possit*: 'who mightn't seem a Suffenus'.

20. *attributus*: 'allotted'.

   error: 'aberration'.

21. *uidemus manticae quod in tergo est*: 'we don't see the bit of the
knapsack that we have on our back'. A fable of Aesop; in
Phaedrus' version (4. 10) it runs:

> peras inposuit Iuppiter nobis duas:
> propriis repletam uitiis post tergum dedit;
> alienis ante pectus suspendit grauem.
> hac re uidere nostra mala non possumus;
> alii simul delinquunt censores sumus.

Horace refers to the fable, *S.* 2. 3. 299.

See:

Vinzenz Buchheit, 'Catulls Dichterkritik in C. 36', *Hermes* 87
   (1959), 309–27.

23

Poem 23 perhaps started as a verse epistle playfully evading
Furius' requests for a loan, on the grounds that his friend 'was
well enough off' as things were (27 *sat es beatus* — the concluding
words of the poem).

But before taking them as even *prima facie* evidence for the
poverty of Furius (who may be the poet Furius Bibaculus) or for
C.'s callousness, it is worth noting how carefully the lines, as they
now stand, are constructed to give readers of the poem with no
independent access to the facts just that grasp of what is going on
which suits C.'s purpose.

A poem may, in short, be revised for publication, and thus
acquire a second lease of life. It becomes a puzzle on which the
reader is invited to sharpen his wits — he is given just enough to
go on, and no more. Clearly Furius is being got at, his domestic
circumstances misrepresented or exaggerated; we seem to catch
here and there the echo of Furius' own words, quoted and turned
against him. But there is no sure way of deciding between fact and
flight of fancy. And to be too gullible means to be lacking in
urbanitas.

Structure: The following is a plausible reading of the lines:
1–4 — hypothesis. 5–6 — affirmation. 7–11 — demonstration.
12–14 — objection raised by Furius. 15–23 — objection overruled.
24–26 — conclusion: case for loan not made out.

Furius' poverty is reverted to in Poem 24, where he is not
named but identified by the key phrase *cui neque seruus est neque
arca*: his poverty makes him no fit associate for men like Juventius.
In Poem 26 we learn that his little villa is heavily mortgaged.
This is the Furius who, along with Aurelius, is entrusted by C.

with a message to his mistress in Poem 11 — and made the butt
of C.'s pique in Poem 16 for taking some naughty poems *au pied
de la lettre*. Identification with Marcus Furius Bibaculus (who
seems to have been a writer of *uersiculi* as well as the author of an
epic poem) is tempting and accepted by Neudling 71–3. As for his
poverty cf. C.'s assertion of poverty 13. 7–8.

Metre: hendecasyllabics.

1. *cui neque seruus est neque arca*: The phrase has the swing of a
quotation about it. Perhaps it is a proverb; perhaps, as Fordyce
suggests, a phrase lifted from Furius himself. If the latter, Furius'wry
rhetoric is undercut by the more down-to-earth imagery of line 2.
The phrase is repeated at 24. 5 (and, with variations, at 24. 8 and
10); cf. the repetition of 41. 4 *decoctoris amica Formiani* at 43. 5.

2. *ignis*: falls a little flat as the third member of this picturesque
trio; Kroll compares a fragment of Alexis (174K).

3. *uerum est et pater et nouerca*: 'but you *do* have a father *and* a
stepmother'. The double emphasis of *uerum* and *et . . . et* should
not escape attention. Most likely the explanation lies in the
relative clause.

3–4. *quorum . . . possunt*: as in line 1, one suspects that Furius'
own words are being turned against him. Did he (1) claim in
asking for a loan that he and his parents were so hard up they
were reduced to eating stones? Or did he (2) claim his parents
were so greedy they would eat anything, even stones? It is
sufficient if the reader feels that Furius' father and stepmother are
perhaps pretty tough characters. In either case C.'s congratula-
tions to Furius on his parents' dental equipment and digestive
powers (8 *pulcre concoquitis*) are ironic.

4. *comesse*: 'devour'; the preverb stresses completion of the
verbal action. Cf. 29. 14 *comessei*.

5. *est pulcre tibi*: 'you get on well with'. A colloquialism, and
probably ambiguous: (1) 'you are on good terms with your
parents'; (2) 'you and your parents are managing pretty well'.

5–6. *parente . . . coniuge . . . parentis*: cf. the jingle 4. 27 *gemelle
Castor et gemelle Castoris*.

6. *lignea*: the word is used by Lucretius (4. 1161) along with *neruosa* ('stringy') in his list of unattractive wenches to whose defects love is blind; to her lover, the girl who is *neruosa et lignea* seems 'a gazelle' (*dorcas*). Presumably then Furius' stepmother, if thin, was sprightly enough.

7–11. Furius and his parents are doing pretty well, then. And no wonder (7 *nec mirum*): they enjoy good health, they have wonderful digestions, and nothing in the world to worry about; lines 9–11 list the stock (and no doubt fully justified) worries of the well-to-do: loss of their property by fire or through structural failure; the activities of criminals; poisonings and other dangers. Cf. an ironical poem by Propertius in which he asserts the lover's exemption from all mundane worries including three of those listed here (2. 27. 9–12):

> praeterea domibus flammam domibusque ruinas,
> neu subeant labris pocula nigra tuis.
> solus amans nouit, quando periturus et a qua
> morte . . .

9. *graues ruinas*: 'ruinous collapses' — of buildings; *graues*, i.e., is ambiguous: (1) 'weighty', (2) 'disastrous'.

11. *casus alios periculorum*: for the idiom cf. Cicero, *Fam.* 6. 4. 3 *ad omnes casus subitorum periculorum magis obiecti sumus*.

12–14. Better taken as a question, picking up Furius' words and perhaps ironically rephrasing them in preparation for the fantasy of 15–23.

12. *atqui*: 'what is more'.

sicciora cornu: the ablative of comparison is used in Latin in such idiomatic expressions where we should make an equation: 'dry as a bone'; see Löfstedt, *Syntactica* I (2nd edn 1942) 311–20.

13. *aut siquid* etc.: for the syntactical pattern cf. 13. 10, 22. 13, 42. 14 and 82. 2 (in all cases except here a complete line).

aridum: = *siccum*; but *aridus* also connotes meanness as in Plautus, *Aul.* 297 *pumex non aeque est ardus atque hic est senex*.

14. *sole et frigore et esuritione*: all instrumental ablative with *sicciora*.

15–22. Observe that, whereas in 7–14 the second person plural is used throughout (7 *ualetis*, 8 *timetis*, 13 *habetis*), from now on C. concentrates on Furius (as in 1–6).

15. *quare non tibi sit bene ac beate?*: ='why then, you should be doing pretty well, shouldn't you?' For the idiom cf. 14. 10. But *beate* is slipped in in preparation for 24 *beata* and the concluding 27 *beatus* — a planned ambiguity: (1) 'well off' = enjoying life; (2) 'well off' = not wanting for money.

16–17. *sudor abest* etc.: On good ancient authority, apparently, reckoned signs of health; cf. Varro in Nonius Marcellus 634L *Persae propter exercitationes puerilis modicas eam sunt consecuti corporis siccitatem ut neque spuerent neque emungerentur.*

19. *salillo*: for this feature of a simple table see Horace, *Carm.* 2. 16. 13–14 *cui paternum / splendet in mensa tenui salinum*. One wonders if the well-polished salt-cellar was not a traditional symbol of the simple way of life.

23. *posses*: The strict classical rules for the use of the tenses of the subjunctive in conditional sentences are not observed by earlier writers; cf. 6. 2–3 *sint . . . posses*.

24–7. The point of the preceding whimsy is now revealed: Furius has failed to make a case for the loan for which he is continually begging (26 *soles* surely constitutes a valid clue).

24–5. *haec tu commoda tam beata . . . noli spernere*: ='you're well off indeed with such advantages, don't despise them'.

25. *nec*: idiomatic (strict logic would require *aut*).

parui: genitive of price.

26–7. *sestertia . . . centum*: = 100,000 *sestertii*; not a fortune, but a substantial sum; cf. Ameana and her *tota milia decem* in 41. 2.

26. *precari*: dependent equally on *soles* and *desine*; *precari* is a fairly strong word.

27. *sat es beatus*: [So Calfurnio in his edition of 1481; FRAENKEL defends the elliptical *nam satis beatus*.]

See:

Eduard Fraenkel, '*nam satis beatus*', *MH* 23 (1966), 114–17.

24

It is a reasonable supposition that the accusation in line 6 rests on no more damning evidence than that adduced in Poem 21 against Aurelius; 6 *sic*, like 21. 5 *nec clam*, by appealing to public knowledge, limits the matter to what can be publicly observed. After the rhetoric of the opening four lines, the refrain of lines 5, 8 and 10 shifts the centre of the poem away from the topic ostensibly at issue (we feel, in short, no real atmosphere of tragedy or disaster) to the subject of the refrain and to C. himself.

More than anything, the lines are an expression (and therefore a confession) of a nagging, smouldering jealousy which either cannot or will not face facts and keeps reverting instead to the one thing easily seized on. Cf. the epigram, attributed to Demodocus on Cinyras the Cilician (*AP* 11. 236), and Martial's well-known lines (1. 32) *non amo te, Sabidi, nec possum dicere quare: | hoc tantum possum dicere, non amo te.*

We meet Juventius again in Poems 48, 81 and 99; it may be presumed that he is the subject also of Poems 15 and 21. The *Iuuentii* were a distinguished Roman family (see Neudling 94-6); which, if any, of them is addressed here we cannot tell. For Furius, identified by the repetition of the phrase *cui neque seruus est neque arca* from 23. 1 (cf. the identification of Ameana by the repetition of 41. 4 in 43. 5), see on Poem 23.

Metre: hendecasyllabics.

1. *flosculus*: the diminutive suggests the protective attitude of one who has Juventius' best interest at heart.

2-3. *non horum modo . . . in annis*: with the formula cf. 21. 2-3, where it contributes to a similar rhetorical build-up.

4. *mallem diuitias Midae dedisses*: i.e. rather money than love; Furius could certainly have done with money; whether Juventius had a lot to give is not part of the data of the poem. Midas and his wealth were proverbial in Greek, but they are not found in Latin literature before this passage.

6. *quam . . . sineres*: *malo quam*, like *potius quam*, normally

repeats with *quam* the construction (subjunctive, indicative, infinitive etc.) of the previous phrase or clause.

    sic: emphatic; with *sineres*, rather than *amari*.

    illo: emphatic, 'that man'.

7. *qui*: instrumental, 'how?'.

    homo bellus: for the phrase see on 22. 9; the final o of *homo* is short. See on 6. 16.

    est: emphatic, 'he *is*'.

9. *hoc*: 'this fact'.

    quam lubet: 'to what extent you like' = 'as much as you like'; more often with adjectives and adverbs.

    abice: 'toss aside' and therefore 'dismiss'. For the verb as a technical term of rhetoric cf. Cicero, *de Orat.* 3. 104 *summa autem laus eloquentiae est amplificare rem ornando, quod ualet non solum ad augendum aliquid et tollendum altius dicendo, sed etiam ad extenuandum atque abiciendum*; ibid. 102, of an actor who 'throws away' a line.

    eleuaque: 'make light of' (*L & S* II B).

25

Poem 25, like Poem 12, deals with napkin-pinching; this time a cloak and some other articles are involved as well; Thallus, in short, is a greater social menace than Asinius. He is also a more interesting phenomenon: sloth personified, until the opportunity presents itself and he springs into action. The note struck is more emotional than in Poem 12. Instead of pained indignation, C. begins with pasquinade and ends with threats of physical violence: 'Thallus, you thieving queer, you'll smart for this.' On this somewhat unpromising theme C. has constructed a poem remarkable not only for its exuberance of language, but also for its imaginative vitality.

Thallus, whom we meet only here, is unidentifiable.

Metre: iambic tetrameters catalectic — a metre C. uses only here. The pure iambic foot predominates; see on lines 5 and 11.

1–5. A thumbnail sketch of Thallus. Two comparative adjectives (1 *mollior* and 4 *rapacior*) form the structural basis; upon the first is built a string of images, each syntactically an ablative of comparison; the second, after a single comparative phrase, introduces a *cum*-clause. But the assertion of heroic grandeur implicit in this elaborate syntax is undercut by the opening insult, the string of diminutives in lines 1–2, the imagery of line 3, and the rollicking rhythm.

1. *cinaede*: for the literal meaning of *cinaedus* and its use as a term of abuse see on 16. 2; linked as here with a proper name in 29. 5 and 9 *cinaede Romule*. Often used of professional dancers, actors in pantomines etc. See COLIN 109.

mollior: the stock epithet for a *cinaedus*; cf. Plautus, *Aul.* 422 *sum mollior magi' quam ullu' cinaedus*. The fun lies in following *mollior* up with a series of images illustrating, or purporting to illustrate, literal softness.

cuniculi: looks like a diminutive, but this is the regular form.

2. *medullula*: = 'softest marrow'; a diminutive found only here The idea is imitated in *Priap.* 64. 1 *quidam mollior anseris medulla*. (No authority for supposing, with Merrill, that *medullula* denotes the delicate inner feathers of the goose.)

imula oricilla: i.e the lobe of the ear; apparently proverbial; cf. Cicero, *Q. fr.* 2. 15a. 4 (Cicero promises to be conciliatory) *tu, quemadmodum me censes oportere esse et in republica et in nostris inimicitiis, ita et esse et fore auricula infima scito molliorem*; cf. also Ammianus 19. 12. 5 *ima quod aiunt auricula mollior*.

3. *situque araneoso*: = 'than cobwebs' — undoubtedly soft but the least attractive of an increasingly uncomplimentary series, in which the last item is linked by -*que* instead of *uel* to mark a more rapid movement at the climax of the series (*uel* prescribes a more measured tempo). The figurative meaning of *situs* (*L & S* II) is the common one in verse.

4. *idemque*: for this use of *idem* see on 22. 15.

turbida . . . procella: 'a swirling hurricane'.

rapacior: the literal meaning 'snatching up', is drawn out by *turbida . . . procella*; but the figurative meaning, 'greedy', is also appropriate.

5. [*mulier aries* O; variations on this in GR; Haupt's *mulierarios* ('womanizers' — a class with whom Thallus may be presumed to have little sympathy) is tempting, but metrically implausible (we have to assume a resolved second foot consisting of three short syllables); the word is used by Cicero of Clodia's henchmen (*Cael.* 66 *mulieraria manus*) and quoted by Isidorus (10. 107) as an old-fashioned synonym of *femellarius* (defined as '*feminis deditus*'); *diua* in this case, according to some = the moon, according to others = Lesbia. Kroll, Schuster and Mynors obelize the line.] PUTNAM, reviving a suggestion by Munro, suggests *diua Murcia*, 'goddess of sloth and inactivity, who shows to Thallus that those around him are off their guard, unprepared for his onslaught.' In place of Putnam's *aridos*, MacKAY's *arbitros* has been adopted here. The result is at any rate a line which makes tolerably good sense: 'When the goddess of sloth shows him that the onlookers are nodding.'

oscitantes: i.e. off their guard; cf. 12. 3 *neglegentiorum*.

6. *pallium*: see on 32. 11.

quod inuolasti: 'that you fell upon'.

7. *sudariumque Saetabum*: cf. 12. 14 *sudaria Saetaba*.

cataraphosque Thynos: Both words apparently are adjectives, the object itself being sufficiently designated by its place of origin and the technical term *cataraphos*. The meaning of the latter is uncertain. We may guess with Lenchantin that the articles in question were handkerchiefs; it seems likely that at any rate something made from cloth is meant, though Merrill argues for a set of writing tablets framed with boxwood.

8. *inepte*: vocative, not adverbial; cf. 12. 4. *quae palam soles habere tamquam auita*: 'which you keep on display as though they were family heirlooms'.

9. *reglutina*: as if whatever came in contact with Thallus fingernails stuck to them.

10. *laneum latusculum*: = 'your delicate, fleecy flank'.

manusque mollicellas: selected as the chief offenders.

11. *inusta turpiter*: i.e. traces to be ashamed of, because slaves were treated in this way.

conscribillent: 'cover with their scribble'. The metre requires the second syllable of *conscribillent* to be short: more likely a liberty (such as is occasionally found) than an indication that the text is unsound.

12. *insolenter aestues*: 'lest you burn in a way you're not accustomed to'; Thallus, it is implied, was more accustomed to the burning of desire. But *aestus* is the word one uses of an angry sea and at a pinch one might say of a ship tossed about in a storm that it *aestuat* (cf. Lucretius 5. 1097 — of a tree tossed around by a gale); so that *aestues* also = 'writhe in agony', as much as 'feel searing pain'.

minuta magno: note the antithesis.

13. *deprensa*: 'caught'.

uesaniente uento: 'a mad wind raging'. The final image invites a trace of sympathy for Thallus: he is a pathetic figure, rather than a rogue, a little to be pitied when the storm of C.'s angry revenge descends upon him.

See (mainly on the textual crux in line 5, but with interesting general comment):

J. Colin, 'L'heure des cadeaux pour Thallus le cinède', *REL* 32 (1954), 106–10.

J. Granarolo, 'L'heure de la vérité pour Thallus le cinède', *REA* 60 (1958), 290–306.

L. A. MacKay, 'Catullus 25. 5', *CPh* 61 (1966), 110–11.

M. C. J. Putnam, 'Catullus 25. 5', *CPh* 59 (1964), 268–70.

26

A pun: taken with 1 *uillula*, 2 *opposita* is appropriate to two quite different contexts, of which lines 1–3 construct one and line 4 constructs the other.

For Furius see on Poem 23.

Metre: hendecasyllabics.

1. *uillula*: 'little place in the country'.

uestra: [The reading of O; *nostra* GR, which Kroll is exceptional among modern editors in adopting, taking the lines as another confession by C. of his poverty (cf. Poems 10 and 13). But the poem makes less sense as a confession than if we suppose Furius is being teased about the mortgage on his *uillula* for our benefit.] The second person plural includes Furius' father and stepmother, whom we met in Poem 23, where C. waxes eloquent on their poverty. It would be nice if we could be surer of the identification of Furius with the poetaster M. Furius Bibaculus to whom are ascribed two epigrams poking fun at the critic Valerius Cato; according to Suetonius, *Gram.* 11 (who quotes the epigrams), Cato, when very old and poor, was forced to live in a wretched hovel after surrendering his Tusculan villa to a creditor. The second of the epigrams is built round a pun, not unlike that in Poem 26:

> Catonis modo, Galle, Tusculanum
> tota creditor urbe uenditabat.
> mirati sumus, unicum magistrum,
> summum grammaticum, optimum poetam,
> omnes soluere posse quaestiones,
> unum deficere expedire nomen.
> en cor Zenodoti, en iecur Cratetis!

where *soluere* = 'solve' and 'pay', and *expedire nomen* = 'deal with a name, or noun' and something like 'pay off a note of hand'.

Cf. the epigram ascribed to Virgil, *Cat.* 8 (*Villula quae Sironis eras, et pauper agelle . . .*).

Austri: the first of the four cardinal points of the compass listed by C.

2. *opposita*: In its first context = 'exposed to', 'facing'. It is clear from 3 *saeui* and the general drift of lines 4 and 5 that to be sheltered from each of these winds was considered desirable. The

situation of Furius' villa was ideal therefore — apart from the fact that it was not really his any longer.

3. *Apheliotae*: = 'Easterly', normally called *Eurus* by the Greeks. An appropriately learned touch to round off the first arm of the verbal ambiguity. With the learned name cf. Cicero's pseudo-neoteric hexameter *Att.* 7. 2. 1 *flauit ab Epiro lenissimus Onchesmites.*

4. *ad milia quindecim et ducentos*: With the second arm of the ambiguity *opposita* = 'mortgaged'. For this (somewhat rare) technical sense see Terence, *Ph.* 661–2 *ager oppositus pignori ob | decem minas est*; cf. Plautus, *Curc.* 356 *ille suom anulum opposuit.* The sum mortgaged, so precisely stated by C., is not large — a trifle in fact compared with the loan of a hundred thousand which Furius is accused of soliciting at 23. 25–7. Cicero, *Cael.* 17, claims that his client Caelius rented a flat for 10,000 *sestertii*. No doubt the figure 15,200 continues the pretence of scholarly precision suggested by *Apheliotae.*

5. *o uentum horribilem atque pestilentem!*: 'oh what a terrible, un-healthy wind!' For the exclamation (which here dismisses the atmosphere of measured statement) cf. 43. 8.

pestilentem: a second pun: (1) 'unhealthy' (cf. Horace, *Carm.* 3. 23. 5 *nec pestilentem sentiat Africum*); (2) 'unpleasant', 'tiresome', 'accursed'; cf. the pun in Cicero, *Fam.* 7. 24. 1 *id ego in lucris pono, non ferre hominem pestilentiorem patria sua*: (= 'I think I am well rid of the damned fellow — a bigger menace to our health than the place [Sardinia] he comes from').

27

A short drinking song: 'Give me stronger drink, boy, water spoils the wine.' For Greek precedents and some good comment see Wheeler 234–5.

Metre: hendecasyllabics.

1. *uetuli*: our 'good old', if over-hearty, catches the note of affection.

Falerni: one of the better known Italian wines. The ancient authorities on wine are Columella, *de Re Rustica* 12, and Pliny, *Natural History* 14 and 23. Italian wines were said to mature more slowly than Greek wines. Charles Seltman, *Wine in the Ancient World* (1957) 153: 'Falernian became fit for drinking in ten years, and might be used when twenty years old.'

2. *inger*: a short form of the imperative (cf. *fer, dic, duc, fac*) found only here.

calices: the receptacles stand for the contents, as often.

amariores: perhaps = 'drier' in our sense, but 'with less water added' fits the context better.

3. *lex Postumiae . . . magistrae*: An ancient drinking party was presided over by a *magister bibendi*, who determined what should be drunk and how. The name *Postumia* suggests a respectable matron, perhaps an unconventional one, like Clodia or Sallust's Sempronia (*Cat.* 25). But, if the presence of a woman of good society at a dinner party is not implausible, we may doubt if she could be appointed mistress of ceremonies; there is perhaps a leg-pull involved here which escapes us. Of course lines 3–4 do not actually require the hypothesis that *Postumia* is present on the dramatic occasion of the poem; she may have been a well-known hard drinker whose personal practice is put forward by C., with appropriate seriousness, as a precedent to be followed.

4. *ebrioso acino ebriosioris*: 'drunker than the drunken grape' (Copley). With the syntactical pattern cf. 22. 14 *infaceto infacetior*, 99. 2 *dulci dulcius*. [*ebriose acino* V points plainly to *ebrioso acino*. There is however a curious tradition preserved by Aulus Gellius (6. 20. 6 — a corrupt passage) that C. actually wrote *ebria acina* — a hiatus of course, but one Gellius found pleasing. Fordyce comments that Gellius' 'preference for *ebria* is clearly misguided. . . . It is most likely that *acina* is a popular by-form and that in both words Gellius, with poor critical judgement, a perverse taste for abnormality, and a fanciful thesis to maintain, preferred the corrupt to the genuine.']

5–7. The ancients, as is well known, mixed their wine with

water — still a practice in those regions (e.g. Apulia) which produce table wines with a high alcoholic content.

5. *lymphae*: the plural suggests water of all kinds.

6. *uini pernicies*: Martial reverts to the charge (1. 18. 5) *scelus est iugulare Falernum*.

seueros: also used of teetotallers by Horace (*Ep.* 1. 19. 8–9) *forum putealque Libonis | mandabo siccis, adimam cantare seueris*.

7. *hic merus est Thyonianus*: 'here is the Thyonian (i.e. Bacchus) undiluted'. Semele, Bacchus' mother, was sometimes called Thyone; Horace, *Carm.* 1. 17. 23, and Ovid, *Met.* 4. 13, call Bacchus *Thyoneus*. (Some take *Thyonianus* adjectivally: 'here is Bacchus' product undiluted', assuming, to account for the masculine form of the adjective, that the Greek word for wine. οἶνος, is understood.)

See:

M. C. J. Putnam, *Latomus* 28 (1969) 850–7.

28

A letter to friends abroad: are they profiting by their experience — if nothing else?

The friends are Veranius and Fabullus. We know from Poems 9 and 12 that at one stage they were in Spain. We now learn that they are abroad with Piso; Poem 47 tells us they are no longer in Piso's good books. The only provincial governor of that name at this time known to us is L. Calpurnius Piso Caesonius, consul in 58 B.C. (the year of Cicero's exile), the father-in-law of Caesar, and governor of Macedonia in 57–55 B.C. This is the right time (C. will be still in Bithynia at the time of writing Poem 28, or just back; he served there under Memmius in 57–56 B.C.), but the wrong country. Did Veranius and Fabullus make two voyages abroad or only one? 'If one a Piso will have to be conjured up, a proconsul governing Hispanior Citerior in 57/6. . . . Which can hardly be done. Therefore two voyages, the earlier to Spain' (SYME 132). The trip referred to in Poem 28 is then the later voyage to Macedonia.

For Piso's activities as governor of Macedonia see Cicero's highly partisan account, *Pis.* 37–50. Fabullus also in Poem 13. Cf. Horace, *Epistles* 1. 3 and 1. 8.

Metre: hendecasyllabics.

1–5. 'How are you getting on with Piso — had enough yet?' The fun in these lines seems to lie in talking to Veranius and Fabullus about their job on Piso's staff (technically called *cohors* — cf. 10. 13) in terms appropriate to regular infantry service (*cohors* properly = the tenth part of a legion); under Piso the privations to be endured in both cases were much the same.

1. *comites*: the technical term for the members of a governor's *cohors*; cf. 46. 9; the word can also = simply companions on a journey, as in 11. 1.

inanis: the primary meaning is 'empty-handed' — a not uncommon meaning (see *L & S*), e.g. Cicero, *Fam.* 15. 17. 1 *etsi quid ego me tibi purgo, cum tui [tabellarii] ad me inanes ueniant, ad te cum epistulis reuertantur?* The context, however, suggests also the connotation 'useless', 'silly'.

2. *sarcinulis*: *sarcinae* = the baggage of soldiers on the march; soldiers in light marching order were called *expediti*. C. playfully suggests that his friends have 'shouldered their little packs, stripped of unessentials'; the overt statement, helped by the brisk rhythm, implies soldiers stepping it out, keen for action. Transferred to the *cohors* to which Veranius and Fabullus actually belonged the implication is rather that they were having a pretty thin time of it.

3. *mi*: vocative of *meus*.

4. *quid rerum geritis?*: the question fixes the dramatic moment of the verse epistle. C.'s friends are still away; he wants news of them.

5. *frigoraque et famem tulistis*: the ordinary soldier has to be prepared to be cold and hungry; the members of a governor's staff expect to live well; -*que et* = *et* ... *et*; see on 102. 3 *meque*.

6–8. As Merrill says, one would expect the question *ecquidnam* etc. to end with *acceptum*, not *expensum*. But the question 'is there any clear profit in your expenses?', though at first it sounds like a jingle, is perfectly meaningful; *lucelli* with *ecquidnam*, not *tabulis*. Veranius and Fabullus, like C. himself, are unlikely to gain anything from their tour of duty in terms of hard cash (cf. 10. 8–13). But they can, like him, profit from the experience, i.e. learn what governors are like.

7. *ut mihi*: = *ut patet mihi in tabulis*.

8. *refero datum lucello*: 'I count expenditure as a little gain', i.e. 'I am out of pocket, but I have learnt my lesson'. (Some editors take *datum* as predicative, so that *refero datum lucello* = 'I record, entered up [*datum*] on the profit side, . . .'; in that case lines 9–10 represent the entry which C. makes. But it seems more natural to take *datum* as a synonym of *expensum* and the direct object of *refero*.)

9–13. In 10. 12 C. called Memmius an *irrumator* — a man who treats his staff with open contempt. (For the colloquial meaning of *irrumare* and its derivatives see on 16. 1.) He now reverts to the charge in lines which elicit the imagery latent in that term — a spectacular example of the readiness with which the literal, obscene meaning of a colloquialism will reassert itself under the stimulus of a little *urbanitas*. (So HOUSMAN.) C. means of course merely that Piso has been as mean with Veranius and Fabullus as Memmius has been with C.

10. *trabe*: = *mentula*.

lentus: i.e. he took his time about it, remained unruffled.

12. *uerpa*: = *mentula*. Cf. 47. 4 *uerpus*.

13. *pete nobiles amicos*: The second person singular shows that this is not just advice offered by C. to Veranius and Fabullus. Very likely the phrase represents the sort of thing traditionally said to young men by their elders, here quoted with bitter irony.

14–15. For the pattern cf. 14. 21–3 and 3. 13. *uobis* = *Pisoni et Memmio* — and all such *opprobria Romuli Remique* (= 'disgraces to us Romans'). For Romulus and Remus see 34. 22, 49. 1 and 58. 5.

See:

A. E. Housman, '*Praefanda*', *Hermes* 66 (1931), 408.

R. G. M. Nisbet, *Cicero, In Pisonem* (1961), Appendix II, 180–2.

Ronald Syme, 'Piso and Veranius in Catullus', *C & M* 17 (1956),
129–34.

29

Mamurra (unlike C. and his friends — see Poems 10 and 28) has
done well out of service abroad; the luxury in which he lives is a
public scandal. An open letter to Pompey and Caesar, expressing
C.'s indignation at the conduct of their protégé.

This is our first meeting with Mamurra, but C. had perhaps
opened the attack some four or five years before in Poem 57 —
and then made his peace with Caesar; he attacks Caesar again in
Poem 54 (54. 7 *unice imperator* picks up 29. 11 *imperator unice*) and
also in Poem 93. For Suetonius' account of Caesar's reactions
see on Poem 57. Mamurra crops up again under a transparent
alias in two poems (41 and 43) ridiculing his mistress Ameana, as
well as in a group of epigrams (Poems 94, 105, 114 and 115)
where he is addressed as Mentula — a pseudonym to which
29. 13 perhaps alludes. A Roman knight from Formiae, he served
under Pompey in the Mithridatic campaign and under Julius
Caesar in Spain, and was subsequently Caesar's *praefectus fabrum*
in Gaul from 58 to 55 B.C., returning to Rome, apparently, after
Caesar's first expedition to Britain. Cicero (*Att.* 7. 7. 6, writing in
December 50 B.C.) couples his name with that of Labienus as men
whose wealth rankled. Mamurra's luxurious house on the
Caelian hill became famous (Pliny, *Nat.* 36. 48).

The most likely date for Poem 29 is late in 55 B.C., while
Pompey was still consul (along with Crassus): the Senate voted
a 20-day thanksgiving upon receipt of Caesar's report on his first
British expedition (*Gal.* 4. 38. 5 *his rebus gestis ex litteris Caesaris
dierum uiginti supplicatio ab Senatu decreta est*); the second expedition
in the summer of 54 B.C. put an end to rumours about the island's
mineral wealth — cf. Cicero, *Fam.* 7. 7. 1 (May 54 B.C., to his
friend Trebatius) *in Britannia nihil esse audio neque auri, neque argenti.*

id si ita est, essedum aliquod suadeo capias, et ad nos quam primum recurras. Caesar's command in Gaul, due to expire in March 54 B.C., had been renewed by Pompey and Crassus for a further 5 years.

The first 10 lines of Poem 29 are addressed to Pompey — Pompey the Great (*Magnus quem metuunt omnes*, as Calvus refers to him in a surviving fragment, *FPL* p. 86): how can he overlook the ostentation and licentiousness of Mamurra's behaviour? Pompey is very much the senior member of the triumvirate at this stage; he is in Rome, Caesar is not; Crassus has perhaps already left for Parthia (he did so at the end of 55 B.C.). A series of repetitions bind lines 1–10 closely together: line 9 = line 5; line 10 echoes line 2.

In lines 11–20 C. turns to address Caesar; unlike the scarcely-veiled contempt meted out to Pompey, the tone now is ironically polite (11 *imperator unice*).

Finally in lines 21–4 son-in-law and father-in-law are jointly addressed (Pompey had married Caesar's daughter Julia — his fourth wife — in 59 B.C.; she was to die in September 54). Line 24 *socer generque, perdidistis omnia* seems to have become notorious — the author of *Catalepton* 6, in using it for his own purposes, introduces it with the remark 'how that line comes in handy everywhere' (*ut ille uersus usquequaque pertinet*).

(Many assume that the *cinaedus Romulus* of lines 5 and 10 is Caesar and that, though 13 *uestra* and 21 *fouetis* include Pompey, 'Pompey is not explicitly addressed until l. 24' (Fordyce). Three arguments can be advanced for this assumption. (1) It becomes easier to find in Poem 29 the *perpetua stigmata* inflicted according to Suetonius (quoted on Poem 57) on Caesar's reputation — these lines, i.e., are the *uersiculi* in question; the lines clearly did become famous, as *Catalepton* 6, a series of reminiscences in Horace of line 7 (*Epod.* 4. 5, 5. 69 and 17. 41), and references in Pliny (*Nat.* 36. 48) and Quintilian (9. 4. 141) show. (2) The echo *unice imperator* at 54. 7 of 29. 11 implies it was Poem 29 which aroused Caesar's anger. (3) Poem 57 plainly calls Caesar a *cinaedus*; therefore, he is the *cinaedus Romulus* of Poem 29. The arguments hardly add up to a watertight case. Poem 57, if written after Poem 29, cannot have

een written long after, unless we are wide of the mark about the
ate of C.'s death; very likely Suetonius is thinking of both pieces.
Of the two, 57 is the more likely to have angered Caesar. As for
he term *cinaedus*, it is a word with which C. is pretty free.)

Metre: pure iambic trimeters (but see notes on lines 3 and 20);
f. Poem 4.

1–10. The fun consists in asking what appear to be rhetorical
uestions (both probably idiomatic clichés) to which the answer is
Nobody' — and then revealing that there *is* somebody who can
ndure the spectacle of Mamurra living in luxury.

2. *nisi impudicus et uorax et aleo*: i.e. somebody like Mamurra
imself. With *uorax* cf. 57. 8 *uorax adulter*.

3. *Mamurram*: the first syllable is long.

   Comata Gallia: = transalpine Gaul, where hair was worn
ong — unlike cisalpine Gaul, where Roman habits had estab-
shed themselves. Cf. Cicero, *Phil.* 8. 27.

4. *uncti*: cf. 22 *uncta* and 10. 11 *unctius*. [V is corrupt; *uncti*,
aerno; Estaço's less ingenious *ante* may well be right.]

   ultima Britannia: cf. 11. 11–12. The final syllable of *ultima*
ounts as long before *Br-*.

5. *cinaede Romule*: 'you homo Romulus'; the insult cancels the
ompliment. For Pompey's claim to the title *cinaedus* see Plutarch's
tory of the claque at Milo's trial in 56 B.C. (*Pompey* 48. 7), to
vhich the epigram of Calvus perhaps refers. On *cinaedus* (here
ess specific, perhaps, than in 25. 1 — or 57. 1 and 10) see on 16.
. For *Romulus* = 'the master statesman' see Sallust, *Cic.* 7 *Romulus
Irpinas* (i.e. Cicero) and Sallust, *Or. Lep.* 5 *scaeuus iste Romulus*
i.e. Sulla). Presumably politicians were called *Romulus* in a spirit
f ironical adulation, though Augustus is said to have toyed with
ssuming the title. For Pompey as a Romulus cf. the remark of
ne of the consuls in 67 B.C., when Pompey's extraordinary naval
owers were being voted, 'If Pompey tries to live like Romulus,
e will end like him' (Plutarch, *Pompey* 25. 4).

6. *et ille nunc* . . .: i.e. this will be the result if Pompey continues
o condone Mamurra's excesses.

superbus et superfluens: 'proud and prodigal'. Note the repetition.

7. *perambulabit*: 'will do the rounds'.

8. *albulus columbus aut Adoneus*: The white dove and Adonis were both associated with Venus. The diminutive *albulus* is ironic. The archaic form *Adoneus* is found in Plautus, *Men.* 144.

9. *cinaede Romule*, etc.: The indignant tone is muted with the repetition — C., i.e., begins to have his doubts: perhaps Pompey *will* tolerate Mamurra's excesses after all.

10. *es impudicus*, etc.: In that case Pompey *is* 'a shameless gambler and a glutton'.

11. *eone nomine*: 'on that account' =i.e. 'on his account'; the same formula in line 23.

imperator unice: ironical flattery, repeated 54. 7; cf. 11. 10 *Caesaris uisens monimenta magni*.

12. *in ultima . . . insula*: cf. 11. 11–12 *ulti- / mosque Britannos*.

13. *uestra*: [*nostra* V; *uestra* is preferable, to prepare the way for 21 *fouetis*.] Pompey and Caesar are united in their protection of Mamurra.

diffututa: =*futuendo exhausta*; contrast 41. 1 *defututa* and 6. 13 *ecfututa*.

mentula: Mamurra's *nom de guerre* in Poems 94, 105, 114 and 115.

14. *ducenties . . . trecenties*: understand: *centena milia sestertium*; = '20 or 30 million *sestertii*'. Large sums of course.

comesset: = Imperfect subjunctive of *comedere*.

15. *quid est alid sinistra liberalitas*: 'what is misguided generosity but this?'. But is the generosity meant Caesar's (in letting Mamurra amass such a fortune) or Mamurra's (in squandering it)? If the former, then *sinistra*, 'perverse', 'upside down', implies that Caesar's generosity was ill-advised, or that it was made possible by robbery — cf. Cato (on Caesar?) in Sallust, *Cat.* 52. 11 *quia bona aliena largiri liberalitas . . . uocatur*. For the idiom cf. Cicero, *Phil.* 10. 5 *quid est aliud librarium Bruti laudare*?

alid: =*aliud*.

16. *expatrauit*: 'ploughed through'. The verb is found only here. Lenchantin suggests there are obscene overtones, quoting the scholiast on Persius 1. 18 *patratio est rei uenereae consummatio*.

17–19. Mamurra, says C., has got through three fortunes already.

18. *praeda Pontica*: i.e. the loot brought back by Pompey and his men after the conquest of Mithridates in 63 B.C.

19. *Hibera*: the reference is to Caesar's campaign as propraetor of *Hispania ulterior* in 61 B.C.

   quam scit: cf. Virgil, *A*. 11. 259–60 *scit triste Mineruae | sidus et Euboicae cautes ultorque Caphereus*.

   aurifer Tagus: Spain was well known as a source of gold. A great river of Spain is given an obviously appropriate epithet.

20. *nunc Galliae timetur et Britanniae*: 'now fears are entertained for Gaul and Britain'. [*hunc timet* V, *nunc* γ. Froehlich's *timetur* is convincing, *nunc* less so: by now Mamurra has presumably brought back his loot (referred to in line 14), and the time for entertaining fears would seem to be past. Perhaps C. means that Gaul and Britain have survived this first blow, but are likely to succumb, should Mamurra return to the attack.] If we read *nunc*, the line begins with a spondee; cf. line 3.

21–4. C. sums up.

21. *malum*: probably not with *hunc*, but the idiomatic use of *malum* as an expletive (perhaps = *malum sit uobis*); cf. Cicero, *Ver*. 2. 1. 54 *quae, malum, est ista tanta audacia atque amentia!* See *L & S* I B.

22. *uncta . . . patrimonia*: Strictly speaking, *patrimonia* is applicable only to 17 *paterna bona*; the facts set out in 17–20 are not of course seriously incompatible with the statement that Mamurra's only talent is for 'devouring fat inheritances'. But perhaps the emphasis falls on *uncta*. There is then a play on words: (1) *uncta* = 'fat', i.e. 'large', and *deuorare* = 'spend quickly'; (2) *uncta* = 'served with a dressing of oil, or with a fatty sauce', and *deuorare* retains its literal meaning: Mamurra, i.e., cannot swallow his inheritances dry; the loot acquired while serving with Pompey

and Caesar provides the sauce. He is useless for anything else, so why waste time with him? (*quid hunc fouetis?*) There is an interesting echo of C.'s words in the pseudo-Ciceronian *Sal.* 20 *patrimonio non comeso sed deuorato.*

23. *eone nomine*: cf. line 11.

urbis o piissimi: [Haupt's *o piissimei* (= *o piissimi*) provides as good a honorific superlative as any that has been suggested in place of the metrically impossible *opulentissime* of V. Haupt wished also to change *urbis* to *orbis*, but this is gratuitous. However, the superlative form of *pius* is somewhat suspect in view of Cicero's assertion, *Phil.* 13. 43 *tu porro ne pios quidem, sed piissimos quaeris et, quod uerbum omnino nullum in lingua Latina est, id propter tuam diuinam pietatem nouum inducis.* Lenchantin accepts B. Schmidt's *putissimei.*]

24. *socer generque*: it became traditional to refer to Caesar and Pompey in this way; cf. Virgil, *A.* 6. 830–1, etc.

perdidistis omnia: cf. Cicero, *Att.* 2. 21. 1 (59 B.C., the reference is to the Triumvirs) *nam iracundiam atque intemperantiam illorum sumus experti, qui Catoni irati omnia perdiderunt.* In C. the primary meaning is the same as in Cicero: Caesar and Pompey 'have brought about the destruction of everything'. But there is probably also a latent play upon words: have Caesar and Pompey 'squandered all they have', to lavish it on Mamurra?

See:

F. Bickel, '*Catulli in Caesarem carmina*', *RhM* 93 (1949), 1–23.
C. Deroux, *Latomus* 29 (1970) 608–31.
J. D. Minyard, *CPh* 66 (1971) 174–81.
W. C. Scott, *CPh* 66 (1971) 17–25.

30

C. is dejected, and in trouble (line 5); Alfenus shows no concern, though it was he who took the initiative in a friendship (lines 6–8) so close, betrayal seemed unthinkable (8 *quasi tuta omnia mi forent*). He behaves now as if it all meant nothing (lines 9–10). Surely he will be punished for such heartlessness (lines 11–12).

   The lines are an odd mixture of styles — declamatory rhetoric
(lines 1–3); measured, logical statement, more in C.'s elegiac
manner (lines 6–11); stilted, alliterative, sententious lines (4 and
12), reminiscent of the early Roman tragedians. While it is not
essential to the hypothesis of the poem that the circumstances and
extent of Alfenus' betrayal should be clear to us, lines 4–5 seem
needlessly disjointed and obscure. If Merrill's suggestion that the
lines are 'but the morbidly exaggerated utterances of a distem-
pered mind' puts the matter too strongly, the poem is remarkable
for a pervasive melancholy of tone (contrast the cooler, more
urbane tone of Poem 38). Cf. Ariadne's speech, 64. 132–201.

   If the Varus of Poems 10 and 22 is the lawyer Alfenus Varus
(see on 10. 1), it is a reasonable assumption that the Alfenus of
Poem 30 is the same man.

   Metre: greater asclepiad; Horace uses this metre in three odes:
1. 11, 1. 18 and 4. 10 — all expository or paraenetic, rather than
lyrical or imaginative.

   1. *immemor*: 'thoughtless'; implies selfish disregard for others;
see on 64. 58.

   unanimis false sodalibus: 'betrayer of devoted friends'; for
unanimis see on 9. 4; *false* is clearly a necessary correction of *salse*,
the reading of V (but cf. 14. 16); the dative is unusual; the
generalization implied by the plural, a characteristic of rhetorical
style, is left unsupported. See on 63. 68.

   2–3. *iam . . . iam . . . iam*: the repetition of *iam* creates a note of
urgency; cf. Poem 46.

   2. *miseret*: yet C. *deserves* pity (5 *miserum*).

   dure . . . dulcis: Note the alliteration and the implied anti-
thesis. We may feel that the self-praise implicit in *dulcis* over-
pitches the assertion of heartlessness.

   amiculi: the diminutive for pathetic effect; as in, e.g., 3. 18
turgiduli ocelli.

   3. *fallere*: picks up 1 *false*; the emphasis probably falls on
dubitas.

   4–5. Hard: *nec* apparently = *nec tamen*. (The suggestion of

H

some editors that *nec* is an archaism = *non* seems hard to substantiate, the usage being confined in literary Latin to fixed formulae and technical clichés.) Line 4 seems a flat rejection of Alfenus' conduct ('But . . .') — a preliminary statement of the threat of retribution which C. repeats in expanded form in lines 11–12. In *quae tu neglegis* the plural is untidy — it cannot really pick up *facta impia*: it is the implications of the statement made in the previous line which Alfenus disregards. Various emendations have been proposed for *quae*.

4. *fallacum*: = *fallacium*; picks up 1 *false* and 3 *fallere*.

caelicolis: the word implies an assertion of high style; contrast, e.g., 51. 1–2 *Ille mi par esse deo uidetur | ille, si fas est, superare diuos.*

5. *miserum . . . in malis*: The details of C.'s misfortune are not part of the poem's hypothesis; but more than plain assertion of the fact is needed to render plausible the intensity of C.'s reaction to Alfenus' indifference.

6. *eheu . . . fidem?*: ironical of course, as the reproach of lines 7–8 shows.

dic: [*dico* V; most modern editors accept Avanzi's *dic*.]

7. *tute*: emphatic.

animam tradere: Something between 'to surrender my soul' and 'to put my life in your hands'; both translations miss, however, the telling simplicity of the Latin. To some extent *animam tradere* picks up 1 *unanimis*. Cf. Horace, *Carm.* 1. 3. 8 *serues animae dimidium meae* (Horace is speaking of his friend Virgil).

inique: vocative.

me: [The line is a syllable short in the MSS.]

8. *inducens in amorem*: the affection, i.e., of true friendship.

quasi tuta omnia mi forent: = 'as if there were no risk for me involved'. The words by implication pick up 7 *animam tradere*: to put one's life in another's hands *does* involve a risk.

9. *omnia*: picks up 8 *tuta omnia.*

10. *uentos . . . sinis*: 'you let the winds and the clouds aloft carry them off useless'. The idea again in 64. 59 and 142, 65. 17

and 70. 4. It is one of the great commonplaces of Greek poetry.
With C.'s formulation cf. Virgil, *A.* 9. 313–14 *aurae* / *omnia*
discerpunt et nubibus inrita donant, and Tibullus 3. 6. 27–8 *uenti*
temeraria uota, / *aeriae et nubes diripienda ferant.*

11. *tu*: emphatic.

oblitus es: picks up the idea of 1 *immemor*, which is then
underlined by *meminerunt* and *meminit*. It remains a weakness of
the poem that, though the idea of broken faith is insisted upon, we
are left unsure what Alfenus has betrayed — an ideal of friendship,
or something more specific?

Fides: The cult of *Fides*, 'Good Faith', that which compels
men to keep their word; Virgil, *A.* 1. 292, calls her *cana Fides*.

12. *quae te ut paeniteat postmodo facti faciet tui*: Note the heavy
alliteration and the hammering rhythm; also the mood of *faciet* —
this is an assertion, not a prayer.

facti . . . tui: 'what you have done'. Coming right at the
end, these words strengthen our feeling that Alfenus has done
something specific (not merely failed to sustain his friend in
trouble) and heighten our curiosity: the *factum* becomes, i.e., too
important a part of the poem's hypothesis to be left unexplained.

See:

D. W. T. C. Vessey, *Latomus* 30 (1971) 45–55.
C. Witke, *Enarratio catulliana, Mnemosyne* supp. 10 (1968).

31

Lines on returning to familiar surroundings after a tour of duty
in Bithynia. Critics stress the expression of feeling (e.g. Merrill:
'The poem is a most unartificial and joyous pouring out of
feeling'), but the simple emotions of joy and relief are counter-
balanced by a sophisticated, consciously complex formulation.

For the reactions of an educated contemporary to natural
beauty cf. Cicero, *Att.* 12. 9 (45 B.C.), with its somewhat self-
consciously abrupt conclusion:

Ne ego essem hic libenter atque id cotidie magis . . . nihil
hac solitudine iucundius . . . cetera noli putare amabiliora

fieri posse uilla, litore, prospectu maris, tumulis, his rebus
omnibus. sed neque haec digna longioribus litteris, nec erat
quod scriberem, et somnus urgebat.

Cf. Horace and his Sabine farm (S. 2. 6, etc.).

Sirmio (now Sirmione) is a small rocky tongue of land on the
south shore of Lake Benacus (Lago di Garda, the largest of the
Lombard lakes, the *pater Benacus* of A. 10. 205), about 20 miles
from Verona; it seems reasonable to infer from lines 10 and 12–14
that C. had a villa on the promontory, overlooking the lake. For
his villa nearer Rome (*o funde noster seu Sabine seu Tiburs*) see Poem 44.

For C.'s visit to Bithynia with the *cohors* of C. Memmius see
Poems 10, 28 and 46.

Structure: 1–6 — C.'s emotions on getting home: an appro-
priately urbane exposition of the basic data. 7–11 — analysis and
reflection. 12–14 — salutation: master greets old retainer.

Metre: limping iambics.

1–2. Expository, rather than descriptive. The personification
is a formal device for building the poem round its addressee; but
the device is exploited ironically by a sustained suggestion, which
becomes fully developed in lines 12–14, that Sirmio is a real
person.

1. *paene insularum*: virtually a compound. (C. perhaps origin-
ated the combination); for C.'s fondness for long learned words
see on 7. 1 *basiationes*.

2. *ocelle*: The vocative of this diminutive suggests a term of
endearment (cf. 50. 19). But the dependent genitives draw out a
second conflicting sense = 'scenic gem'; cf. Cicero, *Att.* 16. 6. 2
cur ocellos Italiae uillulas meas non uideo?; that the primary sense
'eye' (one of the features of physical beauty) underlay this second
sense is suggested by Cicero, *N.D.* 3. 91 *hi duo illos oculos orae
maritimae effoderunt* (Corinth and Carthage), where *effoderunt*
revives the latent metaphor. In Cicero the dependent genitives
denote the body of which the 'eye' is the outstanding feature; in
C. the genitives imply a use of *ocelle* approaching a superlative
adjective. Has C. in mind the islands that dot the Aegean?

liquentibus stagnis: 'limpid pools'; *stagnum* is a word Virgil is fond of; with *liquentibus* cf. 64. 2 *liquidas*.

3. *uasto*: 'empty', 'desolate' as much as 'huge'.

fert: 'supports'.

uterque Neptunus: Either (1) a reference to the two seas of Italy, the Tyrrhenian and the Adriatic (as in *A.* 7. 100–1 *qua Sol utrumque recurrens | aspicit Oceanum*; cf. *A.* 8. 149 (an echo of *G.* 2. 158 *et mare quod supra teneant quodque adluit infra*; cf. *G.* 3. 33); or (2) the god of the ocean, and the god who presides over lakes and inland waters (the latter, according to DELATTE, a north-Italian divinity identified by the Romans with Neptune).

4. *te ... inuiso*: *inuiso* (the word for paying a call on a person) supports the personification.

libenter ... laetus: adverb coupled with adjective. The repetition and the alliteration for emphasis — to establish an initial reaction of joy.

5. *uix mi ipse credens*: The second emotion is more complicated. C. means — not that Sirmio looks like Bithynia — but that all around him invites relaxation; his surroundings are not those, however, he had got used to relaxing in during his year of absence. The phrase *uix mihi credo ...* is a colloquial cliché for the emotion of confused recognition (see, e.g., Plautus, *Am.* 416 and *Rud.* 245–6); here the words are lent a cool, ironical freshness by the word-play on 5 *Thyniam*, etc.

ipse: the reflexive pronoun is regularly nominative in such expressions, rather than accusative or dative, etc.

Thyniam, etc.: A piece of learned word-play. (1) *Bithynia*, not *Thynia*, was the usual Roman name for the province; C. draws out the reaction, invited by the Greek prefix *Bi-*, that if there was a *Bithynia* there must be also a *Thynia*. (The name *Thyni* for the tribe occurs occasionally, and in 25. 7 C. used the adjective *Thynus*.) (2) We expect therefore a jingle, *Thyniam atque Bithyniam*, but C. varies the formula and, by delaying *campos*, tricks us into supposing for a moment he means the people (*Bithyni*), not the place.

6. *in tuto*: i.e. the journey is safely over.

7–11. C. relaxes and reflects on the happiness of finding himself again among familiar objects, with nothing more to worry about.

7. *solutis . . . curis*: = *quid est beatius quam curas soluere?* An apparent simplicity conceals some artifice. (1) The ablative of comparison has a literary flavour — except in stereotypes like *luce clarior*, where no real comparison is intended, the construction with *quam* is the more usual; (2) the combination participle + noun is idiomatic, like *ab urbe condita* ('from the city founded' = 'from the foundation of the city').

8–9. *peregrino labore*: 'toil in foreign parts'. Does C. permit himself a trace of complacency about his duties in Bithynia?

11. = 'this by itself is worth all the toil and sweat'. For the idiom see Cicero, *Att.* 2. 5. 1 *Cato ille noster, qui mihi unus est pro centum milibus*; for the emphatic use of *unum* see 10. 17 and 107. 7. On getting home, C.'s reaction is, 'I'm glad the whole business is over'. To take *labores tanti* as the hardships of travel home misses C.'s conscious and convincing distortion of perspective: the trip to Bithynia turned out a disappointment — see Poem 10 and 28. 9–10.

12–14. In the valediction, the personification becomes sharper: Sirmio is the faithful retainer, attended by a chorus of lesser slaves — all smiles and happy chatter as they welcome their master home.

12. *uenusta*: Elsewhere in C. (5 examples) the word is used of persons (of both sexes) to describe personality rather than appearance (as we should expect from Poem 86); for its use of scenery see Cicero, *Att.* 15. 16a. 1 (of Arpinum) *haec loca uenuste sunt, abdita certe, et . . . arbitris libera.*

ero: the slave's word for his master. See on 61. 151.

13. *gaudente*: *gaude gaudente* was perhaps a conventional formula, comparable to the jingle in Cicero, *Rep.* 1. 4. 7 *in contione populo Romano idem iurante iurauissem.* [The line is corrupt and variously restored: *gaudente* was suggested by Bergk. Many print *gaudete* (with a stop at the end of the previous line). For a

discussion of the passage defending *gaudente* (adopted by Mynors)
see G. P. Goold, *Phoenix* 12 (1958), 94.]

uosque: C. turns from the promontory to the waters of the
lake.

Lydiae: [*lidie* V.] A final piece of learning: 'Lydian' =
'Etruscan' (the Etruscans were commonly supposed to have come
from Lydia in Asia Minor); the reference is to early Etruscan
settlements in the Po valley, long since disappeared (see, e.g.,
Livy 5. 33).

14. *ridete*: An ambiguity extends the personification of the
previous line: the water of the lake splashing round the promon-
tory sounds like the subdued laughter of a group of people. The
same idea is used in a serious context in 64. 273; for examples
from Aeschylus' κυμάτων γέλασμα onwards see Fordyce.

quidquid est domi cachinnorum: a noun-equivalent, forming an
internal accusative: 'ripple forth all the laughter in the house';
cf. 37. 4 *quidquid est puellarum*.

domi: A further ambiguity, supporting the idea of a group
of slaves: (1) 'in the house' — C.'s Sirmio property and its lake
setting are spoken of as his household of slaves; (2) 'on command',
'available' (for this colloquial use see Plautus, *Rud.* 292 *quidquid
est domi, id sat est habendum*; cf. 1335).

cachinnorum: cf. 13. 5 (and 56. 2) and 64. 273 for this word
in a colloquial and a serious context respectively.

See:

R. J. Baker, *Mnemosyne* 23 (1970) 33–41.

Cat. Rev. 34–5.

L. Delatte, '*Uterque Neptunus*', *AC* 4 (1935), 45–7.

32

C., having breakfasted, is lying down while he plans his day. A
note to Ipsitilla seems indicated. Can he spend the siesta with her?
An immediate reply is requested.

These elegant, outrageous *uersiculi* are hardly a historical

document which has come into our hands by accident. Plainly
Ipsitilla, if she existed, is being mocked. For the name, and what
different editors have made of it [the MSS read *ipsithila, ipsi illa,
ipsichila* and *ipsicilla*] see Neudling 87. Feminine names ending in
-*illa* are not uncommon; one need look no further than Aurelia
Orestilla, the merry maid whom Catiline took to wife and of
whom Sallust remarks (*Cat.* 15. 2) *praeter formam nihil umquam bonus
laudauit*; she was said to be Catiline's illegitimate daughter. Did
she survive him, to became C.'s *Ipsitilla*? She seems to be the
lady meant in 64. 402.

For the midday rendezvous cf. 61. 110–12 and Ovid's justly
celebrated elegy *Am.* 1. 5; with C.'s boast cf. Philodemus, *AP* 11. 30.

Metre: hendecasyllabics.

1. *amabo*: idiomatic = 'please'. Common with a following
imperative; the full form is *amabo te*; cf. Laevius, *FPL* p. 62 *mea
Vatiena, amabo*; Cicero, *Fam.* 8. 9. 3 *amabo te, impera tibi hoc*; *Fam.*
7. 32. 2 *urbanitatis possessionem* [= 'the copyright in my witty
remarks'], *amabo, quibusuis interdictis defendamus*.

dulcis: slightly effusive, in preparation for line 2: 'my *dear*
Ipsitilla'.

2. *meae deliciae*: 'my darling'; see on 2. 1.

mei lepores: = 'my clever girl'; the plural applied to a person
is modelled on *deliciae* and *amores* (cf. 10. 1, etc.). But *lepores* in this
sense seems unprecedented; no doubt the word is chosen to cap
the elaborate politeness and the plainly ironical coaxing tone
which C. affects.

3. *iube*: = 'invite'. The request for an invitation is underlined
by the repetition 4 *iusseris* and 9 *iubeto*. For the construction of
iubere with the subjunctive (without *ut*) cf. Plautus, *Per.* 605 *iube
dum ea huc accedat ad me*.

ad te: = *apud te*.

meridiatum: supine with *ueniam*; cf. 10. 2 *uisum duxerat*, 61. 146
petitum eat.

4. *et si iusseris*: 'and if you *do* invite me'; picks up *iube*. No real
doubt about Ipsitilla's response need be intended: for the idio-

matic use of *si* = 'when' in referring to the future see on 14. 17 *si luxerit*.

illud adiuuato: mock solemn = 'it will be helpful, too, if you will kindly attend to the following . . .'.

5. *ne quis liminis obseret tabellam*: 'let no one bolt the street door'; *tabella* = one leaf of a Roman double-door. A further insult: Ipsitilla is not to make an appointment which might conflict.

6–8. Ipsitilla should, in fact, devote her morning entirely to preparations for receiving C.

8. *fututiones*: for the ironical possibilities of the learned poly-syllable see on 7. 1 *basiationes*.

9. *si quid ages*: 'if there's anything doing'; the tense of *ages* is future, of course.

iubeto: picks up 3 *iube* and 4 *iusseris*, and prepares the tran-sition from ironical circumlocution to plain speaking.

10. *pransus*: The word apparently has overtones which may be translated as 'ready for business' as a result of the practice of giving soldiers a meal before an engagement; see *L & S* II and the examples quoted.

satur supinus: cf. Horace, *S.* 1. 5. 85.

11. *pertundo*: apparently the *mot juste* — there was even a *Dea Pertunda*.

tunicamque palliumque: mock heroic, = *et tunicam et pallium*. Possibly C. was wearing both, to be ready to go out the moment he received a reply. But, unless affecting Greek dress, a Roman used his *pallium* more often as a rug to throw over his bed than as an item of clothing; see Ovid, *Am.* 1. 2. 2 *neque in lecto pallia nostra sedent*, etc.; (little can be inferred from the reference to a *pallium* in 25. 6). C., i.e., wants us to imagine him composing his letter after breakfast in bed.

33

'No one is interested in your queer habits, Vibennius; as for your light-fingered father, everybody knows about his tricks. Rome

would be glad to see the last of the pair of you.' Like 32, a
lampoon. Here, however, no time is wasted on innuendo: the
most outrageous charges are fired at Vibennius *père et fils* with
urbane gusto. The lines form a single, somewhat breathtaking
sentence.

Thefts from public baths appear to have been one of the con-
stant irritations of ancient social life; see Ellis. Vibennius is uniden-
tifiable.

Metre: hendecasyllabics.

1. *optime*: Ironically ambiguous: (1) *optimus* is often used as an
honorific epithet = 'most distinguished' (cf. 28. 3); but (2)
Vibennius *père* is also the 'most distinguished' in his profession as
a bathhouse thief.

2. *cinaede fili*: both words are vocative. For *cinaedus* see on
16. 2.

3-4. The chief claim to distinction of each of the pair is briefly
sketched in by means of a descriptive ablative. The implication is
that each of the epithets chosen, *inquinatus* ('filthy', 'unclean') and
uorax ('greedy'), though more specially appropriate to one than
the other, could be applied to either.

3. *dextra*: contrast 12. 1 *manu sinistra*; Vibennius *père* was
perhaps both more skilful and more barefaced in his thefts than
the amateurish Asinius.

inquinatiore: the word is used of both moral and physical
defilement.

4. The son, i.e., is literally a *cinaedus*.

5. *exilium malasque in oras*: = *in exilium malasque in oras*. There is a
play on words in *malas in oras*: (1) literally, 'to unsavoury regions';
(2) but the phrase evokes the idiomatic *in malam rem abire*, 'to go
to the devil'.

6. *rapinae*: 'plunderings'; a serious-sounding word, not one
normally applied to petty thieving.

7. *notae sunt populo*: 'are public knowledge'.

pilosas: the implication is that it is high time Vibennius *fils*
thought of retiring. Cf. 16. 10.

8. *fili*: vocative.

   asse: a derisory figure.

   uenditare: the frequentative implies a final insult.

34

A hymn to Diana, sung by a choir of boys and girls.

The six stanzas form a clear, coherent structure: 1 (hypothesis) + 2–3 (invocation) + 4–5 (celebration) + 6 (prayer). The first stanza sets the stage, a little flatly. Stanzas 2–3 form a single, complex sentence in which a rigorous selection of legends about the birth of Diana (= Artemis, the goddess of mountains, forests, glades and streams) is neatly and simply assembled. Stanzas 4–5 celebrate a more Roman Diana — the mysterious, magical moon goddess, less sharply visualized, perhaps more genuinely believed in. Stanza 6 concludes the hymn with a prayer entreating the goddess's protection for the Roman race.

But this simple layout conceals some artifice. The logical structure combines Greek anthropomorphism with Roman religious feeling deftly and unobtrusively. Clearly Poem 34 is not a translation, but an attempt to sort out two or three themes from the tangle of Greek tradition by giving to them a simple, dignified expression appropriate to the Latin language and to Roman feeling. The result is slight (Callimachus' hymn to Artemis runs into 268 lines) but graceful, if not entirely free from ingenuousness, or even a trace of halting repetitiveness. It is interesting to compare Horace's hymn to Diana, *Carm.* 3. 22; C. cannot manage Horace's apparently effortless compression, or the easy assurance with which he gives personal relevance to traditional form and familiar themes.

Despite the choir of boys and girls in Stanza 1, the hymn is not likely to have been intended for actual performance; it resembles, i.e., Horace's hymn to Diana and Apollo (*Carm.* 1. 21), not his *Carmen saeculare*.

Metre: Each 4-line stanza consists of 3 glyconics ($\smile\bar{\smile}|-\smile\smile-|\smile-$) followed by a pherecratean ($\smile\bar{\smile}|-\smile\smile-|-$); in the first foot, trochees preponderate over spondees; iambs in Stanza 1 only; cf. Anacreon, *Hymn to Artemis*, *LGS* 295. (In Poem 17 each line consists of a glyconic + a pherecratean.) As in Poem 61, the stanza is treated as a single unit: hiatus between lines is avoided; the last syllable of each of the first three lines of each stanza, if not long by nature, is long by position (i.e. the next line begins with a consonant); this is called *synaphaea*. Continuity within the stanza is emphasized by elision at the end of lines 11 and 22.

1. *Dianae*: The i, originally long, is usually short in dactylic verse. It is possible that in this first stanza each line was intended to begin with an iambic foot (not found elsewhere in the poem).

in fide: idiomatic = 'in the custody'.

2. *integri*: 'unmarried'; cf. 61. 36–7 *integrae | uirgines*. (An alternative interpretation, 'having both parents alive' — a necessary qualification for participation in some religious ceremonies — is less likely.)

3. The line is missing in our MSS, though the Renaissance commentator Palladius claimed to have found *Dianae pueri integri* 'in uetustiore exemplari'. *Dianam* is due to Avanzi. The repetitions with variations in the stanza thus constituted form a graceful pattern.

5. *Latonia*: 'daughter of Leto' (called Latona by the Romans); Artemis and Apollo were the twin children of Leto by Zeus; about the place and circumstances of the birth of the twins there are conflicting legends. The commonest was that they were born on the island of Delos. But the Ephesians in Tacitus' time (*Ann.* 3. 61) claimed that they had been born at Ephesus and that the olive-tree against which Leto had supported herself was still to be seen there.

8. *deposiuit*: archaic = *deposuit*.

11. *reconditorum*: 'secluded'; the last syllable is elided.

12. *sonantum*: = *sonantium*; cf. 64. 191 *caelestum*, 100. 2 *Veronensum*; the genitive plural is a little overworked in this stanza.

13–20. These eight lines form an increasing triad — three statements in praise of Diana: 'You are called Lucina Juno; you are called Trivia and Luna; you regulate the farmer's year.' Each statement is introduced by the same emphatic *tu* (anaphora), but the third is of a different order (it expands *Luna* instead of introducing a third embodiment of Diana). Moreover, 16 *dicta* after 14 *dicta* suggests that *notho . . . lumine* (probably instrumental ablative) is on the same syntactical footing as *dolentibus . . . puerperis* (probably dative of the agent). A more serious blemish is the wording of 13–14; *how* can Diana be called 'Lucina Juno'? Diana, like Artemis in Greek, is often referred to as a goddess of childbirth. Varro identifies her with Juno in almost the same words as C. (*L.* 5. 69) *quae* [*Diana*] *ideo quoque uidetur ab Latinis Iuno Lucina dicta.* But it is one thing for an antiquarian and etymologist to discuss this kind of equation and another for a poet in a hymn addressed to a goddess to tell her that she is also a quite different goddess.

15. *Triuia*: The well-known divinity of the cross-roads, often called Hecate; regularly (unlike Juno) identified with Diana.

   notho: cf. Lucretius 5. 575–6 (discussing the theory, said to have been first advanced by Parmenides, that the moon's light is a reflection of the sun's) *lunaque siue notho fertur loca lumine lustrans / siue suam proprio iactat de corpore lucem. . . .*

16. *Luna*: cf. Cicero, *N.D.* 2. 68 *Luna a lucendo nominata sit, eadem est enim Lucina.*

17–18. Cf. Cicero, *N.D.* 2. 69 *lunae cursibus qui, quia mensa spatia conficiunt, menses nominantur.* The repetition *menstruo / metiens* suggests that C. supposed (correctly) that the words were connected etymologically.

19. *agricolae*: perhaps better felt as dative than as genitive, but by its position as well as by its syntactical ambiguity the word binds the phrase together.

21–2. *sis . . . nomine*: based on the usual escape clause of Roman ritual, protecting against possible omission or inaccuracy in addressing a divinity.

22. *Romulique*: the metre requires the final syllable to be elided, though the sequence *Romuliqu' antiqu' ut* is scarcely pleasing to the ear.

23. *antique*: the adverb.

24. *sospites*: subjunctive; an archaism, part of the language of religious ritual.

See:

U. von Wilamowitz-Moellendorf, *Hellenistische Dichtung* (1924) ii 287–91.

35

A verse epistle, included in the collection for C.'s readers to sharpen their wits on. Any reading which takes fair account of the valid clues provided is acceptable. However, the more important clues are prominently placed, to ensure that the alert reader does not end up too wide of the mark.

The opening line, *Poetae tenero, meo sodali*, gets to the heart of the matter at once, inviting us to think of Caecilius first as a poet and then as C.'s friend. He is the author, we discover, of a poem about the goddess Cybele; since C. ends his poem with that fact, we may suppose it important — Caecilius' *Magna Mater* may well prove the real subject of C.'s verse epistle. An epyllion, perhaps, or something more out of the ordinary, like C.'s *Attis* (Poem 63); 1 *tenero* suggests that Caecilius had attempted to give his version of the legend the love interest which was, it seems, *de rigueur* among the *poetae noui*; prominently placed and left unqualified, *tenero* suggests further that in C.'s judgment Caecilius is not without ability in this respect. But his *Magna Mater*, though started, is far from finished: C.'s insistence (13 *incohatam*, 18 *incohata* — the penultimate word of the poem) suggests that Caecilius thought otherwise, or at any rate needed reminding; coupled with the invitation to Caecilius to drop everything and come to Verona, it suggests C. had reservations he would like Caecilius to hear

before it is too late. He has not forgotten that Caecilius has a
girl-friend who is head over heels in love with him (no wonder,
once she has read his *Magna Mater*); but Caecilius mustn't let that
detain him.

Nothing is known about Caecilius; he seems unlikely to be the
Veronese named in 67. 9. It is tempting to suppose that he may
have been an ancestor of the Younger Pliny (C. Plinius Caecilius
Secundus), whose home was in Novum Comum.

Metre: hendecasyllabics.

1. *poetae tenero*: = 'love poet'; cf. Ovid, *Ars* 2. 273 *teneros uersus*, of
love poetry.

   sodali: the word used of Cinna (10. 29), of Veranius and
Fabullus (12. 13 and 47. 6).

2. *uelim ... dicas*: the subjunctive without *ut* is common in
colloquial style.

   papyre: **The trick of making the piece of papyrus on which**
the letter is written the addressee (1) gets the poem going; (2) sets
the tone — urbane and not too serious. Cf. Horace's instructions
to his book of epistles, *Ep.* 1. 20.

3–4. *Noui ... Comi*: In 59 B.C. Julius Caesar settled 5,000
colonists at Comum and renamed the place Novum Comum,
which provides a *terminus a quo* for Poem 35. The modern town
lies on the south-west shore of the Lago di Como (*Lacus Larius*)
about 30 miles north of Milan.

4. *moenia ... litus*: a touch of grandiloquence in preparation
for lines 5 and 6.

5. *quasdam ... cogitationes*: a note of playful solemnity starts to
make itself felt.

   uolo: the final o is short; see on 6. 16.

6. *amici ... sui meique*: Pretty certainly =*meas*; the periphrasis
continues, i.e., the mock pomposity of *quasdam ... cogitationes*. It
is an example in that case of *urbánitas*; but we may suspect C. is
anxious to convey to Caecilius, without ruffling him too much,
that he is not happy about his *Magna Mater*.

7. *si sapiet*: 'if he is sensible'; his behaviour on receipt of the

letter is meant, hence the future tense. Cf. Plautus, *Rud.* 1391 *si sapies, tacebis.*

uiam uorabit: An example of the vivid inventiveness of colloquial speech; the expression is not found elsewhere. Novum Comum to Verona is about 130 miles.

8–10. Cf. Propertius 1. 6. 5–6 *sed me complexae remorantur uerba puellae, | mutatoque graues saepe colore preces.*

8. *quamuis*: = *quamquam* (as occasionally in classical prose); with the subjunctive, however.

candida . . . puella: see on 13. 4.

9. *euntem*: 'as he sets out'.

collo: dative.

10. *roget morari*: the infinitive (instead of *ut* + subjunctive), apparently found only here; the accusative and infinitive construction (e.g. Ovid, *Ars* 1. 433) is also rare.

11–15. C. seems well informed. Is this picture of two hearts beating as one based on what Caecilius himself told C., perhaps in a letter accompanying the draft of his *Magna Mater*? The hint of irony in that case in 11 *si mihi uera nuntiantur* is not out of place.

12. *deperit*: 'is madly in love with'; cf. 100. 2; see also on 45. 5.

impotente: 'uncontrollable', 'raging'; so 4. 18 and 8. 9.

13. *quo tempore*: picked up by 14 *ex eo*, 'ever since'.

legit: perfect; the subject is probably *puella*.

incohatam: Caecilius' *Magna Mater* is begun but not finished. Cicero, *Arch.* 28, provides a useful parallel: *quas res nos gessimus . . . attigit hic uersibus et incohauit, quibus auditis . . . hunc ad perficiendum hortatus sum.*

14. *Dindymi dominam*: = Cybele, the *Magna Mater* of line 18. Caecilius' poem perhaps began *Dindymi dominam* (the ancients frequently referred to a poem by quoting the first few words), though not if the poem were in hexameters (the usual metre for epyllia). C. has *dea domina Dindymi* at 63. 91 (and *Dindymenae dominae* at 63. 13). Dindymus (or Dindymon) is a mountain in eastern Phrygia.

misellae: dative; being in love, Caecilius' *puella* can be described as *misera* (see on 8. 1); the diminutive adds a hint of pathos, as in 45. 21.

15. *ignes*: the fires of love.

    medullam: cf. 45. 16, 64. 93, 100. 7, etc., and Virgil, *A.* 4. 66 *est mollis flamma medullas*; with *edunt* cf. 91. 6 *edebat*.

16–17. *Sapphica puella musa doctior*: What C. means in plain prose is clear: Caecilius' girl has more claim to be called a *docta puella* (i.e. she knows more about poetry) than the poetess Sappho; *doctus* = 'possessing taste', especially in love poetry, not just 'well read'; the *docta puella* is no blue-stocking, though Ovid, *Ars* 3. 329–38, lays down a formidable reading list. What C. actually says is open to some doubt. The most obvious interpretation, out of context, of *Sapphica musa* is 'the Muse of Sappho' or, by an easy transference, 'the poetry of Sappho' — cf. Ovid, *Ars* 3. 330–1 *sit quoque uinosi Teia Musa senis*; | *nota sit et Sappho, (quid enim lasciuius illa?)* We get rather better sense if we assume C. is referring to the familiar conceit that Sappho herself deserved to rank among the Muses (cf. *AP* 9. 506, ascribed to Plato; for other references see Ellis). To say that Caecilius' girl 'knows more about poetry than Sappho, the Muse' (an extremely agreeable companion, i.e., as well as an authority on poetry) is naturally an extravagant compliment; but it is scarcely more seriously intended than the assertion that the girl's admiration for Caecilius' *Magna Mater* has made her fall in love with the author; as C. says, 'the reaction is excusable' (16 *ignosco tibi*).

17–18. *est enim uenuste . . . incohata*: Caecilius, i.e., has made a jolly good start.

18. *Caecilio*: dative of the agent.

    incohata: In what sense is Caecilius' poem *incohata*? Is there more to come, or is it a matter of licking the thing into shape? Does C. repeat the word in the last line of his epistle because he feels Caecilius is unprepared for the point he is trying to get across: that the *Magna Mater* needs a lot more work on it? What Caecilius has sent C., i.e., must be regarded as only a draft: writing an epyllion is a long business (see what C. says in Poem 95 about Cinna's *Zmyrna*); the slipshod craftsmanship of a Suffenus (Poem 22) will not pass.

See:

F. O. Copley, 'Catullus 35', *AJPh* 74 (1953), 149–60.
J. M. Fisher, *CPh* 66 (1971) 1–5.

36

Lesbia made a vow to Venus and to Cupid — if she got her lover back, and the storm of verses pouring ridicule on her ceased, she'd offer 'the worst of poets' choicest work to the limping-footed god of fire for a toasting'. But, though wittily expressed, her vow was imprecisely worded: 'the worst of poets' choicest work'? — surely that must be the *Annals* of Volusius; here is a copy of the disgusting stuff, its fate as good as sealed. That we should so reconstruct the hypothesis of these lines, there is tolerable agreement. Poem 36 then, like Poem 14, began as a covering letter — and then became a little drama in which Volusius' *Annals* receive a personal briefing from C. (cf. Poem 42).

On her basis for making it up Lesbia stood to win all round: she would get C. back; pleading the terms of her vow, she would have the pleasure of consigning C.'s taunting verses to the fire — no risk, therefore, of having to face at some future date (like the *putida moecha* of Poem 42) insolent demands for their return, or of seeing them published to the world, if she returned them. Poem 36 suggests a counter-proposal, couched in terms which make it sound as if C. were helping Lesbia out of a fix, and supported by a 6-line prayer to the goddess of love no less mock-solemn than Lesbia's vow, begging Venus to endorse the eligibility of the *Annals* of Volusius. If Lesbia wants C. back, in short, she must give in gracefully and let herself be outsmarted.

Naturally, we must not take too seriously C.'s mock-heroic reformulation of a lover's quarrel. Lesbia, in demanding a retraction, may very well have threatened to burn the poems sent her by an angry lover; she was very likely in the mood to refer to him

as *pessimus poeta* (the expression recurs in Poem 49; did the
angry sally rankle?). BUCHHEIT's assumption that vow and
counter-proposal are a smoke-screen for literary criticism — a
deliberate, considered attack on Volusius and what he stood
for — is no less dangerous than taking the lines as autobiograph-
ical fact.

Structure: 1–2 — Volusius' *Annals* summoned: they have a task
to perform. 3–10 — the position explained to them, Lesbia's vow.
11–17 — solution: C.'s prayer. 18–20 — Volusius' *Annals*
despatched.

Metre: hendecasyllabics.

1. *annales Volusi*: For Volusius and his *Annals* see 95. 7–8.

2. *pro mea puella*: 'on my mistress's behalf'; Volusius' *Annals*,
i.e., are called on to help Lesbia out of her fix. There need be
little doubt that Lesbia is meant; C. speaks of his mistress as *mea
puella* in Poems 2, 3, 11 and, probably, 13; the name Lesbia is
used less commonly in the polymetric poems than in the elegiac
fragments; see on 51. 7.

3. *sanctae*: the epithet is usual enough of course, but it reminds
us here that a goddess is not to be trifled with.

5. i.e. no more lampoons like Poem 37 (limping iambics)?
Many hold, however, that C. uses *iambi* as a description of a
genre, not a metre; see on 40. 2 and 54. 6–7.

uibrare: is used of hurling a weapon such as a spear, denoting
perhaps the noise made in flight as much as the brandishing of the
weapon before launching.

6–7. *electissima pessimi poetae / scripta*: The key word *electissima*
('most carefully selected', 'choicest') is operative at several levels.
(1) It parodies the language of actual vows (only the best is good
enough for a god). (2) Interacting with *pessimi*, it suggests that
even the best in this case is not up to much. (3) It pinpoints the
work chosen by C. as a substitute sacrifice: Volusius is obviously
pessimus poeta, the *Annals* his 'choicest' work.

7. *tardipedi deo*: Vulcan, the lame god of fire. But the epithet
introduces a mock-solemn note.

daturam: the pronoun-object *se* is omitted — as frequently in verse (and occasionally in prose).

8. *infelicibus . . . lignis*: Another ambiguity. (1) In the technical language of ritual, *infelix* = 'sterile' is appropriate to ceremonies connected with the burning of *portenta prodigiaque* (Macrobius 3. 20. 3); in primitive times, it seems, criminals were hanged on an *arbos infelix* (Cicero, *Rab. Perd.* 13). (2) In everyday speech, *infelix* = 'unlucky'; to end its days helping to burn the *Annals* of Volusius was bad luck for any piece of wood. Cicero seems to have a similar pun in mind when he tells us that the body of Publius Clodius was (*Mil.* 33) *infelicissimis lignis semiustulatum* — perhaps an echo of C.'s words.

ustulanda: The simple verb is found only here in classical Latin: the compound *semiustulare* occurs a number of times (see, e.g., Cicero, *Mil.* 33, just quoted) in what one takes to be disparaging or pejorative contexts. We may reasonably presume therefore that the form *ustulanda* reinforces the hint of a jest contained in *tardipedi* — something less than total destruction by fire seems denoted; perhaps they were to be 'toasted'.

9–10. 'And when she made the vow, the wretched girl thought she was being jolly smart (and Venus and Cupid would enjoy the joke)', i.e. now Lesbia and C. have a problem on their hands: something has got to be done about those verses. Lesbia, we may assume, feigns reluctance to carry out the terms of her vow and C. of course pretends to believe her: the essence of a counter-proposal is that it should appear conciliatory, not a challenge to the position adopted by one's opponent.

9. *pessima . . . puella*: (1) expresses C.'s exasperation — the wretched girl has got herself into a fix; (2) implies the equation *pessimus poeta* = Catullus, adding that, if he is *pessimus poeta*, she is *pessima puella*; the suggestion of some editors that Lesbia was already thinking of Volusius when she made the vow is thus ruled out.

uidit: the tense implies she may have changed her mind.

10. *iocosis*: [A. Riese's emendation (in his edition of 1884);

most editors preserve the MS reading *iocose*, but the asyndeton *iocose lepide* is suspect. Scaliger's *ioco se lepido* is tempting.] Venus and Cupid are frequently represented as divinities who enjoy a joke.

lepide: The smartness of Lesbia's vow is (1) in its witty phrasing — *electissima pessimi poetae scripta* seemed to her neatly to beg the question; the humorous touches noted above in lines 7–8 are more likely due to C. (in his reformulation of Lesbia's vow); (2) she thought she had outsmarted C. by forcing him to accept reconciliation on her terms (see introduction).

11. *nunc*: The primary reference is to the dramatic moment of lines 1–2: a prayer to Venus is indicated before despatching Volusius' *Annals*. But *nunc* also has the implication 'well, let's have a go at getting round this'.

o caeruleo creata ponto: The hymn to Venus begins with a reference in the appropriate style to her birth from the sea.

12–15. Next a list of places famous for the worship of Venus is *de rigueur*; the repeated relative clauses follow the prescribed syntactical pattern for the invocation of a hymn or a prayer. Idalium (mentioned also in 61. 17 and 64. 96), Amathus (cf. 68. 51 *Amathusia*) and Golgi are in Cyprus, the traditional home of the goddess; Italy, Asia Minor and Illyria are also represented; Urii was on the coast of Apulia.

12. *apertos*: 'exposed' (as opposed to 'land-locked'); the term is common in geographical descriptions.

13. *Ancona*: accusative of the Greek form *Ancon*.

harundinosam: the appropriately learned epithet. The word does not occur elsewhere, though Pliny (*Nat.* 16. 156) vouches for the reeds; Praxiteles' famous statue of Aphrodite was at Cnidos.

14. *colis*: 'dwell in' — the appropriate cliché in such contexts.

Amathunta: Greek accusative of *Amathus*.

Golgos: both here and at 64. 96 (also in an address to Venus) the name of the town has been corrupted in the MSS.

15. *Hadriae tabernam*: 'emporium of the Adriatic'; Durrachium, on the coast of Illyria opposite Brundisium, was a famous trading port.

16. *acceptum face redditumque*: 'enter as received and duly paid'; the technical language of business — it must be clear and beyond argument that Lesbia has been freed from her vow; the archaic imperative *face* underlines the legal phraseology, or at any rate makes the matter more solemn.

17. *si non illepidum neque inuenustum est*: Venus, i.e., is asked to be a party to the conspiracy to defraud herself — it is a smart way out of the difficulty and one that is not unworthy of Venus (*non inuenustum est*); for the two meanings of *uenustus* see on 3. 2. Just as her sense of humour (10 *iocosis*) must have been tickled by Lesbia's clever vow, so, C. hopes, it will be tickled now by his equally clever reinterpretation; *non illepidum* picks up to 10 *lepide*.

18–20. For the formula of despatch cf. 14. 21–3 and 27. 5–7.

18. *interea*: While Venus is making up her mind, Volusius' *Annals* can get ready for their journey to the pyre.

19. *pleni ruris et infacetiarum*: cf. Suffenus who is (22. 14) *infaceto . . . infacetior rure*.

20. *annales Volusi, cacata carta*: The last line repeats the first, as in Poems 16, 52 and 57.

See:

Vinzenz Buchheit, 'Catulls Dichterkritik in C. 36', *Hermes* 87 (1959), 309–27.

G. W. Clarke, 'The burning of books and Catullus 36', *Latomus* 27 (1968), 575–80.

Howard Comfort, 'An interpretation of Catullus XXXVI', *CPh* 24 (1929), 176–82.

M. C. J. Putnam, *CPh* 64 (1969) 235–6.

37

There is a jumping shop, nine doors along from the temple of Castor and Pollux; Lesbia's lovers forgather there, by the hundred, to boast of their lecherous achievements, scornful of all who are not members of the club; and she sits with them.

Poem 37 amounts, in short, to a transposition into the comic-satiric mode of the data of Poem 58 and the last stanza of Poem 11. The factual, descriptive note imposed by the slacker form need not seriously challenge our credulity. Transposed to the forensic mode, the data reappear little changed, assuming Lesbia is Clodia, in Cicero's picture of her — e.g. *Cael.* 49, or *Cael.* 36; in one case the setting is the house on the Palatine where Clodia entertains her lovers in droves; in the other, the garden by the river from which she could watch at her leisure the young men who came to swim, and pick out those she fancied. Did she frequent a drinking-shop as well — or is the *taberna* her house and is the word *taberna* part of the insult? Did C. carry out his threat to show his contempt for the habitués by scrawling obscenities on the façade? Or is his threatened exploit another transposition — and Poem 37 the gesture of contempt he means? Are these the *iambi* Lesbia wanted burnt (Poem 36)?

Egnatius, singled out for special treatment in lines 17–20, is dealt with in the grand manner in Poem 39 (probably the earlier of the two — see introduction to Poem 39).

Metre: limping iambics.

1. *salax taberna*: 'jumping shop'; cf. the *fumosa taberna* of the *Copa*, attributed to Virgil. We begin, in the true style of lampoon, with a fine, vigorous line and no words minced.

contubernales: i.e. habitués of the same *taberna*.

2. *a pilleatis nona fratribus pila*: *pila* is vocative, in apposition to *taberna*; i.e. at the ninth pillar, counting from the temple of Castor and Pollux (on the south side of the Forum close to the steep north face of the Palatine — where Clodia had her house), here called *fratres pilleati* because of the caps (*pillei*) which they are usually represented as wearing on coins, etc. The *pila* was often used to advertise a shopkeeper's wares; Horace, e.g., remarks (*S.* 1. 4. 71) *nulla taberna meos habeat neque pila libellos*.

4. *quidquid est puellarum*: cf. 31. 14 *quidquid est domi cachinnorum*.

5. *confutuere*: In this compound (found only here) the preverb *con-* as usual stresses that the job is done properly. The line begins with a dactyl (unless the second u is consonantal).

putare ceteros hircos: Dependent, like *confutuere*, on 3 *putatis*, via 4 *solis licere*, '[and reckon you have the exclusive right] to reckon others goats'; i.e. coarse, unsophisticated creatures, perhaps evil-smelling, too (like the reputed *trux caper* which plagues Rufus in 69. 5–6); *putatis . . . putare* would be awkward, if unintentional, but it is clear from 7 *putatis* and 9 *putate* that the point is being made by repetition that the *contubernales* thought a lot of their own opinion. [Herrmann's *putere*, favoured by HERESCU, '[reckon] all other goats to stink', is ingenious, but the change of construction (*putere* must jump across *licere* to depend directly on *putatis*) is harsh.]

6. *continenter*: 'in a row'.

sedetis: picked up by 8 *sessores* and 14 *consedit*.

insulsi: the *contubernales* sit around and talk big, but they are a stupid lot.

7. *an ducenti?*: 'or are there two hundred of you?' Cf. 11. 18 *quos . . . tenet trecentos*.

non putatis ausurum: 'you think I won't dare'.

8. *una*: the adverb = *eodem tempore*.

irrumare: for the literal meaning and the figurative meaning ('show one's contempt for') see on 16. 1.

9. *atqui putate*: 'well, go on reckoning'.

10. *sopionibus scribam*: By scrawling obscene drawings all over the façade of the *taberna* C. can claim in a sense to have performed the action denoted by *irrumare* in its literal meaning (though there is some doubt about which of the objects commonly depicted on walls is denoted by *sopio* — see Lenchantin; the word is elsewhere found only in *graffiti*, though some restore it in Petronius 22. 1). But the predominant meaning of *irrumare* now becomes the colloquial one, 'show contempt for'.

11. *nam mi*: [*nam me* V has not been satisfactorily emended; in *nam mi*, *mi* must be dative of the person interested — it can scarcely be taken as dative of the agent with *amata*; *mei*, the archaic spelling of *mi*, printed by some editors, is closer to the reading of the MSS.]

fugit: perfect.

12. *amata tantum quantum amabitur nulla*: The line, repeated slightly changed from 8. 5, makes it clear that the *puella* meant is the mistress of C.'s serious love poetry. Cf. 87. 1–2 and 58. 1–3.

13. *pro qua mihi sunt magna bella pugnata*: A further contribution to the emotional build-up begun in the previous line, in preparation for the bitter anticlimax of 14 *consedit istic*.

14. *consedit*: perfect tense; 'has taken her seat', =has settled down.

14–20. Lesbia has two groups of lovers: (1) 'men of rank and fortune' (*boni beatique*) — all of them, and (2) 'small-time back-street lechers' (*pusilli et semitarii moechi*) — and all of them, too; prominent in the second group is Egnatius. Cf. 11. 17–20.

16. *semitarii*: i.e. frequenting *semitae*; found only here. Cf. 58. 4. *moechi*: cf. 11. 17 *cum suis uiuat ualeatque moechis*.

17. *une de capillatis*: 'you outstanding member of the long-haired mob'; *une* is vocative (a rare form). For the sense ('you and you alone') see on 10. 17 *unum me*. Smart young men wore their hair long.

18. *cuniculosae Celtiberiae fili*: 'you son of the Celtiberian bunny-land' (Copley). The word *cuniculus* denoted specifically a Spanish rabbit and Egnatius (as we see in Poem 39) came from Spain; the Spanish rabbit, noted for its long, soft hair (cf. 25. 1 *mollior cuniculi capillo*), was therefore an appropriate emblem for Egnatius.

19. *opaca quem bonum facit barba*: 'whose thick beard gives him social status'. Short ones were the rage among the smart set, full ones were perhaps more conservative, more aristocratic taste (*bonus* =a supporter of the Senatorial party); cf. Cicero's remark (*Cael.* 33, of Appius, the Censor, Clodia's ancestor) *non hac barbula qua ista* [Clodia] *delectatur sed illa horrida quam in statuis antiquis atque imaginibus uidemus*. Egnatius' leg, we may suspect, is being pulled: despite his efforts to shine in good society (cf. line 20 and Poem 39) he never gets things quite right.

20. *defricatus urina*: see 39. 17–21.

See:

N. I. Herescu, 'Autour de la *salax taberna*' in *Hommages à L. Herrmann* (1960) 431–5.

38

There is a wry note in C.'s protestation of affliction which should
warn us against supposing him on his deathbed, or even prostrate
with overwhelming grief; clearly things are not going well, but he
has heart left to upbraid his friend in tones that betray a hint of
irony (6 *irascor tibi*) for his omission to provide an appropriately
plangent exercise in catharsis. C.'s friend was probably Quintus
Cornificius, who was to become well known as an orator and a
man of literary tastes, and served with distinction under Julius
Caesar during the civil wars and married, it seems, the daughter
of Orestilla, Catiline's widow (see Neudling 52–7).

Metre: hendecasyllabics.

1. *malest . . . tuo Catullo*: 'things are not going well for your
Catullo'; for the colloquialism cf. 14. 10 *non est mi male* and 3.
13 *at uobis male sit*.

2. *me hercule, et laboriose*: = 'Lord, they're not! things are really
tough!' Strong words, but they suggest the irony of urbane self-
control, not the depth of despair. BAKER suggests that *laboriose*
after the ejaculation *me hercule* is meant to touch off associations
in the reader's mind with the labours of Hercules (cf. 55.
13 *Herculi labos*). The e of *me* is elided, but not the final e of
hercule; attempts to remove the hiatus are probably needless. Cf.
3. 16 and see on 10. 27.

3. *et magis magis in dies et horas*: A valid clue? If C.'s grief were
occasioned by the death of a friend (as COPLEY suggests) it would
be a careless descent to rhetoric to claim his grief worsened every
day and hour — the passage of time alleviates loss. It should
follow that C.'s unhappiness arises from a situation in which he is
still embroiled — a disintegrating love affair, for example; *magis
magis* also 64. 274.

4. *quod minimum facillimumque est*: 'something very easily done,
a very simple thing to ask'. C. means the act of consoling a friend;
but his words should fit the act of consolation he expected: the

poem, i.e., which he has in mind in 7–8 can scarcely be on an ambitious scale.

5. *allocutione*: i.e. (in view of 7–8) a consolatory poem. For such an *allocutio* in verse see Horace's ode to Tibullus (on the loss of a mistress — stolen by a wealthier lover), *Carm.* I. 33. See on 68. 1–10.

6. *sic meos amores*: Clearly a reproach, justifying C.'s plaintive-peevish *irascor tibi* ('I'm cross with you'). The words do not in themselves make sense — but the sense is easily imagined as completed by an exclamatory infinitive, of which *meos amores* can, syntactically speaking, be either subject (in the accusative case because the whole is an exclamation) or object.

Idiomatically the most natural meaning to attach to *meos amores* is 'my love', i.e. the object of C.'s affection — in other words his mistress; see on 6. 16. COPLEY objects that this inter-pretation disrupts the unity of the poem by introducing a third party. But if the reason for C.'s grief is, as seems *a priori* not unlikely, that his affair with Lesbia is on the rocks, then (1) Lesbia is very much at the centre of the poem; (2) it is understand-able if C. can manage no more than an incompletely formulated reference to her. It must be remembered, however, (1) that the function of the ellipse is to suggest thought incompletely formu-lated, rather than thought fully formulated but incompletely expressed (cf. the angry *quos ego . . .* attributed to Neptune by Virgil, *A.* 1. 135); (2) that, though *meos amores* can stand for Lesbia, what C. has written is *meos amores* — not, e.g., *meam puellam*; the words retain, i.e., an allusive imprecision, effective in a context which depends so much on what is left unsaid. (An alternative is to suppose that *meos amores* = 'my affection', i.e. for Cornificius; in that case Cornificius is reproached for doing so little to return C.'s affection.)

8. *maestius lacrimis Simonideis*: 'sadder than the tears of Simon-ides'. COPLEY 127 remarks that the name Simonides 'must elicit an instant and single response, as *Shakespeare* would elicit "plays," *Keats*, "lyric," or *Milton* "Paradise Lost."' Now there seems to be

no disagreement as to the idea that the name of Simonides would suggest to the ancient reader: it is the idea of death and of songs of lament for death.' C. wants, i.e., a poem from his friend; it need not be long (see above on line 4), but it should be sad — as sad as Cornificius can make it; only thus can C. hope to be distracted from his grief. Since the poem is to serve as a distraction, its subject need not be related to the reason for C.'s grief. So much the better, surely, if it were not.

See:

Sheridan Baker, 'Catullus 38', *CPh* 55 (1960), 37–8.

Frank O. Copley, 'Catullus c. 38', *TAPhA* 87 (1956), 125–9.

39

Egnatius is one of the long-haired, bearded habitués of the *salax taberna* of Poem 37 — a little shaggier than the rest and distinguished by a peculiar habit of oral hygiene upon which C. now expatiates. In Poem 37 C. was in the mood to add Egnatius to the list of Lesbia's lovers — even to single him out for special ridicule; Poem 39 half endears him to us; we feel he is closer to the Arrius of Poem 84 than to the Aemilius of Poem 97. Egnatius is the eternal hanger-on: the man who means well, but never quite grasps what is happening around him; who exudes amiability, wants to be a social success — and gets on everybody's nerves. It is tempting to identify him with a didactic poet mentioned by Macrobius (6. 5. 2 and 12), who quotes two fragments (*FPL* pp. 65–6) from a *de Rerum Natura* — both very Lucretian, the second also worthy of a New Poet: *roscida noctiuagis astris labentibu' Phoebe | pulsa loco cessit concedens lucibus altis.* Perhaps it was his literary aspirations, as much as his passion for being in the swim, that set him in the queue at the *salax taberna*.

The careful build-up for the concluding *coup de massue* in 17–21 suggests a devastating joke sprung for the first time; 37. 20 is in that case a cross-reference and Poem 39 the earlier of the two.

The more indulgent, gaily contemptuous tone of 39 supports this conclusion. The lines are notable for their loose, colloquial style — they read like some early Satires of Horace.

Structure: The 21 lines fall into three stanzas: 1–8, 9–16, and the final insult 17–21. The second stanza is tied to the first by an ambiguity constructed round 8 *urbanum* and 10 *urbanus*. The third stanza is tied to the second by the fresh look it forces us to take at 14 *qui puriter lauit dentes*.

Metre: limping iambics.

1–8. What gets on one's nerves about Egnatius is the flashing grin with which he responds (*renidet*) to every situation. The four-fold repetition of *renidet* suggests how boring this becomes. Egnatius means well, of course; but it makes the irritating fellow sound sillier if C. pretends that Egnatius wants to advertise the whiteness of his teeth (1 *quod candidos habet dentes* — it is the first thing we are told about him in the poem); at the same time the ground is prepared for stanza 3.

2. *renidet*: The word denotes the flash of reflected light when Egnatius bares his teeth. His dense beard (37. 19 *opaca barba*) must have heightened the effect.

usquequaque: 'all over the place', 'on every conceivable occasion'; a colloquialism (cf. Caelius to Cicero, *Fam.* 8. 15. 2 *usquequaque, inquis, se Domitii male dant*), possibly a little old-fashioned (it occurs in a wise saw quoted by Cicero, *Fam.* 7. 16. 1).

2–3. *ad rei . . . subsellium*: Egnatius, i.e., is sitting in court, along with other supporters of the defendant, listening to one of the speakers for the defence; cf. Caelius to Cicero, *Fam.* 8. 8. 1 *simul atque audiui, inuocatus ad subsellia rei occurro*.

4–5. *si ad pii rogum fili | lugetur . . . cum . . .*: The same syntactical pattern as in lines 2–3 because whatever the circumstances Egnatius' behaviour is the same; *lugetur*, like 2 *uentum est*, is impersonal passive.

6. *quidquid est*: 'whatever the occasion'. Egnatius is the subject of *ubicumque est* and the verbs in line 7.

7. *hunc habet morbum*: 'it's a disease the man has'; there is an

echo perhaps in Seneca, *Cl.* 2. 6. 4 *morbum esse, non hilaritatem, semper adridere ridentibus.*

8. *elegantem . . . neque urbanum*: The function of *elegantem* is to limit the reader's reaction to *urbanum* — he takes it for granted that the sense intended is that roughly synonymous with *elegantem.*

9–16. *urbanus* is now given its literal meaning. Egnatius, it turns out, is disqualified by birth from being *urbanus.* But the long *si*-clause once more draws the reader off upon a false scent. As C. ticks off nationality after nationality, we naturally assume C. is listing non-*urbani* (in the literal sense) considered socially acceptable in Roman society. We expect Egnatius to be excluded from the list and we think we know on what grounds.

9. [The line as it stands in the MSS is a syllable short. The addition of *te*, either (as here) after *est* or before *est* seems an acceptable repair.] 'you should be warned'; *monendum* is impersonal and *te* its direct object — a construction found a number of times in Lucretius (e.g. 2. 1129 *manus dandum est*) and occasionally elsewhere in republican Latin.

mihi: dative of the agent.

bone: the vocative of *bonus* seems to have an ironical flavour.

11. *parcus*: [The reading of V, which some change to *pinguis* on the grounds that it is (1) more appropriate to the context (the other adjectives describe physical characteristics); (2) more appropriate to the reputation of the Umbrians; (3) required by a gloss on *pinguis* (*Glossaria Latina* 1. 443 Lindsay) which cites a corrupt but recognizable version of C.'s line. But the line falls flat if the two epithets are synonymous — clearly a contrast (the point of which is lost on us) is implied between *Vmber* and *Etruscus.*]

12. *ater atque dentatus*: 'black (i.e. swarthy) and toothy'.

13. *ut meos quoque attingam*: 'to include my people, too'. The Transpadani did not become Roman citizens till 49 B.C.

14. *puriter lauit*: =*pure lauat*; (*lauit* is present indicative of a third-declension form — the metre excludes the perfect of *lauare*); both words seem to have an old-fashioned ring, which may

be intended also in Horace, *S.* 1. 5. 24 *ora manusque tua lauimus,
Feronia, lympha.*

15. *renidere usquequaque*: the words act as a summary of lines 1–8.

   te nollem: ironically polite in preparation for the blunt,
crushing statement of line 16.

16. *risu inepto*, etc.: with the syntactical pattern cf. 22. 14, 27. 4,
99. 2 and 14.

17–21. The case against Egnatius seemed concluded with lines
15–16. It turns out the most damning charge is yet to come. Why
does Egnatius distribute those flashing grins of his so freely? He
grins, we have been told, because he is proud of his teeth (1 *quod
candidos habet dentes*). And what have his teeth got that other
people's haven't? Well, among the Celtiberians there is a
custom. . . . Oddly enough, if we can believe Diodorus (5. 33. 5)
and Strabo (3. 164), what C. says is correct.

17. *nunc*: 'as it is'; logical, not temporal.

   Celtiber es: [like line 9, this line lacks a syllable; *es* provides
a very probable repair.]

18. *hoc*: ablative.

19. *russam*: a rare by-form (the common words for 'red' are
ruber and *rufus*); the natural interpretation is that Egnatius rubbed
his gums till they were inflamed.

20–1. *iste uester . . . te*: The illogicality of colloquial statement:
'The more resplendent the dental equipment you chaps have, the
more that means that you, Egnatius, have imbibed . . .'; with
iste uester cf. 29. 13 *ista uestra* and 17. 21 *iste meus stupor*.

20. *dens*: collective, as in 64. 315.

21. *bibisse . . . loti*: C. ends with an appropriately imagination-
boggling exaggeration; for *loti* cf. Isidorus (11. 1. 138) *urina . . .
uolgo lotium dicitur.*

                          See:

Cat. Rev. 63–4.

40

A friendly tip to Ravidus (1 *miselle Rauide*): has he not the sense to
see he is heading for trouble? Worse is to come if he does not
watch his step.

The tone — dry and incisive — fixes the level of intent. C. has
the situation well under control; poised for the attack, he pauses
to give his victim fair warning before it is too late. Contrast the
almost hysterical restraint, the utter seriousness of Poem 58.
Though nothing is known of Ravidus, we may assume that C. is
relying on his readers to connect these lines with Poems 15, 21,
etc. — they, rather than the Lesbia cycle, represent the kind of
full-scale attack with which Ravidus is threatened.

Metre: hendecasyllabics.

1. *mala mens*: cf. 15. 14.

miselle: cf., for the note of (slightly amused) pity, 35. 14.

Rauide: The last syllable must he elided (an unparalleled
licence in this metre) or else *Rauide* (assuming the name correctly
given in the MSS) must be pronounced *Raude*; for examples of
such syncopated colloquial pronunciations see Fordyce.

2. *iambos*: Many hold that in C. *iambi* denotes a genre ('verses
in the iambic mode', i.e. 'lampoons') — what Aristotle called
ἰαμβικὴ ἰδέα (*Poetics* 1449b); see on 36. 5 and 54. 6–7.

3. *non bene aduocatus*: 'misguidedly invoked'.

5. *an ut*: elliptical = 'or are you behaving like this in order
to . . .?'

in ora uulgi: An echo, probably, of Ennius' boast (in his
epitaph) *uolito uiuus per ora uirum*. Cf. Propertius 3. 9. 32 *uenies tu
quoque in ora uirum*. Contrast the plural in this and similar expres-
sions with the singular in such expressions as *in ore uulgi*.

6. *qualubet*: 'by any means', i.e. at any cost; cf. 76. 14.

7. *eris*: = *notus eris*.

quandoquidem: C. rather favours this somewhat weighty con-

junction; cf. 33. 6, 64. 218 and 101. 5; Lucretius uses it 23 times —
the word had perhaps a solemn or portentous ring; it does not
seem to occur in Cicero's correspondence.

meos amores: see on 6. 16 and cf. 15. 1 and 21. 4.

8. *cum*: = 'at the risk of', 'though it involved'; cf. Plautus,
Bacch. 503 *illud hercle cum malo fecit suo.*

longa: The lampoon, i.e., will not be quickly forgotten. With
the idea cf. 6. 16–17 *uolo te ac tuos amores | ad caelum lepido uocare
uersu.*

41

Some uncomplimentary *uersiculi* on the subject of Ameana, 'the
girl-friend of the bankrupt from Formiae' (a phrase repeated in
43. 5). The bankrupt is Mamurra (see on Poem 29). His identity
is scarcely concealed by the periphrasis — Horace, *S.* 1. 5. 37,
calls Formiae *urbs Mamurrarum*, and in 57. 4 Mamurra is de-
scribed by C. as having the imprint of Formiae upon him.

Mamurra was with Caesar in Gaul 58–55 B.C. as *praefectus
fabrum* (see on Poem 29). He does not seem to have returned a
bankrupt. Are Poems 41 and 43 earlier than 58 B.C.?

Structure: Lines 1–4 are mock-expository: they make a show of
setting out the data required for the poem's hypothesis, but
amount in reality to a series of defamatory assertions about
Ameana, flung out in quick succession. This fourfold opening
blow is followed (5–8) by some stern words of advice to Ameana's
friends and relations, ostensibly expressing C.'s concern for her
health, but in fact providing C. with a further opportunity for
abuse: Ameana must be off her head — a look in the mirror
would tell her that what she asks is absurd. Note the increasing
mockery of the quadrupled *puella* in lines 1, 3, 5 and 7, and the
way these *uersiculi* climb from the level (in line 1) of something
that might be scrawled on a lavatory wall to something near to
poetry in the last line.

1

Metre: hendecasyllabics. Lines 2 and 3 begin with a trochee, lines 1 (presumably), 5 and 6 with an iambus.

1. *Ameana*: [The MSS have *a mean a* or *a me an a*. Clearly a vocative is required and presumably the girl's name.] As Ameana is not found elsewhere, various emendations have been proposed. See Neudling 3.

2. *tota milia . . . decem*: 'ten thousand sesterces' — a tidy sum. The fee accepted, it seems, by the pimp Silo in Poem 103. It is possible that Ameana is reclaiming a loan (so Ellis) and that C. misrepresents by innuendo the nature of the service rendered; but more likely that the whole assertion is a light-hearted libellous fantasy.

3. *turpiculo*: 'somewhat repulsive' — a pretence of accurate, detached assessment.

4. Again a pretence of factual statement, but in reality the climax to a series of innuendoes. For the ease with which Mamurra ran through several fortunes see 29. 11–19.

5. *propinqui*: the insane became the legal responsibility of their family.

7. *nec rogare*, etc.: 'it is not her practice to ask the image-filled bronze what she looks like'. For references to bronze mirrors see Ellis. Was Ameana more concerned with another kind of bronze (cf. our 'brass' = 'money')? [The MSS have *et*. Froehlich's conjecture *aes*, proposed in 1849, though rejected by Kroll, Friedrich and Lenchantin, is regarded as certain by most modern editors. Housman called it one of the half-dozen finest emendations to the text of Catullus.] The germ of the idea is found in an epigram attributed to Plato (*AP* 6. 1), in which an ageing courtesan dedicates to Venus the mirror for which she has no more use.

8. *imaginosum*: A word found only here. Editors who do not accept *aes* sometimes change *imaginosum* to *imaginosa* and apply the word to Ameana 'full of fancies'. But the circumlocution 'image-filled bronze' is probably intended as an improvement on Callimachus' description of a mirror as 'translucent bronze' (*Hymn to Pallas* 21 διαυγέα χαλκόν). Note how the word order

(=*nec aes imaginosum rogare solet qualis sit*) delays the final blow.

See:

C. Deroux, *Latomus* 28 (1969) 1060–64.

42

Anxious to recover a set of writing tablets from a girl who refuses to restore them, C. enlists the aid of his hendecasyllabics in a *flagitatio* — a piece of rough justice sanctioned by popular custom, in which a complainant sought redress by exposing an offender to public ridicule (see FRAENKEL).

Poem 42 carries the experiment with dramatic form in Poem 36 a stage further, though many shy at taking Lesbia for the original of the pen portrait in lines 7–9. ('The love which had never died in Catullus' heart', says Lenchantin, 'would not have permitted an attack in such vulgar terms on the woman he loved, however degraded'; the most popular rival candidate is the Ameana of Poems 41 and 43.) Much depends on whether we accept *uestra* in line 4, and on how far we press the logic of the poem's hypothesis.

Structure: 1–2 — calling all hendecasyllabics! 3–6 — briefing. 7–10 — here she comes! 11–12 — chorus. 13–18 — consultation. 19–20 — chorus as before. 21–3 — change of tune. 24 — chorus modified.

Metre: hendecasyllabics.

1–2. Strictly speaking, *hendecasyllabi* denotes lines of verse, as when C. warned Asinius that, if he did not return the napkin he had pinched, he would be in for *hendecasyllabos trecentos* (12. 10) — a stream of verse, not necessarily a large number of individual poems. But by a common and natural idiom, a poet's output in a particular genre is referred to by the name of the metre — particularly if there is no obvious unity of theme.

The *hendecasyllabi* by means of which C. hopes to secure the return of his notebooks are, of course, the verses which constitute Poem 42. The hypothesis however on which the poem rests invites us to think of the *hendecasyllabi* as poems already written and now summoned to C.'s assistance. The emphasis C. lays on

rounding up *all* his poems, on gathering them *from all sides* (2
undique) makes it a reasonable inference that C.'s *hendecasyllabi*
had not been published as a collection; we may think of them as
circulating individually among C.'s friends and acquaintances, or
as having individually taken up residence with their addressees,
to whom they would have been sent privately upon completion.

4–5. *uestra . . . pugillaria*: A set of writing tablets, such as could
be held in the fist; more commonly called *pugillares*. Observe that
what has to be recovered is a set of tablets, not a poem, or poems.
The tablets passed perhaps back and forth between C. and the girl
that C. is now disposed to call a *moecha putida*, taking her messages,
as well as poems addressed to her or sent for her approval, and
bringing back answering messages or witticisms — like the *doctae
tabellae* of Propertius (3. 23), which went astray on their return
journey, leaving Propertius to speculate what message they carried
to him from Cynthia. Cf. Ovid, *Am.* 1. 11 and 12.

Most editors alter *uestra*, the reading of V, to *nostra*; the repair
is not clearly called for, and indeed it deprives the *hendecasyllabi* of
a *locus standi* in the *flagitatio*; as FRAENKEL points out, the poems
are the legitimate owners of the tablets on which they originally
came into existence. Cf. the *tabellae* used by C. and Calvus for
working out *uersiculi* in Poem 50. (Once the poem had been worked
out on wax, the poet, if he was pleased with it, transcribed
it onto papyrus. Cf. 35. 2.)

But if we keep *uestra*, we should accept the effect on the logic of
the poem's hypothesis. The missing tablets must in that case be
those on which C. worked out the first clean version of a number
of his poems. How have these come into the girl's hands? Fordyce's
suggestion that she had stolen them, or picked them up when C.
dropped them, will hardly do: if the girl has stolen the tablets, the
fact should be stated or plainly hinted at. A more reasonable
assumption is that C. sent the girl a poem (or poems); perhaps the
girl was Ipsitilla and the poem sent Poem 32, though in that case
C. must have known he was risking his tablets. It seems more
likely that the recipient was Lesbia, and that a lovers' quarrel

(that alluded to in Poem 36, say) prevented the return of the
tablets. The fact that certainty is impossible should warn us that
we are letting our curiosity extend beyond what C. has fixed as
the relevant data for his poem.

4. *reddituram*: *se* is omitted, as in 36. 7 *daturam*.

5. *si pati potestis*: probably idiomatic = 'how do you like that?'

7. *quae sit, quaeritis?*: A formal device, to get in some abuse, and
to advance the drama. Observe, however, that the poems which
ask the question cannot have been addressed to her.

uidetis: not a general statement, but within the drama = 'here
she comes!'

8. *turpe incedere*: Ovid, *Ars* 3. 299 *est et in incessu pars non con-
tempta decoris*; he goes on to give details. Cf. Cicero on Clodia,
Cael. 49 *si denique ita sese gerat non incessu solum sed ornatu atque comitatu
. . . non solum meretrix sed etiam proterua meretrix procaxque uideatur.*
But if the *moecha* has the right idea, she is inexpert in the execution
of it — her way of walking only gets on your nerves (*moleste*).

mimice ac moleste: The *mimae* were the cinema stars of the
ancient world. Cicero, e.g., is surprised and somewhat scandalized
to find among his fellow-guests at a dinner party the famous mime
actress Cytheris, mistress of his host, Volumnius, and later of
Mark Antony (and later still, it seems, of the poet Cornelius
Gallus), *Fam.* 9. 26. 2: *non, me hercule, suspicatus sum illam adfore!*
FRAENKEL 48: 'if we press our lips tightly together to produce
the threefold m-sound, we shall not remain deaf to the contempt in
this half-line'.

9. *ridentem . . . Gallicani*: Her pout looks like a dog showing its
teeth. Arrian, *Cyneg.* 3. 1, remarks that Gallic hounds were
repulsive to look at.

10. *reflagitate*: picks up 6 *reflagitemus*.

11–12. Repetition with the order varied is of course a common
feature of popular songs, jingles, etc.

11. *codicillos*: = *pugillaria*. Cf. Cicero, *Fam.* 9. 26. 1 (opening
words of a letter) *accubueram hora nona, cum ad te harum exemplum in
codicillis exaraui.*

13–14. An aside flung at the girl.

13. *assis*: genitive of price; cf. 5. 3 *omnes unius aestimemus assis!*

lutum, lupanar: strong words. Cicero, *Pis.* 62, calls Piso a *lutum* among other things; *lupanar* is added for alliterative effect — and with 3, etc. *moecha* in mind.

14. *perditius*: 'more corrupt'. Cf. Cicero, *Att.* 11. 18. 2 *sed hoc perditius, in quo nunc sum, fieri nihil potest.*

potest: [*potes* V; *potest* Kroll, Schuster and FRAENKEL.] With the formula cf. 22. 13.

quid: with *si*.

15. *sed non est tamen hoc satis putandum*: 'we must not let it go at this' — i.e. give in: C. once more addresses the *hendecasyllabi*.

16–17. FRAENKEL 48: 'the soft backsound of the English R will not do; we have to round our tongue and produce unashamedly a series of rolling and sustained Italian R's. It is this sound above all that here suggests the ugliness of the dog. To the Roman ear the snarling of a dog was disagreeable; at an early stage they called R the "littera canina".' Cf. 63. 78–83.

16. *quod si non aliud potest*: 'but if nothing else is possible'; cf. 72. 7 *qui potis est, inquis?*

17. *ferreo*: 'hard', 'brazen'.

exprimamus: 'force upon'. The word implies effort; it is also the word used of sculptors, etc., moulding the features of a portrait.

21. *nil proficimus*: 'we're getting nowhere'; the pedagogic first person plural ('we have got this wrong, haven't we?'); also 62. 15; contrast 23 *potestis*, and see on 22 *uobis*.

22. *uobis*: [*nobis* V, adopted by Kroll, Lenchantin and Schuster; *uobis* θ, adopted by Mynors and FRAENKEL.]

24. *pudica et proba, redde codicillos*: cf. Horace's ironical palinode, *Ep.* 17. 40 *tu pudica, tu proba.*

See:

Eduard Fraenkel, 'Two poems of Catullus', *JRS* 51 (1961), 46–53.
Anthony J. Marshall, *CR* 18 (1968) 16–17. (on *flagitatio*)

43

Ameana again, as is indicated by the repetition *decoctoris amica Formiani* from 41. 4. This time she is dealt with more leniently — C. is more concerned with the problem he will attack again in Poem 86 than with abuse. But if the Quintia of Poem 86 has everything except *It*, Ameana fails to score a single point. And yet fools rave about her! The scene is perhaps Verona (see on line 6).

Metre: hendecasyllabics.

1–4. An ironical apostrophe, mock-lyric in tone — the sort of ecstatic list of a girl's good points that we have in Philodemus, *AP* 5. 132, turned upside down. The sixfold repetition of *nec* (each *nec* introducing a descriptive ablative, only to reject it) forms a series of hammer-blows dismissing Ameana on count after count. The lines make an interesting check-list.

1. *salue*: cf. 31. 12 and 67. 2.

nec minimo . . . naso: 'whose nose is by no means small'; cf. 41. 3 *turpiculo puella naso*; Horace, in *S.* 1. 2. 93, derides a girl as *nasuta*.

2. *bello pede*: small and dainty — Horace, ibid., complains that the girl is *pede longo*.

nigris ocellis: cf. Horace, *Carm.* 1. 32. 11–12 *Lycum nigris oculis nigroque | crine decorum*.

3. *longis digitis*: i.e. slender.

ore: 'lips'.

4. *nec sane nimis elegante lingua*: 'and certainly none too elegant of tongue'. C. puts it the way he does to preserve an appearance of continuity. But in this list of negative attributes the final item represents a climax of understatement. Ameana's looks were bad enough; but when she opened her mouth. . . . Cf. 60. 5 *nimis fero corde*; with *elegante* (ablative in -e) cf. 68. 99 *infelice*.

5. *decoctoris amica Formiani*: see on 41. 4; the repetition identifies Ameana without naming her (cf. the repetition of 23. 1 at 24. 5).

Most punctuate as part of the opening sentence, as in Poem 41,
where the line caps the preceding line. But it is better taken as a
fresh sentence. Poem 43 then, like Poem 41, falls into two
quatrains, and gains in liveliness as well as balance. Cf. *passer
deliciae meae puellae*, vocative in 2. 1, nominative in 3. 4. Though
fond of repeating lines (they act as cross-references), C. usually
avoids verbatim echoes; see, however, on 16. 14.

6. *ten*: = *tene*.

prouincia: Ameana, i.e., though they rave about her in 'the
province' = *Gallia cisalpina*, might fare differently in Rome.
Mamurra, Ameana's lover, was *praefectus fabrum* with Caesar in
Gaul, returning to Rome apparently after Caesar's first expedition
to Britain. Did he meet Ameana in 'the province' — at Caesar's
winter headquarters in Verona perhaps?

8. *o saeclum insapiens et infacetum!*: 'how witless the times, how
devoid of taste!' Praise, i.e., of Ameana condemns the critic. With
infacetum cf. 22. 14 *idem infaceto est infacetior rure*.

See:

C. Deroux, *Latomus* 28 (1969) 1060–64.

44

A letter of thanks addressed to C.'s little place in the country: his
stay there has enabled him to shake off the dreadful cold he
caught while reading one of Sestius' speeches. C. can tell a joke
well at his own expense. The butt, however, of this discursive,
bantering fantasy is Sestius, for whom he reserves more than a hint
of malice.

Structure: The formal skeleton consists of line 1 + lines 6–7 +
16–17:

> O funde noster seu Sabine seu Tiburs . . .
> fui libenter in tua suburbana
> uilla, malamque pectore expuli tussim . . .
> quare refectus maximus tibi grates
> ago, meum quod non es ultu' peccatum.

This is expanded by an explanatory parenthesis following the

opening line (lines 2–5), and then by a second explanatory
parenthesis at line 7 (lines 8–9). The latter, however, calls for a
fuller explanation (lines 10–15), picked up in the tailpiece (lines
18–21, 'next time . . .').

Cf. Cicero, *Fam.* 7. 26 (Cicero has retired to his villa in Tuscany,
to recover from an attack of gastritis following a dinner party).

Metre: limping iambics.

1. *o funde*: The vocative personifies, and C.'s farm becomes the
recipient of a verse epistle — perhaps even a divinity to whom C.
can offer mock thanks for his cure (which would explain C.'s
anxiety to ensure the farm is properly addressed); cf. Poem 31. A
small estate near Rome was fashionable, as is evident from
Cicero's numerous references to *fundi* and *suburbana*; the most
famous is probably Horace's unpretentious Sabine farm; cf. the
uillula quae Sironis eras of Virgil, *Cat.* 8.

noster: 'my'.

seu Sabine: C. pretends to hesitate, hence the vocative
(instead of the more deliberate *seu Sabinus es*, etc.).

Tiburs: adjectival, 'near Tibur' (Tivoli) — quite the smart-
est place for a villa; the *ager Sabinus* lay just beyond.

2. *autumant*: an old-fashioned word (mock-solemn here).

2–3. *quibus . . . laedere*: 'who take no pleasure in hurting
Catullus'; the complaint is double-edged — there'd be no point
in denying C. a fashionable address if he were not anxious to
possess one. With *cordi esse* cf. 64. 158, 81. 5 and 95. 9.

6. *fui libenter*: = 'I enjoyed staying', a common idiom in
Cicero's letters.

7. *malamque pectore expuli tussim*: The reading of a late codex.
[*aliamque pectore expulsus sim* V].

9. *dum . . . appeto*: The verb is present, though the reference is
to the past — common when the *dum*-clause specifies the time
within which the action of the main verb takes place. Another
example in the next sentence.

dedit: the dislocated order (hyperbaton) perhaps reinforces
the limping iambic metre. Cf. (also colloquial style) Horace, *S.* 1.

5. 72 *paene macros arsit dum turdos uersat in igni*; 2. 3. 211 *Aiax immeritos cum occidit desipit agnos.* Contrast 66. 18.

10. *Sestianus*: old-fashioned and literary for *Sestii*. The object of C.'s malice is Publius Sestius, the well-known stooge of the senatorial party, defended by Cicero in 56 B.C. along with Hortensius, Licinius Calvus (the friend of C. — see Poem 50) and M. Crassus — an impressive quartet; Sestius had raised an armed band against Clodius. C.'s assertion that he was a frigid speaker is supported by Cicero's complaint, while absent from Rome in 51 B.C., that the witticisms of other people, 'even jokes from Sestius' repertoire (*Sestiana*)', (*Fam.* 7. 32. 1) were being attributed to himself.

dum uolo: practically causal, 'wishing'.

11–12. Several ambiguities here. The surface meaning is that Sestius' speech was 'utterly venomous and mischievous'; this sense of *pestilentia* is supported by the use of *pestis* of a person (='nuisance'). But the speech was no less unhealthy for those who merely read it, as C.'s experience proves. The play on words is helped by two further ambiguities: *legi* ('I read') can also mean in high style 'I traversed'; *pestilentia* ('mischief') is also used of places whose climate etc. is unhealthy: e.g. Cicero, *Agr.* 2. 26. 70 [*agrorum genus*] *propter pestilentiam uastum atque desertum.*

11. *orationem in Antium petitorem*: Nothing is known of the speech, or of 'the candidate Antius'. Line 21 implies that Sestius sent C. a copy along with the invitation to dinner.

13. *hic*: need =no more than 'thereupon'; but the sense 'here' supports the suggestion, half implied in the previous line, that the speech is an unhealthy region through which C. has had to make his way.

grauedo: our common cold. For the symptoms see Celsus 4. 5. 2 *nares claudit, uocem obtundit, tussim siccam mouet.* . . .

14. *usque, dum*: 'continually until'.

15. *otioque et urtica*: traditional treatments (see Celsus 4. 5. 8 and 4. 10. 4), but the zeugma and the poetic use of *-que* (=*et otio et urtica* — see on 102. 3 *meque*) should not be missed.

16–17. *maximas tibi grates ago*: mock-solemn; *grates* archaic for *gratias*. Cf. 49. 4–5.

17. *ulta'*: Most editors accept *ulta*, the reading of the MSS, though this necessitates a change of addressee from the *fundus* to the *uilla* of line 7 — harsh after the long address of 1–5. Muret's *ultu'* restores unity; *ulta* is easily explained as the correction of a careless scribe looking back only at line 7; the objection that the final s is dropped only once elsewhere in C. (116. 8), though the practice is common in Lucretius, is hardly conclusive in view of the free use of archaic words and forms in this poem (see on lines 2, 10 and 19).

peccatum: cf. 8 *non inmerenti*.

18–19. *nec deprecor . . . quin*: = 'I have no objection if'.

18. *iam*: = 'in the circumstances'.

nefaria scripta: the final a of *nefaria* here counts as a long syllable before the double consonant of *scripta*; see on 17. 24.

19. *recepso*: 'if I lay my hands on again', an archaic future form, equated in usage to a future perfect.

21. *qui tunc . . . legi*: The jest in the previous line misfires unless it prepares the way for a more telling point. Most likely both meanings of *legi* ('read' and 'traversed') are drawn out here, as in line 12. A play on *malum* ('of poor quality', and 'evil', i.e. 'malicious' or 'wreaking mischief') may also be intended. A pun (or more than one) seems required to underpin the clearly intended implication that Sestius runs a risk inviting such a guest — and that C. is in no mind to ward off the danger (18 *nec deprecor*) from his host.

legi: [*legit* V; *legi* Lachmann. If we keep *legit* here, we must read *legit* also in line 12. But *legit* could only mean that Sestius read his speech aloud in C.'s presence and 18–19 *si . . . recepso* is against this.]

See:

Vinzenz Buchheit, 'Catulls Dichterkritik in C. 36', *Hermes* 87 (1959), 313–15 (on Poem 44 as an attack on Sestius as a stylist).
C. P. Jones, 'Parody in Catullus 44', *Hermes* 96 (1968), 379–83.

45

A conversation between two lovers, in which each swears he loves
the other more. The elegance of the structure, the traditional
form, the lovers' unashamed rhetoric, an unusual descriptive
lushness — all emphasize that the scene is viewed through rose-
tinted glasses. At the same time we should miss neither the over-
tones implied by the confidence with which Cupid's approval is
assumed, nor the extravagant optimism of the final stanza. Line
22 points to a date round 55 B.C. — another reason for doubting
C.'s uncritical commitment to this charming vignette of romantic
love.

Structure: An improvement upon a traditional genre (amoebean
song) — a small-scale drama in which two rival singers cap one
another's songs; see on 62. 20–58 and cf. Theocritus 5 and 8 and
Virgil, *Ecl.* 3 and 7. Like Horace in *Carm.* 3. 9 (close comparison
is instructive), C. uses the form for an urbanely ironical study in
psychology. Each of the first two stanzas consists of a 7-line
sentence, introducing a speaker and quoting his words, followed
by a 2-line sentence reporting the reaction of Cupid. A third
8-line stanza (four couplets, each a sentence) expresses the poet's
enthusiastic appraisal of the situation.

Metre: hendecasyllabics.

1–7. After a suggestion of dramatic context (we enter in the
middle of the love scene), the duet begins with Septimius'
asseveration of desperate (3 *perdite*), life-long (4 *omnes . . . annos*)
love.

1. *Acmen*: Greek accusative. The name, though found in
inscriptions, presumably implies here that the girl was in the
bloom of youth and beauty (ἀκμὴ βίου =*flos aetatis*).

   suos amores: = 'mistress'; see on 6. 16.

   3. *perdite*: cf. 104. 3 *perdite amarem* and 91. 2 *in . . . hoc perdito amore*.
   porro: 'in time to come'. Cf. 68. 45.

   5. *quantum qui pote plurimum perire*: = 'just as much as ever a man

can be madly in love'; *qui = is* [*potest*] *qui*; *pote = potest* (see on 17. 24); *plurimum = maxime*; *perire* is lovers' cant for *perdite amare* (*L & S* II B 2). For similar idiomatic expressions involving *quantum* see *L & S* under *quantum* adv.

Septimius' protestation of life-long, passionate love is expressed in a burst of verbal fireworks that leaves us somewhat confused. Essentially, it is an elegant expansion of the colloquial *peream ni te amo*, 'may I die if I do not love thee' (cf. 92. 2 *me dispeream nisi amat*). (In Septimius' version of the colloquialism, *perire* is commandeered for the conditional clause (in its other sense, 'love desperately'), so that the sense 'die' has to be expressed by different means in the principal clause.) Lines 3–5 are Septimius' appropriately embroidered version of *ni te amo*. Lines 6–7 are his appropriately picturesque version of a sticky end.

The suspicion is hard to resist, however, that a play on the two senses of *perire* is intended (as in Propertius 2. 27). While the immediate context demands the sense 'love desperately', the sense 'die' is elicited by the wider context and refuses to be dismissed. The primary meaning of line 5 is 'as much as he who loves as desperately as man can' — an expansion of line 4; but we half entertain as well a meaning something like 'ranking with him who endures the worst of deaths' — an anticipation of lines 6–7. If the ambiguity is not fully resolved, that is not unfitting on an occasion when love has muddled thinking (see on lines 8–9).

6–7. Perhaps a reminiscence of Semonides, Fragment 12D (in Fordyce).

6. *Libya Indiaque*: The Romans often used -*que* where we should say 'or', but here it probably suggests light-hearted indifference on Septimius' part to the place of his demise. Libya and India are the two places where one might hope to find a lion.

7. *caesio*: 'green-eyed', usually only of persons; a translation of γλαυκῶπις; but perhaps a piece of erudition evoking the lion simile in *Il.* 20. 164–73, where a green-eyed lion attacks a young hunter.

8–9. Variously punctuated (*ut ante* can go with *sinistra* or with *dextra*) and much argued over. For a Cupid in attendance see 68. 133. Does Cupid, after an earlier disapproving sneeze to the right (or left), now sneeze approval to the left (or right)? Or do both sneezes indicate approval? What does *ut ante* mean? Whose left is meant anyway, and whose right? The moment we pause to question the evidence, we find we are uncertain, even about what actually occurred.

The phenomenon reported by C. as proof of Cupid's benevolence sounds like something less than proof to the reader uncommitted to the mood of romantic optimism which pervades the poem and to which C. pretends to surrender. Was the sneeze that counted in fact propitious? Was Cupid merely stifling his mirth at the lovers' innocence? (Cf. Venus' shifty laugh [*perfidum ridens*] in Horace, *Carm.* 3. 27. 67.) But if the purpose of C.'s words is to undercut idyllic optimism, they should preferably make some straightforward statement, rather than one that depends for clarification on special knowledge or ingenious argument. The old view that Cupid, on hearing Septimius' words, sneezed first on one side then the other — in rapid succession, presumably, and with equal enthusiasm each time (*ut ante*) — seems best: *ut ante*, i.e., does not refer to some separate prior occasion. In that case the question 'Which side first?' hardly arises since one sneeze follows the other; we may suppose that Cupid, doubtful himself which was the propitious side, was anxious to make doubly sure. Some hold that C. leaves it open to the reader to take *ut ante* with *sinistra* here and with *dextra* in 17–18 (vice versa rather less likely): that would add to the fun, and is consistent with C.'s habit of repeating a line or phrase with the meaning modified on second occurrence by a change of wording (e.g. 8. 3 and 8; 29. 2 and 10; 2. 1 and 3. 4) or by the intervening context (e.g. 16. 1 and 14).

10–18. Acme proceeds to cap Septimius' protestation of undying love, and wins equal approbation from Cupid.

10. *leuiter . . . reflectens*: 'tilting her head gently backwards' (she is still on Septimius' lap as in line 2), like Mars on the lap of Venus in Lucretius 1. 33–7:

> in gremium qui saepe tuum se
> reicit aeterno deuictus uulnere amoris,
> atque ita suspiciens tereti ceruice reposta
> pascit amore auidos inhians in te, dea, uisus,
> eque tuo pendet resupini spiritus ore.

11. *dulcis*: genitive rather than accusative.

  ebrios: drunk with love, as in Anacreon 17D: μεθύων ἔρωτι.

12. *illo purpureo ore*: cf. Simonides 44D; Horace, *Carm.* 3. 3. 12; and the discussion of *purpureus* in Fordyce.

13–16. The penalty Acme invokes (if what she asserts is not true) is the loss of the lover whose mistress she wishes to remain for ever. For *sic . . . ut* see on 17. 5.

13. *mea uita*: = 'my love', as in 104. 1 and 109. 1; cf. Cicero, *Fam.* 14. 2. 3 (to his wife) *obsecro te, mea uita*; again 14. 4. 1.

  Septimille: an endearing diminutive; cf. 47. 1 *Socration*.

14. *huic uni domino usque seruiamus*: The master meant is probably Cupid; *huic* because she knows he is there — she has heard him sneeze; to him, and to him alone (*uni*), she prays, may Septimius and she be forever slaves. (Another possibility is that *seruiamus* is plural for singular, and the master meant Septimius.)

16. *ignis . . . medullis*: cf. 35. 15.

17–18. Some punctuate these lines differently from 8–9, assuming that Cupid somehow behaves differently, as a result perhaps of Acme's acknowledgment of his presence. He still apparently sneezes approval each time.

19–26. The suspicion that C. has been speaking tongue in cheek, or is at any rate less emotionally committed to his tableau of idyllic love than he pretends, finds some confirmation in this concluding string of bland, emphatic pronouncements.

19. *ab auspicio bono*: the *auspicium bonum* must be that provided by Cupid.

21. *unam*: emphatic, like 14 *uni* and 23 *uno*.

  misellus: for *miser* of the unhappy lover see on 8. 1; the diminutive adds a hint of pathos, as in 35. 14.

22. *Syrias Britanniasque*: The plural captures Septimius'

extravagant unconcern for the life of romance and adventure —
unlike Horace's Iccius in *Carm.* 1. 29. C. refers, presumably, to
Caesar's campaigns in Britain (55 and 54 B.C., cf. Poems 11 and
29) and Crassus' expedition against the Parthians (he set out late
in 55 B.C.).

23. *uno in Septimio fidelis*: i.e. this time love will last; in Roman
love poetry lovers seldom protest inexperience.

24. *facit delicias*: = 'has fun' — a meiosis as in 74. 2 (in Plautus
the phrase seems to mean something like 'pull one's leg' — see
Men. 381, etc.). For *deliciae* see on 2. 1.

libidinesque: makes the meiosis a little plainer.

26. *auspicatiorem*: 'better omened'. The comparative (not found
again till Pliny, *Nat.* 13. 118) of the technical term *auspicatus*,
'shown by augury to be auspicious', is a piece of playful erudition.

See:

Sheridan Baker, 'The irony of Catullus' "Septimus and Acme" ',
CPh 53 (1958), 110–12.

C. M. Bowra, *AJPh* 79 (1958), 377–91, on the form of the love
duet.

H. Comfort, 'Analysis of technique in Catullus XLV', *TAPhA* 69
(1938), xxxiii.

H. Dietz, *Symbolae Osloenses* 44 (1969) 42–7.

J. B. Edwards, 'The irony of Catullus 45', *TAPhA* 59 (1928),
xxiii.

D. O. Ross Jr., 'Style and content in Catullus 45', *CPh* 60 (1965),
256–9.

D. Singleton, *G & R* 18 (1971) 181–7.

For the facts about sneezes as omens, and conflicting views
about the propitiousness of right and left, see Fordyce; also P. J.
Enk on Propertius 2. 3. 24. Among ingenious interpretations of
the passage are Tenney Frank, *CQ* 20 (1926), 201–3; H. J. Rose,
HSPh 47 (1936), 1–2; J. B. Stearns, *CPh* 24 (1929), 48–59.

46

A poem setting out C.'s plans for sightseeing during the first stage of his return home from Bithynia in the spring of 56 B.C. (see on Poems 10 and 31), and his reactions to the prospect. Cf. Horace, *Ep.* 1. 13.

Structure: 1–3 — spring. 4–6 — now's the time to be off. 7–8 — anticipation. 9–11 — farewell.

Metre: hendecasyllabics.

1. *iam*: repeated at the beginning of lines 2, 7 and 8, to express the note of excitement that underlies the poem (cf. 30. 2–3). C. adapts to his purpose some of the familiar clichés of a spring poem.

egelidos: the rare, precise, carefully considered word, 'no longer chill'; cf. 2 *aequinoctialis*; 7 *praetrepidans*. See on 7. 1 *basiationes*.

refert: 'brings back' — the cycle of the seasons is hinted at.

tepores: the plural = 'warm days'.

2. *furor*: 'frenzy', 'madness'; not 'fury'.

3. A compact, sinewy line, recalling Poem 64, rather than the simple verbal fabric of many of the short poems; *silescit* implies a personification — some being in the equinoctial heavens who is 'starting to quieten down', soothed by the warm gentle spring breeze; *iucundis . . . aureis* (archaic spelling = *auris*) is instrumental ablative, as though *silescit* were passive. The spring Zephyrs are 'welcome', both because they are more pleasant than the 'equinoctial gales' and because they mean the resumption of navigation, suspended during the winter; one of the clichés of spring poetry, but appropriate here — C. will be travelling by sea, not overland.

4–5. Nicaea was the capital of Bithynia. (It was to be the venue of the Council of Nicaea in 325 A.D. and the seat for a time after the fall of Constantinople of the Byzantine emperor.) The city stood in a plain at the other end of the sea of Marmara from Homeric Troy. 'Phrygian' almost = 'Trojan', so that *Phrygii . . . campi* suggests the plains of Troy, as in 64. 344; cf. 31. 5–6 *Bithynos campos*, 63. 2 *Phrygium nemus*, Virgil, *A.* 3. 11 *campos ubi Troia fuit*; in C.'s day the area had long been something of a backwater.

4. *Catulle*: for the device of self-address see on Poem 8.

5. *aestuosae*: Though cold in winter, the north coast of Turkey has a hot, moist summer climate; cf. 7. 5 *aestuosi*.

6. C.'s decision to depart is announced in the central line of the poem. Note the consonantal u-sounds which start in this line and reach their excited climax in line 11.

claras: (1) 'bright' (as in 61. 85); (2) 'famous'. Cf. Horace, *Carm.* 1. 7. 1 *laudabunt alii claram Rhodon*; but a common epithet of towns — used, e.g., by Cicero of Lampsacus, *Ver.* 1. 24. 63.

Asiae: The richest of the Roman provinces. Its most famous city was Pergamum, capital of the Attalid kings till Attalus III bequeathed his kingdom to Rome in 133 B.C. — about 75 years before the date of Poem 46. Other cities were Sardis and Ephesus. C. probably thinks also of the adjacent islands Lesbos, Mytilene, Rhodes, etc. In C.'s day it was an area that was beginning to attract the Roman tourist because of its glamorous past. Cato, a few years before C., had conceived a similar plan (Plutarch, *Cato* 12); cf. (a generation or so later) Horace, *Ep.* 1. 11. 1–3, Ovid, *Tr.* 1. 2. 78, *Pont.* 2. 10. 21. C.'s friend Cinna seems to have written a poem for Asinius Pollio to guide him on a similar tour of Greece and the Orient.

7. *praetrepidans*: 'excited in anticipation'; cf. 64. 145 *animus praegestit apisci*.

uagari: 'rush away' — stronger than 'wander': cf. Virgil, *A.* 4. 68 (of Dido in love) and C.'s use of *uagus* in Poem 63 (e.g. 4, 13, etc.).

8. For vividness C. ascribes to his feet what we might describe as some kind of impulse to be off which feels physical (*laeti studio pedes uigescunt*) by contrast with the level of rational thought (represented by 7 *mens auet uagari*).

9–11. Note the change of key: (1) the poem becomes less self-centred; (2) a hint of sadness in 9 *ualete*. The various members of the *cohors* all set out together, but will return to their homes by different routes (some may head north overland; for those proposing to go by ship there are a number of possibilities), but in their various ways all will eventually return to Italy: *diuersae* = 'quite different', 'opposite'; *uarie* = simply 'by dissimilar, not

identical, routes'. [*diuerse uarie* V; some editors make both words
adjectives (*diuersae uariae*), giving 3 words in the line which end in
ae- (as in 2. 1).]

See:

J. P. Elder, 'Notes on some conscious and unconscious elements
   in Catullus' poetry', *HSPh* 60 (1951), 103–4, 109 and 120–1.

M. C. J. Putnam, 'Catullus' journey (Carm. 4)', *CPh* 57 (1962),
   10–19.

Critical Essays 31–4.

47

C.'s friends Veranius and Fabullus, who served with Piso in
Macedonia, it seems (see on Poem 28), are no longer in his good
books. Was the fall from grace permanent, or temporary? When
did it occur — before the trip to Macedonia? while there? or
after their return? The tone of Poem 47 and the tense of 4
praeposuit imply a definite occasion: lines 5–7 suggest Rome
rather than Macedonia. Whatever the facts, Veranius and
Fabullus have been passed over and Poem 47 expresses C.'s
indignation on learning this.

Piso took up his appointment as proconsul of Macedonia in
57 B.C. and returned to Rome in the summer of 55 B.C.; for a
partisan account of his activities as governor see Cicero, *Pis.*
37–50.

Socration (a diminutive, 'little Socrates', rather than an actual
name) was perhaps the Epicurean philosopher and poet Philo-
demus — there are grounds for supposing that he accompanied
Piso to Macedonia. Attempts to identify Porcius are guesswork.

Metre: hendecasyllabics.

1. *sinistrae*: The Romans, like us, had right-hand men (Cicero,
Att. 14. 20. 5 *Quintus filius, ut scribis, Antoni est dextella*). So that to
be called *sinistrae* is in itself disparaging. For possible overtones see
on 12. 1–2.

2. *scabies famesque mundi*: A picturesque insult — Porcius and Socration personify something repulsive and rapacious in the world.

3. *Veraniolo*: The diminutive also 12. 17; cf. *Socration* (probably) and 45. 13 *Septimille*.

4. *uerpus*: the insulting use of a technical term — Piso (like Flavius in 6. 13) is suffering from the effects of wear and tear. Cf. 28. 12 *uerpa*.

praeposuit: cf. 81. 5 *praeponere*.

Priapus: a traditional figure of lust. As in 28. 12–13 the language is colourful rather than specifically accusatory.

5–7. Porcius and Socration are enjoying themselves while C.'s friends are left to beg for invitations to dinner.

5. *conuiuia lauta*: Cicero makes much of Piso's dinner parties, though it suits him to paint a different picture — *Pis.* 67 *nihil apud hunc lautum*, etc.

6. *de die*: = 'while it's still day' — i.e. before the time for dinner.

7. *uocationes*: for *uocare* = 'invite to dinner' cf. 44. 21; *uocatio* (not found elsewhere in this sense) is one of C.'s learned polysyllables (see on 7. 1).

See:

Ronald Syme, 'Piso and Veranius in Catullus', *C & M* 17 (1956), 129–34.

Cicero, *In Pisonem*, ed. R. G. M. Nisbet (1961), esp. 180–6.

48

An elegantly frivolous demonstration of the contrapuntal possibilities of soberly measured syntax and wildly passionate statement. Less, one suspects, a confession than a calculated provocation of those who can be scandalized by such talk, or who pretend to be; it seems from Poem 16 that the *pilosi* rose to the bait.

For Juventius see on Poem 24. Contrast Poems 5 and 7.

Structure: The 6 lines form a compound sentence, whose second half inverts the order of the first: lines 1–2 express the protasis answered by the apodosis of line 3; line 4 expresses the apodosis corresponding to the protasis of lines 5–6. The sense climbs breathlessly through this complex syntactical pattern to the flamboyant imagery of the final couplet; the concluding poly-syllable suggests, however, a hint of ironic detachment from this wild surge of emotion.

Metre: hendecasyllabics.

1–2. With *mellitos oculos tuos . . . basiare* cf. 45. 11–12. With *mellitos* cf. 99. 1 (also of Juventius) and 3. 6 (of Lesbia's sparrow). Note how *si quis . . . sinat* (instead of *si tu sinas*) unobtrusively accords the hypothesis the status of a day-dream.

3. *usque . . . basiem*: note the obsessive repetition of *usque basiare*.

4. *nec numquam*: = *nec umquam*, 'not ever'; cf. 76. 3 *nec . . . nullo*. [*numquam* V; *mi umquam* Estaço.]

5. *aridis*: i.e. ripe.

6. *osculationis*: for C.'s use of learned polysyllables see on 7. 1.

See:

L. Richardson Jr, '*Furi et Aureli, comites Catulli*', *CPh* 58 (1963), 96–7 (expresses a somewhat eccentric preference for 48 — 'a better and far more sophisticated poem' — over 7).

49

A short, intriguing, flowery, abject letter of thanks to Cicero. The service rendered is unspecified. Was it common knowledge, or is the reader left to guess? Poem 49 has not the ring of sincere thanks; C. can't really believe he is *pessimus omnium poeta*. Does the final couplet provide a clue? Are the lines, in short, bitterly ironical, as many have supposed?

Cicero was out of Italy from March 58 to September 57 B.C. In the months preceding Cicero's exile C. seems to have been living in Verona (this is the likely date of Poem 68). By the time Cicero came back from exile C. was already in Bithynia; he returned about the time of Cicero's defence of Caelius Rufus in April 56 B.C.

Metre: hendecasyllabics.

1. *disertissime*: 'most eloquent' — the obvious epithet to apply to Cicero, but perhaps also a valid clue, inviting us to assume that the. thanks refer to a particular demonstration of Cicero's oratorical prowess.

Romuli nepotum: Contrast 34. 22–4 *Romuli . . . gentem*, where sense and context justify the rhetoric. Here one suspects mock-solemnity — or plain irony, as in 58. 5 *magnanimi Remi nepotes*.

2–3. *quot sunt . . . in annis*: cf. 21. 2–3 and 24. 2–3 — in both cases ironically flowery.

2. *Marce Tulli*: formal. Cicero so imagines himself addressed by the state, *Cat.* 1. 27 *si omnis res p. loquatur*, '*M. Tulli, quid agis . . .?*'

4–5. The almost oriental abjectness and the build-up of 1–3 suggest something less than full commitment on C.'s part to the formal, positive, impersonal statement of lines 4–5. Cf. 44. 16–17.

5. *pessimus omnium poeta*: 'the rottenest poet of them all'; cf. 14. 23 *pessimi poetae* (plural), 36. 6 *pessimi poetae* (genitive).

6–7. We sense a change of tone. Ostensibly a comparison is expressed with mathematical exactness: C.'s inferiority to all other poets is commensurate with Cicero's superiority to all other *patroni*; but if that is all they are intended to convey, lines 5–6 seem a clumsy, needless expansion of the compliment already more elegantly expressed by the contrast 1 *disertissime Romuli nepotum . . . 5 pessimus omnium poeta*. We get better sense if we give *tanto . . . quanto* a causal force. Cicero's (? latest) success as an orator has been accompanied by (i.e. has caused) C.'s (? final) failure or disgrace as a poet. Lines 5–6, syntactically a wry after-thought, become the real point of the epigram.

Is the occasion Cicero's *pro Caelio*? C. might be expected to welcome the ridicule heaped with such eloquence and wit upon Clodia, the woman he had idealized and by whom he had been betrayed. But would C. *really* feel grateful? Could the Lesbia poems survive Cicero's brilliant witty demonstration that falling in love with Clodia stamped you as the dupe of a worthless nymphomaniac?

7. *optimus omnium patronus*: The context ostensibly invites the meaning 'the leading *patronus* of them all'. But whereas in *pessimus omnium poeta*, *omnium* attaches itself naturally to *pessimus*, in *optimus omnium patronus*, *omnium* attaches itself at least as readily to *patronus*. Indeed *omnium patronus*, 'every man's *patronus*', is applied (as a piece of flattery) to Cicero in a letter to him from A. Caecina (*Fam.* 6. 7. 4 *ubi hoc omnium patronus facis, quid me, ueterem tuum, nunc omnium clientem, sentire oportet?*). The effectiveness of the poem depends then on an unresolved ambiguity: the surface meaning remains complimentary, but the other meaning cannot be rejected.

Fordyce argues that the case for irony is not proven. But if *pessimus omnium poeta . . . pessimus omnium poeta . . . optimus omnium patronus* is merely rhetorical and the only effect aimed at is emphasis, the repetition hardly earns its keep; something more easily felt as *urbanitas* seems needed in the concluding lines.

To the charge of being every man's lawyer Cicero rather laid himself open: in order to appear as the champion of Caelius against Clodia, he had virtually changed sides, having appeared in an earlier related action in which he and Caelius had been opposing *patroni*. A couple of years later he defended Vatinius, whom he had attacked in 56 B.C. while defending Sestius; the latter occasion is possibly the subject of Poem 53. If we take Poem 49 as a carefully phrased, veiled jibe, it is tempting to see the source of the jibe in a sally by Cicero ridiculing Clodia, *Cael.* 32 *quam omnes semper amicam omnium potius quam cuiusquam inimicam putauerunt* (where *omnium* = 'of all and sundry').

See:

E. Laughton, *CPh* 65 (1970) 1–7.

D. F. S. Thomson, 'Catullus and Cicero', *CW* 60 (1967), 225–30.

D. E. W. Wormell, 'Catullus 49', *Phoenix* 17 (1963), 59–60.

50

A letter in verse to C.'s friend Calvus, the orator and poet (full name C. Licinius Calvus Macer; in Poem 53 C. pays an ironical tribute to Calvus' ability as an orator; in Poem 14 he complains that Calvus has sent him a volume of verse by worthless poets; in Poem 96 he consoles Calvus for the loss of Quintilia). After the excitement of an afternoon spent tossing off scraps of verse, C. could not sleep. He wrote Calvus a poem to tell him this, adding a plea for a further meeting.

Was this a first meeting? A hint of unsureness in the tone of Poem 50 (contrast Poem 14) rather suggests it; see also on line 19. What were the *uersiculi* about? Squibs like Poems 41, 43, 78, 93, 113, etc.? The sort of writing defended in Poem 16? If Poem 50 *is* early work, C.'s lightness and accuracy of touch are impressive, despite minor clumsinesses (see on 2 *meis*, cf. the repetitions *lusimus*, *ludebat* and *scribens*, *reddens*). There is a remarkable resemblance between these lines and the opening words of a letter from Cicero to Atticus in 49 B.C. (*Att.* 9. 10. 1):

> Nihil habebam quod scriberem . . . sed cum me aegritudo non solum somno priuaret, uerum ne uigilare quidem sine summo dolore pateretur, tecum ut quasi loquerer . . . hoc nescio quid nullo argumento proposito scribere institui.

For a letter from Cicero following up a dinner-party discussion see *Fam.* 7. 22 (? 44 B.C., to the lawyer Trebatius):

> Illuseras heri inter scyphos quod dixeram controuersiam esse, possetne heres quod furtum antea factum esset recte furti agere. itaque, etsi domum bene potus seroque redieram, tamen id caput ubi haec controuersia est notaui, et descriptum tibi misi, ut scires id quod tu neminem sensisse dicebas Sex. Aelium, M'. Manilium, M. Brutum sensisse. ego tamen Scaeuolae et Testae assentior.

For the fantasy of formal competition between poets on *tabellae* cf. Horace, *S.* 1. 4. 13–16:

> ecce:
> Crispinus minimo me prouocat: 'accipe, si uis,
> accipiam tabulas; detur nobis locus, hora,
> custodes; uideamus uter plus scribere possit.'

Structure: The sense falls into 4 sentences, each organized round a vocative. 1–6 — data. 7–13 — C.'s reactions to the evening with

Calvus. 14–17 — explanation of Poem 50. 18–21 — a further
meeting requested.

Metre: hendecasyllabics.

1–6. Lines 1–6 tell the reader what he needs to know — one
sign that this apparently spontaneous poem has been carefully
rearranged for publication (cf. Poem 1).

1. *hesterno . . . die*: A usual enough phrase (e.g. Cicero, *Catil.*
2. 3. 6), but also an instance of C.'s use of the effective long word
(see on 15 *semimortua*) — it helps to build up a strong opening.

otiosi: In C. the word implies time spent enjoying oneself
(instead of concentrating on the serious business of life like the
senes seueriores of 5. 2), rather than in relaxing, or doing nothing;
cf. 10. 2 *otiosum* and 51. 13–16.

2. *lusimus*: (1) 'had a good time' (cf. 17. 1 and 17, 68. 17 and
156); (2) 'made jokes', esp. in verse (cf. 61. 225 *lusimus satis*). The
word is used by later writers of *vers de société*.

meis tabellis: A set of waxed wooden tablets, the kind used for
rough jottings, also called *pugillaria* (42. 5) and *codicilli* (42. 11,
etc.); *meis* may imply that the tablets used were the ones C. is now
using for Poem 50 (for the use of *tabellae* for an interchange of
letters see Propertius 3. 23); or the word may be a false clue — a
detail not meant to attract attention.

3. *delicatos*: The basic meaning is 'delightful', 'charming'.
Overtones are: (1) 'sophisticated', 'precious', 'smart', almost
'decadent'; (2) something like 'risqué'. The word is used by Cicero
of a smart dinner party in 59 B.C., about which Atticus has
aroused his curiosity (*Att.* 2. 14. 1 — βοῶπις is Clodia): *quantam
tu mihi moues exspectationem de sermone Bibuli, quantam de colloquio
βοῶπιδος, quantam etiam de illo delicato conuiuio!* Cf. *Pis.* 70 *delicatissimis
uersibus* (of the verse of Philodemus). Cf. on 17. 15; also on 2. 1 *deliciae*.

4. *uersiculos*: 'scraps of verse', 'epigrams'. Cf. 16. 3 and 6. The
word suggests the degree of seriousness and the length of the
individual compositions, not the length of line. C. and Calvus
were not writing poetry, but *vers de société*. Contrast *nugae* (see on
Poem 1). One example of *uersiculi* by Calvus survives — an

epigram (with indecent undertones, if the traditional interpretation is correct) on 'The Great Pompey' (*FPL* p. 86):

> Magnus, quem metuunt omnes, digito caput uno
> scalpit: quid credas hunc sibi uelle? uirum!

Cf. C.'s *uersiculi* on Pompey, Poem 113, and the epigrams of Furius Bibaculus on Cato (*FPL* pp. 80–1). Cf. Pliny's comments on his experiments with *vers de société*, 5. 3 and 4. 14.

5. *ludebat*: explains the statement of *lusimus*, hence the change of tense, but the repetition hardly earns its keep.

numero . . . hoc, etc.: i.e. the *uersiculi* were in a variety of metres, not e.g. only elegiacs.

6. *reddens mutua*, etc.: implies a process of capping one another's lines — i.e. short epigrams, perhaps on related subjects.

per iocum atque uinum: The zeugma (1) fixes the atmosphere and the attitude of the participants; (2) is itself an example of a neatly-turned phrase; a variation occurs in 12. 2.

7-13. The data needed for the poem having been sketched in, the poem proper begins. To express the intensity of his reaction, C. resorts to the language and imagery of love poetry: he is on fire (*incensus*); his thoughts are deranged (*furore*); he is to be pitied (*miserum*); he is off his food, he cannot sleep; he wants only to be with Calvus again. Cf. Dido in the opening lines of *A.* 4; for this sense of *miser* see on 8. 1.

7. *lepore*: 'charm', i.e. wit and sophistication; described in 16. 7 as one of the necessary qualities of *uersiculi*.

8. *facetiisque*: another word that fixes the nature of the occasion and the verse it produced.

9. *cibus*: fixes the time — before dinner, i.e. the afternoon.

10-13. Note emphasis on the sleepless night; cf. 68. 5–6. An echo of Homer, *Il.* 24. 4–6 (Achilles, thinking of Patroclus). Cf. Propertius 1. 1. 33–4. Yet the writing is crisp, not maudlin, and it carries conviction.

10. *quiete*: For the idea, cf. Virgil, *A.* 4. 529–32.

11. *indomitus*: 'uncontrollable'; cf. 64. 54 *indomitos furores*.

14-17. Physical fatigue ends in lucidity. Again the basis is the

convention of love poetry as communication with the beloved
(*dolor* is often used of the pain of love — see ,e.g., Virgil, *A*. 4. 419).
The bald statement of line 16 is meant to impress.

14. *labore*: 'suffering'.

postquam: (with imperfect) = 'afterwards when' (less com-
mon than the perfect, but in good usage). The imperfect is
epistolary (i.e. the writer adopts the point of view of the recipient,
for whom the writing of the letter lies in the past). Cf. on 1. 3–4.

15. *semimortua*: The word seems to have been coined for the
occasion. For C.'s use of rare polysyllables for effect see on 7. 1.
For the form see on 61. 213. The second syllable is short.

lectulo: the diminutive, though common, perhaps adds a
hint of pathos.

16. *iucunde*: strikes (like 19 *ocelle*) a more intimate note than the
formal vocative *Licini* of lines 1 and 8. Cf. 14. 2. (The addressee
has to be identified at some point, of course.)

poema: i.e. Poem 50 is something more than *uersiculi*; cf. the
(ironic) use of the word for the compositions of Suffenus, 22. 15
and 16.

17. *perspiceres*: 'see clearly', = 'understand fully'. A final relative
clause.

dolorem: = 'the way I feel about you'.

18–21. Though the formal objective of C.'s *poema* is to reveal
C.'s feelings to Calvus, this is not its psychological objective,
which is foreshadowed in the climactic *ut tecum loquerer simulque ut
essem* of line 13 (cf. Cicero's words to Atticus). C. does not formally
propose a second meeting. Instead he strikes a mock-tragic note,
and threatens Calvus with divine punishment if he meets C.'s
request with arrogant refusal. The bantering tone is in self-
protection — Calvus may not want him as a close friend. At the
same time the *poema* is intended as a demonstration that C.
deserves Calvus' friendship.

18. *audax*: probably 'foolhardy', 'courting trouble', but perhaps
with an overtone of 'shameless' (i.e. rejecting responsibility for
C.'s predicament).

caue: The final syllable is short though the verb is 2nd conj. (again line 19 — 'iambic shortening' see on 6. 16). The subjunctives without *ne* are paratactic and colloquial.

precesque nostras: no formal request is made, but one is clearly implied in line 13.

19. *despuas*: A strong, uncommon word — 'reject out of hand' (lit. 'spit out'). C. perhaps does not feel entitled (on the strength of an afternoon spent together) to expect close, lasting friendship; in any case, a delicately worded hint is conveyed that something more than ordinary friendship would be welcomed by C. — an intimacy which C. feels Calvus may scornfully reject.

ocelle: the final vocative keeps up the (bantering) use of the language of love poetry. See on 31. 2.

20. *Nemesis*: for this semi-playful invocation of a deity cf. the *patrona uirgo* of 1. 9. For Nemesis see on 64. 395.

reposcat a te: The order is emphatic = 'punish *you* for punishing me' (by refusing my request). Cf. the emphasis in *laedere hanc caueto* — 'take care not to offend *her*' (by offending me).

21. *uemens*: = *uehemens* (two long syllables).

laedere: the offence of *lèse-majesté*.

caueto: Future imperative: the poem ends on a note of mock-solemnity ('you will please be careful'); contrast the simple imperative *caue* in 18 and 19; cf. 64. 231 *facito*.

See:

Tenney Frank, 'Cicero and the Poetae Novi', *AJPh* 40 (1919), 396–415.

Eduard Fraenkel, 'Catulls Trostgedicht für Calvus', *WS* 69 (1956), 278–88 (281–2 good on Poem 50).

Erich Gruen, 'Cicero and Licinius Calvus', *HSPh* 71 (1966), 215–24.

Piero Pucci, 'Il carme 50 di Catullo', *Maia* 13 (1961), 249–56 (Poem 50 as 'the literary manifesto of the *neoteroi*').

W. C. Scott, *CPh* 64 (1969) 169–73.

C. P. Segal, *G & R* 17 (1970) 25–31.

C. Witke (see above, under Poem 30).

51

WILKINSON's statement of the hypothesis of Poem 51 is suc-
cinct and persuasive. 'I believe, with others,' he says, 'that this
was the first poem Catullus sent to Clodia, a free translation of
one by Sappho. It was intended as a test, a "feeler". If she were in
love with him, she would understand what he meant; if not —
after all it was only a translation.'

If Wilkinson is right, we are entitled to expect (1) that C.'s
version will be sufficiently close to pass for a translation; (2) that
it will contain hints none the less that more is intended than a
literary exercise. Such seems to be the case: C. has translated,
apparently, only the first three stanzas of Sappho's poem (on
C.'s final stanza see below); but in these his version, in the main,
follows Sappho closely. There are, however, several clear depar-
tures from Sappho, especially in the opening lines, and the
suspicion that these are deliberate is strong: (1) the rest of his
version shows C. fully capable of a close translation of the opening
lines, which contain no insuperable difficulties; (2) the opening
lines being naturally the most familiar, departures from the Greek
text would be quickly noticed by anyone attempting to read
between the lines.

For the support lent this interpretation by Poem 11 see on
Poem 11.

One gathers from Cicero that Clodia was not unaccustomed to
seizing the initiative, *Cael.* 36: *uicinum adulescentulum aspexisti; candor
huius te et proceritas, uoltus oculique pepulerunt; saepius uidere uoluisti.*

Metre: sapphic stanzas (see on Poem 11 and WORMELL 199–
201).

Sappho's poem is as follows:

> φαίνεταί μοι κῆνος ἴσος θέοισιν
> ἔμμεν' ὤνηρ, ὄττις ἐνάντιός τοι
> ἰσδάνει καὶ πλάσιον ἆδυ φωνεί-
> σας ὑπακούει

καὶ γελαίσας ἰμέροεν, τό μ’ ἦ μὰν
καρδίαν ἐν στήθεσιν ἐπτόαισεν·
ὡς γὰρ ἔς σ’ ἴδω βρόχε’, ὥς με φώναι-
σ’ οὐδ’ ἔν ἔτ’ εἴκει,

ἀλλ’ ἄκαν μὲν γλῶσσα †ἔαγε†, λέπτον
δ’ αὔτικα χρῷ πῦρ ὑπαδεδρόμηκεν,
ὀππάτεσσι δ’ οὐδ’ ἔν ὄρημμ’, ἐπιρρόμ-
βεισι δ’ ἄκουαι,

κὰδ δέ μ’ ἴδρως ψῦχρος ἔχει, τρόμος δὲ
παῖσαν ἄγρει, χλωροτέρα δὲ ποίας
ἔμμι, τεθνάκην δ’ ὀλίγω ’πιδεύης
φαίνομ’ ἔμ’ αὔτ[ᾳ.

ἀλλὰ πὰν τόλματον, ἐπεὶ †καὶ πένητα†

1. C. (1) sharpens the original statement slightly, by substituting the singular *par . . . deo* for the plural ἴσος θέοισιν (the plural *diuos* in line 2 is appropriate to the general statement there); (2) makes the opening line self-contained by bringing up into it his translation of ἔμμεναι and omitting a translation of ὤνηρ. Otherwise his translation is remarkably close, and at the same time direct and natural.

2. The repetition of *ille* throws an emphasis foreign to Sappho's poem upon 'the man'. In Sappho he is merely a peg on which to hang the theme of envy (or rather 'pronouncing happy' — μακαρισμός) until the true theme (self-analysis) can be developed. For C. the man is more important: C. hopes to supplant him, and succeed to his unique happiness.

On *fas* see Austin on *A.* 2. 157: '*fas est* implies not what is compulsory but what is allowable without transgressing the law of heaven; . . . in all republican Latin *fas* is always predicative, never subject.' Ostensibly, therefore, *si fas est* = *si superare diuos est fas* — a formula protecting the speaker from the sin of irreverent overstatement. But why make the overstatement? (Nothing corresponds to it in Sappho.) And why, having made it, undercut by a protective formula? Probably, to emphasize C.'s intensity of feeling: the strategy of C.'s poem required that he should set out from Sappho's opening line, but the line had no doubt become a commonplace; the way to inject fresh feeling into a commonplace is to go one better. At the same time, the measured seriousness of the statement (each word weighed, and meant), which C.'s translation is intended to convey, requires restraint in hyperbole. Hence *si fas est*. See on 68. 141–6.

3. *identidem*: Another departure from Sappho, and too big and matter-of-fact a word to be padding. It contributes to the build-up of *ille*; *he* enjoys as a matter of course what is to C. an isolated privilege, provided perhaps by an invitation to dinner at Metellus' house. The word occurs again (at the same point in the stanza) at 11. 19 — an obvious cross-reference.

4. *spectat*: A further departure from Sappho. Perhaps only a substitute for words like πλάσιον and φωνείσας. But one is struck by the parallel with Lucretius 4. 1101–2 (on the obsession of lovers with looking at those they love): *sic in amore Venus simulacris ludit amantis / nec satiare queunt spectando corpora coram.*

5. *dulce ridentem*: also 61. 212. The man in Sappho hears the girl speak as well as laugh. C. eliminates φωνείσας and transfers to *ridentem* Sappho's ἆδυ in place of the untranslatable ἰμέροεν. In part, no doubt, the simplifications are the result of technical necessity. But the decision to concentrate on Lesbia's sweet laughter suggests sound poetic instinct as well, though Horace, in an echo of C., *Carm.* 1. 22. 23–4, also in sapphics, supplies the *dulce loquentem* which C. had omitted.

5–12. As far as we can tell in the absence of line 8, a close paraphrase of the original, rather than a word-by-word translation. For other attempts to describe the onset of passionate feeling see Apollonius 3. 962–72; Valerius Aedituus (*FPL* p. 42) *dicere cum conor curam tibi, Pamphila, cordis*, etc.; Horace, *Carm.* 1. 13; cf. Lucretius' description of the physical symptoms of fear, 3. 154–8.

5. *misero*: the stock epithet of the unhappy lover (see on 8. 1);

nothing corresponding in Sappho; the word practically amounts, therefore, to a declaration.

quod: the relative sums up lines 3–5.

6. *eripit sensus*: cf. 66. 25 *sensibus ereptis*. A free rendering of the Greek. See also on 76. 19–21.

simul: = *simul ac*.

7. *Lesbia*: If Lesbia is Clodia (see Introduction), then the name Lesbia represents the customary substitution, in the published version of a poem, of a metrically equivalent name for the real name of the poet's mistress; the principle, well known in antiquity, was illustrated by Bentley on Horace, *Carm.* 2. 12. 13. The name Lesbia is a natural enough, harmless-sounding name in a poem purporting to be a translation of Sappho. There is no vocative in Sappho, however; the name Lesbia, i.e., is an addition C. chose to make. If we accept that Poem 51 is the first addressed by C. to his mistress, no further explanation of the name Lesbia is needed, though it would be a nice touch of *urbanitas* if the name contained as well a reference to ancient beauty contests at Lesbos (see ALFONSI).

C. uses the name Lesbia in 12 other poems (5, 7, 43, 58, 72, 75, 79, 83, 86, 87, 92 and 107; always either nominative or vocative). In 7 other poems (2, 3, 8, 11, 13, 36 and 37) his mistress is simply referred to as *puella* (usually *mea puella*): nominative in 8. 4, 8. 7, 36. 9 and 37. 11; vocative in 8. 12; genitive in 2. 1, 3. 3, 3. 4 and 3. 17; dative in 11. 15 and 13. 11; ablative in 36. 2; in 11. 15 clearly and probably in all other cases, except perhaps 36. 2 and 9 (see on Poem 36), the *puella* is Lesbia. Lesbia is almost certainly also the *domina* of 68. 68 and the *mulier mea* of 70. 1.

super: adverbial.

8. The general sense of this line, missing in the MSS, is plain from Sappho. Friedrich's *Lesbia uocis* is perhaps better than others (e.g. *quod loquar amens* or *uocis in ore*) since the repetition of *Lesbia* would account for the loss of the line.

9–10. Cf. 76. 21 *quae mihi subrepens imos ut torpor in artus*.

10. *suopte*: = *suomet*.

11. *tintinant*: a by-form of *tintinio*, itself a variant of *tinnio*.

gemina: Ablative with *nocte*, the so-called transferred epithet — described by Fordyce as 'a piece of sophistication which seems suspiciously out of place in a poem whose language is otherwise so simple'. [Those who share Fordyce's suspicion that 'Catullus has allowed a reminiscence of an Alexandrian conceit to intrude on Sappho' may read *gemina et* with Spengel, or simply *geminae* with Schrader.]

13–16. The final stanza raises problems comparable to those raised by 2. 11–13. Does the stanza belong to the poem at all? 'I have found myself changing sides so often that I now feel despondent' (FRAENKEL 211). Comparison with Sappho hardly helps. Lines 1–16 of Sappho's poem form a satisfactory whole; but in the MSS of Longinus these lines are followed by a seventeenth corrupt line: it is possible that this is the equivalent of C.'s fourth stanza (Sappho's fourth stanza in that case being left untranslated by C.), but hardly likely. Friedrich's solution was that C. added his fourth stanza later. That C. re-read Poem 51 when he came to write Poem 11 is put beyond doubt by the repetition of *identidem*; it is not 'incredible' (so Fordyce) that he should have added a wry final comment.

From the *otium* in his personal life, C. passes to the life of peoples, kings and cities. The idea that prolonged peace weakened the energy of a city or nation figures prominently in Poseidonius, an older contemporary of C.; LATTIMORE compares Theognis 1103–4 ὕβρις καὶ Μάγνητας ἀπώλεσε καὶ Κολοφῶνα / καὶ Σμύρνην. πάντως, Κύρνε, καὶ ὕμμ' ἀπολεῖ; cf. also Agamemnon, in Ennius, *Iphigenia* 241–5W:

> otio qui nescit uti . . .
> plus negoti habet quam cum est negotium in negotio;
> nam cui quod agat institutumst non ullo negotio
> id agit, id studet, ibi mentem atque animum delectat suum;
> otioso in otio animus nescit ⟨quid agat⟩ quid uelit.

There is an echo of C. in Horace, *Carm.* 2. 16.

13. *tibi molestum est*: 'does not agree with you'.

K

See:

Luigi Alfonsi, 'Lesbia', *AJPh* 71 (1950), 59–66.

E. Bickel, 'Catulls Werbegedicht an Clodia', *RhM* 89 (1940), 194–215.

G. Devereux, *CQ* 20 (1970) 17–31.

J. P. Elder, 'The "figure of grammar" in Catullus 51', in *The Classical Tradition*, ed. L. Wallach (1967), 202–9.

R. I. Frank, *TAPhA* 99 (1968) 233–9.

Eduard Fraenkel, *Horace* (1957), 211–13 (on the final stanza).

E. A. Fredricksmeyer, *TAPhA* 96 (1965) 153–63.

H. A. Kahn, *RhMus* 114 (1971) 159–78.

D. A. Kidd, 'The unity of Catullus 51', *AUMLA* No. 20 (1963), 298–308.

Richmond Lattimore, 'Sappho 2 and Catullus 51', *CPh* 39 (1944), 184–7.

L. P. Wilkinson, Fondation Hardt, *Entretiens sur l'antiquité classique* 2 (1956), 47.

G. Wills, *GRBS* 8 (1967) 167–97.

D. E. W. Wormell, 'Catullus as translator', in *The Classical Tradition*, ed. L. Wallach (1967), 187–201.

On Sappho's poem (31 LP, quoted by Longinus as a perfect example of the expression of feeling) see C. M. Bowra, *Greek Lyric Poetry*, 2nd ed. (1961), 185–9, A. Lesky, *Hist. Greek Lit.*, 143–4, D. L. Page, *Sappho and Alcaeus* (1955), 26–33.

52

A brief, sardonic comment on the contemporary political scene. One suspects that Pompey and Caesar, the supporters of these worthless, grotesque creatures, are the real objectives of C.'s abuse (cf. Poems 29 and 54).

On P. Vatinius, 'the best-hated man of his time', see also Poem 53. Already as a candidate for the quaestorship in 64 B.C. he was boasting, according to Cicero, *Vat.* 11 (56 B.C.), about how he would conduct his second consulship. He was tribune in 59 B.C., Caesar's tool. Poem 52 perhaps belongs to his praetorship

in 55, by when he doubtless felt the consulship was already
his. He eventually became *consul suffectus* for a few days in 47 B.C.

Nonius may have been the tribune Nonius Sufenas, a supporter
of Pompey; or else Nonius Asprenas, a *legatus* of Caesar in Africa
and Spain; see Neudling; there is no record of either holding
curule office. Pliny, *Nat.* 37. 81, quotes C.'s reference to Nonius
in connexion with a grandson, the possessor of a fabulous opal
which was coveted by Augustus.

Metre: iambic trimeters (only here — Poems 4 and 29, prob-
ably, are in *pure* iambic trimeters).

2. *sella in curuli ... sedet*: probably =Nonius feels he is well on
the way to political success (whereas Vatinius thinks of himself as
already at the top). The aedileship, largely because of its con-
nexion with the games, was regarded as useful to a man with
political ambitions; it was the first office to confer full senatorial
dignity and the *ius imaginis*.

struma: described as follows by Celsus 5. 28. 7: *tumor in quo
subter concreta quaedam ex pure et sanguine quasi glandulae oriuntur.*
Nonius is an excrescence on the body politic. Oddly enough,
Cicero refers several times to the boils which disfigured Vatinius'
appearance.

3. *per consulatum*: i.e. Vatinius swears by the consulship which
he regards as as good as his: that he lies (*peierat*) can be taken for
granted.

53

Laughter in a Roman court. C.'s friend, Licinius Calvus, is in
full flight against Vatinius. His eloquence elicits an approving
interjection from a member of the audience. But *urbanitas*
dictated something short of unqualified approval, even of a
friend's oratorical triumph: the compliment and C.'s way of
telling the anecdote manage to convey a hint that Calvus was
laying it on a shade thick. Vatinius was too much in and out of
court and the circumstances too little known to us for us to be sure

of the occasion: was it Calvus' first prosecution of Vatinius in
58 B.C.? or, more likely, the trial of 54 B.C., when Vatinius was
successfully defended by Cicero? (Tacitus (*Dial.* 21. 2) implies
there were at least three speeches which *in omnium studiosorum
manibus uersantur.*)

On Calvus see on Poem 50. There is a nice story told by Seneca,
Con. 7. 4. 6, that during one of Calvus' speeches against Vatinius,
the victim himself jumped up to complain: *rogo uos, iudices, num,
si iste disertus est, ideo me damnari oportet.* FRAENKEL 279 remarks
that in all probability it was Calvus who took the initiative in the
campaign of invective conducted by C. and Calvus against
Pompey, Caesar and their henchmen.

On Vatinius see on Poem 52 (mentioned also 14. 3).

Structure: FRAENKEL 280 remarks that the poem follows the
traditional αἶνος — a form in which a few short sentences setting
out the basic data lead up to a remark in direct speech. The
opening, like that of Poem 56, suggests Archilochus' χρῆμά τοι
γελοῖον ἐρέω (Fragment 153 LB); cf. our 'a funny thing happen-
ed to me . . .'. But the formula complete with verb in the initial
position is found again in the conversational style of Cicero, *Q. fr.*
2. 13 (opening words): *Risi 'niuem atram', teque hilari animo esse . .
me iuuat.*

Metre: hendecasyllabics.

1. *corona*: for the stress laid by Cicero on the importance of the
corona (the crowd of bystanders) see *Brutus* 192 and 290; cf. his
uneasiness at its absence, *Mil.* 1. For *nesciŏ* see on 6. 16.

2. *mirifice*: also 71. 4 and 84. 3; common in Cicero's letters.

Vatiniana: cf. 14. 3 *odio Vatiniano*, and 44. 10 *Sestianus conuiua*.

3. *meus*: with the order cf. 44. 9.

5. *di magni*: also 14. 12.

salaputium: The reading of V appears to have been *sala-
pantium*. The form *salaputium* or *salaputtium* is restored from
Seneca, *Con.* 7. 4. 7 *erat enim [Caluos] paruolus statura, propter quod
etiam Catullus in hendecasyllabis uocat illum 'salaputtium disertum'.* The
meaning is much debated. To give the anecdote point, a pictur-

esque or obscene meaning seems desirable; BICKEL's suggestion
that *salaputium = mentula salax* is etymologically plausible.

See:

E. Bickel, '*Salaputium, mentula salax*', *RhM* 96 (1953), 94–5 (see on
   line 5).
H. Comfort, 'The date of Catullus 53', *CPh* 30 (1935), 74–6 (either
   58 B.C. or 54, not 56).
Eduard Fraenkel, 'Catulls Trostgedicht für Calvus', *WS* 69
   (1956), 279–80.
Erich S. Gruen, 'Cicero and L. Calvus', *HSPh* 71 (1966),esp. 217–20.
J. Knobloch, *RhMus* 112 (1969) 23–9.

54

Poem 54 ends with an echo of 29. 11 *imperator unice*. Did Caesar
(who was in Gaul) convey his displeasure at C.'s attack on his
henchman Mamurra? If so, C.'s answer was, it seems, a calculated
act of defiance. See on Poem 29 and cf. Poems 57 and 93.

It is not easy to get much further with these lines. Some (e.g.
Lenchantin) find them wildly obscene. The text is certainly
corrupt, nor can any of the persons named be confidently
identified. Despite BICKEL's optimism, one feels tempted to agree
with Merrill that 'an extremely un-Catullan blindness and awk-
wardness . . . makes it altogether probable that the tradition of
the text is incurably defective'.

Structure: It is a reasonable assumption that lines 1–3 each pick
out a particularly repellent feature of the person named: 'that
feature,' i.e., 'at any rate,' says C., '*si non omnia, displicere uellem
tibi et* . . .'. There is no way of telling why Fufidius (if that is his
name) is paired off with Caesar and put on a different footing
from the other three henchmen of Caesar.

Metre: hendecasyllabics.

1. In the MSS 50. 16–17 are repeated after this line.

   caput: According to Lenchantin, perhaps for *caput mentulae*;
Calvus' epigrams on Tigellius and Pompey (*FPL* pp. 84 and 86)
have been similarly interpreted.

2. *Hirri*: The MSS are corrupt. *Hirri* seems as good a guess as any, once we accept Turnebus' *rustica* in place of the MSS *rustice*. According to BICKEL the person meant is C. Lucilius Hirrus (a cousin of Pompey). See Cicero *Q. fr.* 3. 8. 4.

3. *Libonis*: perhaps L. Scribonius Libo (father-in-law of Sex. Pompeius).

5. *Fufidio*: BICKEL's suggestion, the Fufidius of Horace, *S.* I. 2. 12–17. The MSS have *Suffucio*, a name not found elsewhere. Some identify the person meant as C. Fuficius Fango, but the second syllable of Fuficius is probably long.

seni recocto: possibly 'hard-baked' (BICKEL); more likely a reference to the story of Aeson, Medea's father-in-law, whom she rejuvenated by boiling him in a cauldron.

6–7. ='you are going to have more harmless, iambic verses to make you angry', i.e. not this poem (which, like Poem 57, is in hendecasyllabics) but verses like Poem 29 (pure iambic trimeters), specifically recalled by the echo *unice imperator* from 29. 11. It is often assumed, however, that in C. *iambi* denotes a genre, not a metre; see on 36. 5 and 40. 2; contrast 12. 10–11 *hendecasyllabos trecentos | exspecta* and Poem 42. *irascere*: future indicative; *immerentibus*: mock-innocent, of course.

See:

E. Bickel, '*Catulli in Caesarem carmina*' *RhM* 93 (1949), 13–20 (he identifies all the persons named and finds the poem a political lampoon, innocent of obscene assertion or innuendo.)

55

A polite request to Camerius to reveal his whereabouts (1–2). He is nowhere to be found (3–12). It won't do at all (13–14). He must show up and explain himself (15–16). Has he fallen in love (17)? If so, he mustn't keep the details to himself (18–22).

Alert, ironical concern for a friend who shows signs of having got involved with a girl is a common theme in Roman personal poetry. Everybody is anxious to stop the man making a fool of himself, and also curious to know what is going on; understandably, the man isn't keen to tell.

Camerius, unlike Flavius in Poem 6, has disappeared from circulation altogether: like Horace's Sybaris, he has gone under cover (*Carm*. 1. 8. 13 *latet*). Contrast Poem 10, where Varus takes C. on a visit of inspection. Line 6 points to a date not earlier than 55 B.C.

For the theory that 58b belongs to 55 see on 58b.

Metre: A variation on the hendecasyllabic metre: in at least 12 of the 22 lines (in line 9 the text is uncertain) the nucleus $- \cup \cup -$ is contracted to $- - -$, giving an opening sequence of five long syllables. See on 58b.

1. *oramus*: the first person plural here and in lines 3 and 15 (contrast 22 *sim*) is probably mock solemn; C. normally uses either the first person singular, or refers to himself by name in the third person. Contrast the frequent use of the plural pronoun (*nos*, etc.) and possessive adjective (*noster* etc.), of himself.

   si forte non molestum est: 'provided it's no trouble'; ironically polite; cf. Cicero, *Fam*. 5. 12. 10 *his de rebus quid acturus sis, si tibi non est molestum, rescribas mihi uelim*.

2. *demonstres*: subjunctive without *ut*.

   tenebrae: 'hiding place' (*L & S* I C 3; cf. 2 and 4).

3. *Campo . . . minore*: presumably a particular *campus*, but the term *Campus minor* is not found elsewhere.

   quaesiuimus: The MSS have an unmetrical *in* after *quaesiuimus*, on the model presumably of lines 4, 5 and 6; some editors retain *in*, by various expedients.

4. *Circo*: the Circus Maximus.

   tĕ in omnibus: The e of *te* here (though not at the beginning of this line or the following line) is shortened before the following vowel instead of being elided, a licence (presumably reflecting ordinary speech) found occasionally in Augustan verse, as well as in Plautus and Terence; see on 10. 27 *mane*.

   libellis: C. no doubt means places where books were displayed for sale (cf. Martial 5. 20. 8), but no need to assume (as some do) that *libeili* = 'bookshops'.

5. *templo summi Iouis*: the temple of Capitoline Jove.

6. *Magni . . . ambulatione*: A rectangular court surrounded by colonnades, part of Pompey's theatre in the Campus Martius, dedicated in 55 B.C.; recommended by Ovid (*Ars* 1. 67 and 3. 387) as a fashionable rendezvous; cf. Propertius 4. 8. 75. For *Magni* = *Pompeii* cf. Calvus' epigram quoted on 50. 4 (*Magnus, quem metuunt omnes . . .*).

7. *femellas*: the diminutive only here.

prendi: 'cornered'.

8. *uultu . . . serenas*: i.e. they did not have Camerius on their conscience. [The MSS vary between *serenas* and *sereno*.]

9–12. Corrupt and defective, but the general sense is plain: one of the girls interrogated about the whereabouts of Camerius replies in effect 'you can have a look for yourself'. A pun is perhaps involved on Camerius' name (COPLEY suggests a word καμάριον = *strophium*). Friedrich's *nudum reclude pectus*, or something similar, is needed to complete line 11, with a further pun perhaps on *pectus* ('breast' and 'heart', i.e. 'thoughts'). Attempts at repairing line 9 are inconclusive. The position of 11 *inquit* outside the direct speech is also suspect, and the pattern of contracted nuclei in alternate lines is upset.

10. *Camerium*: apparently to be pronounced as three syllables.

pessimae: 'wretched', 'wicked' (mock indignant); cf. 36. 9 *pessima puella*, 14. 23 and 49. 5.

12. *latet*: apparently the word used of a young man who had gone out of circulation; cf. Horace, *Carm.* 1. 8. 13. Another pun in that case.

14. *tanto te in fastu negas*: 'you deprive us of your company with such aloofness'.

15. *dic nobis ubi sis futurus*: the ostensible objective of C.'s verse epistle, i.e., is to ask Camerius to fix a time when he and C. may meet.

17. *te lacteolae tenent puellae?*: = 'the darling blondes have got

you, have they?' The plural because Camerius' desertion of his
friends can only mean (C. fears) that he is now in the clutches of
his mistress and her equally glamorous associates, who — looked
at another way — are of course the *pessimae puellae* of line 10;
lacteolae = 'fair-skinned' — Roman poets preferred blondes (cf.
86. 1); the diminutive which might be used by the enthusiastic
admirer of a particular girl is used ironically of a whole class.
With *tenent* cf. 64. 28 *tenuit. num* instead of *nunc* is tempting.

18–20. C. assumes the role of the authority on love (*praeceptor
amoris*), one of the stock poses of the Roman elegiac poets: cf.,
e.g., Propertius 1. 9. 34 *dicere quo pereas saepe in amore leuat.*

18. *tenes*: i.e. 'if you go on keeping silent, as you are now
doing'.

20. The assertion that the goddess of love enjoys publicity is of
course *argumentum ad hominem.*

21–2. The appeal for private information (in a verse epistle
obviously destined for subsequent circulation as a poem) is not to
be taken too seriously. Cf. Horace, *Carm.* 1. 27: at a drinking party
Horace invites a friend to entrust a similar secret to him alone
(17–18 *quidquid habes . . . depone tutis auribus*) and then promptly
adds to his victim's discomfiture by ironically sympathetic
exclamations about the girl concerned.

22. *uestri*: plural!
    sim: [*sis* V.]

See:

F. O. Copley, 'Catullus 55, 9–14', *AJPh* 73 (1952), 295–7.
Cat. Rev. 78–81 (on the social background).
J. Foster, *CQ* (1971) 186–7.

56

Like Archilochus Fragment 153 LB:

    Ἐρασμονίδη Χαρίλαε, χρῆμά τοι γελοῖον
      ἐρέω, πολὺ φίλταθ' ἑταίρων, τέρψεαι δ' ἀκούων,

the equivalent of our anecdotal stereotype, 'A funny thing

happened to me . . .' (cf. Poem 53). The recipient of C.'s hair-raising confidence is presumably Valerius Cato, the hard-up poet and critic. Unless of course these elegantly phrased, urbane, obscene lines are a provocation of Cato Uticensis — numbered thus, by implication, among the *pilosi* of Poem 16; cf. Valerius Maximus' story (2. 10. 8) — how Cato walked out in the middle of a performance of the *Ludi Florales*, so that a strip-tease act could proceed.

Metre: hendecasyllabics.

1. *rem ridiculam*: exclamatory accusative.

2. *dignamque auribus et tuo cachinno*: =*dignamque auribus tuis et tuo cachinno*.

3. *quidquid amas . . . Catullum*: a variation on *si me amas* = a strong form of 'please'; cf. Cicero, *Att.* 5. 17. 5 *si quicquam me amas, hunc locum muni* = 'please leave no loophole'. Cato's laugh is appealed for, as a sign of agreement that the *res* is *ridicula et iocosa*.

Cato, Catullum: note the jingle. *Catullus* is possibly a diminutive formed from *Cato*.

4. A Janus-line at the centre of the poem, looking back to line 1 and forward to what is to come.

5–7. The joke seems to be that the youngster who is so anxious to show he is a man receives an appropriately witty equivalent of the traditional punishment of those caught *in flagrante delicto* (so Lenchantin).

5. *puellae*: dative of advantage.

6. *trusantem*: intensive of *trudentem* (i.e. *mentulam*).

si placet Dionae: = 'if Dione will allow the boast'; Dione is the mother of Venus.

7. An elaborate pun: *cecidi* =*pedicaui*; but *pro telo* etc. links this colloquial use of *caedere* (*OLD* sense 2) with such expressions as *gladio caedere* ('cut down', i.e. 'slay'), from which the colloquial meaning is presumably derived. A further pun, probably, involving *pro telo*: the obvious sense 'in place of a weapon' is secured by the following instrumental *rigida mea* (i.e. *mentula*); but *protelo*, a rarish adverbial form (literary or archaic, cf. Lucretius 4. 190) also suggests itself, and with it the meaning 'I straightway

despatched'. For another poem built around a pun see Poem 26.

See:

Kroll, and A. E. Housman, '*Praefanda*', *Hermes* 66 (1931), 402
  (for different interpretations of lines 1 and 7).

R. P. Robinson, 'Valerius Cato', *TAPhA* 54 (1923), 98–116 (for
  all the known facts about Valerius Cato).

W. C. Scott, 'Catullus and Cato', *CPh* 64 (1969), 24–9.

57

The most libellous of C.'s attacks on Julius Caesar. In Poem 29
the centre of the attack is Mamurra; Pompey is abused, and
Caesar reproached, for supporting him. In Poem 54 the attack is
on a mixed bag of Caesar's henchmen; the tone is ironically
defiant, but there is no direct abuse of Caesar. Poem 93 hardly
amounts to an attack.

Poem 57 is a different matter. It is a sustained outrageously
insulting lampoon in which Caesar and C.'s *bête noire* Mamurra
are jointly libelled. The charges levelled or implied (sodomy,
ridiculous literary pretensions, promiscuous womanizing, or
worse) were not, in themselves or individually, beyond forgive-
ness. Such accusations were levelled pretty freely. 'Freedom of
speech', says Ronald Syme, 'was an essential part of the Republican
virtue of *libertas*, to be regretted more than political freedom when
both were abolished.' (*Roman Revolution* [1939], 152). What one
would have supposed unforgivable, even in a society where it was
a point of honour to take such things gracefully, is C.'s tone of
unmitigated contempt.

Yet Caesar forgave, it seems, in accordance no doubt with his
expressed view that an obligation rested on those in power to act
with greater restraint and detachment than private individuals
(Sallust, *Cat.* 51); but also, perhaps, because of that love of
literature which C. had ridiculed. Indeed, these are probably the
uersiculi referred to in Suetonius' well-known anecdote, *Jul.* 73:

Valerium Catullum, a quo sibi uersiculis de Mamurra

perpetua stigmata imposita non dissimulauerat, satis
facientem eadem die adhibuit cenae hospitioque patris
eius, sicut consuerat, uti perseuerauit.

Suetonius implies an appreciable interval between attack and
reconciliation, which fits Poem 57, but almost rules out Poem 29.
Poem 29 cannot be placed earlier than the autumn of 55 B.C.;
the meeting between Caesar and C. cannot be placed later than
the following winter in Verona; Caesar could at most only just
have heard about Poem 29. Poem 57 belongs probably to the
period between Caesar's return from Spain at the end of 61 B.C.
and his departure for Gaul at the beginning of 58 B.C.: Caesar and
Mamurra must be together if C.'s charges are to make sense; they
were together in Spain and again in Gaul until Mamurra's return
to Rome in 55 (see on Poem 29), but the whole tenor of Poem 57
suggests scandalous goings-on in Rome. The reconciliation be-
tween Caesar and C. spoken of by Suetonius can be assigned to the
winter of 58–57 B.C. (C. seems to have been in Verona then,
following the death of his brother, prior to setting out for
Bithynia); or to the winter of 56–55 (following C.'s return from
Bithynia; that he went for a time to Verona can be assumed from
Poem 31); the later date is suggested by Suetonius' remark
hospitioque patris eius, sicut consuerat, uti perseuerauit (i.e. Caesar
visited C.'s father's house in Verona both before the reconciliation
and afterwards — after C.'s death perhaps; in the years 58–49
Caesar regularly came south each winter into Gallia Cisalpina; he
was prevented by the *Lex Cornelia* from entering Italy proper).
The reconciliation may even have encouraged C. to resume the
attack on Caesar's henchmen in Poems 29 and 54; where Caesar
himself is concerned, the tone of these poems is much more
moderate — elaborate, irreverent irony rather than anything
justifying talk of *perpetua stigmata* (29. 5–10 refer to Pompey, not
to Caesar — see on Poem 29; one can imagine that Caesar in
55 B.C. was not greatly distressed by the attack on Pompey).

   (The view that Suetonius meant Poem 29 depends on the mis-
taken assumption that 29. 5–10 refer to Caesar; see on Poem 29.)

C.'s friend Calvus attacked Caesar along similar lines: cf.
Suetonius, ibid. and *Jul.* 49.

For Mamurra see on Poem 29.

Structure: 1–2 — thesis. 3–9 — demonstration. 10 — the thesis,
having been proved, is repeated.

Metre: hendecasyllabics.

1. *pulcre*: = *bene*, as in 23. 5 and 8.

    cinaedis: see on 16. 2, where, as here, the term is linked with
pathicus.

2. *Mamurrae pathicoque*: if = *Mamurraeque pathico*, the licence is a
rare one; cf. perhaps 76. 11 *teque*. Perhaps a variation on an idiom
found several times in Horace, in which e.g. *pacis eras mediusque
belli* (*Carm.* 2. 19. 28) is used for *pacis eras medius mediusque belli*; see
Page thereon. In any case Ellis is right, probably, in remarking:
'The *que* joined as it is with *pathico*, and thus standing between
Mamurrae and *Caesarique*, distributes the vice equally to both.'
For Caesar as *cinaedus* see Suetonius, *Jul.* 49.

3. *nec mirum*: so 23. 7.

    utrisque: the plural, of two individuals (common enough in
prose), only here and in line 6 in C. (Five examples of the singu-
lar.)

4. *Formiana*: 'one caught it at Rome and the other at Formiae'
(Copley). See on 41. 4 (= 43. 5).

6. *morbosi . . . gemelli*: = 'twin brothers in vice'.

7. *uno in lecticulo*: Apparently a pun on the two meanings of
lecticulo: (1) 'bed'; (2) = *lecticula*, 'study couch' — cf. *erudituli*. But
lecticulus does not occur elsewhere and the MSS, apart from O,
have *lectulo*, which is unmetrical, unless one assumes that the final
o remains as a short syllable as in 55. 4. BICKEL's *alueolo*
('gamingboard') is gratuitous. Copley thus translates 6–7:

> two little twins with the same disease
> same sweet little school for their Ph.D.'s

    erudituli: Caesar became an authority on style and grammar
as well as a writer of memoirs; for Mamurra's literary pretensions
see Poem 105. The diminutive *eruditulus* occurs only here.

8. *uorax*: cf. 29. 2 and 10, and 33. 4.

　　adulter: For Caesar's exploits see Suetonius, *Jul.* 50–2, to whom we owe the often quoted jingle sung by Caesar's soldiers:

　　urbani, seruate uxores: moechum caluom adducimus.

　　aurum in Gallia effutuisti, hic sumpsisti mutuum.

Suetonius concludes with a remark attributed to the elder Curio that Caesar was *omnium mulierum uirum et omnium uirorum mulierem*. For Mamurra cf. C.'s indignant question (29. 7) *perambulabit omnium cubilia?*

　　9. *riuales socii et puellularum*: 'joined in friendly rivalry in the pursuit of maidens, too'. For this sense of *riuales* cf. Plautus, *St.* 434 *eademst amica ambobus, riuales sumus*; *et* (which some remove) in this case = *etiam*. Alternatively, take *et* as adversative, implying that the peculiar tastes of Caesar and Mamurra made them *riuales* of the *puellulae*, as well as sharing the *puellulae* between them; for this sense of *socius* see *L & S* II A 1.

　　puellularum: the diminutive is also found three times in Poem 61: lines 57, 175 and 181.

　　10. For repetition of the opening line see Poems 16, 36 and 52.

See:

E. Bickel, '*Catulli in Caesarem carmina*', *RhM* 93 (1949), 20–3.

58

'Caelius, our Lesbia is a common prostitute.' More detailed, more savage, more contemptuous — less detached than 11. 17–20. Cf. 37. 11–16.

What better person to share his feelings with publicly in a poem than Caelius Rufus, the man who had succeeded C. as Clodia's lover, only to be discarded by her in his turn? The identification of the Caelius whose name forms the opening word of Poem 58 with the victim of Clodia so eloquently defended by Cicero in April 56 B.C. is both tempting and plausible — granted the identification of Lesbia with Clodia Metelli (so WILAMOWITZ).

(See Introduction.) Caelius had called Clodia a *quadrantaria Clytemnestra* (Quint. 8. 6. 53) and Cicero picked up the jest, *Cael.* 62. For the question whether he is also the Caelius of Poem 100 and the Rufus of Poems 69 and 77 see on these poems. Since Poem 11 belongs to 55 B.C., it seems reasonable to put Poem 58 after C.'s return from Bithynia early in 56 B.C. — Clodia and Caelius had quarrelled while he was away: Poem 58 is not the sudden, flaming anger of discovery, but the bitter, sullen, smouldering anger of a man unable to shake himself free from the fragments of a shattered illusion, incapable of accepting the sordid evidence which confronts him of what he already knows.

We can hardly suppose that C. and Caelius were any longer friends. The likelihood, however, that Poem 77 more nearly reflects C.'s true feelings towards Caelius (regarded by AUSTIN as telling against identification of the Caelius of Poem 58 with Clodia's victim) need only heighten the irony of the situation.

Structure: one complex sentence, the main verb *glubit* in the last line.

Metre: hendecasyllabics.

1. *nostra*: probably = *mea*. On C.'s use of *noster*, etc., for *meus*, etc., see Fordyce on 107. 3f. But surely if Caelius is Caelius Rufus, the reader must be invited to entertain the sense 'yours and mine', even if only to reject it. [*uestra* OG, *nostra* R.]

2-3. *quam Catullus unam* | *plus quam se atque suos amauit omnes*: The echo of 8. 5 *amata nobis quantum amabitur nulla* (repeated slightly changed at 37. 12) adds bitter overtones of irony to the plangency of these words — how things have changed! At the same time the echo is structurally effective: the thing is so incredible it is necessary to insist that there can be no possible mistake; even the repetition *Lesbia nostra, Lesbia illa, illa Lesbia* is not enough; it must be put beyond doubt that C. means the woman of whom he once said (72. 3-4): *dilexi tum te non tantum ut uulgus amicam*, | *sed pater ut gnatos diligit et generos.*

4. *in quadriuiis et angiportis*: adversative — 'on street corners' (i.e. in broad daylight), as well as 'in back alleys'; cf. 37. 16 *semitarii moechi*.

5. *glubit*: emphatic, opposed to 3 *amauit*. The word is used by
Cato of stripping the bark off an oak, by Varro of skinning sheep.
An obscene meaning is usually assumed here; for some suggestions
see LENZ. But perhaps C. means no more than that Lesbia strips
her lovers of their clothes (and their cash); the effect aimed at i.e. is
bathos — a devastating contrast between the past evoked in lines
1–3 (ending with *amauit*) and the tawdry, sordid present. Cf.,
however, Cicero, *Fam.* 9. 22. 1 (a discussion of obscenity):
meministi Roscium (the actor), '*ita me destituit nudum*'. *totus est sermo
uerbis tectus, re impudentior.*

   magnanimi Remi nepotes: = *Romanos*, but the grandiloquence
is ironic: Lesbia degrades the heirs to Rome's glorious past along
with herself.

See:

R. G. Austin, commentary on Cicero, *Cael.* (3rd edn 1960),
   Appendix III: 'Caelius and Catullus'.
F. W. Lenz, '*Catulliana*', *RCCM* 5 (1963), 62–7.
U. von Wilamowitz-Moellendorff, *Hellenistische Dichtung* (1924)
   ii 308.

58b

The temptation is strong to attach these lines to Poem 55. They
have the same addressee, Camerius, who is not found elsewhere.
Their theme is an elaboration, with an appropriate display of
urbanitas and *doctrina*, of the theme of 55; according to COMFORT
45, C. is parodying the 'high-flying manner of the self-conscious
vates'; (he supports his assertion with a vocabulary analysis).
Finally, the lines display the same metrical peculiarity, contracted
nucleus; though this occurs in only two lines, 1 and 9, whereas in
Poem 55 twelve lines, probably, have a contracted nucleus.

   One or two late MSS give the lines after 55. 12; Ellis put them
after 55. 14; the obvious place, however, seems after 55. 13.
That they should have strayed from their proper place is hardly

stranger than that 50. 16-17 should crop up a second time
after 54. 1 — a clearly impossible position for them. There
are plenty of examples, however, in the Catullan collection
of a poem echoing an earlier poem and separated from
it by apparently unrelated poems. Whether we incorporate the
lines in Poem 55 or not, a certain amount of textual surgery seems
called for.

Metre: hendecasyllabics with contracted nucleus in lines 1 and
9; see on Poem 55.

1-4. The fourfold *non*, if it is to follow 55. 13 *sed te iam ferre
Herculi labos est*, must negate some such statement as 'could I keep
track of you', which we must suppose to have dropped out, either
before 58b. 1 or after 58b. 2. Those who assume that all four
non's introduce a protasis usually transpose lines 2 and 3.

1. *custos . . . ille Cretum*: =Talos, the (animated) bronze giant,
made for King Minos, to ward off invaders; he ran round Crete
three times a day.

  si fingar: 'if I were given the shape cf', i.e. changed into.

2. ='not if I were swept along, Pegasus-like'.

3-4. As printed, best taken as supplementary assertions: 'I am
no Ladas' etc.

3. *Ladas*: a famous Spartan runner.

  pinnipesue: high-style; cf. 5 *plumipedas*; both compounds occur
only here.

4. As printed, 'I am not Rhesus' snow-white, speedy chariot
pair'; those who transpose 2 and 3 regard *bigae* as genitive singular,
or make the phrase ablative. The horses of Rhesus were famous.

5. ='While you are about it, you can throw in feather-footed
and flying fowl'.

6-7. 'Requisition at the same time the winds' onslaught:
you might unite them and put them at my disposal'.

8-10. The climax, apparently, for which all that precedes
prepares: 'I'd still be dead-tired, if I tried to track you down'.

The words *defessus quaeritando* occur in a passage of Plautus
(*Am.* 1009-14 — Amphitruo has been sent on a wild-goose chase)

which can be regarded as a colloquial model for Poems 55 and
58b:

> Naucratem quem conuenire uolui in naui non erat,
> neque domi neque in urbe inuenio quemquam qui illum uider
> nam omnis plateas perreptaui, gymnasia et myropolia;
> apud emporium atque in macello, in palaestra atque in foro,
> in medicinis, in tostrinis, apud omnis aedis sacras
> sum defessus quaeritando: nusquam inuenio Naucratem.

See:

K. Barwick, 'Zu Catull C. 55 and 58a', *Hermes* 63 (1928), 66–80
(two separate poems).

H. Comfort, 'Parody in Catullus LVIIIa' *AJPh* 56 (1935), 45–9.

F. O. Copley, 'Catullus LV, 9–14', *AJPh* 73 (1952), 295–7 (for
integration).

59

An elegantly structured epigram, rather than a lampoon. Upon
an opening line devastating in its simplicity and finality (it reads
like an inscription, or rather like something scrawled upon a wall)
is built an elaborately phrased sentence, in which Rufa's reputa-
tion is torn to shreds with a detachment that renders the lurid
imagery all the more telling.

Cf. some actual inscriptions —

> *CIL* 4. 2421: Rufa ita uale, quare bene felas.
>
> 1427: Saluia felat Antiocu luscu.
>
> 2402: Ionas cum Fileto hic fellat.

Metre: limping iambics.

1. Rufa and her Rufulus (an ironical diminutive — if correctly
restored: the MSS have *Rufum*, which is unmetrical) are unknown,
though we may suspect a reference to the Rufus of 69. 2 etc.; with
the diminutive cf. 12. 17 and 47. 3 *Veraniolum*. The fact that Rufa
came from Bologna need not be a valid clue; the detail may simply
be recorded to enhance the mock-solemnity of the opening.

2. *uxor Meneni*: the detail clashes ironically with the statement of line 1.

saepe: Rufa was perhaps a *bustuaria moecha*, like those mentioned by Martial 3. 93. 15 (cf. 1. 34. 8).

sepulcretis: the word is found only here; both food and drink were burned with the bodies of the dead.

3. *ipso . . . de rogo*: Emphatic, to underline (1) the ironic contrast with *cenam*: Rufa's 'dinner' is a loaf of bread snatched up as it tumbles down from the flames; (2) Rufa's impudence — she does her thieving during the actual cremation.

5. *semiraso*: 'half-shaven', i.e. 'ill-shaven', 'unkempt'; *ustores* seem to have been a pretty rough lot, but the detail underlines the squalor to which Rufa sinks. (Some suggest that *semiraso* = 'shaven on one side of the head only' as a sign that the man had been a runaway slave.)

See:

Cat. Rev. 33.

60

The last of the polymetric poems complains that an appeal (for help, or comfort) in a final crisis is passing unheeded: how is it possible to be so hard-hearted?

There is a rush of passionate rhetoric here more characteristic of the high style of epic or epyllion than the wry, bantering irony of Poem 38 (cf. Poem 30), or even the tortured, hard-hitting invective of Poem 77: this is how Ariadne reproaches the absent Theseus, 64. 155-8; cf. Dido to Aeneas, *A.* 4. 365-7. The only clue is provided by 4 *supplicis*; can it be reconciled with WEINREICH's hypothesis that Lesbia is the recipient of these lines?

Metre: limping iambics.

1-3. The cliché (a poetic elaboration of the idea that cruelty etc. shows that one is an unnatural son or daughter) goes back to Homer (*Il.* 16. 33-5, Patroclus to Achilles). The immediate model is perhaps Euripides, *Medea* 1341–3: Jason calls Medea 'a lioness (λέαιναν), more savage than the Scylla'; Medea takes up both words in her reply, 1358–9; see also *Bacchae* 988–90. Cf. Virgil, *A.* 2. 540–9 (Priam's reproach, and Neoptolemus' contemptuous rejoinder) and 4. 365–7.

1. *num*: 'surely not'; expresses incredulity, or a lingering hope.

leaena: also 64. 154.

Libystinis: a rare form of the adjective; cf. 7. 3 *Libyssae*.

2. *Scylla*: In Homer (*Od.* 12. 85–100) a six-headed, twelve-footed monster that barks like a dog. The Roman poets (Lucretius 5. 892–5; Virgil, *Ecl.* 6. 75, *A.* 3. 426–8; etc.) tend to make her a kind of monstrous mermaid somehow ending up in a bunch of yelping dogs (σκύλλω = 'tear to pieces', σκύλαξ = 'puppy').

infima inguinum parte: = 'where her belly terminates'.

4. *supplicis uocem*: implies an appeal for help, or comfort.

in nouissimo casu: 'in this latest emergency'; for *nouissimus* = 'last of a series' and therefore 'last of all' see on 4. 22–4. Cf. Varro, *L.* 6. 59 *a quo etiam extremum nouissimum quoque dici coeptum uolgo, quod mea memoria ut Aelius sic senes aliquot, nimium nouum uerbum quod esset, uitabant.*

5. *contemptam haberes*: 'regard with indifference'; cf. 17. 2 *paratum habes.*

nimis fero corde: cf. 43. 4 *nimis elegante lingua*; for *cor* in this sense cf. 64. 54, 94 and 124, etc.

See:

O. Weinreich, 'Catull c. 60', *Hermes* 87 (1959), 75–90.

61

Like Poem 62 (and the Song of the Fates, 64. 323–81), a marriage hymn; or rather a literary version of one — a Greek framework incorporating motifs from Roman ritual (the *Fescennina iocatio* of 124 ff., the scene at the threshold, 159–61), written apparently in

honour of a real marriage, that of Manlius Torquatus (possibly
L. Manlius Torquatus, praetor 49 B.C., the exponent of Epicur-
eanism in Cicero's *Fin.*) and his bride, called *Iunia* in line 16 and
addressed as *Aurunculeia* in 82–3; she was possibly the woman from
Asculum mentioned as the bride of a Manlius by Cicero, *Sul.* 25.

Some suppose Manlius to be also the addressee of Poem 68, but
this is hard to reconcile with the readings of the MSS (see on 68.
41 *Allius*).

Structure: A dramatic monologue, in the form of a long
invocation of the God of Marriage, followed by a series of
addresses (interspersed with asides to the other participants in the
ceremony), first to the bride, then to the groom, and finally to the
bridal pair:

1–75 — invocation (includes aside to the bridesmaids, 36–45).
76–81 — aside announcing arrival of the bride. 82–113 — to the
bride (interrupted by a short, fragmentary aside to the marriage-
bed, 107–12). 114–83 — held together by the refrain *io Hymen*
etc.; the addressee varies. 184–98 — to the groom. 199–223 — to
the bridal pair.

Metre: Four glyconics $(- \underline{\cup} \mid - \cup \cup - \mid \cup -)$, followed by a
pherecratean $(\cup \underline{\cup} \mid - \cup \cup - \mid \underline{\cup})$ — i.e. the same line minus a final
syllable. As in Poem 34, the stanza is treated as a single unit:
hiatus between lines is avoided; the last syllable of each of the first
4 lines of each stanza, if not long by nature, is long by position (i.e.
the line ends with a consonant, and the next line begins with a
consonant). This is called *synaphaea*. The same basic units are
employed in Poem 17.

1–75. The *Invocation to the Marriage God* is divided into two parts
by the aside to the bridesmaids, 36–45. The first is constructed
round a string of eight imperatives (6 *cinge*, 8 *cape*, 9 *ueni*, 14 *pelle*,
15 *quate*, 24 *age*, 27 *perge*, 31 *uoca*) interrupted by the two ex-
planatory stanzas, 16–25. The second part of the invocation,
46–75, is a formal hymn of praise.

1–2. *collis . . . cultor*: 'dweller on Mt Helicon'; the seat of the
Muses, in Boeotia.

2. *Vraniae genus*: = 'son of the Muse Urania'; the Marriage God's ancestry is variously given; with *genus* cf. 64. 23 *deum genus* (of Peleus).

3. *rapis*: Clearly a reference to the Roman marriage ritual, which prescribed a show of force in taking the bride from her mother's arms to her new home. See on 58–9.

4. *o Hymenaee Hymen*: The refrain is repeated three times in the invocation (at 39, 49 and 59); in the form *io Hymen* etc. it occurs at 117 and then ten times more at the conclusion of each stanza from 137 to 182; ὑμήν seems to have been originally a ritual 'cry in marriage ceremonies; a lengthened form of the cry (ὑμέναι' ὦ etc.) was subsequently interpreted as an invocation of the Marriage God; the longer form also came to be used, in Latin as in Greek, of the marriage song itself (as in 62. 4), and then as a synonym of *nuptiae*, or even *conubium* (as in 66. 11), commonly in the plural (as in 64. 20 and 141); cf. the transferred use of *taeda* and *thalamus*. The form *Hymen*, of the Marriage God, seems not earlier than Ovid.

6–10. The Marriage God, i.e., is bidden to dress like the bride.

7. *amaraci*: the fragrant red marjoram.

8. *flammeum*: The bridal veil, apparently orange in colour (it is variously described as 'red' and 'yellow'); cf. line 115. In the Aldobrandini wedding frieze (Maiuri, *Roman Painting* 30–1) the bride is veiled in white, but there is a yellow object, possibly the *flammeum*, lying on the bed behind her. See on 68. 133–4.

10. *luteum . . . soccum*: A yellow slipper, like that worn by the bride in the Aldobrandini frieze; note C.'s exploitation of colour contrast, as in 64. 49, etc.; cf. 188 *luteumue papauer*.

11–16. Hymen is invited to join in singing the marriage hymn.

13. *tinnula*: i.e. clear and high-pitched; a 'pathetic' use of the diminutive; cf. 22 *ramulis*, 57 and 181 *puellulam* (175 *puellulae*); 88 *hortulo*; 160 *aureolos*; 174 *brachiolum*; 186 *floridulo*; 209 *paruulus*; 213 *labello*.

14. *pelle humum pedibus*: i.e. in dance.

15. *pineam . . . taedam*: the marriage torch.

16. On Junia and Manlius see introductory note; *Manlio* is dative with 20 *nubet*.

17. *qualis Idalium colens*: 'like her who dwells in Idalium'; see on 36. 12. The bride, i.e., is as lovely as Venus when she appeared before Paris, to be judged more beautiful than Hera or Athena.

19–20. *cum bona ... alite*: 'under favourable auspices'; an *auspex* was traditionally present at weddings.

21. *enitens*: 'radiant'.

22. *myrtus Asia*: The ancient grammarians distinguish *Asia*, the province and its corresponding adjective, *Asius* (short initial a), from *Asius* (long initial a), an adjective referring to the area of Lydia, at the mouth of the Maeander. With the comparison cf. 87–9, 186–8, 62. 39–44 and 64. 87–90.

23–5. 'which the wood nymphs feed on dew, to be their plaything'.

25. *nutriunt umore*: no other case in either Poem 61 or Poem 34 of three long syllables in the second foot of the pherecratean.

26. *huc aditum ferens*: cf. 43 *huc aditum ferat*, 63. 47 *reditum tetulit*, 63. 79 *reditum ferat*.

27. *perge linquere*: = 'make haste to quit'; cf. 193 *perge, ne remorare*.

27–8. *Thespiae ... specus*: 'the Aonian caves (accusative plural) in the Thespian rock' — i.e. Mt Helicon; the town of Thespiae lay at the foot of the mountain. The god, i.e., is asked, as is usual in hymns, to quit his customary haunts.

29–30. *nympha ... frigerans Aganippe*: Aganippe is at once the nymph and the spring which bore her name.

31. *domum dominam uoca*: i.e. call the bride to the home of which she is henceforth mistress. Cf. 68. 68.

32. *cupidam*: cf. 54 *cupida*.

33. *mentem amore reuinciens*: 'entwining her thoughts with love'.

34. *tenax hedera*: a simile often applied to lovers, entwined in each other's arms.

36–45. *Aside to the bridesmaids*. Cf. the chorus of *innuptae*, 62. 6, etc.

36–7. *integrae uirgines*: 'unmarried girls'; see on 34. 2.

37. *aduenit*: present tense: 'approaches'.

38. *par dies*: i.e. 'your own marriage day'.

in modum: hardly 'in tune' (Fordyce), but 'in the right and proper way'; cf. 116.

42. *citarier*: the archaic passive infinitive; cf. 65, 70 and 75 *compararier* and 68 *nitier*; probably also 68. 141 *componier*.

44. *bonae . . . boni*: contrast, i.e., 97–101 and 146.

45. *coniugator*: the word occurs only here.

46–75. A formal *hymn of praise* to the Marriage God.

46. *quis deus*: see on 62. 20 *quis ignis*.

46–7. *est ama-* | *tis*: [Bergk's transposition of V *amatis* | *est* restores the metre; cf. 82–3 *Au-* | *runculeia* for the division, and 45. 20 *amant amantur* for the collocation *amatis . . . amantibus*. But Haupt's *anxiis* | *est* is perhaps more plausible.]

48. *colent*: the future has something of the force of 'are to worship'.

49. *caelitum*: also 11. 14.

51–6. With the anaphora, *te . . . tibi . . . te . . . tu* cf. 64. 25–9.

51. *suis*: i.e. on behalf of his children.

tremulus: presumably 'shaky with age' as in 154; see on 17. 13 *tremula*.

53. *zonula soluunt sinus*: 'free the folds (of their dress) from the girdle (which gathers it up)'; part of the symbolism of the marriage ceremony. *soluunt* scans as 3 syllables; cf. 95. 6 *peruoluent*.

54–5. *cupida . . . aure*: 'with eager ear'; cf. 32 *cupidam*.

55. *captat*: 'listen for'.

56. *fero*: probably 'rough' (i.e. 'not gentle' — by comparison with a woman); see on 3 *rapis*. No conflict therefore with the image of the eager, nervous husband of 54–5; possibly, however, 'shy', 'nervous' (like a wild creature) — see on 64. 14 *feri uultus*.

58–9. *a gremio suae matris*: part of the ritual. See Festus 364. 26 Lindsay *rapi simulatur uirgo ex gremio matris*; cf. 62. 21.

61–3. The construction is: *sine te Venus nil commodi capere potest quod bona fama comprobet*; i.e. nothing good can come of it; the practical common-sense view of things, rather than a moral pose incompatible with C.'s usual persona.

65. *compararier*: see on 42 *citarier*.

ausit: = *audeat*, an old optative form common in verse.

66–70. The first half of the stanza follows the pattern of 61–3; the second half reproduces the refrain of 63–5.

68. *stirpe nitier*: for the metaphor see Cicero, *Cael.* 79 *qui hoc unico filio nititur*.

71–5. A second variation on the basic pattern of 61–5; this time a slight change in the refrain.

71. *quae . . . careat*: 'that was without'. The (generic) subjunctive suggests an unlikely state of affairs.

72. *praesides*: 'defenders' (cf. *praesidium*); *L & S* II A.

76–81. *Aside*, announcing the arrival of the bride. The metre shows that 4 lines (at least) are missing after 78.

77. *uiden ut*: = *uidesne ut*; cf. 62.8. In the colloquial form (1) the verb introduced by *ut* is indicative; (2) the second syllable of *uiden* is clipped ('iambic shortening'). For the formula without *ut* see 94–5; a further variation in 164–6 *aspice ut* etc. Often singular, though several persons addressed; cf. 62.12 *aspicite ut* etc.

82–113. *To the bride.* (Interrupted by the short fragmentary aside, 107–12.) Held together by the refrain *prodeas noua nupta* (92, 96, 106, 113, and probably 91) and the leitmotive *abit dies* (90, 105 and 112).

82–6. A pleasantly ironical variation on the commonplace 'the prettiest woman under the sun'; the dawn is that of the wedding day (cf. 11 *exitus hilari die*).

82–3. *Aurunculeia*: see introductory note.

87–9. Cf. 62.39–44.

87. *uario*: 'many-coloured'; cf. 66.59 *uario in limine caeli*.

88. *hortulo*: for the diminutive see on 13 *tinnula*.

89. *hyacinthinus*: the adjective. Not our hyacinth, possibly the blue iris.

91. The line is missing in the MSS. The procession begins.

94–5. [*uiden ut* V, as in 77, but here unmetrical. Some keep *ut* and reduce *uiden* to *uide*.]

96–7. *in mala . . . adultera*: with the ablative cf. 64.98 *in flauo hospite*.

100–1. Cf. 64. 379–80.

102. *adsitas*: 'planted beside them', to support the vines.

107–12. *Aside* to the marriage-bed. The metre shows that 3 lines (at least) are missing after 107.

109–10. 'how great (*quanta*) the joys which (109 *quae*) await your (i.e. the bed's) master; for *ero* see on 151 and 31. 12.

110 and 111. *quae*: contained accusative with 112 *gaudeat*.

110–11. *uaga nocte*: 'wandering night'; the reference is to Night in her chariot. Cf. 64. 271 *uagi Solis*.

111. *medio die*: cf. 32. 3 *meridiatum*.

112–13. The echo *sed abit dies*: | *prodeas noua nupta* from 105–6 concludes the section which began at 76.

114–83. Held together by the refrain *io Hymen* etc., rephrased from line 4. The addressee varies.

114–23. To the male attendants; cf. 179–83 to the female attendants.

115. *flammeum*: the bridal veil; see on 8.

116. *in modum*: see on 38.

120. *Fescennina iocatio*: the ribald *uersus Fescennini* formed part of the traditional marriage ceremony; they were sung while the procession was moving through the streets; C. has accommodated the traditional obscenities to their present artistic setting, contenting himself with a bantering reference to a displaced *concubinus* (124–33).

122–3. *desertum . . . amorem*: 'hearing that his love for his master has been rejected'.

123. *concubinus*: The *puer delicatus* (a slave — cf. 122 *domini* and 127 *seruire*), a youngster his own age (hence the symbolism of 131–2), to whom the bridegroom had been devoted; no doubt a traditional theme of the *Fescennina iocatio*; cf. Poems 15, 21, etc., however, and the *deliciae domini* of Corydon in Virgil, *Ecl.* 2.

124–43. The *Fescennina iocatio*. First the *concubinus* (124–33) and then the groom (134–43) are addressed on behalf of the *pueri* of 114 (as is shown by 139 *scimus*); the poet, i.e., becomes the mouthpiece of a chorus; cf. Poem 42.

124. *da nuces pueris*: Walnuts were used as playthings in children's games. The scattering of them during the wedding procession symbolized, like the ritual shaving of 131–2, that the time had come for the *concubinus* (and the groom) to put childish things aside. The nuts no doubt were discarded (here by the *concubinus*, in Virgil, *Ecl.* 8. 30 by the *maritus*) and then picked up by the *pueri* in the procession (all this being part of the ritual), not necessarily for use as confetti.

     iners: 'lazy'; cf. Cicero, *N.D.* 1. 36. 102 *Epicurus quasi pueri delicati nihil cessatione melius existimat.*

125–6. *satis diu* etc.: i.e. the *concubinus* is now too old for such things. Cf. 225 *lusimus satis.*

126–7. *lubet . . . seruire*: oxymoron; the time has come for the *concubinus* to change his master.

127. *Talasio*: Talasius, or Talassius, was the Roman equivalent of Hymenaeus.

129. *sordebant tibi uilicae*: farm-stewards' wives, i.e., were not good enough for him — though he was a slave. Cf. Virgil, *Ecl.* 2. 44 *sordent tibi munera nostra.*

130. *hodie atque heri*: = 'until now'.

131–2. Till now the *concubinus* has needed a barber only to wave his hair; but the time has come for manly things and, to symbolize this, the *cinerarius* ('hair-waver', 'friseur') must set to and shave the *concubinus'* cheeks. Martial (11. 78. 4) makes the bride attend to the shaving personally: *tondebit pueros iam noua nupta tuos.*

134–43. Now it is the groom's turn to be lampooned.

134. *male*: = 'with difficulty'.

135. *unguentate*: i.e. all sleeked-up for the marriage ceremony.

     glabris: = *pueris delicatis.*

139–40. = 'we know about your secrets and there is nothing wrong about them'; *quae licent*, i.e., implies the groom, in sowing his wild oats, had stayed within what the law permitted. The plural *licent* is rare.

144–73. *Second address to the bride.* The refrain *io Hymen* etc.

continues, but the ribald persiflage is dropped in favour of a tenderer and more sympathetic tone.

144–5. With the sentiment cf. 8. 6–7. For *cauĕ* see on 6. 16.

146. A warning complementary to the reassurance of 97–101.

petitum: supine, as in 10. 2 *uisum duxerat*, 32. 3 *ueniam meridiatum*.

ni . . . eat: = *ne eat* (archaism).

149. A gesture towards dramatic verisimilitude: the singers reach the house of the groom. Cf. 31 *domum dominam uoca* and 159–60 *transfer . . . pedes*.

ut: 'how'.

151. *quae tibi sine seruiat*: 'let it be your slave'; the house, i.e., becomes the slave of its *domina*. For a development of the idea see on 31. 12 *ero gaude*.

152–3. The only time the refrain falls in mid-sentence.

154–6. *usque dum . . . annuit*: 'until white-haired old age, making your forehead shake, nods Yes to everything'; i.e. the shaking of the head, a sign of old age, will make her seem to be agreeing to everything. A fine vivid image. The present indicative with *dum*, 'until', (instead of the future perfect or the present subjunctive) is common, especially in early Latin.

155. *anilitas*: only here in classical Latin.

159–61. A further gesture towards dramatic realism (cf. on 149). The reference is to the Roman ceremony of conducting the bride across the threshold of her new home. (C. seems to visualize the bride stepping across the threshold herself, not being carried.)

160. *limen aureolos pedes*: double accusative (only here with *transferre*).

aureolos: 'yellow'; cf. 10 *luteum pede soccum*. For the idea cf. 68. 70–2. For the diminutive see on 13 *tinnula*.

161. *rasilem*: Either (1) 'polished', or (2) 'well-worn' (cf. 68. 71 *trito in limine*); in either case *subi* makes it clear that *forem* is the doorway, rather than the door itself.

164–6. Either (1) the bride arrives to find the groom upon the marriage couch (cf. 64. 47–9, though it seems that in classical times the *lectus genialis* was symbolic rather than for actual occupancy by the bridal pair). Or (2) the bride arrives to find the groom still participating in a banquet — either the marriage feast, or some sort of bachelor party; the marriage feast normally took place at the home of the bride before the *deductio*, but the reverse seems implied by Poem 62. Cf. Cicero, *Q. fr.* 2. 3. 7 *Prid. Id. Febr. haec scripsi ante lucem. eo die apud Pomponium [Atticum] in eius nuptiis eram cenaturus.* In either case C.'s gesture at realism need not be incompatible with some simplification of fact. Roman art is often simultaneously factual and fanciful in its representation of ceremonial occasions. Fordyce's 'merely pictured as lying on a couch, while he waits for the bride's procession to arrive' misrepresents a stylized economy of imagery equally characteristic of both poetry and art.

166. *totus immineat*: 'is intent only upon'.

169–71. The image of fire is of course latent in the cliché *uror* = 'I am in love', but C.'s reformulation of it revivifies the metaphor; the passive *uritur* with a subject like *flamma* is an example of tensioned statement.

170. *pectore . . . intimo*: locative.

171. *penite*: = *penitus*; the form is not found elsewhere; in early Latin *penitus* is often treated as an adjective.

174–6. *Aside* to a boy (175 *praetextate*) among the attendants.

174. *mitte*: 'release'.

    brachiolum: for the diminutive see on 13 *tinnula*.

    teres: see on 64. 65 *tereti*.

175. *puellulae*: genitive; cf. 57 and 181 *puellulam*.

176. *cubile*: see 107–8.

179–81. *Aside* to the matrons (those who have been 'long and happily married').

180. *cognitae*: see on 72. 1 and 5.

181. *puellulam*: the 'pathetic' diminutive (also 57 and 175 — and 57. 9) is extremely effective here; see on 13 *tinnula*.

184–98. *To the groom.*

186–8. With the simile cf. 21–5. With *nitens* cf. 2. 5 *nitenti*.

186. *floridulo*: see on 13 *tinnula*.

187. *parthenice*: perhaps the white camomile. No doubt chosen here for its name (παρθένος =*uirgo*).

188. *luteum*: see on 10 *luteum*.

192. *sed abit dies*: echoes 90, 105 and 112.

193. *ne remorare*: =*noli remorari*; an archaism characteristic of verse style; also 62. 59 *ne pugna* and 67. 18 *ne dubita*.

195. *bona . . . Venus*: cf. 44 *dux bonae Veneris* and 61–4.

196. *iuuerit*: the perfect subjunctive in a wish means much the same as the present (cf. 189 *iuuent*).

199–223. *To the bridal pair.*

199–203. For the idea see on 7. 3–6.

201. *subducat numerum prius*: 'let him first reckon up the total'; cf. Cicero, *Att.* 5. 21. 11 *sed subducamus summam.*

207–8. *indidem . . . ingenerari*: sc. *decet*; i.e. without recourse to adoption (common among old Roman families).

209. *uolo*: the final o is short; see on 6. 16.

    paruulus: see on 13 *tinnula*.

212. *dulce rideat*: cf. 51. 5 *dulce ridentem*.

213. *semihiante*: a word apparently coined by C.; cf. 50. 15 *semimortua*, 54. 2 *semilauta*, 59. 5 *semiraso*.

    labello: see on 13 *tinnula*.

215. *insciens*: [The reading of V. Those who keep 216 *omnibus* read *insciis*, a correction found in R.]

216. *obuiis*: [*omnibus* V — suspect because a final long syllable is required; *obuiis* Pleitner.]

218. *indicet ore*: i.e. may his looks proclaim he is his father's son.

219–20. =*talis illius laus a bona matre genus a bona matre approbet*, 'may the character which he will owe to his mother prove his descent from a virtuous mother'. The sense is compact rather than obscure, only becoming awkward when one attempts to state it fully according to the conventions of prose; the rule that prepositional phrases should be fairly tightly linked to a verb is a convention of classical Latin, as earlier legal expressions such as *lex de ui, quaestio de rebus repetundis*, etc., show. Cf. 221–3 *unica ab optima matre . . . fama.*

221–3. *qualis unica . . . manet fama*: 'no less than the peerless fame that abides . . .'.

222. *Telemacho*: son of Odysseus by Penelope, the classical model of the virtuous wife.

223. *Penelopeo*: =*Penelopae*. See on 64. 1 *Peliaco*. The adjective (a verse archaism) ends the stanza with a flourish.

224–8. *Tailpiece*: 224–5 to the bridesmaids; 225–8 to the couple.

225. *lusimus satis*: ='we have had our fun'; cf. 125–6 *satis diu lusisti nucibus*. See on 17. 1 *ludere*.

227–8. ='may you live happily and devote your youthful energies unstintingly to your duty as a married couple'.

227. *munere assiduo*: instrumental ablative, with both *ualentem* and *exercete*.

See:

Wheeler, Chapter 7, for the marriage hymn as a literary form.

U. von Wilamowitz-Moellendorff, *Hellenistische Dichtung* (1924) ii 280–7.

Gordon Williams, 'Some aspects of Roman marriage ceremonies and ideals', *JRS* 48 (1958), 16–29 (16–17 deal with Poem 61).

62

Like Poem 61 and 64. 323–81, a marriage hymn. 'The scene which we are going to watch unfolds gradually. We are listening first to a group of young men talking excitedly together, then to a group of equally excited young women. It is evening, shortly after sunset; a rich wedding feast is coming to its end; the arrival of the bride is imminent. In the large room or hall the two groups have been dining at some distance from one another, the men near to the open door, the women farther inside: they cannot directly observe the rising of the evening star, but have to infer it (7, *nimirum*) from what they see the young men doing. At this preparatory stage, before the actual singing of the choirs begins, the young men cannot distinctly hear the voices of the girls at whom they are looking (12): the din among the company is overwhelming. When the young women, after some flurried consultation (6 ff.) and a quick last minute rehearsal (12 ff.), are ready, they intone their first stanza (20) 'Hespere, quis caelo fertur crudelior ignis?' etc. What we have heard up to this point was not to be taken as singing but as snatches from the talk of the young people. Whether at lines 5 and 10 and 19 they are supposed to hum, by way of preparation or anticipation, the ritual refrain 'Hymen o Hymenaee' we cannot decide; it seems, however, more likely that in these places the refrain belongs, as it were, to the poet rather than to the choirs and merely serves to separate the words of the young men from those of the young women.' (FRAENKEL 2)

The dramatic setting includes details from both Greek and Roman ritual. Poem 62, in other words, (like Poem 61) is a poem in dramatic form, not the text of an actual hymn.

Poem 62 is included in a ninth-century anthology (the *codex Thuaneus*) — some 500 years older than the earliest surviving text of the rest of C.

Metre: hexameters.

1–4. Conversation among the young men, organized into a continuous statement on behalf of all by one of the choir — presumably the leader — as the imperative *consurgite* shows (see on 15 and 17).

1. *Vesper*: the evening star.

   consurgite: = 'rise from your couches' (where they have been feasting), in preparation for the hymn.

   Olympo: 'in the sky'; locative ablative, like 20 *caelo*.

2. *uix tandem*: 'only just'; repetition for emphasis; a colloquialism (see Austin on Virgil, *A.* 2. 128); also 68. 121.

   lumina: high-style plural.

3. *surgere*: the simple form of the verb picks up the compound 1 *consurgite*; see on 10. 20.

iam pinguis linquere mensas: = 'now is the time to give up feasting', in order to come forward and join the *innuptae*.

4. *iam ueniet uirgo*: the bride is apparently about to arrive at her future home at the conclusion of the *deductio*; cf. 61. 159–63.

dicetŭr: see on 64. 20 *despexīt*.

hymenaeus: = 'the marriage hymn'; see on 61. 4.

5. The metre requires a variation in quantity: *Hymen o Hўmenaee*. For the refrain, which occurs 8 times in the poem (and is often added after line 58) see on 61. 4.

ades: imperative.

6–9. Conversation among the girls.

6. *contra*: the two choirs, i.e., face one another.

7. *nimirum*: = 'clearly', or 'the fact is', as in 22. 18; 14 *nec mirum* is rather different. From where they are sitting, the girls cannot see the evening star, but infer it has risen from when the young men have risen to their feet.

Oetaeos: From the mountain between Thessaly and Aetolia; but the word 'had become to the Roman poets, presumably after some Hellenistic model, a common epithet of *Hesperus*, to be used at random'. (FRAENKEL)

ignes: high-style plural, like 2 *lumina*.

8. *uiden ut*: see on 61. 77.

9. *non temere exsiluere*: = 'they haven't sprung to their feet to waste their time'.

canent quod uisere par est: 'their song will be worth seeing'; an illogical colloquialism. [So T; *uisere parent* V, corrected to *uincere par est* by Renaissance editors before the readings of T became known, by which *par est* was confirmed, but not *uincere*; many still print *uincere*; FRAENKEL remarks, 'A conservative critic keeps *uisere*.']

11–18. Conversation among the boys. They can see that the girls are getting their song ready, though they cannot hear what the girls are saying.

11. *parata*: 'assured'; the boys, i.e., will have to exert themselves to win the prize.

L

12. *aspicite . . . ut*: see on 61. 77.

meditata requirunt: i.e. refreshing their memories of what they have prepared; *meditari* = 'rehearse a part' etc.

14. *nec mirum*: 'and no wonder'.

penitus . . . tota mente: repetition for emphasis; see on 63. 44–9.

quae . . . laborant: an indicative verb in casual relative clauses is common in early Latin; contrast 21 *possis*, 27 *firmes*; *laborare* = not just 'work', but 'work hard', 'struggle'.

15. i.e. the boys have been listening to their choir-master, but not concentrating — unlike the girls: the leader identifies himself with the group — a common pedagogical device ('we haven't been listening, have we?'); cf. 42. 21 *nil proficimus*.

17. *animos . . . conuertite uestros*: 'listen to me', or perhaps 'get your minds on the job' (the leader now speaks more firmly); *nunc saltem* = 'now, if you haven't before'.

18. *dicere*: used absolutely of formal utterance — speaking in court etc., reciting poetry etc.

20–58. The contest now begins. Such singing matches (amoebic poetry) are a tradition of pastoral poetry (Theocritus 5 and 8; Virgil, *Ecl.* 3 and 7). There is often, as here, some preliminary banter, and then the contest begins, each contestant, or group of contestants, trying to outdo the other; for exploitations of the form see Poem 45 and Horace, *Carm.* 3. 9.

20–4. The girls begin, developing (no doubt with mock plaintiveness) the theme that marriage is a cruel custom.

20. *quis . . . ignis*: = 'cruellest star in the sky'. [*quis*, the reading of T, is to be preferred to V *qui*.] The forms *qui* and *quis* are more freely interchangeable than grammars suggest, the form *qui* being usual, for both pronoun and adjective, before a word beginning with s. Cf. 61. 46 *quis deus*.

caelo fertur: 'is borne along in the sky'.

21. *possis*: *posse* often = 'bring oneself to'.

complexu auellere matris: see on 61. 58–9. Cf. 64. 88 and 118.

22. *retinentem*: 'holding on', 'clinging'.

24. *capta . . . urbe*: 'when a city is captured'.

26–30. The boys reply with praise of Hesperus, following closely the syntactical pattern of the girls' complaint. Their reply is best taken as a general statement: the evening star by his appearance (*tua flamma*) makes marriage contracts (*desponsa conubia*) binding; husbands-to-be and fathers of the brides are agreed about terms (*pepigere*), but the contracts have not been put into effect (*nec iunxere*); for the scansion of *conubia* see on 57; with *iunxere* cf. Cicero, de Orat. 1. 37 *Sabinorum conubia coniunxisse*.

30. *felici optatius hora*: echoes *capta crudelius urbe*, but with a change in the force of the ablative (comparative, instead of locative).

32. Doubtless the lost lines of the girls' second contribution argued that Hesperus was the ally of thieves.

33. The opening words of the boys' defence of Hesperus alias Eous is also missing. Far from helping thieves, they argue, Hesperus ensures by his arrival that the watch is on its toes (*uigilat custodia*); the only officials at all resembling policemen in Republican Rome were the *tresuiri capitales* also known as the *tresuiri nocturni*, whose duties included imprisoning thieves; property-owners doubtless maintained their own guards. (FRAENKEL suggests C. had in mind the night-watch φυλακή employed in Hellenistic towns.)

35. *mutato comprendis nomine Eous*: C.'s words are, of course, playfully ironical: the star whom thieves tend to regard as their accomplice, Hesperus, often turns up (*saepe reuertens*) under a different identity (*mutato nomine*, like a professional informer) to catch them red-handed (i.e. daybreak finds them still on the job). The fact that the planet Venus is visible sometimes in the morning (=Lucifer), sometimes in the evening (=Hesperus) was frequently made use of by ancient poets — e.g. by C.'s friend and contemporary Cinna, in his *Zmyrna* (see on Poem 95):

> te matutinus flentem conspexit Eous,
>
> et flentem paulo uidit post Hesperus idem

though Cinna was mistaken if he thought that the morning star could reappear as the evening star on the same day. [*Eous* is a brilliant conjecture (*eospem* T; *zosdem* V) due to the eighteenth-century scholar Ioannes Schradeı.]

36. *innuptis*: in particular the *innuptae* (cf. line 6) who are taking part in the contest. Cf. 61. 31–5.

37. *quid tum, si carpunt, tacita quem mente* . . .?: = 'so what? they criticize you, but in their unspoken thoughts . . .'.

39–47. An exquisite, sensuously beautiful Homeric-type simile. There is almost certainly an allusion to a poem attributed to Sappho of which a fragment survives (Fr. 105c *LP* = *LGS* 225; see on 11. 23). FRAENKEL 5 remarks that, if C. had the fragment in mind, 'he recast his model freely, which is exactly what those who are familiar with his ways would expect. The flower in the well-protected garden is as different from the wild hyacinth on the hills as is 'tenui carptus . . . ungui' (43) from πόσσι καταστείβοισι and *defloruit* from χάμαι . . . πόρφυρον ἄνθος. And yet the feeling behind the two passages seems to be kindred. Personally, I am confident that Catullus adapted the same model a second time, and in a context which makes its Sapphic origin almost certain.' Cf. 61. 87–9 and see on 61. 22–6.

39. *hortis*: the plural of an elaborate, ornamental garden (cf. our 'botanical gardens' etc.).

40. *nullo conuolsus aratro*: Did C. remember Creon's words to his son: Sophocles, *Antigone* 569 ἀρώσιμοι γὰρ χἀτέρων εἰσὶν γύαι?

41. *mulcent*: 'caress'; *L & S* I.

42. *optauere*: C. is apparently the first Latin writer to use the 'gnomic' perfect.

43. *tenui . . . ungui*: i.e. a girl does the picking, as in the story of Europa; cf. Virgil, *A.* 11. 68 *qualem uirgineo demessum pollice florem*.

45. *dum . . . dum*: correlative, 'as long as . . . so long', an archaism remarked on by Quintilian (9. 3. 16), quoting C.'s lines.

46. *polluto corpore*: Merrill remarks well, 'the fierce virginity of the chorus views even marriage as a compromise of chastity'. The attitude is assumed, of course, for the sake of the contest, rather than seriously held.

49–58. The boys' answer, as in 26–30, follows closely the

pattern of the girls' complaint, but runs into 10 lines (not count-
ing the refrain), as against 9 from the girls; this has caused some
to suppose a lacuna between 41 and 42, but the extra line may
compensate for the absence of the refrain after 58. The boys'
answer points to the common ancient custom of 'marrying' the
vines to a supporting elm-tree (props were also used); *marita* as a
technical term is at least as old as Cato 32 *arbores facito ut bene
maritae sint*. The details of the imagery are graceful and charming;
but, as in 33–6, the spirit in which the boys cap the girls' complaint
is one of playful irony aimed at outwitting the girls, not at
convincing them.

49. *uidua*: 'unwed'.

   nudo: 'bare' (i.e. of trees).

   nascitur: picks up 39 *nascitur*.

50. *educat*: echoes 41 *educat*.

52. 'all but touches its topmost shoot with its root'; *flagellum* is
the technical term for a young vine-shoot. More natural the other
way around :— *radicem contingit flagello*; but the slight absurdity is
probably part of the fun.

53–5. Where the girls had 42 *multi . . . multae* and 44 *nulli . . .
nullae*, the boys reverse the order, putting their *nulli . . . nulli*
before their *multi . . . multi*.

53. *nulli coluere iuuenci*: i.e. the vine is a wild one, not under
cultivation; the oxen were used to break up the ground round the
vines; Varro, *R.* 1. 8. 5, speaks of spaces between the props, *qua
boues iuncti arare possint*.

54. *eadem*: picks up 43 *idem*.

   marito: if right [T has *marita*] the masculine noun ('as
husband'), not an adjective agreeing with *ulmo* (which is feminine).

56. *sic uirgo dum intacta manet*: repeats the first half of 45, to cap
it with an opposite conclusion.

57. *par conubium*: 'an appropriate marriage'; an allusion per-
haps to the first epigram of Callimachus; cf., however, 61. 38
par dies. The plural *conubia* regularly scans in hexameter verse as
though the u were long (as in 27 and 64. 141 and 158); here, if

the u is long, the i must be consonantal, but possibly the word could be pronounced with either long or short u as a metrical convention; see Austin on Virgil, *A.* 4. 126.

58. *cara*: echoes 47 *cara*.

   inuisa: the notion that an unmarried daughter is a nuisance to her father is consistent with the light-hearted tone of the contest; contrast 61. 51–2.

59–65. To the bride. FRAENKEL argues that the plain truth of 57–8 silences the girls completely. 'If they were right, there ought to be no wedding at all. So the girls, for all their fine effort, are doomed from the outset: the boys must win.' The boys, knowing that they have carried the day, 'do not even pause to repeat the refrain [usually restored by editors after line 58], but turn straight to the bride.'

59. *ne pugna*: = 64 *noli pugnare*. For the form see on 61. 193.

60. *cui*: = *cum eo, cui*; for the omission of the antecedent see on 110. 2. For the role of the father see on 68. 143.

61. *cum*: 'along with'.

62–5. The argument from arithmetic, though very Roman, is hardly seriously intended.

62. *ex parte parentum est*: = 'a share belongs to your parents'.

63. *patrist*: = *patri est*; the first syllable counts as long (uncommon), cf. 29. 22 *patrimonia*.

64. *noli pugnare duobus*: the bride, i.e., must accept the verdict of the majority of shareholders; the dative with *pugnare* (= *cum* + ablative) is not uncommon in verse.

See:

Eduard Fraenkel, '*Vesper adest*', *JRS* 45 (1955), 1–8.

63

Perhaps the most remarkable poem in Latin. 'A study of fanatic devotion and subsequent disillusionment' (ELDER), it has the intense vividness of a nightmare.

WILAMOWITZ's thesis of a Greek model (references in

ELDER), though reasserted by SCHUSTER ('Stark unter spätgriechischem Einfluss steht ohne Zweifel das 63. Gedicht') and Fordyce ('it seems certain that Catullus was translating or adapting a Greek original. . . . What that original was we cannot guess'), is now generally discredited. SELLAR 369–70 well remarked a hundred years ago, 'There is nothing at all like the spirit of this poem in extant Greek literature. No other writer has presented so real an image of the frantic exultation and fierce self-sacrificing spirit of an inhuman fanaticism; and again, of the horror and sense of desolation which a natural man, and more especially a Greek or Roman, would feel in the midst of the wild and strange scenes described in the poem, and when restored to the consciousness of his voluntary bondage, and of the forfeiture of his country and parents, and the free social life of former days.'

The starting point is a wild, primitive legend, the castration of Attis, embodied in the cult of the Great Mother, a Phrygian mystic religion, whose rites had invaded Italy in the third century B.C. (see FRAZER, and the description of Cybele and her procession in Lucretius 2. 600–43). The original Attis is commonly regarded as a vegetation god, though this has been challenged. (LAMBRECHTS maintains Attis was a minor mortal follower of Cybele, whose rise to godhead is not earlier than the second century A.D.) C.'s Attis, at all events, is a Greek, not a Phrygian, who renounces his way of life *Veneris nimio odio* (line 17). Beyond the brief retrospective sketch in lines 62–7 C. tells us nothing: our curiosity — about who Attis was, who his companions were, when and why their flight to Phrygia took place — is left unsatisfied. If such highly compressed, elliptical narrative was a trick of Hellenistic epyllion (see on Poem 64), it is also the method of tragedy — a familiar legend is taken over, adjusted to lend it contemporary significance, and used as a framework for exploring an emotional situation.

Structure: The basic narrative structure consists of two pathetic 11-line vignettes — 1–11 — Attis' frenzied self-mutilation; and 39–49 — Attis, the rueful penitent.

Each vignette is followed by a speech in full tragic style —
12–26 (15 lines) — Attis' address to his companions; and 50–73
(23 lines) — Attis' soliloquy. The first speech is followed by a
pendent narrative passage — 27–38 (12 lines) — the rush to the
slopes of Mt Ida. The second speech is followed by an epilogue,
relating Attis' escape and recapture — 74–7 — escape; 78–83 —
speech of Cybele; 84–90 — recapture; 91–3 — the poet's prayer
to the goddess.

The poem can also be regarded as possessing a tripartite
structure: 1–38 — frenzy; 39–73 — repentence; 74–90 — escape
and recapture.

Metre: The basic line is best regarded as two closely related
sequences of eight syllables, intended clearly to represent the
dialogue of kettledrum and cymbals:

$$\cup\cup- \mid \cup- \mid \cup- \mid - \parallel \cup\cup- \mid \cup\cup\cup \mid \cup\breve{\cup}$$
leue tym|panum|remu|git, ‖ caua cym|bala re|crepant
'The light drum bellows forth, the hollow cymbals rattle back.'
(Contrast line 21.)

In this pattern, ∪∪ and – are fairly freely interchangeable: line
63 represents the extreme limit of resolution (first and second
foot both resolved), line 73 the limit of contraction (three con-
tractions). Most of the variations occur in the first two feet. Only
10 lines have more than one long syllable within the second half
(not counting, i.e., the final syllable); the most striking variation
is that which breaks the concluding rattle of short syllables (lines
14, 35, 73, 76 and 91). See also on line 54.

Hephaestion tells us that in Greek the metre was used by the
'neoteroi', and quotes two lines; a scholiast on the passage tells us
that the metre was used by Callimachus. For the two lines see on
line 12. Varro seems to have introduced the metre into Latin —
in describing the rites of Cybele; the four fragments, 6 lines in all,
which survive are interesting evidence of C.'s indebtedness to
Varro:

Men. 79 —
  tua templa ad alta fani properans citus itere
Men. 131 —
  Phrygius per ossa cornus liquida canit anima
Men. 132 —
  tibi typana non inani sonitu matri' deum
  tonimus chorus tibi nos, tibi nunc semiuiri
  teretem comam uolantem iactant tibi famuli
Men. 275 —
  spatula euirauit omnes Veneri uaga pueros

Maecenas also used the metre (*FPL* p. 102). Nothing else in
Latin, unless one accepts Morel, *Incerta* 19 (=*FPL* p. 174).

The style is heavily end-stopped. Though there is always a
clear caesura, most lines make a single, closely knit statement.

1–5. The first five lines form one sentence (as do the next six),
in which the preliminary steps of the narrative are set out at
breathtaking speed.

1. Contrast the rhythm of 101. 1 *multas per gentes et multa per
aequora uectus.*

  alta . . . maria: cf. 12 *alta . . . nemora*, 71 *sub altis . . . columinibus.*

  Attis: The first of a pattern of repetitions: Attis is named six
times (also 27, 32, 42, 45 and 88), always at the caesura. ELDER
401–2 remarks, 'This sort of repetition is not used for liturgical
purposes, for the *Attis* is anything but a hymn, nor is the repetition
mere ornamentation. Rather, its function is to help convey the
picture of a unique and morbid state of mind, by returning the
reader forcefully and frequently to key themes.'

2. *Phrygium . . . nemus*: evocative, rather than descriptive; see
on 46. 4 *Phrygii campi*; the glade is near Mt Ida (see line 30); cf.
20 *Phrygiam*, 22 *Phryx*, 71 *Phrygiae*; 12, 20, 32, 52, 58, 79, 89
nemora, 72 *nemoriuagus.*

  citato: cf. 8 *citata*, 18 *citatis erroribus*, 26 *citatis tripudiis*; *citus*
in lines 30, 42 and 74; *pede* again in lines 30 and 86, *pedem* in 52.

  cupide: the adverb also in 64. 267 *cupide spectando.*

  tetigit: cf. 35 *tetigere.*

3. *opaca*: 'shady'; cf. 32 *opaca nemora*, 54 *opaca . . . latibula.*
 redimita: cf. 66 *corollis redimita domus.*

4. *stimulatus*: 'goaded' (as literally in 77 *stimulans*).
 rabie: cf. 44 *rapida sine rabie*, 57 *rabie fera carens.*
 uagus: cf. 13 *uaga pecora*, 25 *uaga cohors*, 31 *uaga*, 86 *pede uago.*
See on 64. 225.

 animis: [*amnis* V supports the plural (as perhaps in Cicero,
Tusc. 1. 96 *pendemus animis*), rather than the more normal *animi*.]

5. 'with a sharp flint struck off the weight from his groin'.
WILAMOWITZ suggests that a stone instrument was prescribed
by tradition. Cf. Ovid, *Fast.* 4. 237–44.

[In the MSS the line is almost meaningless — the reading of
V was *deuoluit iletas acuto sibi pondere silices.* The first step towards
restoration was taken by the Renaissance scholar Avanzi, to whom
we owe *pondera silice*; the remaining steps, by the nineteenth-
century German scholars Haupt, to whom we owe *deuolsit*, and
Bergk, to whom we owe *ilei* (i.e. a would-be archaic spelling of
ili, genitive of *ilium*.) Cf. 11. 20 *ilia rumpens.*]

6–11. A second sentence. The narrative now becomes more
detailed.

6. *itaque, ut*: the same formula in line 35.

7. *etiam*: 'still'.
 terrae sola: cf. Lucretius 2. 592 *ardent sola terrae*; the plural
again in 40 *sola dura.*

8. *niueis . . . manibus*: cf. 10 *teneris . . . digitis*, 74 *roseis . . . labellis*
and 88 *teneram . . . Attin.*

 citata: The feminine because of Attis' self-emasculation. The
device is more subtle than it sounds in an English translation.
We feel at first that *citata* probably belongs to a neuter plural
noun — there are four of them in the sentence: *membra, sola, initia,
terga* — and the ambiguity is not resolved till the sentence assumes
its final shape at 11 *adorta est.* C. got the idea perhaps from a Greek
poem in the same metre (the two lines which survive are quoted
on line 12) in which the priests of Cybele are spoken of in the
feminine — cf. 12 and 34 *Gallae.*

The feminine agreement is used of Attis in 11 *adorta*, 31 *uaga*, 32 *comitata*, 49 *allocuta*, 68 *ministra* and *famula*; 11 *tremebunda*, 31 and 54 *furibunda* and 58 *remota* might be neuter plural (like 6 *relicta*); only in 89 *fera* (probably neuter) would the masculine scan. The feminine plural occurs in 12 and 34 *Gallae*, 14 *quae* (momentarily ambiguous after 13 *pecora*?), 15 *exsecutae*, 35 *lassulae*, and probably 34 *rapidae*, unless we read the adverb *rapide* (*rapide* in the MSS in either case); any of these could be masculine. Elsewhere the MSS give the masculine (42 *excitum*, 45 *ipse*, 51 *miser*, 78 *hunc*, 80 *qui*, 88 *tenerum*, 89 *ille*); but in all these places the feminine is equally possible metrically. (In 52 *famuli* the statement is a general one.)

In all instances, in short, a feminine agreement is metrically possible. Most editors since Lachmann restore the feminine in some at any rate of seven places where the masculine occurs in the MSS. The arguments for leaving some masculine agreements are (1) it stops the trick from becoming too mechanical; (2) Attis is of uncertain sex (27 *notha mulier*), rather than female; (3) the masculine agreement is dramatically more effective in describing Attis before his emasculation (51 *miser*), or during his rebellion (78 *hunc*, 80 *qui* — and perhaps 88 *tenerum* and 89 *ille*, though Mynors prints *teneram* and *illa*).

    leue typanum: cf. 29 *leue tympanum*.

  9. *tuum, Cybebe*: [This simplification of the reading of the MSS, *tubam Cybelles*, is due to Lachmann.]

    Cybebe: The metre sometimes requires a long second syllable, as here, sometimes a short. Most editors adopt the dictum of Bentley (on Lucan 1. 600) that the Lydian form *Cybebe* (cf. Herodotus 5. 102) should be used in the former case, and reject the spelling *Cybelle* (adopted by Merrill and Lenchantin).

    tua . . . initia: i.e. the instrument of initiation.

  10. Note the t alliteration.

  11. *adorta est*: archaic for *coepit*.

  12–26. *Attis' speech*. His attempt to assert his leadership over his companions (especially in the piled-up line 15 *sectam meam*

exsecutae duce me mihi comites) is a pathetic betrayal of his depend-
ence on them — he clutches at command to conceal his helpless-
ness from himself; note the repetition 12 *ite . . . simul*, 13 and 19
simul ite.

12. *Gallae*: The feminine form of this name for the devotees of
Cybele is found in the 2-line fragment quoted by the metrician
Hephaestion to illustrate the galliambic metre (see introductory
note):

> Γαλλαί, μητρὸς ὀρείης φιλόθυρσοι δρομάδες,
> αἷς ἔντεα παταγεῖται καὶ χάλκεα κρόταλα.

The ascription of these lines to Callimachus is doubtful. In any
case, they do not justify the assumption that Poem 63 is in
general a translation or an adaptation of a Greek original.

13. *Dindymenae*: From Mt Dindymus or Dindymon, in eastern
Phrygia (91 *dea domina Dindymi*); cf. 35. 14.

   dominae: cf. 91 *domina*, 18 *erae* and 92 *era*.

   uaga pecora: cf. 77 *laeuumque pecoris hostem*.

14. *aliena . . . loca*: epithet-noun enclosing line again in lines
43, 67 and 83. See on 64. 5.

   quae: probably neuter plural with *pecora*, rather than
femine plural with *exsecutae*.

   exules: The first of five lines in the poem where the conclud-
ing rattle of short syllables is broken. Each time the rhythm seems
to stumble on a word that is dramatically significant (76, 91) or
pathetically effective (here, and in 35 and 73).

15. *sectam . . . exsecutae*: The *figura etymologica*, a form of con-
tained accusative, as in 61. 110–12 *quanta gaudia quae gaudeat*. The
combination *sectam sequi* is not uncommon in formal style, but the
repetition of the sound *sec-* may be intended to elicit associations
with *secare* (*secare* and *sequor*, though in fact etymologically
distinct, are not infrequently treated in high style as if they were
connected, e.g. Virgil, *A.* 6. 899 *ille uiam secat ad nauis*).

16. *rapidum salum*: cf. 64. 358 *rapido Hellesponto*.

   tulistis: 'endured'. Cf. 64. 99.

   truculentaque pelagi: Bears much the same relationship to

truculentum pelagus as *aequora*, *regna* and such high-style plurals bear to the corresponding singular. A common combination in Lucretius (e.g. 5. 35 *pelagi seuera*), only here in C.; cf. 64. 179 *ponti truculentum aequor*.

17. *corpus*: English idiom favours the plural ('bodies'), Latin idiom the singular in cases like this.

  nimio odio: cf. 36 *nimio e labore*. For the sense cf. 66. 15.

18. *erae*: [Avanzi's emendation, the MSS are corrupt.] Cf. 92 *era*. Servius on Virgil, *A.* 3. 113. remarks that Cybele was addressed as *era*.

19. *tarda*: with *mora*, not *mente*.

21–5. Six successive *ubi*-clauses, the first two occupying a line between them, the other four a line each. With 21–2 cf. on 64. 261–4 and Varro, *Men.* 132 (quoted above, under *Metre*).

21. *cymbalum sonat uox*: 'the voice of the cymbals rings out'.

  reboant: 'boom back' (in answer); cf. Lucretius 2. 28 and 4. 546. Cf. 29.

22. *canit . . . graue*: the *tibia* was a reed-instrument more like an oboe than a flute.

  curuo . . . calamo: 'with his curved reed'; the Phrygian pipe was a straight tube, curved at the opposite end to the mouth-piece; *calamo*, properly the reed, stands for the instrument.

23. *Maenades*: strictly worshippers of Dionysus, whose rites are often connected with those of Cybele (see, e.g., Euripides, *Bacch.* 55–9); cf. 69 *Maenas*.

  ui iaciunt: 'toss violently'.

  hederigerae: The first of several polysyllabic compound adjectives, a Graecism contributing to the exotic flavour of the poem, as well as providing convenient sequences of short syllables; cf. 34 *properipedem*, 41 *sonipedibus*, 51 *erifugae*, and 72 *nemoriuagus* and the heavier *siluicultrix*. See on 64. 52.

26. Attis breaks off a description that has become increasingly wild and detailed, to conclude with a line which is all the more effective because of its archaic, characteristically Roman simplicity.

decet: the pathos of understatement.

celerare: usually transitive.

tripudiis: a purely Roman word — *tripudia* are the wild dances of the *Salii* and the *Fratres Arvales*.

27–38. Three sentences, each 4 lines:

27–30 — departure (temporal clause + 4 principal clauses in asyndeton).

31–4 — the journey (3-line temporal clause + single-line principal clause).

35–8 — arrival (temporal clause + 3 principal clauses in asyndeton).

27. Picks up line 11.

simul: = *simul atque*, as in 31 and 45; contrast 12, 13 and 19.

Attis: not named since line 1.

28. *thiasus*: properly, a band of worshippers of Dionysus, as in 64. 252.

ululat: cf. 24 *ululatibus*.

29. *leue tympanum*: cf. 29.

remugit . . . recrepant: 'bellows forth' . . . 'rattle back'; the *re-* to emphasize that the drum and the cymbals answer one another — first one, then the other, as in the two halves of each line of the poem; see on 21 and the parallels from Lucretius quoted there.

30. *adit . . . chorus*: = 'the dancers make their way to'.

31–3. The jerky rhythm (short phrases piled up without connecting words) to suggest desperate, protracted physical effort.

31. *furibunda . . . uaga*: both probably feminine, like *comitata* in the next line (though *furibunda* might be a contained accusative plural with *anhelans*).

simul . . . uadit: 'as soon as he strides off'; if he is to use *uadere* C. is restricted to the present; contrast 26 *simul . . . cecinit*, 'as soon as he finished his declamation'.

animam agens: literally, 'drawing breath'; but usually = 'at one's last gasp', and probably so here — i.e. almost dead with exhaustion.

32. *Attis*: the name this time in the middle of a 3-line temporal clause.

    opaca nemora: echoes of 3 *opaca* and 12 *nemora*.

33. *ueluti . . . iugi*: the simile ironically underlines the contrast between Attis' actions and his state of mind (he is rushing to *accept* the yoke, not to avoid it). This and 51–2 *dominos . . . solent* are the only formal similes in the poem (14 *uelut exules* implies an equation rather than a likeness). Cf. 68. 118. It seems from Ovid, *F.* 4. 335–6 that heifers were sacrificed to Cybele.

34. Four echoes of Attis' speech in this line: 16 *rapidum*, 15 *duce me*, 19 *sequimini* and 12 *Gallae*.

35. *tetigere*: 'reached' (*L & S* I B 2a).

    lassulae: again the rhythm falters (as in 14), here heightening the pathos of the diminutive. See on 3. 18.

36. *nimio e labore*: cf. 17 *nimio odio*.

    sine Cerere: = 'without bread'. FRAZER 461: 'Throughout the period of mourning the worshippers fasted from bread.' This use of *Ceres*, an archaism apparently surviving in popular expressions (e.g. Terence, *Eu.* 732 *sine Cerere et Libero friget Venus*, [Virgil] *Copa* 20 *est hic munda Ceres, est Amor, est Bromius*), becomes part of the common style of verse (several times in Virgil, e.g. *A.* 1. 701–2 *famuli . . . Cererem . . . canistris / expediunt*, contrast *G.* 1. 7–12) and thus available for fresh verbal poetry such as *A.* 8. 180–1 *onerant . . . canistris / dona laboratae Cereris, Bacchumque ministrant*.

37–8. A chiasmus (line 37 ends with a verb, 38 begins with a verb, expanding the bald *somnum capiunt* (= 'they go to bed') of 36; in 38, after the sensuous *abit in quiete molli*, the sentence finally unwinds on *rabidus furor animi* — the poet's concluding comment on Act I of his tragedy. Cf. 59–60.

37. *labante languore*: = 'tottering with fatigue'. Effectively tensioned statement (literally 'weariness tottering').

38. *quiete*: 'sleep'.

39–43. A single sentence: the peacefulness and beauty of dawn described with a wealth of imagery (much of it belonging to the

world of fantasy), to establish a definite break with the action of
1–38. For the same device on a smaller scale cf. Virgil, *A*. 4.
6–7.

39. *oris aurei Sol*: 'the golden-faced sun'; descriptive genitive.

radiantibus oculis: 'with the rays of his eyes' (Copley); the
image implicit in *oculis* is sharpened by the preceding *oris aurei Sol*.

40. *lustrauit*: (1) 'lit up'; (2) 'ranged over'; also (3) 'purified',
as a relevant overtone — i.e. the madness of the previous day has
been dispelled.

42. *Somnus*: the god of sleep, as in Virgil, *A*. 5. 838–61.

excitam: The MSS here revert to masculine agreements.
See on 8 *citata*.

43. *Pasithea*: In Homer, *Il*. 14. 263–9, Hera promises Hypnos
(Sleep) the Grace Pasithea in marriage if he will put Zeus to
sleep (a passage imitated by Virgil, *A*. 1. 71–5). Pasithea's only
other appearance in Greek is in an epigram of Antipater of
Thessalonica (*AP* 9. 517. 5–6), conceivably a reminiscence of C.

44–9. To convey the confused, sorting-out process in Attis'
mind when he woke up, C. piles up the Latin words for 'mind',
'intelligence', 'emotions' — 45 *pectore*, 46 *liquida . . . mente*, 47
animo aestuante. Cf. 62. 14, 64. 69–70 and 68. 37–8.

44. *de quiete molli, rapida sine rabie*: picks up line 38.

45. *simul*: = *simul atque*. as in 27 and 31.

ipsa: [*ipse* V.]

sua facta: 'the things that he had done'; cf. 30. 12 *facti tui*.

46. *quis*: = *quibus*; see on 64. 145.

47. *animo aestuante*: 'his mind seething'.

rusum reditum ad uada tetulit: symbolizes the impulse to
reverse the irreversible; the situation of course is not unlike
Ariadne's in 64. 128–31; *rusum* = *rursus*, an archaic by-form
common in Lucretius; *tetulit* = *tulit*, as in line 52 *tetuli* and 66. 35
tetulisset, common in comedy. Cf. 79 *reditum . . . ferat*, 61. 26
aditum ferens, 61. 43 *aditum ferat*.

49. *miseriter*: archaic.

50–73. Attis' second speech is a wild soliloquy of repentance, ending with the terrible, stumbling *iam iam dolet quod egi, iam iamque paenitet*. His first speech is full of references to his companions; the second stresses Attis' isolation, and his preoccupation with his own plight: *ego* 15 times; no mention of his companions.

50. The verbal parallelism underlines the different metrical structure of the two halves of the line: in *creatrix* the stress falls on the second syllable, which is long; in *genetrix* the stress falls on the first syllable, the second syllable being short. Note also the change from *mei* to *mea*.

   patria: also 55 and 59.

51. *miser*: Changed to the feminine *misera* by some editors, but the masculine can be regarded as appropriate to Attis before the onset of his frenzy.

51–2. *dominos ... solent*: Like the simile in line 33, the image ironically describes Attis' state of mind as much as his action: he ran away like a slave escaping from his master (cf. 17 *Veneris nimio odio*) — in order to become a slave.

53–4. The double final clause represents an ironical statement of Attis' objective.

53. *gelida*: the final syllable counts as long before the st following; see on 17. 24 *pote stolidum*.

54. *opaca*: cf. 3 and 32 *opaca*. [the MSS have *earum omnia*, but *omnia* sounds too feeble to justify the metrical licence it involves (without parallel, unless we accept Lachmann's needless *aere citatis* in line 18); *opaca* was proposed by L. Müller in 1910. Some suspicion still attaches to *earum*, a form rarely found in verse.]

   furibunda: if *opaca* is read, *furibunda* has to be feminine, as probably in 31. See on 8.

56. *pupula*: the word is rare in verse; it is perhaps used here for pathetic effect.

   sibi: provides two short syllables, without contributing much sense; Fordyce compares 15 *mihi*, but there the pile-up of related words is effective.

57. *carens ... est*: = *caret*; cf. 64. 317 *fuerant exstantia*.

58. *remota*: more likely feminine with *ego* than neuter with *nemora*.

59–60. Chiastic arrangement, as in 37–8.

59. *genitoribus*: 'parents', as in Lucretius 2. 615.

60. The symbols of the normal way of life of a young man in a Greek city.

gyminasiis: the 5-syllable form is found in Varro, *R.* 1. 55. 4; cf. forms like *dracuma*, *Alcumena* in early Latin.

61. *miser a miser*: vocative with *anime*; so 61. 132–3 *miser a miser / concubine*.

63. The four *genera figurae* through which Attis has passed, including his present state of *mulier* (cf. 27 *notha mulier*), are set out in reverse order. Line 63 is the longest in the poem (both first and second foot resolved). Contrast 73, the shortest.

64. *fui … eram*: A change from perfect to imperfect in successive principal clauses is not uncommon in passing from a general to a more detailed statement; e.g. Cicero, *Tusc.* 1. 4 *in Graecia musici floruerunt, discebantque id omnes* etc.

flos: cf. 100. 2 (and 24. 1 *flosculus*).

decus olei: = *decus palaestri*; tensioned statement — a somewhat overstrained example of the figure called metonomy ('crown' for 'king'); cf. Horace, *Carm.* 1. 8. 8–10 *cur oliuum uitat?*

65–7. After a run of *ego*'s, now a run of *mihi*'s (4 in 3 lines).

65. *ianuae*: the plural because Attis is recalling a way of life — all those occasions on which there were crowds waiting at the door — but also no doubt to balance *limina*.

limina tepida: his doorstep is warm because his admirers have spent the night on it — an allusion to the conventions of the serenade poem or paraclausithuron (see on Poem 67).

66. *corollis*: the diminutive again 64. 283.

redimita: cf. line 3.

67. *ubi esset*: frequentative subjunctive, as in 84. 1; rare before Livy, but cf. Caesar, *Civ.* 2. 15. 3 *ubi imbecillitas materiae postulare uideretur*.

68–71. Six *ego*'s in 4 lines.

68. *deum*: plural, though only one divinity — and that a goddess — is meant. The plural in such cases has something of

the classifying function of an adjective; cf. 75 *deorum* and Virgil, *A.* 4. 201 *excubias diuum aeternas* (only Jove is meant), etc.; allied to the 'generalizing' plural (as in 10. 10 *praetoribus*, 12. 3 *neglegentiorum*, 30. 1 *unanimis false sodalibus*) and the much commoner high-style plural (as in 62. 2 *lumina*, 64. 172 *Cecropiae tetigissent litora puppes*, etc.). See on 64. 53.

  ministra: feminine.

  famula: picks up the simile in 51–2.

  ferar: 'be called'.

69. *Maenas*: see on 23.

70. *algida*: with *niue*.

71. *columinibus*: =*culminibus*, 'peaks'.

72 To Attis, the city dweller, life in the wilds is devoid of the romantic attraction we may feel in the imagery of this line — it spells only terror. But also a line of verbal poetry (both *siluicultrix* and *nemoriuagus* only here), to prepare a contrast for line 73.

73. The shortest, and therefore the heaviest, line in the poem (3 contracted feet) and the third line to break the concluding sequence of five shorts. The four *iam*'s come like a series of blows, leading up to the terrible, final *paenitet*. Both *iam iam* and *iam iamque* are common as reinforced forms of *iam* (see *L & S*); cf. 62. 52 *iam iam contingit*.

74–90. Cybele intervenes.

74. *citus*: [Added by Bentley, to supply the two shorts needed in the second half of the line.]

75. *deorum*: for the plural see on 68 *deum*.

  noua nuntia: 'unexpected news'; the neuter is rare.

76. *ibi*: temporal, 'thereupon', as in lines 4, 48 and perhaps 90.

  iuncta iuga: 'the yoked yoke', i.e. the yoke which had been fastened in position.

  leonibus: The lions are those which traditionally draw the car of Cybele. In the second half of the line the sequence of short syllables is broken, throwing *leonibus* into prominence; dative of advantage.

77. *laeuumque pecoris hostem*: 'the left-hand enemy of her flock';

'left', as the symbol of ill-luck or disaster. With *pecoris* cf. 13 *Dindymenae dominae uaga pecora*.

78–83. Note the r alliteration in Cybele's speech; see on 42. 16–17.

78. [The line is unmetrical in the MSS; *i* and *agitet* are the traditional repairs.]

79. *reditum . . . ferat*: see on 47 *reditum . . . tetulit*.

81. *caede terga cauda*: = 'lash your back with your tail', i.e. in anger; *caedere* is the word used of a severe thrashing.

   tua uerbera patere: 'endure your blows'; a studied artificiality of expression.

82. *fac . . . retonent*: *fac* this time without *ut* (contrast 78 and 79).

83. *torosa ceruice*: 'on (with) your muscular neck'; cf. Virgil, *A.* 12. 6–7 (also of a lion) *gaudetque comantis excutiens ceruice toros*.

85. *sese adhortans rapidum incitat animo*: = 'rousing himself till he was in the mood to rush off'; *rapidum* is best taken equally with *adhortans* and with *incitat* — proleptic in both cases; *animo* equally with *rapidum* and *incitat*. But there are rather too many words used for the effect gained, unless C.'s intention is to contrast the apparent hesitation of the lion while it works itself up into a fury with its sudden lunge forward in line 86.

86. A staccato line (the first foot in each half contracted), all action.

87. The last scene of the narrative opens on a melting rhythm.
   albicantis: suggests the misty white of breaking waves.

88. *marmora pelagi*: i.e. the marbled expanse of ocean.

89. *demens*: contrast 46 *liquida . . . mente*.
   illa: [*ille* V.]
   fugit: present.
   fera: probably neuter, though the feminine singular nominative ('a wild thing') may be intended to be present as a second, latent meaning.

90. *semper omne uitae spatium*: cf. the piling-up in 109. 5–6.
   famula: cf. 52 *famuli* and 68 *famula*.

91–3. A concluding prayer.

91. The line is remarkable for its stuttering rhythm (first half: 2nd foot resolved; second half: 1st foot resolved, giving a sequence of 5 shorts, the normal concluding sequence of shorts is broken by the heavy initial syllable of *Dindymi*); note also the d alliteration.

92. *tuos*: = *tuus*[*tuo* V.]. Cf. 53. 3 *Caluos*, etc.

See:

J. P. Elder, 'Catullus' *Attis*', *AJPh* 68 (1947), 394–403.

J. G. Frazer, *The Golden Bough*, (abridged edn 1922), Chapters 34–6.

A. Guillemin, 'Le poème 63 de Catulle', *REL* 27 (1949), 149–57.

P. Lambrechts, *Attis: van Herdesknaap tot God* (1962), reviewed by J. A. North, *JRS* 55 (1965), 278–9.

G. N. Sandy, *AJPh* 92 (1971) 185–95, and *TAPhA* 99 (1968) 389–99.

M. Schuster, 'C. Valerius Catullus' in *RE* (1948), (2376–7 on Poem 63).

W. Y. Sellar, *Roman Poets of the Republic* (1863), 369–70.

U. von Wilamowitz-Moellendorff, *Hellenistische Dichtung* (1924) ii 291–5.

64

A miniature epic, or *epyllion* — a tale from legend elegantly and compactly retold. This sophisticated refinement upon a traditional form seems to have been evolved by Hellenistic poets in response to Callimachus' condemnation of epic as long-winded and flabby; among C.'s contemporaries it served as a demonstration of technical virtuosity and devotion to the poet's craft: it was the sort of poem that might take years to write.

There is no evidence that miniature epics were called *epyllia*: the term was first used in this way by Moritz Haupt in 1855, in a lecture on Poem 64; see Fordyce 272. Poem 64 is the only example we have from the time of C. For Cinna's *Zmyrna* see on Poem 95; Calvus wrote an *Io* (six unconnected lines survive, *FPL* pp. 85–6), Cornificius a *Glaucus* (one line survives, *FPL* p. 90), Valerius Cato a *Dictynna*, received by Cinna with the

enthusiasm with which C. received Cinna's *Zmyrna (FPL* p. 90):
saecula permaneat nostri Dictynna Catonis. The episode of Aristaeus in
Virgil's fourth *Georgic*, that of Cacus in *A.* 8 and that of Nisus and
Euryalus in *A.* 9 are probably examples of epyllia incorporated in
larger works; cf. also such *tours de force* as the episode of the ships
turned into nymphs in *A.* 10. Much of Ovid's *Metamorphoses* can
reasonably be regarded as a series of epyllia ingeniously organized
into a single mammoth structure. Cf. also the *Culex* and the *Ciris*
of the Virgilian Appendix.

Synopsis:

Structure: Poem 64 draws upon themes from two distinct legends: there is an *outer story*, the marriage of Peleus and Thetis, and an *inner story*, the elopement of Ariadne with Theseus. (For the relationship between the two see on 50–1.) The poem consists of nine colourful tableaux, held together by condensed passages of narrative interspersed with two exercises in tragic rhetoric (Ariadne's lament, Aegeus' farewell) and a formal marriage hymn. In the outer story the movement of the narrative is strictly linear, but the inner story moves both backwards and forwards in time. The normal pattern is the complex, periodic sentence, each sentence connected to the one before and the one after; but there are also interesting experiments in the outer story with a staccato unconnected narrative structure (32–42, 399–406).

Metre: hexameters (also Poem 62).

1–21. *Opening Tableau: Departure of the Argonauts*. The first sentence is shot through with reminiscences of Ennius' version of Euripides' *Medea*, which began —

> Vtinam ne in nemore Pelio securibus
> caesae accedissent abiegnae ad terram trabes,
> neue inde nauis inchoandi exordium
> coepisset quae nunc nominatur nomine
> Argo, quia Argiui in ea delecti uiri
> uecti petebant pellem inauratam arietis
> Colchis imperio regis Peliae per dolum;
> nam numquam era errans mea domo efferret pedem
> Medea animo aegro amore saeuo saucia.

For echoes of Apollonius see below.

1. The poem opens with a 5-word hexameter, a line of which C. is extremely fond — nearly 1 line in 4 in this poem is a 5-word hexameter (counting the refrain 327 etc. as one line). There are four 4-word hexameters, 15, 77, 115 and 319. The line is also an

example of neoteric verbal ingenuity: *prognatae*, an old-fashioned word, by drawing attention to itself, gives support to the implied personification of *pinus* — the pines are living creatures; at the same time the fact that *prognatus* is normally associated with an ablative of origin invites us to assign to *Peliaco prognatae uertice* the meaning 'born from Pelion's head' (an ironic allusion to the birth of Athena from the head of Zeus), along with the common-sense meaning 'born on Pelion's summit' (locative ablative; *uertex*, 'head', in 63, 309 and 350; 'summit', in 244, 278 and 390).

Peliaco ... uertice: high style for *Peli uertice* (contrast 278 *e uertice Pelei*). Other examples: 3 *Aeeteos*, 77 *Androgeoneae* and 368 *Polyxenia*; cf. 66. 8 *Bereniceo*, 68. 74 *Protesilaeam*.

quondam: emphasizes the legendary setting.

pinus: for the notion tree-from-mountain-slope-into-ship see on 4. 10–17.

2. *liquidas*: 'clear'; cf. 63. 46 *liquida mente*. But the adjective's denotation is less important than its structural function (adjective before principal caesura, rhyming noun at end of line).

nasse: builds on the personification latent in *prognatae*. To conjure up a half-image of the pines as living creatures is an effective piece of poetic irony. At the same time the way is prepared for a description of the construction and departure of Argo as something miraculous. The Roman poets use *nare* and *adnare* not infrequently of travel by sea, no doubt connecting *nare* and *nauis*; cf. 66. 46 *classi barbara nauit*.

3. *Phasidos ... Aeeteos*: *Phasidos*, Greek genitive; Aeetes, the father of Medea. A flamboyant line, beginning and ending with an exotic name, to underline the keynote of adventure and romance. A reminiscence of Apollonius 2. 1277–8 Κολχίδα μὲν δὴ γαῖαν ἱκάνομεν ἠδὲ ῥέεθρα / Φάσιδος; *Aeeteos* echoes Αἰήτάο from the line following (also a spondaic ending). For the rhythm (a concluding quadrisyllable and a 5th-foot spondee) cf. lines 11, 15, 24, 28, 36, 67, 71, 78, 79, 80 etc. Altogether 30 5th-foot spondees, 9 involving proper names — about as many as in the whole of the *Aeneid*. The distribution is interesting. With two

exceptions, 119 (where the ending is restored by conjecture) and 358, the pattern is confined to two sections of the poem: 1–115 (18 examples) and 249–302 (10 examples). No spondaic 5th foot in Poem 62, 5 examples in 65–6 (none a proper name), 4 examples in 68 (3 proper names), rare in 69–116 (76. 15, 100. 1, 116. 3).

4. Note the echoes in this line of Ennius' *quia Argiui in ea delecti uiri*. For *pubes = iuuentus* see *L & S* II C; cf. Virgil, *A.* 8. 518–19 *robora pubis lecta | dabo*; in 267 *pubes* is practically a synonym of *populus*.

5. *auratam . . . pellem*: The first of 23 examples in the poem of a line beginning with an adjective etc. and concluding with the corresponding noun; cf. 54, 72, 99, 234; the line is built round the participle *optantes* –– a way of avoiding a final clause (e.g. *ut auerterent*) and the characteristic hierarchic structure of prose; cf. 7 *uerrentes*, 101 *cupiens . . . contendere*, etc.

auertere: 'carry off', 'steal'; *L & S* I B.

6. *ausi sunt*: indicative because 4 *cum* defines an actual occasion; cf. 1. 5 *cum ausus es*.

uada salsa: An epic kenning found in Accius; Ennius has *salsa* and *mare salsum*; *uada* in its etymological sense of 'way' (cf. *uadere*), as in Virgil, *A.* 5. 158 *longa sulcant uada salsa carina*.

decurrere: normally an intransitive verb, 'run or race down' (so several times in the *Aeneid*); the transitive use and the sense 'race through or across' (*de-* as in *debellare* etc.) seem to have belonged to the technical language of navigation, chariot-racing, etc.; the latter connotation perhaps prepares the way for 9 *currum*.

7. Adjective, participle, adjective, and then the two nouns in the same order; a variation on the strict Golden Line (in which the verb or participle separates adjectives from nouns — e.g. 59, 129, 163, 235, 351); other examples: 10, 113, 162, 245, 295, 332, 345. See on 332.

uerrentes: *uerrere*, of oars, since Ennius.

palmis: see on 4. 4 *palmulis*.

8–10. Such a ship needed divine help in building.

8. *diua*: Athena (= the Roman Minerva, who supervises the construction of the wooden horse in Virgil, *A.* 2).

quibus: refers to 4 *iuuenes*. Postponement of the relative is not common. On the continuing relative see on 267.

retinens: a somewhat strained device to avoid a further relative clause, on the model of Greek (where a participial phrase often defines a noun, but is distinguished from the ordinary participle by a preceding definite article).

9. *ipsa*: to heighten the exceptional character of the enterprise.

leui . . . uolitantem flamine currum: 'a car that flew before the breeze'.

10. 'fitting pine-wood frame to curving keel'; *texta* (from *texo*) suggests the interlacing of ribs and beams. Cf. Virgil, *A.* 2. 16 (of the horse) *sectaque intexunt abiete costas*. Observe that we have returned to the pines of line 1 ('composition embrassée').

11. 'hanc proram [in cursu inexercitatam] Minerva imbuit sive initiavit mari' (Baehrens). For the rhythm see on 3. [The line is corrupt in the MSS: *proram* O, *primam* GR; *Amphitritem* (or some such form) V, *Amphitrite* is a correction found in O. Many print *illa rudem cursu prima imbuit Amphitriten*, 'she (i.e. Argo) first introduced inexperienced Amphitrite (to ships) by her passage', arguing that *rudem cursu* is doubtful Latin for 'inexperienced in sailing'. The choice is really between Argo, the first ship ever, and Argo, the ship that was launched personally by Athena. To make Argo the first ship ever is appropriate enough to the immediate context of wonder and divine help and seems to be the way Ovid remembered this passage in writing *Am.* 2. 11. 1–2. But it gets us into difficulties when we come to 52–70: how can Argo be the first ship ever when Theseus' voyage must precede that of Peleus? See on 52–3.]

illa: for this 'pictorial' use of *ille* etc. in the second of two clauses with a common subject see Williams on Virgil, *A.* 5. 186 and 457. Cf. 288 *ille* and Fordyce thereon.

Amphitrite: wife of Neptune, and hence, by metonymy, 'the sea', on the same principle as 63. 36 *sine Cerere*, 'without bread'.

12. *uentosum . . . aequor*: 'the windy plain'.

    proscidit: 'ploughed'; cf. Varro, *R.* 1. 29. 2 *terram cum primum arant, proscindere appellant*; for ploughing of the sea cf. Virgil, *A.* 5. 158 *longa sulcant uada salsa carina.*

13. An ironical refinement upon a cliché: *incanuit* picks up Homer's πολιός, a stock epithet of the foam-flecked sea, while *torta* suggests that the flecks of foam (*spumis*) produced by the twisting action of Argo's oars are actual curls (and the oars, if we like, the curling tongs).

[*torta* (cf. Virgil, *A.* 3. 208 and 4. 583 *torquent spumas*) is one of two improvements in this line due to Renaissance editors. The reading of V was *tota* (which left *remigio* unsupported) and *incanduit*, regarded as intolerable in view of 14 *candenti*.]

14. *feri . . . uultus*: more likely nominative (and *aequoreae . . . Nereides* an appositional expansion) than descriptive genitive; those who read *freti* mostly take *uultus* as accusative after *emersere*.

[Schrader's *freti*, proposed in 1776, is adopted by Mynors and Fordyce, and seems supported by pseudo-Senecan *Oct.* 720 *talis emersam freto spumante Peleus coniugem accepit Thetim*. But the case against *feri*, the reading of V, (i.e. 'timid', 'shy', cf. Virgil's goats, *A.* 4. 152) is not conclusive. See on 61. 56.]

15. The first of four 4-word hexameters in the poem; cf. 77, 115 and 319. No other 4-word hexameters in C. For 4-word pentameters see on 66. 8. An echo of Apollonius 1. 549–50 (the nymphs on Mt Pelion watching Argo's departure are all excitement); but in Apollonius Peleus is already married and his son Achilles already born. C. seems to be drawing equally on Apollonius 4. 930–63 (the Nereids, Thetis among them, help Argo through the Wandering Rocks).

    monstrum: = anything unprecedented.

    Nereides: -*ĕs*, as in Greek; cf. 3 *Phasidŏs.*

    admirantes: for the rhythm see on line 3.

16. *luce*: = *die*; cf. 325.

[V is unmetrical and doubtful sense. Bergk's *haud* meets both difficulties better than other suggested repairs, though one would

feel happier with a line that made the sighting of nymphs by
sailors unprecedented rather than unparalleled, since parallels
are found e.g., in Sophocles and Euripides (refs. in Fordyce);
cf. Virgil's tale of Aeneas' meeting with his ships transformed into
nymphs, *A.* 10. 215-55.]

17. *oculis*: a common enough idiomatic reinforcement of
uidere, though the position and the two consecutive ablatives are a
little awkward; the nominative *oculi* is tempting.

18. *nutricum*: for *mammarum*, apparently because τιτθῶν,
genitive plural of τίτθη (=*nutrix*), is also genitive plural of τιτθός
(=*mamma*); the trick hardly comes off in Latin, one feels, even
if the two Greek words were to some extent interchangeable.

e gurgite cano: picks up 14 *candenti e gurgite*.

19-21. The repeated *tum*'s emphasize how quickly it all
happened, and prepare the way for the lyrical outburst of 22-30;
at the same time the changes are rung on the name *Thetis* — a
Hellenistic trick. With the anaphora cf. 39-41, 63-5 and 387-94.

19. *incensus fertur*: probably = *incensus esse fertur*, but *fertur*
seems out of harmony with the positive statements of 20 and 21.
Perhaps 'swept along on fire' (for this sense of *feror* see *L & S* I B),
though the present rather clashes then with 20 *despexit* and 21 *sensit*.

20. *humanos . . . hymenaeos*: 'marriage with a mortal'. For
hymenaei = 'marriage' see on 61. 4.

despexit: the final syllable counts as long in arsis, a Greek
usage found also in 62. 4 and 66. 11 (both in foot 5 and followed
by the same Greek word).

21. 'Then Jove himself realized Peleus must marry Thetis';
Jove had wanted Thetis for himself (see 27), but abandoned the
idea on learning from Prometheus that Thetis was fated to bear
a son greater than his father. See on 293-7.

22-30. *Hymn in praise of the forthcoming marriage of Peleus and
Thetis*. A double apostrophe, almost lyrical in tone, (1) saluting
the Heroic Age (22-4); (2) congratulating the bridegroom,
Peleus, (a μακαρισμός — cf. 334-6 and see on Poem 51). Cf. 69,
94-8 and 253.

22. *optato*: a word C. is fond of; he uses the verb 16 times, the participle *optatus* 7 times; cf. 31, 141, 328, 372; also 5 *optantes*, 82 and 401 *optauit*.

saeclorum: Apparently a reference to Hesiod's Five Ages of Mankind: Gold, Silver, Bronze, Heroic, Iron. (*WD* 156–73 After the men of the Bronze Age had destroyed one another, there came the men of the Heroic Age, that of the Theban and Trojan wars; this represented an improvement on the two ages which had preceded it, but it was followed by the Iron Age, in which we now live, the worst of all. Cf. Aratus 100–36.) The Heroic Age was a time *nimis optato* ('too much missed'); one could perhaps hardly hope to have been born in the Golden Age; cf. Virgil, *A.* 6. 649 *magnanimi heroes, nati melioribus annis*.

23. *heroes*: the traditional chieftains etc. of Homeric poetry and various other legendary figures; see *OCD* under Hero-cult.

deum genus: An echo of Hesiod, *WD* 159 ἀνδρῶν ἡρώων θεῖον γένος. In Homer the heroes are not necessarily divine or semi-divine; in post-Homeric poetry the use of the word 'hero' of a legendary figure with one mortal and one immortal parent becomes common: e.g. Hercules, son of Alcmena and Jove; Aeneas, son of Anchises and Venus. Achilles is a hero in this sense, being the son of Peleus and Thetis; Peleus himself was the son of Aeacus and the nymph Endeis, daughter of Chiron.

o bona matrum: We owe *matrum* [*mater* V] to a scholiast on Virgil, *A.* 5. 80, who quotes also the half-line 23b.

23b. [Peerlkamp's *iterum saluete bonarum* is as good a second half to the line as any suggested; the chiasmus *bona matrum progenies . . . bonarum* is plausible; *deum genus . . . bonarum* then amounts to a kind of definition of *heroes*.]

24. A common formula of hymns. Clearly, despite the lacuna, *uos = heroes*. Presumably C. means 'I will often address you in my poetry' — i.e. 'I will often write poetry addressing you'.

25. *teque*: another anaphora begins here (cf. 28 and 29 *tene*).

adeo: marks a climax; *L & S* III C.

eximie: the adverb.

taedis felicibus aucte: cf. 66. 11 *nouo auctus hymenaeo*; *auctus* =
'enriched', 'blessed' (*L & S* I B).

27. *suos . . . amores*: 'his love' (i.e. the woman he loved);
perhaps ironical — see on 6. 16.

28. *tenuit*: cf. 72. 2 *tenere* and 55. 17 *nunc te tenent*; 'held enthrall-
ed' rather than 'held in her arms' (though cf. 45. 2 *tenens in
gremio* and 11. 18 *complexa tenet*); perhaps colloquial or ironical,
like 27 *amores*.

Nereine: = *Nereis*. [*nectine* V; *Nereine* Haupt.]

29–30. Oceanus and Tethys are the parents of Doris, the
mother of the Nereids. It seems to have been a Hellenistic trick
to state explicitly the more remote family relationships of
legendary characters (here 29 *neptem*), treating them for ironical
effect as real persons, just as it was a trick to bring together in a
single context attributes not rationally reconcilable (here
Oceanus, the grandfather of Thetis, and Oceanus, the river). For
Tethys see also 66. 70.

29. *concessit*: repeats 27 *concessit*.

30. An echo of Euphorion 122 Powell: Ὠκεανός, τῷ πᾶσα
περίρρυτος ἐνδέδεται χθών.

31–42. *Second Tableau: Arrival of the wedding guests.* An elaborate,
detailed picture of the guests assembling from all over Thessaly,
leaving the countryside deserted and all normal agricultural
tasks suspended. Whereas the perfect tense was used in the
Opening Tableau, the present is here used throughout (apart
from 32 *aduenere*).

31. *quae . . . luces*: usually taken as a generalizing plural (see
on 63. 68); more likely that C. means the whole period of the
marriage feast — the description which follows implies a sus-
pension of normal activities for a longish period; the continuing
relative *quae* is loosely used, to pick up the general idea of
'marriage day' from what precedes.

simul: = *simul atque*; see on 63. 27.

finito tempore: 'at the time appointed'.

32–4. The neutral statement *domum . . . Thessalia* is repeated in more emphatic form in *oppletur . . . coetu*. Then two half-lines, each a clear-cut image. With the string of short unconnected statements (asyndeton) here and in 35–42 cf. 399–406 and 63. 27–38.

35–42. An extension of the scene of 32–4, rather than a separate scene: the focus is now widened to take in the surrounding countryside as it is emptied of its inhabitants. We return with these to the palace at line 37, as the repetition 37 *frequentant* of 32 *frequentat* (at the same point in the line) emphasizes; then move out again into the countryside, now deserted.

Lines 32–42 contain 14 separate, unconnected statements (asyndeton).

35. *Cieros*: an obscure place in Thessaliotis, mentioned by Strabo.

[V had *Scyros* perhaps, an Aegean island possessing associations with Achilles, but hardly appropriate in a description of the Thessalian countryside; *Cieros* Meineke.]

Pthiotica Tempe: Adjective and noun are chosen for their literary associations, with some unconcern for geography: Phthia, famous as the birth-place of Achilles, was actually in southern Thessaly; Tempe (a Greek neuter plural), the famous valley of the Peneus between Olympus and Ossa, lay to the north; cf. 285 *uiridantia Tempe*.

36. Crannon and Larisa (or Larissa) were two towns of central Thessaly, the latter connected with the name of Achilles.

domos ac moenia: for the sake of balance, rather than implying any real distinction.

37. *Pharsaliam*: The town is usually called Pharsalus and some print *Pharsalum* here, to avoid the change in quantity *Pharsăliam . . . Pharsālia*; however, repetition with change of quantity was a recognized Hellenistic trick; cf. on 62. 5.

38–42. Apparently a traditional theme; cf. Tibullus 2. 1. 5–7, Ovid, *Fast.* 1. 667–8, and Virgil's picture of a return of the Golden Age, *Ecl.* 4. 40–1 *non rastros patietur humus, non uinea falcem, | robustus quoque iam tauris iuga soluet arator.* C.'s exploitation of the theme is urbane, ironical, and at the same time imaginatively vivid and poetically sensitive. For the string of *non*'s in 39–41 see on 19–21.

39. *humilis . . . uinea*: The vines were sometimes trained on trees, sometimes (as here) kept low; cf. Varro, *R.* 1. 8; the latter practice is still followed to some extent in Italy, and elsewhere.

40. Except for foot 5, the line is spondaic throughout, to suggest the heavy, straining motion of the plough.

41. *falx . . . frondatorum*: The other method of growing grapes, by marrying the vines to trees, whose foliage has to be thinned, so that the sun may reach the grapes and ripen them.

42. Not as far-fetched as it sounds: highly-polished iron (tools, railway lines, etc.) rusts overnight in the open.

43–9. *Third Tableau: The royal palace and the marriage-bed.* The description continues in the present tense. Lines 43–4 pick up and expand 33 *oppletur laetanti regia coetu*. The guests assemble in the palace of Peleus, where all is glittering gold and silver, crystal and ivory; last to be described is the marriage-bed. This tableau and that preceding build up a panoramic view, in which distance is foreshortened (as in art). Our eye is caught first by the crowded palace (32), then by the crowds which stream towards it, then by the deserted countryside; lastly we follow the crowds in the palace through the scenes of splendour to the centre-piece, the marriage-bed.

43. *ipsius*: the country-folk would naturally refer to Peleus as *ipse* (*L & S* II A). See on 2. 9.

quacumque . . . recessit: 'in whatever direction it receded', i.e. from the eye of the spectator; frequentative perfect. Cf. Virgil's description of Dido's palace, *A.* 1. 637–42; with *recessit* cf. *A.* 2. 300 *obtecta recessit*.

44. *fulgenti . . . argento*: cf. Lucretius 2. 27 *nec domus argento fulget auroque renidet*.

45. *soliis . . . mensae*: dative.

collucent: stronger than *lucent*; *fulgenti*, *splendent*, *candet* and *collucent* all emphasize the idea of dazzling brightness.

46. A summing-up line, like 11.

gaudet: cf. Virgil's *pater Apenninnus*, *A*. 12. 702–3: *gaudetque niuali/uertice se attollens*. The palace shares, i.e., the joy of visitors and occupants.

47. *puluinar . . . geniale*: the *lectus genialis* in the centre of the *atrium* was a feature of a Roman wedding; *puluinar*, a special couch reserved originally for the images of gods in such ceremonies as the *lectisternium*, is here substituted for *lectus*, since the bride is a goddess (*diuae*).

48. *sedibus*: picks up 43 *sedes*.

Indo . . . dente politum: 'ornamented with Indian ivory'; for this meaning of *politus* cf. Varro, *R*. 3. 2. 9 *uilla polita opere tectorio*.

49. Suetonius (*Jul.* 84, on the funeral of Julius Caesar) describes a similar bed and coverlet: *lectus eburneus auro ac purpura stratus*. *purpura* (originally the shell-fish, then the dye produced from it) often = a piece of purple cloth (*L & S* II B); *tincta . . . roseo conchyli . . . fuco* emphasizes the colour contrast between the ivory of the bed and the purple of the bed-spread; the adjective *roseo* comes at the principal caesura, and the noun with which it goes, *fuco*, at the end of the line. The elaborately poetic diction focuses our attention on the bed-spread, in preparation for the switch from story 1 to story 2.

50–1. *Bridge passage*, like 265–6. These two couplets, 50–1 and 265–6, enclose the inner story, the elopement of Ariadne with Theseus: 50–1 take us away from the wedding scene, 265–6 bring us back. Editors usually make a fresh paragraph at 50, but this spoils the poet's trick, by warning us of the break and thus dissipating the emotional energy built up by the tensioned description of the marriage-bed.

What is the connexion between inner story and outer story? Are they simply contrasting pictures of happy and unhappy love? Or can the relationship be more sharply defined — a heroic version of *furtiuus amor* perhaps (like C.'s affair with Lesbia, but with the roles reversed) and a heroic version of happy marriage (like that celebrated in Poems 61 and 62), held together by the

M

part played by gods in each: Peleus marries a god, Ariadne is
saved and married by a god? Undoubtedly there are strong
undercurrents of irony in C.'s evocation of the Heroic Age; but
his romantic nostalgia is surely genuine none the less; if it is not,
what do we make of 22–30 and 384–408?

51. The natural meaning to attach to C.'s words is that the
scenes on the *uestis* illustrate the courageous deeds of the Heroic
Age. We may ask how that assertion is backed up by the two
scenes selected for description, Theseus' desertion of Ariadne,
and her rescue by Bacchus. C.'s statement is no doubt ironical, like
348 *egregias uirtutes claraque facta* (the Fates' comment on the
bloody deeds they proceed to prophesy); but can C. in either
case speak wholly tongue in cheek without contradicting 22–30
and 384–408?

52–70. *Fourth Tableau: Ariadne on the Beach, Part 1.* We pass from
description of an artefact to description of a scene, a trick first
found in Homer's description of the shield of Achilles (*Il.* 18. 478–
613) and apparently common in Hellenistic poetry; the Greek
name for the trick seems to have been ἔκφρασις. The kernel
of the Ariadne story is found in *Od.* 11. 321–5; cf. Apollonius
4. 430–4. For Ariadne in art see WEBSTER. See also on 252.

52–3. The difficulties caused at this point by supposing that
line 11 describes Argo as the first ship ever (and not just a ship
whose construction and launching were presided over by Athena)
are insuperable (how can Theseus' voyage *not* be earlier than that
of Peleus?) — unless we attribute to C. the sort of careless slip
which seems incredible at the very point of juncture of inner and
outer story. According to Herodotus 7. 171 the death of Minos
took place three generations before the Trojan War (the exploits
in which of Achilles, son of Peleus and Thetis, are described by
the Fates in 348–61).

52. *fluentisono*: for other compound adjectives see 125 *clarisonas*,
320 *clarisona*, 263 *raucisonos*; see on 63. 23 *hederigerae*.

　　　Diae: the name of the island in Homer, equated in Hellen-
istic times with Naxos. Again 121.

53. *classe*: Occasionally in the high style = 'ship's company', of the crew of a single ship (see Norden on Virgil, *A.* 6. 334 *Lyciae ductorem classis Oronten*). The question, How many ships did Theseus have? is probably not one we are expected to put. The singular suits the pathos of 84 *naue leui nitens* (contrasting effectively with the following line, *magnanimum ad Minoa uenit sedesque superbas*); the plural suits the tragic rhetoric of 171–2 *utinam ne tempore primo | Cnosia Cecropiae tetigissent litora puppes*. Here *celeri cum classe* (ablative of *accompaniment* — not instrumental) probably opposes Theseus surrounded by his companions straining to get away (*celeri*) and Ariadne alone and motionless; *cedentem celeri cum classe* also provides an effective alliteration; *naue* is metrically equivalent, but probably not idiomatically compatible with *cum*. Such considerations seem often to dictate the choice between singular and plural (or collective) in Latin poetry — however strange this may seem to the modern mind accustomed to treat the distinction between singular and plural like that between black and white, or that between true and false. See E. Löfstedt, *Syntactica* I (2nd edn 1942), Chapters 2–3. See also on 63. 68.

tuetur: the present tense, natural in describing an artefact, makes the transition smoother.

54. In this first Ariadne scene, she is still madly in love; by line 124 her mood has changed; with *furores* cf. 94 *exagitans immiti corde furores*.

56. *utpote . . . quae*: = 'naturally enough, since she'; cf. 67. 43. The expression and the tone it implies are alien to the high style.

57. *in sola . . . harena*: cf. 154 *sola sub rupe* and 184 *sola insula*.
miseram: see on 8. 1 *miser*.

58. Note the jerky rhythm, suggesting the guilty haste of Theseus' departure. (See *Critical Essays* 44.)

immemor: 'with no thought for Ariadne'; the word is used again of Theseus in 123, 135, 248; cf. 148 *meminere* and 231 *memori*. The first occurrence of the *memor*-leitmotive.

uada: see on 6 *uada*.

59. An elegant Golden Line, to sum up (see on 7); picked up

by 142 *quae cuncta aerii discerpunt irrita uenti.* For the imagery see on 30. 10.

60. *alga*: the line of seaweed at the high-water mark; a picturesque detail (inappropriate to the high style); again 168.

maestis: the word recurs as a kind of thematic echo in 130, 202, 210, 249 and 379.

ocellis: for the pathetic use of the diminutive see on 3. 18; *ocellus* also 3. 18, 31. 2, 43. 2, 45. 11, 50. 10 and 19.

61. *saxea ut effigies bacchantis*: Ariadne's wild appearance (described in 63–7) suggests a Maenad; but she is motionless, like a statue; cf. Euripides, *Hecuba* 560–1 (Polyxenia about to be sacrificed is like a statue): μαστοὺς δ'ἔδειξε στέρνα θ'ὡς ἀγάλματος / κάλλιστα.

eheu: heightens the pathos. [*heue* V; *eheu* Bergk.]

62. *magnis curarum fluctuat undis*: 'she is tossed about by great waves of anguished emotions'; cf. 65. 4 *tantis fluctuat ipsa malis.* Virgil picks up the phrase, *A.* 8. 19 *magno curarum fluctuat aestu*; cf. *A.* 4. 531–2 *ingeminant curae rursusque resurgens / saeuit amor, magnoque irarum fluctuat aestu*; *cura* = any painful emotion, especially that caused by love; the plural suggests conflicting or confused emotions.

63–7. An ironical description of the pathetic figure Ariadne cuts: epic heroines are not normally made the subject of such detailed studies in realism. (See *Critical Essays* 43.) With the pattern of anaphora introduced by the triple *non* cf. 39–41.

63. *flauo . . . uertice*: epic heroines were traditionally blondes; cf. Theseus (98 *flauo . . . hospite*).

mitram: = (among other forms of headgear) a kind of hairnet worn by women in bed; cf. Propertius 2. 29. 15–16. Ariadne's has fallen off.

64. 'clothed no longer in the flimsy garment by which her torso had been veiled'; *uelatum* repeats the idea contained in *contecta*; Ariadne, i.e., has lost the dress she had been wearing. An accusative dependent on a past participle as though it were the direct object of a deponent participle (*contecta . . . uelatum pectus*) becomes

one of the regular features of the common style of Augustan verse. (See *Cat. Rev.* 66–7.) The same construction in the next line, 122 *deuinctam lumina somno* and 207–8 *mentem . . . consitus*.

65. *tereti*: used of things which are rounded or tapered, like the cymbals in 262, the weight in 314, or the tomb of Achilles in 363; 61. 174 of an arm.

strophio: = 'brassière'; cf. the mosaics of dancing girls from Piazza Amerina (J. P. V. D. Balsdon, *Roman Women*, opp. p. 193). As one might expect, Aristophanes makes great play with the garment in the *Thesmophoriazusae*. Isidorus 19. 33. 3 ascribes an almost identical phrase to Cinna: *strofio lactantes cincta papillas*; cf. 66. 81.

66–7. Ariadne had made her way to the water's edge on waking; her clothing 'had fallen everywhere from place' and was now trailing in the water at her feet.

66. *omnia quae*: accusative.

67. *alludebant*: the spondaic 5th foot suggests the flatness of despair.

68. *neque tum . . . neque tum*: repetition for rhetorical effect.

fluitantis: 'fluttering' or 'hanging loose', not 'floating'; the reference is to 64 *leui . . . amictu*.

69–70. The repetition *toto . . . pectore . . . toto animo . . . tota . . . mente* for pathetic emphasis; see on 63. 44–9.

69. *uicem curans*: *L & S* II 2a. Usually adverbial as in Cicero, *Fam.* 4. 5. 3 *an illius uicem . . . doles?* ibid. 11. 19. 1 *meam et uestram uicem timeam necesse est*, etc.

ex te . . . Theseu: apostrophe, a Hellenistic trick; cf. 253 — and 28. 9–10.

71–5. *Bridge passage: How this came about.* (Preparing the way for the flashback at 76.)

71. *externauit*: an uncommon frequentative form of *sternere*; originally 'flatten'; then, by association with *externus*, something like 'craze', 'dement'; cf. *alienare*; again 165.

72. An elegant, distancing line; the latent metaphor in *spinosas* is drawn out by *serens*.

Erycina: The epithet (from Eryx in western Sicily, famous for its temple of Venus) is commonly applied to Venus; there was also a temple of Venus Erycina at Rome. Venus is addressed simply as Erycina in Horace, *Carm.* 1. 2. 33.

73. *illa tempestate . . . quo ex tempore*: =*illo ex tempore . . . quo tempore*, 'ever since the time that'. Repetition of the noun-antecedent in the relative clause is not uncommon in contemporary prose; it is a mannerism of Caesar. Though C. varies the pattern by the use of a synonym (*tempestas*, as a synonym of *tempus* is an archaism), the words hardly earn their keep; cf. 335–6 and see on 96. 3.

ferox . . . Theseus: cf. 247 *ferox Theseus*. The epithet implies insensitivity or callousness, as much as courage.

74. *Piraei*: the port of Athens.

75. *iniusti*: the challenging epithet (Minos was traditionally the law-giver in Hades).

Gortynia: = 'Cretan'.

templa: =any enclosure or building, hence 'palace'. Cf. Ennius, *Trag.* 101–2W: *o Priami domus! | saeptum altisono cardine templum.* Archaic in this sense.

76–115. *Flashback.* A highly selective narrative sequence that moves forward from Theseus' departure from Athens to his triumphant emergence from the labyrinth, incorporating two short tableaux (86–93: Ariadne in love at first sight, 105–11: death of the Minotaur) and shorter vignettes (Ariadne praying to the gods, Theseus retracing his steps).

76. *nam perhibent olim*: cf. 212 *namque ferunt olim* and 2 *dicuntur*; *namque* also in 52.

crudeli peste: C. follows the version of the story in which the Athenians were reduced by hunger and pestilence to accept Minos' terms.

coactam: with 79 *Cecropiam.*

77. A 4-word hexameter. Androgeon (or Androgeos), a famous wrestler, was assassinated, the story goes, by Aegeus, king of Athens; his father Minos, king of Crete, after besieging Athens,

exacted an annual tribute of seven young Athenian men and seven young women to be delivered over to the Minotaur (a monstrous creature kept in the labyrinth, or maze, from which no one had ever found his way out alive) and devoured. Virgil summarizes the story, as depicted by the architect Daedalus on the walls of the temple of Apollo at Cumae, *A*. 6. 20–30 (including an echo of C.'s line 115), attributing the trick of the thread to Daedalus himself. For the adjectival form *Androgeoneae* see on 1 *Peliaco*.

78–80. Three lines in a row with a spondee in foot 5.

78. *electos*: probably a reference to choice by lot (Virgil, *A*. 6. 22 *stat ductis sortibus urna*); but cf. 4 *lecti iuuenes*.

    decus innuptarum: Virgil omits the girls.

79. *Cecropiam*: 'Cecrops' land' (the legendary first king of Athens).

    solitam esse: i.e. the tribute had been paid for some time before Theseus' intervention.

    dapem: 'banquet' (cf. 304 *multiplici constructae sunt dape mensae*); ironical.

80. *quis . . . malis*: = *quibus malis*; i.e. the loss of the young men and women year after year. See on 145.

    angusta . . . moenia: i.e. Athens was still small.

81. *Theseus*: son of King Aegeus.

82. *proicere*: i.e. cast his own body before the monster.

    potius quam: with the subjunctive, regularly = 'to prevent'.

83. *funera . . . nec funera*: = 'living corpses'; *funus*, 'corpse', is first found here in poetry; cf. Virgil, *A*. 2. 539, 6. 150 and 9. 491; perhaps an archaism — cf. Varro, *R*. 1. 4. 5 *domus repletae . . . aegrotis ac funeribus*; Servius' explanation of 2. 539 (*funus est iam ardens cadauer*) seems to be an attempt to derive *funus* from *funis*, 'torch'; the combination *funera . . . nec funera* is a Graecism, based on combinations like Sophocles' ἄδωρα δῶρα (*Ajax* 665).

84. *naue leui*: see on 53 *classe*.

85. *magnanimum . . . superbas*: both 'stock' epithets are ironical.

86–90. The youth and innocence of Ariadne are effectively conveyed by a pattern of imagery in which neither is explicitly asserted, apart from 87 *castus*; cf. 61. 21–5 and 62. 39–41. The long aside ends by describing something which happened in a moment (Ariadne's falling in love at first sight).

86. *cupido . . . lumine*: 'with eager eye'; the epithet is transferred from such expressions as *cupido animo*; perhaps an echo of Ennius, *Medea* 281 W *cupido corde*; cf. 147 *cupidae mentis*, 267 *cupide*, and 398 *cupida de mente*.

conspexit: 'caught sight of'.

88. *in molli complexu matris*: 'in the tender arms of her mother'; see on 61. 58–9; cf. 62. 21–3.

alebat: i.e. had been rearing to womanhood (*adolescentia*).

89. The *suauis odores* of 87 are 'like the myrtles which the streams of Eurotas bring forth'; i.e. 'like those of the myrtles', with the usual idiomatic suppression of the unimportant middle term of a comparison. [*pergignunt* V, *progignunt* θ; Baehrens's *praecingunt*, though ingenious, by making *quales . . . myrtus* nominative, makes the transition to 90 impossibly harsh.]

90. *auraue*: =*uel quales aura*; an appositional expansion of the simile in the Homeric manner, no longer closely referable to the original object described. With the image cf. 62. 39–44 and Lucretius 1. 7–8.

colores: cf. Virgil, *G.* 4. 306 *ante nouis rubeant quam prata coloribus*.

91–3. Ariadne is set on fire by the flame which emanates from Theseus, passing through her eyes into the depths of her body. C. seems to have had in mind objects set on fire by the rays of the sun passing through a lens. An ironic development of the cliché according to which a handsome man or woman is said to radiate beauty (cf. 2. 5 *desiderio meo nitenti*, etc.). Cf. Ovid, *Met.* 7. 79–83 (of Medea).

91–2. *flagrantia . . . lumina*: i.e. her eyes burn like burning-glasses.

91. *declinauit*: i.e. she took a first long look, instead of modestly averting her gaze. Spondaic 5th foot.

92–3. Note the alliteration: first the heavy thump of c- **and** f-sounds in *cuncto concepit corpore flammam funditus*, then the crackle of s- and t-sounds in *imis exarsit tota medullis*.

92. *concepit*: 'took up', 'received'; cf. Virgil, *A.* 8. 389 (Mars in love with Venus) *accepit solitam flammam*.

93. *exarsit*: 'burst into flames'.

94–8. With this apostrophe of Cupid and Venus cf. 22–30. An echo of Apollonius 4. 445–7 in 94–5.

94. *misere*: the adverb. Apparently a colloquialism = 'excessively'; cf. Horace, *S.* 1. 9. 8 *misere discedere quaerens*; ibid. 14 *misere cupis abire*.

95. *misces*: cf. 68. 18 (of Venus) *quae dulcem curis miscet amaritiem*.

96. See on 36. 12–15. Golgi and Idalium are in Cyprus. C. echoes Theocritus 15. 100.

97. *mente*: with *incensam*.

98. *fluctibus*: cf. 62 *magnis curarum fluctuat undis*. Draws out the metaphor latent in *iactastis*. One of the few lines in the poem where the sense flows over from the previous line; cf. 175–6.

flauo: cf. 63 *flauo*.

99. *tulit*: =*perpessa est* (*L & S* II B 5b).

languenti: *languidus*, 'tired out', 'exhausted' (a stronger word than its English equivalent) and the corresponding verb *languere* are common in love poetry, e.g. Propertius 1. 3. 37–8: *namque ubi longa meae consumpsti tempora noctis | languidus exactis, ei mihi, sideribus?* Cf. 188 *languescent*, 219 *languida*, 331 *languidulos*.

100. *quanto*: ablative of measure of difference with *magis*: 'how much more'; *fulgore* is comparative ablative, also with *magis*. A clumsy line. [Faerno's *quam tum* is an improvement, and also provides a correlative for 101 *cum*.]

fulgore . . . auri: Ariadne, an olive-skinned Mediterranean beauty, would naturally turn pale yellow (the colour of pure gold), rather than white, with fear. Cf. 81. 4 *inaurata pallidior statua*.

101. *contra*: cf. Virgil, *A.* 5. 370 *solus qui Paridem solitus contendere contra. L & S contendo*, II B 2β.

102. Echoes Apollonius 4. 205.

2 M

praemia laudis: cf. Cicero, *Mil.* 81 *ex quo etiam praemia laudis essent petenda*.

103. *non ingrata tamen frustra*: i.e. despite her fears; *non* with the whole phrase ('she did not promise unacceptable gifts to no purpose'), not with *ingrata*. For *ingrata* see on 73. 3.

munuscula: the diminutive for pathetic effect, like 104 *labello*; cf. 131 *frigidulos* and 316 *aridulis . . . labellis*, and see on 3. 18.

104. *tacito . . . labello*: i.e. she dare not let on what she is doing.

succepit: = *suscepit*. [*succendit* V is attractive, but inappropriate (Ariadne is undertaking a vow, not discharging it), unless we suppose C. means incense burnt while making the vow, as Merrill suggests.]

105–11. The simile is Homeric in structure; the immediate model is Apollonius 4. 1682–8, but cf. *Il.* 13. 389–93; Virgil's version in *A.* 2. 626–31.

105. *brachia*: of trees, *L & S* II C 1.

107. *indomitus*: personifying epithet: 'untamed', therefore, 'wild'.

contorquens flamine robur: 'twisting the solid timber with its blast'.

108–9. Appositional expansion of the basic syntactical pattern; typical of Homeric-type similes.

108. *procul*: with *cadit*: the whole tree is wrenched out by the roots and falls 'some distance away' from where it grew, wreaking havoc along its path (line 109).

109. *prona cadit*: to emphasize the parallel with the Minotaur.

late quaeuis cumque obuia frangens: 'smashing everything in its path for a considerable distance'. [*lateque cum eius* V, which is meaningless and unmetrical; the rewrite (due to Robinson Ellis) is as good as any that has been suggested. R. O. Fink, *AJPh* 84 (1963), 72–4, proposes *lateque cacumen it, obuia frangens*.]

110. *domito*: the echo of 107 *indomitus* is somewhat unhappy.

saeuum: here used as a noun, like *fera*.

111. The Greek original of this line happens to be quoted by

Cicero (no indication of authorship and no comment on the
5th-foot spondee), *Att.* 8. 5. 1: πολλὰ μάτην κεράεσσιν ἐς ἠέρα
θυμήναντα.

113. For the order see on 7; *errabunda* closely with *regens*: his
feet kept straying, but the thread kept guiding him back onto the
right path; Virgil picks up the phrase *errabunda uestigia* in *Ecl.* 6.
58 (in retelling the story of Pasiphae) and *regens* in his version of
the Minotaur story, *A.* 6. 30.

115. 'the undetectable wandering of the structure' (taking
error as a quality of the building — it rambled, as we say, in all
directions, and there was no way of telling one winding path from
another), rather than 'an undetectable mistake with regard to
the structure' (taking *tecti* as genitive of respect). One of four
4-word hexameters in the poem (cf. 15, 77 and 319); the flashback
76–115 ends with a flourish. Cf. Virgil, *A.* 6. 27 *inextricabilis error*
and 5. 591 *irremeabilis error* (both of the labyrinth).

116–23. *Bridge passage* (an expansion of the rhetorical *quid
plura?*), returning us, via a quick résumé of intervening events, to
where we left Ariadne on the beach at line 70.

116. *a primo . . . carmine*: = 'from where I began my poem' (the
inner, not the outer, tale).

117. 'how', followed by further *ut*'s in 118 (2 of them), 121 and
122 — a convenient way of stringing together the main points in
C.'s recapitulation; cf. 66. 3–6. See also 87–8.

    linquens genitoris filia uultum: the simple statement is
curiously effective; cf. 180–1.

118. Sister and mother embrace Ariadne; her father (it is
implied) shows by his look that he is unapproachable. Ariadne's
mother, Pasiphae, had several daughters; the best known was
Phaedra, who became the wife of Theseus and the stepmother of
Hippolytus.

119. *misera*: with *gnata*.

    laetabatur: [*leta* V *lamentata est* Conington.] The spondaic
5th foot, if right, and the oxymoron *deperdita laetabatur* effectively
emphasize Pasiphae's attempt to rejoice for her daughter's sake.

120. *praeoptarit*: the first two syllables are run together.

122. *deuinctam lumina*: for the construction see on line 64.

123. *immemori*: the *memor*-leitmotive. See on line 58.

   coniunx: see 139-42.

124-31. *Fifth Tableau: Ariadne on the Beach, Part 2.* This time an action tableau, unlike the static 52-70. By now Ariadne has grasped what has happened to her and 124-31 set out her reactions: first she cries out in distress (124-5); next she scales a steep cliff (126-7); then she runs down into the water (128-9). C.'s psychological insight is acute: as Theseus' ship disappears over the horizon, Ariadne naturally climbs up to a vantage point to keep it in view; when it disappears again, she surrenders to the instinct to run into the water after it; but this time she is sufficiently aware of what she is doing to lift her dress clear of the water (129 — contrast 66-8). Her formal tragic lament follows.

125. *clarisonas*: cf. 320 *clarisona*.

126. *conscendere*: contrast 125 *fudisse* and 130 *dixisse*; the change of tense corresponds to a switch from perfect indicative to historic present in *oratio recta*; cf. 128 *procurrere*.

127. *aciem . . . protenderet*: cf. Attis, 63. 56 *cupit ipsa pupula ad te sibi dirigere aciem*. [*in* is added in late MSS.]

128. *tremuli*: see on 17. 13.

129. = 'raising her light dress, thus leaving her legs exposed'; *mollia*, 'soft', i.e. not stiff or heavy. Ariadne would naturally put her clothes in order (the *leuis amictus* etc. had slipped from her shoulders at 64-7) before scaling the cliff.

130. *extremis*: i.e. her last words as a mere mortal; when her lament is over, she is rescued by Dionysus (see 251-3); there is an echo in Propertius 3. 7. 55 *flens tamen extremis dedit haec mandata querellis*.

131. *frigidulos*: another pathetic diminutive (see on 103 *munuscula*): 'with tear-stained face emitting little chill sobs'; with *cientem* cf. Lucretius 5. 1060 *dissimilis . . . uoces uariasque ciere*.

132-201. *Ariadne's Lament.* The longest section of the poem. The first 56 lines (to 187) follow a rather rambling course —

132–42: accusations of treachery and cruelty hurled at the absent Theseus; 143–8: 'men are like that'; 149–70: Theseus' ingratitude; 171–87: the lament proper — her situation is hopeless — culminating in the fine:

> nulla fugae ratio, nulla spes: omnia muta,
> omnia sunt deserta, ostentant omnia letum.

These lines, the high point in the lament, lead effectively into the concluding curse (188–201). There are obvious echoes of Euripides' *Medea*, and of Apollonius' Medea (4. 354–90). See HROSS. Cf. Virgil's Dido and Horace's Europa (*Carm*. 3. 27).

132. *sicine*: cf. 134 and 77. 3.

patriis . . . ab aris: cf. Virgil, *A*. 11. 269 *patriis . . . redditus aris*.

134. *neglecto numine diuum*: neglecting, i.e., their power to punish perjury.

135. *immemor*: cf. on 58.

deuota: 'accursed', 'hateful'; no specific reference to 188–201.

139–40. *blanda . . . uoce*: i.e. coaxing her, so as to get what he wanted. [*blanda* O, *nobis* X — a curious variant.]

140. *miserae*: one would expect the accusative with *iubebas*; the dative perhaps is a carry-over from *mihi*.

141. Cf. 158 *conubia nostra* and 20 *humanos . . . hymenaeos*. The unusual rhythm (no strong caesura in either foot 3 or 4, no coincidence of stress and initial syllable in foot 5) is preserved in Virgil's echo, *A*. 4. 316 *per conubia nostra, per inceptos hymenaeos*; for *hymenaeos*, 'marriage', see on 61. 4.

142. An echo of 59 *irrita uentosae linquens promissa procellae*. For the imagery see on 30. 10.

143. *nunc iam*: cf. 8. 9 *nunc iam illa non uolt*.

femina: see on 69. 1.

145. *quis*: = *quibus*; so 80, 63. 46, 66. 37, 68. 13 (all ablative, here dative of the person interested); the passage from negative singular to positive plural is natural enough.

praegestit: cf. 46. 7 *praetrepidans*; Cicero, *Cael*. 67 *praegestit animus iam uidere*.

147. *cupidae mentis*: see on 86 *cupido . . . lumine*.

libido: need =no more than 'wish', 'desire'; cf. 17. 5 *ex tua libidine*.

148. *dicta nihil meminere*: i.e. they are *dictorum immemores*. Cf. 30. 11 *si tu oblitus es, at di meminerunt, meminit Fides*. [*meminere* was conjectured by Czwalina in place of the palaeographically equivalent *metuere* of V, which most print. See G. P. Goold, *Phoenix* 12 (1958), 105.]

periuria: picks up 135 *periuria*.

149. *in medio . . . turbine leti*: = 'right in the middle of . . .', a common idiom; cf. Virgil, *A.* 4. 61 *media inter cornua fundit*.

uersantem: = *qui uersabatur*; the nominal forms of the verb were originally independent of distinctions of voice.

150–1. *potius . . . quam*: see on 82.

150. *germanum*: i.e. the Minotaur (strictly Ariadne's half-brother).

creui: archaic for *decreui*.

151. *supremo in tempore*: = 'in the moment of crisis'; cf. 169 *extremo tempore*.

152–3. To refuse a corpse burial meant that the soul was denied the peace of death; see, e.g., Virgil, *A.* 6. 325–30; that birds and beasts of prey feed on unburied corpses is a theme which goes back to the opening lines (1. 4–5) of Homer's *Iliad*; much is made of it, e.g., by Sophocles in the *Antigone* (28–30, 205–6, 696–8, 1017–18). Cf. Virgil, *A.* 9. 485–6 (Euryalus' mother, of her son) *heu, terra ignota canibus data praeda Latinis | alitibusque iaces!*

154–7. For the imagery and the cliché that cruelty etc. shows that one is an unnatural son or daughter see on 60. 1–3.

154. *sola sub rupe*: cf. 57 *in sola . . . harena* and 184 *sola insula*.

155. An alternative suggestion.

conceptum . . . exspuit: = *concepit et exspuit*.

spumantibus exspuit undis: note the alliteration. Cf. 68. 3.

156. Three further suggestions, all names of treacherous stretches of water personified; the personification of Scylla is the best established (see on 60. 2), that of Charybdis less so; *Syrtis*

normally = either of two famous shoals off the coast of Africa (one near Carthage, the other further east). An echo of C.'s line in Virgil, *A.* 7. 302–3 *quid Syrtes aut Scylla mihi, quid uasta Charybdis | profuit?* For Scylla and Charybdis see also *A.* 3. 420–8, 558–60 and 684–5.

158. *si tibi non cordi fuerant*: cf. 44. 2–3, 81. 5, 95b. 1. The pluperfect *fuerant* takes us back to a time before the coaxing promises of 139–40, suggesting that Theseus had rejected any thought of marriage from the outset (despite what he said to Ariadne) because of the supposed *praecepta* of his father.

    conubia nostra: cf. 141.

159. *praecepta*: Aegeus' parting words to his son, as imagined by Ariadne, not what Aegeus was likely to say if Theseus brought the sister of the Minotaur home as his bride. Aegeus, Ariadne suggests, was a father of the old school (*prisci*) who had strong ideas (*saeua . . . praecepta*) about their sons and foreign women; a further calculated intrusion of realism, probably, as in 63–70. With this picture of Theseus mindful of what his father had told him cf. 209. Note the alliteration in *prisci praecepta parentis*. With *prisci* cf. 50 *priscis . . . figuris*.

160. *uestras . . . sedes*: i.e. the home of Theseus and his father.

    ducere: sc., *me*. An obvious pronoun object is often omitted; cf. 214 *complexum*.

161. *famularer serua*: An echo of Euripides' *Andromeda* (Fragment 133 N). But to take home a foreign slave (and concubine) was customary in the Heroic Age (cf. Aeschylus' Cassandra).

162–3. Washing feet and making beds are tasks commonly performed for men by female slaves in Homer. But the imagery effectively exploits the inherent pathos of the idea of 161.

162. *permulcens . . . lymphis*: for the order see on 7. Cf. Pacuvius, Fragment 266–7 W (Ulysses' old nurse is speaking):

    cedo tuum pedem mi lymphis flauis fuluum ut puluerem
    manibus isdem quibus Vlixi saepe permulsi abluam.

With *permulcens* cf. 284 *permulsa*.

    uestigia: = *pedes* (*L & S* I B 1); rare.

163. A Golden Line. Is the echo of 47–9 deliberate?

164–70. Ariadne pulls herself together, and proceeds to expatiate on the fact that there is nobody present to listen to her. In 164–6 C. intends probably a reference to the old habit of lamenting to sun and sky (for parallels and parodies see Page on Euripides, *Medea* 57–8 and Ennius, *Medea* 264–5W *cupido cepit miseram nunc me proloqui | caelo atque terrae Medeai miserias*. C. perhaps connects the practice with the phenomenon of echo. The 'up-to-date' rational language in which Ariadne registers her protest is part of the distancing irony.

165. *externata*: see on 71 *externauit*.

    quae: the antecedent is 164 *auris*.

    nullis sensibus auctae: an echo of Lucretius 3. 626 and 630, where the *anima* is spoken of as *sensibus aucta*. See Friedrich 396.

166. Further echoes in this line of Lucretian phraseology; cf. 3. 931–2 *si uocem rerum natura repente | mittat*, 4. 577 (of echoes) *loca uidi reddere uoces*; *reddere uoces* also in Virgil, *A.* 1. 409 and 6. 689

167–70. = 'there are certainly no human beings to hear me'.

167. *mediis*: see on 149 *in medio . . . turbine leti*.

168. *uacua . . . in alga*: tensioned statement. Cf. 60 *ex alga*.

169. *extremo tempore*: cf. 151 *supremo in tempore*.

170. *etiam*: with *auris*.

171–6. She appeals, therefore, to Jove.

171–2. *utinam . . . puppes*: An echo of Ennius' *Medea* 253–4W (quoted on 1–18); cf. 281W (Chorus speaking) *utinam ne umquam Mede Colchis cupido corde pedem extetulisses*, Virgil, *A.* 4. 657–8 (Dido speaking) *si litora tantum | numquam Dardaniae tetigissent nostra carinae*.

171. *tempore primo*: = 'in the first place'.

172. *Cnosia*: = 'Cretan'.

    puppes: see on 53 *classe*.

173. See on 5. Here the epithets and nouns form a chiasmus.

174. *perfidus*: cf. 133 *perfide*.

    in Creta religasset . . . funem: 'tied his ship up on the shore of Crete'. [O has *in Creta*; the other MSS give *in Cretam*, adopted by Mynors, 'untied his ship for the voyage to Crete'; *religare* 'untie' and 'tie up' are both common.]

175-6. The over-flow of 175 into 176 and the elaborate syntax of 171-6 help the anticipation of *hospes* by *malus hic*; *hospes* also predicatively with *requiesset* ('as a guest'); an echo of 176 in Virgil, *A.* 4. 10 *quis nouus hic nostris successit sedibus hospes*.

177-87. 'What shall I do? There is no way of escape.' An echo of Euripides' *Medea* 502-5 (νῦν ποῖ τράπωμαι; etc.); Ennius' version is (284-5W):

> quo nunc me uortam? quod iter incipiam ingredi?
> domum paternamne anne ad Peliae filias?

C. Gracchus used the commonplace in a speech (quoted by Cicero, *de Orat.* 3. 214): *quo me miser conferam? quo uertam? in Capitoliumne? at fratris sanguine madet. an domum? matremne ut miseram lamentantem uideam et abiectam?*

177. *referam . . . nitor*: 180 *sperem* and 182 *consoler* suggest that *referam* and 178 *petam* are better regarded as subjunctive. [Some print *nitar*, but *nitor* has the better MS authority.]

178. *Idaeosne . . . montes*: = Crete.

179. *discernens*: emphasizes *diuidit*, and supports 178 *gurgite lato*. An unemphatic *me* (the object of both *discernens* and *diuidit*) is omitted; cf. 160.

 ponti truculentum . . . aequor: 'the angry expanse of ocean'; cf. 63. 16 *truculentaque pelagi*. [*truculentum ubi* V, but most editors omit *ubi*.]

180. *an patris auxilium sperem*: i.e. that he will follow Ariadne and rescue her.

181. *respersum . . . fraterna caede*: i.e. the blood of the Minotaur; cf. 150 *germanum*, 399 and 68. 19. An echo in Virgil, *A.* 4. 21 *sparsos fraterna caede penatis*.

182. *coniugis . . . fido . . . amore*: 'with a husband's faithful love' Ariadne's argument is that all the normal sources of comfort (home, father, husband) are denied her.

183. *lentos incuruans . . . remos*: = 'straining at the oars'. As in

58 Theseus is spoken of as if he were rowing his own ship; cf. Aulestes in Virgil, *A.* 10. 207–8: *lentus* = 'bending slowly, or reluctantly'; cf. *A.* 3. 384 *Trinacria lentandus remus in unda*.

184. *nullo litus, sola insula, tecto*: For the order cf. Virgil, *Ecl.* 2. 3 *inter densas, umbrosa cacumina, fagos*; it became a mannerism of the common style of Augustan verse; *nullo . . . tecto* is descriptive ablative with *litus*. [Mynors and Fordyce prefer A. Palmer's emendation *colitur*, 'is inhabited by no dwelling'.]

   sola insula: cf. 57 *in sola . . . harena* and 154 *sola sub rupe*.

186. *nulla spes*: the final syllable of *nulla* counts as long before the double consonant of *spes*; cf. 67. 32 *supposita speculae* (a conjecture); contrast 357 *unda Scamandri*, and see on 17. 24 *pote stolidum*.

187. *ostentant omnia letum*: an echo in Virgil, *A.* 1. 91 *praesentemque uiris intentant omnia mortem*.

188–201. The curse. There is a marked rise in the quality of the rhetoric.

190. *multam*: = *poenam*; a prose word (strictly, a fine); perhaps here for the sake of 192 *multantes*.

   191. *caelestum*: = *caelestium*; cf. 34. 12 *sonantum*, 100. 2 *Veronensum*. *postrema . . . hora*: i.e. now.

192. *uindice*: used adjectivally (uncommon).

193. *Eumenides*: 'the well-disposed goddesses', a propitiatory euphemism applied (as in Aeschylus' play) to the Erinyes; their function was to punish murder, especially murder of a kinsman, but the punishment of various lesser offences was also attributed to them since ancient times; among these is perjury (Homer, *Il.* 19. 259–60, Hesiod, *WD* 803–4); Aeschylus is said to have been the first to represent them with snakes entwined in their hair. Cf. Sophocles, *Ajax* 835–40.

194. *exspirantis*: intransitive with *iras*; the angry hissing of the snakes 'displays' (*praeportat*) the anger exhaled from the *pectus* (the site of the lungs, and also the seat of the emotions) of the Eumenides.

   praeportat: = *prae se fert*; cf. Lucretius 2. 621 *telaque prae-*

portant uiolenti signa furoris (where *tela* is nominative and *signa* accusative).

195. *huc huc*: cf. 61. 8–9 *huc huc ueni*.

196. *extremis . . . medullis*: =93 *imis . . . medullis*; cf. Ovid, *Ep.* 4 70 *acer in extremis ossibus haesit amor*.

198. *quae*: i.e. the *querellae*.

    pectore ab imo: cf. 196 *extremis . . . medullis*. Lucretius (3. 57–8) argues that under stress *uerae uoces tum demum pectore ab imo | eliciuntur et eripitur persona, manet res*.

200–1. *quali . . . mente . . . tali mente*: = 'by that same attitude of mind in which . . .'; i.e. *immemori mente*; cf. 246–8 and see on 58 *immemor*. C. seems to be rationalizing the legend, according to which Theseus 'forgot about' Ariadne and then 'forgot about' what his father had told him (because in each case a god caused him to forget), into an assertion about the sort of person Theseus was: a person, i.e., with no thought (*immemor*) except for himself.

201. *funestet*: cf. 246 *funesta . . . tecta*.

    seque suosque: the double -*que* is a mannerism of epic, introduced into Latin verse by Ennius, on the model of Homeric τε . . . τε; often at the end of a line, as here; see Austin on Virgil, *A.* 4. 83.

202–14. *Bridge passage*. Ariadne's curse acknowledged (202–6). Effect on Theseus (207–11). Second flashback begins: Theseus' departure from Athens (212–14).

202. *has postquam*: cf. 267 *quae postquam*, 303 *qui postquam*; *postquam* also in 397. See on 267.

204. The starting-point is *Il.* 1. 528–30 (said by Strabo to have inspired Pheidias' famous statue of Zeus at Olympia), from which C. takes over only the general situation and the nod of assent. For his reformulation he revitalizes traditional Latin material (cf. the formula reported by Livy 7. 30. 20 *annuite, patres conscripti, nutum numenque uestrum inuictum Campanis*) by the placing of *inuicto numine*, which attaches itself on the one hand to *caelestum rector* (cf. Homer's formulae for Zeus) in a descriptive ablative ('ruler of unvanquished power') and on the other to *annuit* in an instru-

mental ablative, drawing out the etymological connexion of *numen* and *nuere* ('nodded assent with all-powerful nod'). Cf. Virgil, *A.* 9. 106 *adnuit et totum nutu tremefecit Olympum.*

205–6. Echoes here of Lucretius: 3. 834–5 (of the Carthaginian wars) *omnia cum belli trepido concussa tumultu | horrida contremuere sub altis aetheris oris*; 1. 788 *a caelo ad terram, de terra ad sidera mundi*; 5. 1204–5 *nam cum suspicimus magni caelestia mundi | templa super stellisque micantibus aethera fixum.* Horace has *horrida aequora* in *Carm.* 3. 24. 40-41.

205. *quo motu*: [*quo modo tunc* V; *quo motu* Heyse; Fea's *quo nutu et* is tempting.]

206. *mundus*: 'firmament'; cf. 66. 1.

207–11. Picked up by 238–40.

207–8. *caeca mentem caligine . . . consitus*: = 'murky dark sown in his mind'. For the accusative see on 64; the combination *caeca caligine* occurs in Virgil, *A.* 3. 203, 8. 253; cf. Lucretius 3. 304 *caecae caliginis umbra*, 4. 456 *in noctis caligine caeca.*

208–9. *cuncta, quae mandata*: = *cuncta mandata, quae.*

209. Cf. Lucretius 2. 581–2 *illud . . . conuenit . . . memori mandatum mente tenere.* The word *mandata* is repeated as a kind of leitmotive in 214 and 232 and the whole line picked up in 238 *haec mandata prius constanti mente tenentem.*

210. *dulcia . . . signa*: explained in 233–7.

211. *Erectheum . . . portum*: = *Piraeum* (cf. 74), after Erectheus, a legendary king of Athens (cf. 229 *sedes . . . Erecthei*).

212. *namque ferunt olim*: cf. 76 *nam perhibent olim.*

moenia diuae: accusative with 213 *linquentem*; the goddess is Athena.

classi: cf. 53 *classe*; *classi* (also Virgil, *A.* 8. 11) is the less common form of the ablative. Again 66. 46.

214. *complexum*: sc. *eum* (cf. on 160).

215–37. *Aegeus' Farewell.* As usually printed, it consists of two elaborate sentences — among the longest in the poem; cf. 397–406, several instances of 8- and 9-line sentences; 215–22 and 228–37 probably represent the most complicated patterns of syntax in the poem, though 228–37 make up a very loosely articulated structure (4 separate *ut*-clauses). An attempt, perhaps, at stylization of an old man's rambling way of speaking. Cf. Virgil's Evander, *A.* 8. 558–84.

215–17. *gnate . . . unice . . . reddite*: all vocative. Cf. Virgil, *A.* 5. 724–5 (ghost of Anchises) *nate, mihi uita quondam . . . | care magis, nate Iliacis exercite fatis.*

217. *reddite*: Theseus had been separated from his father from infancy till manhood; for the details of this picturesque story see, e.g., *Oxford Companion to Classical Literature*, s.v. Theseus.

  extrema . . . fine: more often masculine, as in 3 *fines Aeeteos.*

218. *quandoquidem fortuna*: = 101. 5.

219. *languida*: see on 99 *languenti.* Here an (ominous) echo of 188 *non tamen ante mihi languescent lumina morte* — to remind us of the curse that hangs over Theseus?

221. *gaudens laetanti pectore*: repetition for the sake of emphasis; cf. 179 *discernens . . . diuidit*; see also on 69–70.

223. With the note of distancing irony introduced when Aegeus says he will 'first of all lament at length' cf. on 164–70.

224. So Achilles, grieving at the death of Patroclus, *Il,* 18. 23–5; cf. Priam, *Il.* 24. 163–5; Virgil, *A.* 10. 844 (Evander, grieving for Pallas) *canitiem multo deformat puluere,* 12. 611 (Latinus) *canitiem immundo perfusam puluere turpans.*

225. *infecta*: 'dyed'.

  uago: 'wandering', i.e. about to set out on its journey. A word C. is fond of; cf. 271 *uagi . . . Solis,* 340 *uago . . . certamine,* and see on 63. 4.

227. *obscurata*: with *carbasus,* which is feminine.

  ferrugine Hibera: 'Spanish rust'; defined by Servius on *A.* 9. 582 (of a cloak which is *ferrugine clarus Hibera*) as *uicinus purpurae subnigrae*; not, i.e., the colour of fresh rust (the *squalida rubigo* of 42), but the deep blue colour of heavily weathered iron.

228. *sancti . . . incola Itoni*: Athena; she had a famous sanctuary at Itonus (or Iton) in Boeotia (or Thessaly).

229. *Erecthei*: see on 211. Genitive of *Erectheus,* like 120 *Thesei.*

230. *annuit*: C.'s Athens is still small (80 *angusta . . . moenia*), and Athena has just agreed, apparently, to take it under her protection (*defendere . . . annuit*) which accounts for Aegeus' calling Athena 'the Itonian'; *annuere* with dependent infinitive is uncommon.

tauri respergas sanguine dextram: thematic echo of 181 *respersum iuuenem fraterna caede*.

231. *memori*: the leitmotive again; see on 58 *immemor*.

facito: the future imperative introduces, as usual, a solemn or earnest note; cf. 50. 21 *caueto*.

232. *mandata*: cross-reference to 209 *mandata*.

oblitteret aetas: i.e. as the passage of time wears away the *lettering* of an inscription; an effective use of an uncommon, precise word.

233. *lumina*: 'your eyes'.

234. *funestam*: thematic echo of 201 *funestet*; cf. 246 *funesta*.

undique: i.e. *all* of the sails. See on 243 *ueli*.

235. *intorti . . . rudentes*: 'twisted ropes'; stock epithet.

236. *quam primum*: 'as soon as possible'.

237. *aetas prospera*: *aetas* normally = a period of time (often the lifetime of a person), not a point in time. Perhaps 'a lucky period in our lives' — Aegeus hopes, i.e., that Theseus' luck will continue to hold.

238–48. *Second flashback concludes. Ariadne's curse fulfilled.*

238–40. A detailed cross-reference to 207–11.

238. *haec mandata*: better regarded as subject of 240 *liquere*, though the words are made also to serve provisionally as an object for *tenentem*. For the *mandata* leitmotive see on 209.

239. *Thesea*: Greek accusative.

239–40. The simile is perhaps suggested by *Il.* 5. 522–6.

240. *liquere*: the tense fits *haec mandata . . . Thesea*, but *liquere* is involved by its position in the simile; more likely a gnomic perfect (see on 62. 42) than that *liquere cacumen* is a hyperbaton (*cacumen* and *liquere* transposed).

niuei: a word C. is fond of; again 303, 309, 364; also 58b. 4, 61. 9, 63. 8 and 68. 125.

241. *prospectum*: an anticipation of the cross-reference 249 *prospectans*, intended to point a parallel between Aegeus gazing grief-stricken out to sea (242 *anxia in assiduos absumens lumina fletus*) and Ariadne? With *prospectum . . . petebat* cf. Virgil, *A.* 1. 180–1 *omnem | prospectum late pelago petit.*

242. Rhythmical elegance (the line is almost a Golden Line) and effective pathos are combined. Cf. 68. 55 *maesta neque assiduo tabescere lumina fletu.*

243. *inflati . . . ueli*: We gather from 225 and 235 that the ship had several sails, and this would be normal enough (227 *carbasus* refers to the material of the sails); *ueli* here may be a variation without significance — Latin poetry is curiously lax about the distinction between singular and plural (see on 53 *classe*); or C. may mean that Aegeus committed suicide as soon as he caught sight of the topmost sail of Theseus' ship. [Many print *infecti*, a traditional conjecture which would act as a cross-reference to 225 *infecta*. But *inflati*, the reading of V, gives excellent sense ('bellying' in the wind).]

244. *scopulorum e uertice*: cf. Ariadne in 126–7.

245. For the order see on 7.

246–50. These lines form a complicated pattern of cross-reference and thematic echo: *funesta* picks up Ariadne's *funestet seque suosque!* (201); 247–8 *qualem . . . mente immemori, talem* picks up 200–1 *quali . . . tali mente*; 246–7 *ingressus . . . ferox Theseus* (the end of Theseus' journey) picks up 73–4 *ferox . . . Theseus egressus* (the beginning of the journey). Then a series of cross-references take us back to the beginning of the Ariadne story: 247 *Minoidi* picks up 60 *Minois*; 248 *immemori* (last occurrence) picks up 58 *immemor* (first occurrence); 249 *prospectans* picks up 52 *prospectans* and 61 and 62 *prospicit*; 249 *cedentem* picks up 53 *cedentem*; 249 *maesta* picks up 60 *maestis*. Naturally in a similar situation the same words tend to recur, though in 250 *multiplices animo uoluebat saucia curas* C. manages to restate the sense of 54 *indomitos in corde gerens Ariadna furores* with all the key words changed. The effect of the verbal echoes is to emphasize the beginning and end of the inner story: we start with Ariadne on the *uestis*, we come back to her.

246–7. funesta goes with *tecta* (*domus* is genitive), *paterna morte* with *funesta* ('full of death through a father's dying'); *ferox* is used absolutely as in 73.

247. Minoidi: the final i is short — Greek dative (rare).

249–50. Bridge passage. We return to the *uestis*, in preparation for 251–64; a recapitulatory cross-reference to 52–70.

251–64. Sixth Tableau: Dionysus and his Worshippers.

251. parte ex alia: = 'elsewhere' (i.e. on the *uestis*) cf. Virgil, *A.* 1. 474.

florens: = 'youthful and vigorous'; the common representation of Dionysus in art and literature.

uolitabat: = 'hastens to and fro'.

Iacchus: like *Bacchus*, a cult title of Dionysus.

252. thiaso: a band of frenzied devotees, usually of Dionysus, but cf. 63. 28.

Nysigenis: i.e. brought by Dionysus from Nysa (in India?). Apollonius 4. 430–4 refers to a wonderful robe made by the Graces for Dionysus on Dia: 'And from it a divine fragrance breathed, ever since the King of Nysa himself lay to rest upon it, flushed with wine and nectar, beautiful Minos' daughter in his embrace, whom Theseus had left behind on the island of Dia after she had followed him from Cnossos.'

253. See WEBSTER for representations in art of Dionysus and Ariadne. With the apostrophe cf. 22–30 and 69.

Ariadna: cf. 54 *Ariadna* (the first and last references to her in the poem).

254. cui Thyades: Bacchus' female worshippers are now described; cf. 391 *Thyadas*; *cui* = *Iaccho*, dative of advantage. [*qui tum alacres* V. Most accept Bergk's *quae tum* (a somewhat unpleasing echo of 249) and suppose a lacuna of one or more lines preceding, containing a feminine plural antecedent for *quae*. O. Skutsch's *cui Thyades*, *Philologus* 106 (1962), 281–2, is a neat repair.]

lymphata mente furebant: for the frenzy of the Bacchantes see, e.g., Euripides' *Bacchae*.

255. *euhoe . . . euhoe*: the repeated cry of the Bacchantes stands outside the syntactical construction. Cf. 391 *euantis*.

bacchantes: 'in a Bacchic frenzy'; a true participle (not a proper name), balancing *inflectentes*.

256. *tecta . . . cuspide thyrsos*: the *thyrsus* is a vine-rod or spear (a stroke from which induced frenzy) tipped (*tecta cuspide*) with a pine-cone or a bunch of vine-leaves, sometimes with ivy.

257. Almost a translation of Euripides' line, *Bacchae* 739: ἄλλαι δὲ δαμάλας διεφόρουν σπαράγμασιν.

259. 'Others were crowded in worship of the sacred objects concealed within their baskets'; *orgia* is used both of the cult-objects themselves, and in the more general sense of 'rites'; the latter sense is not appropriate here, since a particular detail of the ceremony is being described; *cauus* is often used of an object that encloses another, or contains it within it.

260. *orgia quae . . . audire*: *audire* seems to invite the general sense of *orgia* ('rites') rather than the specific sense required by 259. Kroll suggests there is a shift of meaning as we pass from 259 to 260; Lenchantin that *audire* = 'hear about' (= *OLD*, sense 9; he quotes Caesar, *Gal.* 2. 12. 5 *magnitudine operum, quae neque uiderant ante Galli neque audierant*). Virgil, *A.* 4. 302–3 *audito stimulant triterica Baccho | orgia* is no help: Virgil means that the worshippers respond to the cry of *Bacche*; C. is talking about the *profani*. If we follow Kroll, C. means they may not approach within earshot; if we follow Lenchantin, C. means they may not learn about the holy objects from the initiates.

261–4. A word picture, rich in vowel music, alliteration and rhythmical effects, of the sounds produced by different instruments — drums, cymbals, horns and pipes. A re-working perhaps of two passages in Lucretius, 2. 618–20:

> tympana tenta tonant palmis et cymbala circum
> concaua, raucisonoque minantur cornua cantu,
> et Phrygio stimulat numero caua tibia mentis

and 4. 545–6:

> cum tuba depresso grauiter sub murmure mugit

et reboat raucum regio cita barbara bombum

and a passage in Varro, *Men.* 132 (quoted in introductory note to Poem 63); cf. 63. 21–2.

261. *proceris*: i.e. 'outstretched'.

262. *tereti . . . aere*: i.e. the cymbal; see on 65.

263. *multis*: dative: cf. 307 *his*; = 'many had horns and these blared forth hoarse boomings.'

264. *barbara*: i.e. Phrygian (and therefore non-Greek).

265–6. *Bridge passage*, corresponding to 50–1, and effecting the transition back from inner to outer story. The remainder of the poem comprises a sequence of three Tableaux: (1) 267–77 — departure of the mortal guests; (2) 278–302 — arrival of the immortal guests; (3) 303–22 — the Fates, followed by the Song of the Fates, 323–81, and the poet's concluding comment, 382–408.

267–77. *Seventh Tableau: The mortal guests depart.* The pendant of the Tableau describing their arrival (31–49). There is a nice irony in C.'s picture of the Heroic Age: though the gods moved freely among mankind (see 384–6) there were social distinctions all the same; the mortal guests are expected to be out of the way before the important guests arrive.

267. *quae postquam*: B. Axelson, *Unpoetische Wörter* (1945) 48–9, challenging Kroll's comment that C.'s use of the continuing relative is prosaic, points out that in more than 30 occurrences out of 90 of *postquam* in Ovid's *Metamorphoses* a continuing relative precedes. *quae* = the scenes on the *uestis*, the implication being that there were more than the two selected by C. for description. (Those who suppose that the inner and the outer stories were composed separately might argue that *quae* shows that 267 originally followed 49, summing up the description of 43–9.)

cupide: see on 86 *cupido . . . lumine.*

Thessala pubes: cf. 32–3 *tota . . . Thessalia*; for *pubes* see on 4.

268. *expleta est*: cf. Lucretius 4. 1102 *nec satiare queunt spectando.*

269–77. An elaborate simile, likening the movement of the crowd of guests from the *uestibulum* out into the open to a westerly wind at dawn driving the waves of the ocean with increasing force towards the rising sun. See *Critical Essays* 53–4. The Homeric models are *Il.* 4. 422–6 (the Greeks advancing in waves are likened to breakers beating on the headland) and 7. 63–4 (the massed ranks of Greeks and Trojans bristling with spears are like the sea rippling before the rising west wind).

269–70. To begin with, the sea is calm (269 *placidum mare*); then a breeze rises from the west, ruffles up the surface of the water (270 *horrificans . . . undas*) and sends a series of waves or wavelets tumbling forward (270 *procliuas incitat undas*).

271. The time is dawn. The waves move, therefore, out of darkness into light, like the crowd. For *uagi* see on 225 and cf. 277 *uago . . . pede*.

272. The movement of the waves, like that of the crowd, is gradual to begin with.

273. The splash of the wavelets as they topple over (corresponding to the ripples of laughter that run through the crowd — a correspondence reinforced by the ambiguity of *cachinni*, as in 31. 14) stands out against a background of more continuous noise (*leni . . . plangore*, corresponding to the continuous hum of conversation in the crowd); *plangor* is used of a variety of noises; the essential characteristics seem to be that the noise (1) is continuous, (2) varies in pitch; cf. Cicero, *Phil.* 2. 85 (the reaction of the crowd when Caesar was offered the crown by Antony) *tu diadema imponebas cum plangore populi; ille cum plausu reiciebat*. With *leni*, it suggests the whine of the wind, rather than the noise of the sea. [Most read *leuiter*, for which the MS authority is stronger. They are then almost forced (1) to take *cachinni* as genitive singular, since *plangore* unsupported by an adjective can hardly stand alone; (2) to take *quae* (=*undae*) as the subject of *sonant*. Cf. 68. 64 *lenius aspirans (leuius* V).]

274. *magis magis*: also 38. 3; cf. 68. 48 *magis atque magis* (the more common formula).

275. The light of the rising sun is reflected on the water; *procul* with *refulgent*; with *nantes* cf. Ennius, Epic Fragment 536W *fluctusque natantes*.

277. The breaking up of the crowd is emphasized by repetition:
ad se quisque, uago ... pede, passim, discedebant. The 5th-foot
spondee helps to suggest this disruptive movement.

278–302. *Eighth Tableau: The immortal guests arrive.* Like the
mortal guests (31–49), the immortal guests come from different
places and bring gifts.

278–84. First comes the Centaur Chiron, the future tutor of
the son of this marriage, Achilles.

278. *e uertice Pelei*: cf. 1 *Peliaco ... uertice*; *Pelei* archaic spelling
of *Peli*.

280–2. *quoscumque ... quos ... quos ... flores*: The reader is
prepared three times for a masculine plural accusative noun, but
does not know what is being described till he comes to *flores*. The
effect is to give a new vitality to what would otherwise be con-
ventional descriptive writing: instead of a list of places where the
flowers came from, the reader is offered a series of images of
Thessaly, its fields and mountains, the river Peneus, and left
free to explore these; the strictly denotative word *flores* necessarily
inhibits this process, so it is delayed as long as possible.

281. *fluminis*: the river Peneus. Cf. 285–92.

282. *aura ... Fauoni*: cf. Lucretius 1. 11 *et reserata uiget genita-
bilis aura Fauoni*; the model is perhaps Callimachus, *Hymn to
Apollo* 80–2.

283. *indistinctis*: did C. perhaps write *in distinctis*?

284. *quo ... odore*: more natural, if less logical, than *quorum
odore*; cf. 87–90.

permulsa: cf. 162 *permulcens*.

risit: The metaphor is as old as Homer (*Il.* 19. 362), but
it is revitalized here by the collocation *permulsa ... iucundo risit
odore*: flattered and disarmed (*permulsa*) by the mass of flowers, the
palace was all fragrance and smiles. Cf. 46 *tota domus gaudet*.

285–92. Next comes the river god Penios, or Peneus (see on
281). His gifts are no less lavish. The Peneus flows through the
famous valley of Tempe to the sea.

287. *linquens . . . celebranda choreis*: 'abandoning (verdant

Tempe), to crowd with their dancing'. No really satisfactory restoration of the rest of the line has been suggested. [The name of a group of nymphs, or something of the sort, to whom Tempe is abandoned is required. Heinsius' *Haemonisin* will do, but leaves *doris* to be tidied up — it cannot really pass as a by-form of *Doriis*; *doctis* and *duris* have been suggested.]

288. *ille*: = 'there he was with trees in his hands'; for this 'deictic' use of *ille* see Fordyce. Cf. 11 *illa*.

289. *recto ... stipite*: 'straight-trunked'. A descriptive ablative is often the Latin poet's answer to the problem of finding an equivalent for the compound adjectives of Greek.

290-1. *lentaque ... Phaethontis*: 'the supple sister of Phaethon who went up in flames' is the poplar. The story is told by Ovid, *Met.* 2. 340-66 and alluded to by Virgil, *A.* 10. 190.

291. *cupressu*: the first syllable is usually short.

292. *contexta*: 'woven together', to form a kind of screen.

293-7. Next comes Prometheus. His presence at the wedding is an allusion to the story that Prometheus was able to warn Zeus of the danger which threatened him if he married Thetis (whose son was destined to be greater than his father) and thus win his release from bondage; the description of Prometheus' appearance in 295-7 reinforces the allusion. See on 21.

294. *sollerti corde*: = 'ingenious'; Prometheus is the inventor of the arts; his name means 'foresighted' in Greek.

295. *extenuata ... uestigia*: = 'faint scars'. For the order see on 7.

296-7. This is how Prometheus appears at the beginning of Aeschylus' *Prometheus Bound*.

298-302. An ironic 'royal-family' group — Jove, Juno and an unspecified number of their children (*natis* covers both sons and daughters); Apollo and Artemis (children of Jove by Latona) are conspicuous by their absence. In Homer and Pindar, Apollo attends the wedding; in C. Apollo's sister joins him in slighting Peleus (301-2), a version of the story not otherwise known — no doubt an allusion to Apollo's responsibility for the death of Achilles.

298. *natisque*: the hypermetric *-que* is elided.

299–300. *caelo te . . . relinquens | unigenamque simul . . . montibus Idri*: The basis is a chiasmus in which *caelo* and *montibus* are both locative.

299. *te . . ., Phoebe*: for the apostrophe see on 22–30.

300. *unigenam*: Should mean 'only begotten', which might do for Hecate, with whom Artemis is often identified, but will hardly do in a context which links Artemis with her brother. One suspects C. is trying to use the word to mean 'born in a single birth' — Artemis and Apollo were twins; cf. 66. 53.

simul: 'likewise', 'in like manner'.

cultricem: predicative, 'living in the mountains of Idrus as a dweller', i.e. 'where her home was'; but *cultricem montibus Idri* can also be felt as a kind of compound, like 66. 58 *Canopeis incola litoribus*.

montibus Idri: Idrias was a town in Caria, linked with the worship of Hecate; *Idri* is presumably genitive singular of *Idrus*, the name (not found elsewhere) of its founder. The reading is suspect however.

303–22. *Ninth Tableau: The Fates*. As is appropriate at the wedding of a goddess, the marriage hymn is sung by the Fates themselves. For these formidable creatures in whose hands lie both the distribution of good and evil for mankind and life itself (Lachesis assigns the lot, Clotho spins the thread, Atropos severs it) see *OCD*, s.v. Fate. Their personification as the Spinners is ancient and natural. C.'s detailed portrait of three elderly ladies busy with the most familiar of female household tasks in antiquity, singing while they work, but singing of a bloody destiny for the child that will be born of the marriage, is an example of realistic treatment of legend, in the same spirit as the Tableau of Ariadne on the beach (52–70), but on a larger scale, more striking in its conception, subtler in its irony, even more brilliant in its treatment of detail.

303. *qui*: i.e. the divine guests.

niueis . . . sedibus: i.e. in ivory chairs; the practice of reclining at table is later than the Heroic Age.

304. *constructae . . . mensae*: 'the tables are piled up'; cf. Cicero, *Tusc.* 5. 62 (of the banquet offered to Damocles beneath the hanging sword) *mensae conquisitissimis epulis exstruebantur*. For the singular of *daps* (uncommon) cf. 79 *dapem dare Minotauro*.

305. *cum interea*: cf. 95. 3.

    infirmo quatientes corpora motu: 'their bodies shaking as they moved unsteadily'.

306. *ueridicos*: a word used by Lucretius of Epicurus (6. 6) *omnia ueridico qui quondam ex ore profudit*.

    Parcae: Thought by the Romans to come from *pars* (hence the identification with the Greek name for the Fates, Moirai); in fact, it seems, from *parere*, and originally the name of a Roman goddess of birth.

307–9. Curious echoes of 49–50.

307. *his*: dative; cf. 263 *multis*.

307–8. *uestis | candida*: note the over-flow.

309. *roseae niueo*: [*roseo niueae* V.]

311–19. Each spinner holds the distaff wrapped in unspun wool in her left hand. She draws down the fibres from the distaff with her right hand, shaping them roughly into a thread with the fingers of the right hand, which is held palm uppermost. At intervals she reaches down with her right hand and imparts a turning motion to the weighted spindle, which is balanced on the thumb of the hand held palm downwards during this part of the operation. C.'s description is organized round four focal points: (1) the action of the left hand (311); (2) the twin actions of the right hand (312–14); (3) the action of the tooth (315–17); (4) the image of the baskets of wool waiting to be spun (318–19).

312–14. The subject of both *formabat* and *uersabat* is *dextera*; the two operations, *deducens fila . . . formabat* and *torquens . . . uersabat . . . fusum* are performed alternately (*tum . . . tum*).

312. *leuiter*: 'carefully' — to avoid tearing the fibres.

314. *libratum*: 'weighted'.

    turbine: a 'weight' or 'flywheel', to keep the spindle spinning.

fusum: 'spindle' (on to which the spun thread is wound from time to time).

315. *atque ita decerpens aequabat . . . dens*: a separate process, interrupting the other two (*deducens . . . formabat* and *torquens . . . uersabat*); the singular *dens* preserves the symmetry of construction: *laeua retinebat, dextera tum formabat tum uersabat, aequabat dens*; but the singular is also imaginatively effective, focusing our attention on a single tooth (which performs the operation by closing with a snap upon the opposing jaw); hence the same construction, participle + verb; *atque ita* = 'and, as part of this process', as in 84; *decerpens*, 'tugging off' — a regular, jerky motion, like 310 *carpebant*; the jerkiness is emphasized by the monosyllabic ending *dens* and the heterodyne 5th foot; cf. 68. 19.

316. *aridulis . . . labellis*: 'little, dried-up lips'; see on 103 *munuscula*. Cf. Cinna, *FPL* p. 89 *aridulo . . . libello*.

317. *fuerant exstantia*: = *exstiterant*. Cf. 63. 57 *carens est*.

319. The description ends with a flourish — a 4-word hexameter (cf. 15, 77, 115) and a double alliteration.

custodibant: archaic = *custodiebant*; cf. 68. 85 *scibant*, 84. 8 *audibant*.

320. *haec*: archaic feminine plural = *hae*.

clarisona: cf. 125 *clarisonas*; the compound was perhaps coined by Cicero, *Arat.* 280 *e clarisonis auris Aquilonis*.

petlentes uellera: i.e. prodding at the masses of wool. [Fruterius' conjecture *uellentes uellera* is ingenious, but the triple alliteration *uellentes uellera uoce* is probably too much, even for C.]

321. *talia . . . fuderunt . . . fata*: 'poured forth the following prophecy'. A phrase in the high style: cf. Lucretius 5. 110 *fundere fata* and Virgil's regular use of *talia* etc., even though the ostensible actual words of the speaker are given (see Pease on *A.* 4. 219). Cf. 382 *talia praefantes*.

322. *arguet*: a vivid use of the future.

323–81. *The marriage hymn*. Cf. Poems 61 and 62. After an appropriate introduction (323–36), a prophecy of the achievements and death of Achilles, the son of the marriage (338–71), followed by a conclusion (372–81).

323. *o decus . . . augens*: 'O you, who add to your distinction . . .'.

324. *Emathiae tutamen*: cf. 26 *Thessaliae columen*; Emathia was actually in Macedonia.

Opis carissime nato: 'you who are most dear to the son of Ops'. The son of Ops is Jove; for the genealogy of Jove, son of Ops, see Ennius, *Euhemerus* 8–38W; cf. Plautus, *Mil.* 1082 *Iuppiter ex Ope natust* and *Per.* 251. [*tutum opus* V; Housman's *tutamen*, *Opis* (*CQ* 9 [1915], 229–30), based on a correction found in GR *tu tamen opis*, makes sense out of nonsense without changing a letter.]

325. *quod . . . sorores*: the relative clause anticipates 326 *ueridicum oraclum*.

luce: = *die*, as in 16 *illa atque haud alia . . . luce*.

326–7. *uos . . . fusi*: = *sed uos currite, fusi, subtegmina ducentes quae fata sequuntur*, 'run, shuttles, drawing the thread that destiny follows'; the subject of *sequuntur* is *fata*, the object is *quae* (= *subtegmina*). Line 327 forms a refrain which is repeated at intervals of 4 or 5 lines (on two occasions 6 lines) (the repetition at 378 in mid-sentence is usually omitted by modern editors); cf. the refrains in the wedding hymns, 61. 5 etc. and 62. 5 etc. The refrain was a feature of Hellenistic poetry; see, e.g., the 1st and 2nd idylls of Theocritus; cf. Virgil, *Ecl.* 8; C.'s refrain is echoed by Virgil in *Ecl.* 4. 46–7 (not repeated):

> 'talia saecla' suis dixerunt 'currite!' fusis
> concordes stabili fatorum numine Parcae.

327. Traditionally, the Fates determined the length of a man's life-thread, snipping it off at the appropriate point. Seneca, in a delightful mock-epic parody (*Apoc.* 4) in which the Fates, after winding up and breaking off the life-thread of Claudius, switch production to the life-thread of Nero, uses *stamina* (in *weaving*, the cross-thread, or 'weft') of the life-thread in both cases and *subtegmina* (in *weaving*, the lengthwise thread, or 'warp') apparently of the unshaped thread as it is drawn (*ducta*) from the fleece (5–7):

N

> candida de niueo subtegmina uellere sumit
> felici moderanda manu, quae ducta colorem
> assumpsere nouum.

It seems not unlikely that C.'s *ducentes subtegmina* is used in the same way; *ducentes*, i.e., = *deducentes* (cf. 312 *deducens*; see also Horace, *Ep.* 13. 15). Spinning implies weaving, of course, and it is not hard to imagine an elaboration of the traditional image, in which human existence becomes a pattern of warp and weft upon the loom.

328–32. Cf. the opening of Poem 62.

328. *iam*: with the future indicative = 'soon'.

329. *Hesperus*: the Evening Star.

 fausto cum sidere: i.e. *cum Hespero*.

 coniunx: i.e. Thetis; contrast 373.

330. *flexanimo*: i.e. that turns one's thoughts aside from other things. The compound is first found in Pacuvius (of oratory, quoted by Cicero, *de Orat.* 2. 187). Cf. Virgil, *G.* 4. 516 *nulla Venus, non ulli animum flexere hymenaei*; *A.* 4. 22 *solus hic inflexit sensus*.

331. *languidulos*: note the diminutive; cf. 188 *languescent* and 219 *languida*.

332. The standard pattern for a Golden Line, *leuia robusto substernens brachia collo*, gives exactly the same rhythm, but is perhaps too formal or showy, especially after the 'tender' note struck by 331 *languidulos*. See on 7.

334–6. A Makarismos, like 22–30.

334. *contexit*: 'sheltered' (from *contego*), the *mot juste* for a *domus*.

335–6. For the construction *tali coniunxit foedere . . ., qualis adest . . . concordia* see on 73 and 96. 3; the first *qualis* in 336 anticipates *concordia* (it cannot pick up *foedere*, which is neuter).

335. *foedere*: cf. 373 *felici foedere*, and see on 76. 3 and 109. 6.

336. *Peleo*: scans as two syllables (synizesis). In 382 C. uses the dative form *Pelei*.

338–71. The prophecy.

340–1. 'winner in a running contest that ranges far and wide (*uago*), he will outstrip the flashing feet of the swift deer'; *uago*

(cf. 63. 86 *pede uago*) suggests that the lines describe Achilles'
ability to pursue deer while hunting; this is better than taking
340 as a general assertion of his ability as a runner (equivalent to
the stock description 'swift of foot' in Homer), backed up by an
assertion amounting to 'often he will run faster than a deer'. For
Achilles' exploits as a hunter see Pindar, *N*. 3. 43–52 ('Achilles of
the golden hair . . . while still a child wrought mighty deeds . . .;
he slew stags without help of hounds, for he excelled in fleetness of
foot').

341. *flammea*: with the image cf. Virgil, *A*. 11. 718, where
Camilla is described as *pernicibus ignea plantis*, and 11. 746 *uolat
igneus aequore Tarchon*.

343–6. General statement of Achilles' supremacy in the Trojan
War.

343. *se conferet*: 'will confront', i.e. in single combat; cf. Virgil,
A. 10. 734–5 (of Mezentius) *seque uiro uir | contulit*.

heros: see on 23.

344. *Phrygii . . . campi*: cf. 46. 4. [*campi* added by Estaço.]

345. For the order see on 7.

346. Like the preceding line, a 5-word hexameter. 'The third
heir of lying Pelops' (i.e. the third in line of succession) is Aga-
memnon, the Greek commander-in-chief at Troy, more usually
referred to as the son of Atreus; his grandfather Pelops won
Hippodamia in a chariot race by bribing the opposing driver and
then murdering him. The line of succession is variously given;
that implied by C.'s *tertius heres* seems to be Pelops, Atreus,
Thyestes (brother of Atreus), Agamemnon.

348–51. C., though claiming to recount the *egregias uirtutes
claraque facta* of Achilles, the invincible warrior, stresses the misery
and suffering he caused.

348. *uirtutes*: see on 51 and cf. 323 and 357.

349. *fatebuntur*: 'will acknowledge'.

matres: Herodotus (1. 87) makes Croesus complain to
Cyrus of the wrongness of war, in which 'fathers bury their sons,
instead of sons burying their fathers'; the device of using the grief

of the *women* of Troy as a comment on the cruelty of war is at least as old as Euripides' *Troades*. See, however, on 394–6.

350–1. Traditional signs of grief.

350. [The first half of the line is corrupt in the MSS; most modern editors print Baehrens' *incultum*, i.e. 'uncombed', as a sign of grief.]

351. Golden Line.

putrida: 'withered'.

uariabunt: i.e. 'bruise'; cf. Plautus, *Mil.* 216 *uarius uirgis*. Contrast 50 *priscis hominum uariata figuris*.

353–5. The simile of the reaper perhaps from *Il.* 11. 67–71 (of the Trojans and Achaeans assailing one another).

353. *praecerpens*: i.e. 'slicing off as he advances'. Cf. Virgil, *A.* 10. 513 (of Aeneas after the death of Pallas) *proxima quaeque metit gladio*. [*precernens* V, *praecerpens* Estaço; *messor* O, *cultor* X.]

354. A fine vivid line.

355. A variant on the Golden Line: genitive plural *Troiugenum* in place of first epithet.

infesto: 'raised', 'menacing'.

357–60. The reference is to Achilles' exploits in *Il.* 21, with an echo perhaps of Accius 313–14W (Achilles speaking): ... *Scamandriam undam salso sanctam obtexi sanguine, / atque aceruos alta in amni corpore expleui hostico*. Cf. Virgil, *A.* 5. 804–11. The turn of phrase *permixta caede* is Lucretian (3. 643); see on 360 *tepefaciet*.

357. *testis erit*: for the formula (again 362) see Ennius' *Scipio* 14W *testes sunt campi magni*; cf. Horace, *Carm.* 4. 4. 37–8 *quid debeas, o Roma, Neronibus, / testis Metaurum flumen*.

Scamandri: Scamander (also called Xanthus) is a famous river at Troy. The other is Simois.

358. An ornamental, distancing line; *rapido ... Hellesponto* locative ablative, or dative = *in rapidum Hellespontum*. Spondaic 5th foot. Cf. 11. 7–8.

360. *tepefaciet*: contrast 68. 29 *tepefactat*. The germ of the idea perhaps in Lucretius 3. 643, where he speaks of chariots which are *permixta caede calentis*.

362-70. The fate of Priam's daughter Polyxena, offered as a living sacrifice on the tomb of Achilles (a story best known in Euripides' moving version, *Hecuba* 521-82), is cited with grim irony as further proof of the greatness of Achilles; the general statement of 362-4 is followed, after the refrain, by an explanatory couplet (366-7) and the gruesomely realistic description of the sacrifice in 368-70. For a possible echo of the *Hecuba* see on 61.

362. *denique*: This is the third and final proof of Achilles, greatness. The *matres* will acknowledge his greatness (349 *fatebuntur*) by their grief; the corpse-filled waters of Scamander and the blood-thirsty sacrifice of Polyxena will serve as mute evidence (357 and 362 *testis erit*). Each of the first two proofs is allotted 4 lines; the third is given 8 lines, divided into 3+5 by the refrain at 365.

morti quoque reddita praeda: i.e. the fact that Achilles, though dead, received his share of the spoil. According to Euripides, *Hecuba* 37-44, the ghost of Achilles appeared, to demand Polyxena as his prize.

363. A string of words describing the tomb, so that it can be felt to dominate the Tableau; for *teres*, 'rounded', see on 65.

364. *niueos*: see on 240.

366. *fessis*: an echo in Horace, *Carm.* 2.4.11.

367. Troy was built by Dardanus, and then rebuilt for Laomedon by Neptune, who protected the city until the fated time for its destruction arrived, when he joined in its destruction (see Virgil, *A.* 2. 608-12); *Neptunia soluere uincla* = therefore, to break down the walls of Troy, but with an allusion to the idea that Neptune had till then kept the city locked together and safe; the phrase echoes the concluding words of Achilles' speech to Patroclus, *Il.* 16. 49-100.

368. Unlike the normal Golden Line, the arrangement of epithets and nouns is chiastic.

alta . . . sepulcra: the *bustum* of 363.

Polyxenia . . . caede: = *Polyxenae caede*; see on 1 *Peliaco . . . uertice*.

369. The simile underlines the brutality of the act: Polyxena is treated like a sacrificial animal (*uictima*).

quae: i.e. Polyxena, implicit in 368 *Polyxenia*.

succumbens: 'collapsing beneath'.

370. Literally, 'she will throw her headless body forward'. Polyxena is of course the headless body, but it is poetically effective to represent her as existing apart from it; cf. Virgil, *A.* 11. 827–31 (of the death of Camilla). Copley's translation, 'will drop headless on crumpled knee, a corpse', captures the horror of the image which concludes the prophecy; note the heavy deliberate rhythm of *truncum summisso*. With the detail of the collapsing knee cf. Lucretius' description of the sacrifice of Iphigenia, 1. 92: *terram genibus summissa petebat.*

372–81. The song of the Fates ends, as it began (328–32), as a typical Roman wedding hymn; cf. 61. 97–146; the opening *quare* seems almost ostentatiously to ignore the horror of what has just been prophesied.

372. *animi*: Phrases such as 2. 10 *animi curas*, 102. 2 *fides animi*, and perhaps 68. 26 *delicias animi* suggest taking *animi* with *amores*; but it is more natural to link *animi* with *optatos* ('desired in your thoughts'), on the analogy of phrases like *animi pendere, animi se excruciare*, in which the genitive is later supplanted by the ablative *animo*.

optatos . . . coniungite amores: cf. 68. 69 *communes exerceremus amores*, 78. 3 *dulces iungit amores*; for *optatos* see on 22 *optato*.

373. *coniunx*: Peleus, the husband; contrast 329, where *coniunx* = Thetis.

foedere: see on 335 *foedere*

374. *cupido*: cf. 70. 3.

iam dudum: 'without delay', with *dedatur*; for *iam dudum* with an imperative etc. see, e.g., Virgil, *A.* 2. 103 *iam dudum sumite poenas* (and Austin's note thereon); other parallels in Fordyce.

376–7. The superstition is referred to by Nemesianus 2. 10 (late 3rd century A.D.), but is not found elsewhere. Thetis, like Medea, etc., will keep her nurse after marriage.

378. Most editors follow Bergk in omitting the refrain, since it separates co-ordinate clauses and breaks the pattern of 3-, 4- or 5-line blocks. But a stepping-up of the tempo at the conclusion of the hymn is quite possible; and the sense is slightly improved by separating 376-7 (which refers to the following day) from 379-80 where *mittet sperare* implies a longer period.

379-80. The construction is: *nec mater anxia, discordis puellae secubitu maesta, caros nepotes mittet sperare.* The marriage, i.e., will not start with a quarrel (or with the husband continuing a previous liaison; cf. 61. 97-101).

382-3. *Bridge passage*, rounding off the description of the wedding day, and concluding the outer story.

382. *praefantes*: normally *praefari* = to pronounce 'a formula preliminary to a solemn ritual act' (Fordyce); the sense 'utter a prophecy' is unparalleled, but difficult to reject here.

    Pelei: dative; contrast 336 *Peleo*. Two syllables.

383. *carmina*: with the plural ('a marriage hymn') cf. 61. 13.

    diuino ... pectore: = 'with prophetic mind'; cf. Ennius, Epic Fragment 18-19W: *doctusque Anchisa, Venus quem pulcherruma dium | fari donauit, diuinum pectus habere.*

384-408. *The poet's final comment*. The days when gods mixed with men are no more.

It seems likely C. had in mind, for the first part of his postscript (384-96), King Alcinous' words in *Od.* 7. 195-206 (of Odysseus): 'And we will preserve him on the way from further hardship or accident, till he sets foot in his own land. After that he must suffer whatever Fate [αἶσα] and the cruel Spinners [κλῶθες] span for him with the thread at his birth. But if he is an immortal come down from heaven, then the gods must be up to something new. For in the past they have always appeared plain to see as gods when we sacrifice sumptuous hecatombs, and they feast with us sitting where we sit. Even when a lonely traveller meets them, they make no concealment, for we are close to them, like the Cyclopes and the wild tribes of the Giants.'

With the second part of C.'s postscript (397-408, 'the gods have

deserted us and the present age is corrupt and doomed') cf.
Hesiod, *Works and Days* 174–201 ('the time will soon come when
sons will no longer be like their fathers, there will be no trust
among men, children will despise their parents and have no fear
of the gods; honesty will disappear, force, dishonesty and hatred
will be supreme. Shame [*Αἰδώς*] and Retribution [*Νέμεσις*]
will abandon mankind and rejoin the gods'). Cf. 68. 153–4,
Aratus, *Phaenomena* 100–36, and Hesiod, Fragment 218 [in
Merrill]. Virgil, proclaiming the return of the Golden Age in his
4th *Eclogue* (especially 15–17 and 46–7), seems deliberately to
evoke C.

384. *praesentes*: picked up by 396 *praesens*. Cf. Horace, *Carm.*
3. 5. 2–3 *praesens diuus habebitur | Augustus.*

    namque: for the position cf. 23. 7, 66. 65.

    ante: the adverb, 'in former times'.

385. *mortali . . . coetu*: either dative with *ostendere*, like 66. 37
caelesti reddita coetu (datives in -u not uncommon in Lucretius and
Virgil), or locative ablative.

386. *caelicolae*: cf. 30. 4 and 68. 138.

    nondum spreta pietate: i.e. *a mortalibus.*

387–96. Three proofs of the general statement of 384–6, the re-
peated *saepe* (387, 390 and 394) each time backing up 386 *solebant.*

387. *reuisens*: = 'paying his regular visit'.

389. = Homer's hecatombs, *Od.* 7. 202 (see on 384–408) — an
especially grand sacrifice of course.

390. *uagus*: see on 225.

    Parnasi uertice summo: cf. 1 *Peliaco . . . uertice.* Mt Parnassus
is just north of Delphi.

391. *Thyadas*: see on 254.

    euantis: 'crying *euhoe*!' (see 255).

    egit: 'drove'.

392. *Delphi*: i.e. the people of Delphi.

393. *diuum*: accusative.

    fumantibus aris: either instrumental with *acciperent*, or
locative.

394–6. Note that C.'s concept of the wholesomeness of former days is compatible with the suffering of war.

394. *in letifero belli certamine Mauors*: The high style. *Mauors*, the archaic form of *Mars*, is found in Lucretius 1. 32; several times in Virgil.

395. *rapidi Tritonis era*: Athena; 'mistress of the swift Triton' = Homer's Τριτογένεια; C. possibly had in mind the river Triton in Boeotia.

Ramnusia uirgo: Nemesis, as in 66. 71 and 68. 77 (after her famous shrine at Rhamnus in Attica), the *uemens dea* of 50. 21. C. is very likely thinking of Hesiod's Nemesis, who will desert mankind at the end of the Iron Age, *Works and Days* 197–200. See *OCD* for this somewhat puzzling deity. [*Rhamnusia* was restored in the first printed edition of C. in 1472; *ramunsia* O *ranusia* X. Some prefer Baehrens' *Amarunsia* (i.e. Artemis) on the ground that Nemesis is never represented as taking part in battle, as Ares and Athena often are in Homer.]

396. *praesens*: picks up 384 *praesentes*.

397–406. A denunciation of the modern corruption in family relationships. Best taken as one long sentence: a double *postquam*-clause, 397–8, expressing the idea of the corruption of mortality in general terms, is followed by (1) four specific statements; (2) a reformulation of the general statement of 397–8. Of the four specific statements, 399–404, the first three begin with a verb (*perfudere, destitit, optauit*); the first and the second are each allotted one line, the third flows over into a subordinate clause; a fourth specific statement follows, spread like the third over two lines.

398. *cupida de mente fugarunt*: cf. 68. 25 *tota de mente fugaui*; for *cupida* see on 86.

399. Cf. Lucretius 3. 72 (in a denunciation of *auarities* and *cupido*) *crudeles gaudent in tristi funere fratris*. Also Virgil, *G.* 2. 510 (another denunciation) *gaudent perfusi sanguine fratrum*. Perhaps the most famous instance of fratricidal murder in classical literature, the mutual slaying of Eteocles and Polynices in the siege of Thebes, belongs to the Heroic Age.

401–4. The insistence on the corruption of marriage is appropriate to the main themes of Poem 64. Cf. Poems 74, 78, 88–91 and 111.

402. ='so that he might enjoy his son's pretty young stepmother without hindrance from the son'. Perhaps an allusion to the story, preserved for us by Sallust, *Cat.* 15, of Catiline's (allegedly incestuous) marriage with Orestilla: *quod ea nubere illi dubitabat, timens priuignum adulta aetate, pro certo creditur nectato filio uacuam domum scelestis nuptiis fecisse.* She was said to be the daughter of Catiline's former mistress: he murdered, i.e., his son to marry his daughter; see Ronald Syme, *Sallust* (1964), 84–5. C. allows himself to call the father's second wife *nouerca* by the same sort of anticipation that enables Sallust to call the son *priuignus*; in both cases the son was dead before the relationship actually existed. For *innupta* with the connotations of young unmarried girl, see line 78 and 62. 6, 12 and 36. For another possible reference to Orestilla see on Poem 32.

403–4. Perhaps Gellius and his mother (see on Poem 74), though *ignaro* seems inappropriate. Hardly Oedipus and Jocasta, who *both* acted in innocence.

404. *penates*: [*parentes* V. There are references in inscriptions to *di parentes*, but *penates* seems more likely here, and *parentes* an intrusion from line 400.]

405. *fanda nefanda*: the jingle reinforces the notion of confusion.
　　malo permixta furore: 'thrown into confusion by evil madness'.

406. *iustificam*: the compound only here.
　　auertere: perfect.

407–8. Perhaps an allusion to the Epicurean belief that the gods dwell apart, with no concern for human affairs.

408. *lumine claro*: 'in the bright light of day', i.e. they continue to exist, but unseen; cf. Virgil, *A.* 4. 358–9 *ipse deum manifesto in lumine uidi | intrantem* (cf. *A.* 3. 151).

See:

J. P. Boucher, 'A propos du carmen 64 de Catulle', *REL* 34 (1956), 190–202.

J. C. Bramble, *Proc. Camb. Phil. Soc.* 16 (1970) 22–41.

L. C. Curran, *YClS* 21 (1969) 169–92.

Léon Herrmann, 'Le poème LXIV de Catulle et l'actualité', *Latomus* 26 (1967), 27–34.

Helmut Hross, *Die Klagen der verlassenen Heroiden in der lateinischen Dichtung* (diss. München, 1958).

G. Kilroy, *Symbolae Osloenses* 44 (1969) 48–60.

T. E. Kinsey, 'Irony and structure in Catullus 64', *Latomus* 24 (1965), 911–31.

Fr. Klingner, 'Catulls Peleus-Epos', *SBAW* (1956, Heft 6), 1–92.

H. Patzer, 'Zum Sprachstil des neoterischen Hexameters', *MH* 12 (1955), 77–95.

M. C. J. Putnam, 'The art of Catullus 64', *HSPh* 65 (1961), 165–205.

D. F. S. Thomson, 'Aspects of unity in Catullus 64', *CJ* 57 (1961), 49–57.

D. F. S. Thomson, *RhMus* 13 (1970) 89–91.

R. Waltz, 'Caractère, sens et composition du poème LXIV de Catulle', *REL* 23 (1945), 92–109.

T. B. L. Webster, 'The myth of Ariadne from Homer to Catullus', *G & R* 13 (1966), 22–31.

U. von Wilamowitz-Moellendorff, *Hellenistische Dichtung* (1924) ii 298–304.

65

An open letter written while C. was overwhelmed with grief at his brother's death (cf. Poems 68 and 101). It is addressed to Hortalus, generally taken to be Q. Hortensius Hortalus, the orator and — despite the backhanded compliment — the productive poet of 95. 3. A version of Callimachus (almost certainly Poem 66) accompanies the note.

Structure: Assuming the loss of one hexameter after line 9, the 24 lines make up a single sentence. A double concessive clause (1–4) is separated from the principal clause (15–16) by a long parenthesis, in which C. first turns aside to explain to Hortalus why he cannot bring himself to write (5–9), then breaks off to address his dead brother (10–14). The principal clause is followed by an explanatory parenthesis (17–18) and then by a beautiful simile (19–24). The whole forms a carefully organized structure, in which the illusion of grief continually breaking through the bonds of rational restraint is an effect of art, supported by the delicate irony of 1–4 and the concluding simile. For another example of a letter accompanying a poem see Cinna, *FPL* p. 89:

haec tibi Arateis multum inuigilata lucernis
  carmina, quis ignis nouimus aetherios,
leuis in aridulo maluae descripta libello
  Prusiaca uexi munera nauicula.

It seems a reasonable guess that Poem 65 (like Poem 68) was written in Verona, some time before C.'s departure for Bithynia.

Metre: Poems 65–116 are all in the elegiac metre, which is used in none of the previous poems.

1–4. 'Unremitting grief makes it impossible for me to concentrate on writing poetry.'

1. *assiduo confectum cura dolore*: strong language; cf. Cicero, *Att.* 3. 5 *ego uiuo miserrimus et maximo dolore conficior*; for *cura*, 'grief' see 66. 23 *quam penitus maestas exedit cura medullas!*

2. *seuocat*: said by *L & S* to be a favourite word of Cicero; it does not, however, occur in his letters.

doctis . . . uirginibus: the Muses; they are called παρθένοι by Pindar (*I.* 8. 127); for the meaning of *doctus* see on 35. 16–17. We should not miss the sad irony with which C. implies that his grief left him no time for female company, however high-minded.

Hortale: [The MSS drop the h, just as O drops the h in *Hortensius* in 95. 3.]

3–4. A pattern of half-imagery, flowing on from 1–2, suggests that normally the poet would be only too willing to display the offspring of his union with the Muses.

3. *potis*: = *pote* (for which see on 17. 24); *potis* also 72. 7, 76. 24, 115. 3. Both forms uncommon in classical prose.

expromere: combines the notion of 'expressing' (as in 64. 223 *expromam mente querellas*) with that of 'displaying'.

4. *mens animi*: an old-fashioned expression for 'mind', found in Plautus and Lucretius.

fluctuat: cf. 64. 62 *magnis curarum fluctuat undis*.

ipsa: C.'s mind, i.e., has its own worries.

5. *Lethaeo gurgite*: syntactically ambiguous: 'by the waters of Lethe' (locative; cf. 24 *manat tristi . . . ore*) or 'with the waters of Lethe' (instrumental). C. has 4 other examples of *gurges*, all in the form *gurgite*, all in Poem 64 (14, 18, 178, 183), all referring to the sea.

6. *pallidulum*: pathetic diminutive (see on 3. 18).

alluit unda pedem: with *nuper* — i.e. at the moment when his brother stepped into the waters of forgetfulness, to board Charon's boat.

7–8. 'whom the soil of Troy weighs down, below the beach at Rhoeteum'; strictly speaking, Rhoeteum was a promontory on the Hellespont, but the word is often used simply as a synonym of Trojan; 68. 91–2 implies C.'s brother died at Troy. For the grave see Poem 101. Virgil pretty clearly intends a compliment to C. when he makes Aeneas say (*A*. 6. 505–6, of the symbolic burial of Deiphobus): *tunc egomet tumulum Rhoeteo litore inanem | constitui et magna manis ter uoce uocaui*.

8. *ereptum*: cf. 68. 106.

obterit: cf. Lucretius 3. 893 (of a dead body) *urgeriue superne obtritum pondere terrae*.

10–14. C. breaks off to address his brother; cf. 68. 20–4 and 92–100.

10. *uita . . . amabilior*: cf. 64. 215 *longa iucundior uita*; 68. 106 *uita dulcius atque anima*.

12. The promise is kept in Poem 68, if not in the poems written after C.'s return from Bithynia.

13. *sub densis ramorum . . . umbris*: the detail is Homeric (*Od*. 19. 520 δενδρέων ἐν πετάλοισι καθεζομένη πυκινοῖσιν).

14. *Daulias*: More likely Procne than her sister Philomela, though the two are oddly confused in different versions of this famous tale; turned into a nightingale, she spends her time lamenting the fate of her son Itylus (or Itys), whom she had killed

to punish her husband Tereus for raping her sister; called Daulias from Daulis in Phocis, where Tereus lived.

15–18. = 'I am sending you my translation, none the less, (in case you think I have forgotten all about what you said) . . .': *sed tamen* introduces the principal clause after the long parenthesis.

16. *haec . . . carmina Battiadae*: = 'this poem of Callimachus'; cf. 116. 2 *carmina Battiadae* (= probably 'a poem of Callimachus'), 61. 13 and 64. 383 (of a marriage hymn), and the fragment of Cinna quoted in introductory note; for *Battiadae* = Callimachus, son of Battus of Cyrene, cf. 7. 6.

17. *credita uentis*: cf. 30. 9–10, 64. 59 and 164–6, and 70. 4.

19–23. What does this beautiful simile represent? Hortalus' words (17 *dicta* — urging C. to attempt a translation of Callimachus' poem?), sent tumbling from C.'s thoughts by his brother's death? Surely the apple stands for the version itself which C. had been working at when his brother's death caused him to put it aside. To the arrival of the mother and the girl's jumping up corresponds the letter from Hortalus to which Poem 65 is C.'s reply: it said perhaps, 'What has happened to that translation of Callimachus?' The letter elicits the translation, which C. will watch tumble forth upon the world, as embarrassed as the girl at its untimely appearance.

19. *furtiuo munere*: i.e. as a secret gift from the man she loves.

20. *casto*: 'innocent'.

gremio: 'lap' or 'bosom'? 66. 56 *Veneris casto . . . in gremio* suggests the former, lines 21–2 the latter. The Latin word seems to denote the front part of the body in general (cf. *tergum*, 'the back part of the body').

21. i.e. thrust aside, and forgotten about.

22. *dum*: 'while' (dependent on *excutitur*).

excutitur: subject *quod*; the two verbs suggest the abrupt movement which dislodges the apple.

23. Fifth foot spondaic, to suggest the bumping of the apple.

24. Why *tristi*? Has the girl been crying like Catullus?

See:

L. W. Daly, 'Callimachus and Catullus', *CPh* 47 (1952), 97–9.

A. R. Littlewood, 'The symbolism of the apple in Greek and Roman literature', *HSPh* 72 (1967), 147–81.

J. B. Van Sickle, *TAPhA* 99 (1968) 487–508.

U. von Wilamowitz-Moellendorff, *Hellenistische Dichtung* (1924) ii 304–5.

C. Witke, (see above, under Poem 30).

66

Almost certainly the version of Callimachus referred to in Poem 65. Queen Berenice of Egypt vowed to cut off a tress of her hair if her husband Ptolemy III returned safely from the invasion of Syria on which he had set out soon after becoming king in 246 B.C. and straight after marrying Berenice. The king returned in triumph, the vow was paid, but the shorn tress vanished mysteriously from the temple where it had been dedicated. Then Conon the astronomer-royal discovered a new constellation, and recognized it at once as the tress of Berenice: it is the constellation known still to astronomers as the *coma Berenices*.

To celebrate the miracle, Callimachus wrote an appropriately ingenious poem, later included in the fourth book of the *Aetia* (explanations in elegiac verse of the origins and names of festivals, customs, etc.). Comparison with the fragments recovered on papyrus suggests that C.'s version in general kept close to the original. See on 77–8 and 94; see also KIDD and PUTNAM. For the Greek text (some 46 lines or bits of lines, pieced together from two papyrus fragments and other sources — about 25 complete or tolerably complete lines) see R. Pfeiffer, *Callimachus* (vol. i, 1949), 110–22; Mynors 107–8 and Fordyce 407–8 omit the heavily mutilated lines — those corresponding to C.'s 65–74 and 89 ff. (nothing in the papyrus corresponds to C.'s 15–38 and 79–88).

Structure: 1–14 — hypothesis. 15–38 — flashback. 39–76 — the *coma* laments its fate. 77–94 — mainly about scent.

The *coma Berenices* (the constellation) speaks throughout.

1–14. Hypothesis: 'My newly-married mistress Berenice offered me, the hair of her own head, to the appropriate goddesses when her husband set out on an expedition against the Assyrians; Conon, the distinguished astronomer, observed my ascent to the heavens.' The data are woven into an elaborate 14-line period, in which C. slowly converges upon his true theme: the first 6 lines (two relative clauses, the second flowing over into an expanding triad of explanatory *ut*-clauses) extol the achievements of Conon; a block of 4 lines leads us back from Conon's observation of the new star to Berenice and her vow; lines 11–14 explain why Berenice made her vow. Meanwhile we move smoothly back in time to the moment of Ptolemy's departure on the morrow of his wedding night.

1–6. With the formal encomium cf., e.g., that of Epicurus, Lucretius 1. 62–79.

1. *dispexit*: 'looked upon' and hence 'observed' (in the scientific sense).

lumina mundi: *mundi* practically =*caeli*, as in 64. 206.

2. Probably refers to the apparent daily motion of the stars, due to the rotation of the earth.

3–6. i.e. Conon observed the eclipse of the sun, the movements of the planets, and the phases of the moon. But the words extol Conon by their rhetorical and imaginative power, rather than by recapitulating fact.

3. *ut*: 'how'; see on 64. 117.

rapidi: elsewhere in C. (7 other examples) of rapid or frenzied motion; perhaps here of the swirling heat of the sun, as in Virgil, *Ecl.* 2. 10 *rapido aestu*.

obscuretur: spondaic 5th foot; again 41, 57 and 61; see on 64. 3.

4. *cedant*: 'retreat'.

certis . . . temporibus: ablative, 'at fixed times'.

5–6. We pass from the didactic, pseudo-scientific note struck in the opening lines to something more fanciful.

5. *Triuiam*: strictly, Selene; see on 34. 15.

sub Latmia saxa relegans: 'banishing to the rocks of Latmus'.

A trace of irony in this evocation of Selene's visits to Endymion in a cave on the slopes of Mt Latmus in Caria — *dulcis amor* made Selene face hardships a heavenly body should not descend to.

7. *Conon*: the astronomer-royal of Ptolemy III of Egypt; he claimed to have identified Berenice's missing tress between Virgo and the Bear (see introductory note).

caelesti in limine: 'on the threshold of the sky', as if looking down at Conon from her new home; cf. 64. 271 *uagi sub limina Solis*. [*caelesti numine* V, *caelesti in lumine* Vossius, *caelesti in limine* Baehrens; cf. 17 *limina*, where the MSS have *lumina*; so 59 *in limine caeli*.]

8. A 4-word pentameter, the first of 10 in Poem 66; cf. 60 *ex Ariadnaeis aurea temporibus*; 29 such lines altogether in C., only one certain example in the Callimachean original of Poem 66. For 3-word pentameters in C. (3 examples) see on 68. 74; for 4-word hexameters (4 in Poem 64) see on 64. 15.

Bereniceo: for the adjectival form of a proper noun see on 64. 1 *Peliaco uertice*.

caesariem: 'long, flowing or luxuriant hair' (*OLD*). According to Callimachus, Berenice offered a single lock of hair (8 βόστρυχον, 62 πλόκαμος). C., no doubt connecting the word with *caedere* (a false etymology), seems to have used *caesaries* to mean something like 'mass of shorn hair', i.e. one long, flowing tress. He had in mind perhaps Achilles cutting off his hair (χαίτην) at the grave of Patroclus, *Il.* 23. 141–51 (see on line 38). It seems clear from 51–2 that Berenice is not to be thought of as having cut off her hair entirely; the singular in 93 *coma regia* is not in itself conclusive, since both the singular and the plural of *coma* are used of a whole head of hair: cf. 4. 12 *loquente coma* (of the foliage of a forest), and 61. 78 and 95 *splendidas quatiunt comas* (of marriage torches). See also on 62 *flaui uerticis exuuiae*.

9. *fulgentem clare*: leaps across the parenthetical expansion in line 8 of 7 *me* to attach itself to 7 *uidit*; take *e Bereniceo uertice* with *caesariem* ('the tress shorn from Berenice's head') — not with *fulgentem*.

multis . . . dearum: a nice touch: Berenice tried to tempt goddess after goddess with her tresses. [Haupt's *cunctis deorum* is probably a needless attempt to reduce C.'s improvement on Callimachus' πᾶσιν θεοῖς to a mere translation; contrast, however, 33 *cunctis ... diuis*.]

11. *qua ... tempestate*: the temporal clause prepares the way for a flashback, as in 64. 73-5.

auctus hymenaeo: There is a hiatus before *auctus* and the second syllable of *auctus* counts as long (cf. 64. 20 *despexit hymenaeos*); with *auctus*, 'enriched', 'blessed', cf. 64. 25 *taedis felicibus aucte*.

12. Four-word pentameter.

uastatum: supine; cf. 10. 2 *uisum duxerat*, 32. 3 *ad te ueniam meridiatum*, 61. 146 *ni petitum aliunde eat*.

iuerat: archaic = *ierat*; pluperfect because Ptolemy had already departed.

Assyrios: strictly, Syrian — a common confusion; cf. 68. 144 *Assyrio odore*. The campaign was to avenge the murder of Ptolemy's sister, in 246 B.C.

13. 'bearing the sweet traces of a night encounter', i.e. Ptolemy left the morning after his wedding night (the meaning supported by line 14) — no doubt an improvement on historical fact for the sake of pathos. An epigram of Agathius perhaps preserves an echo of the Callimachean original (*AP* 5. 293) σύμβολον ἐννυχίης εἶχον ἀεθλοσύνης.

14. *de uirgineis ... exuuiis*: ostensibly mock heroic = *ut eius uirginitatem spoliaret* (*exuuiae* as a military term). But a less heroic sense = *ut uirgo nudaretur* (*exuuiae* simply 'cast-off clothing') also suggests itself: cf. 81 *reiecta ueste*, and Propertius 2. 1. 13 *nuda erepto mecum luctatur amictu*. The frequent use in Roman love poetry of military imagery for the *bella Veneris* underpins the interplay of the two meanings.

15-38. An expansion of the flashback which began at line 11. After some thoughts on how brides feel about marriage (15-20) and a digression on the discrepancy between Berenice's grief at her husband's departure and her earlier fortitude (21-32), her vow, the successful conclusion of Ptolemy's campaign and the promotion to the heavens of Berenice's tress are briefly alluded to (33–8). The movement of the sense is somewhat disjointed. There is nothing in the fragments of Callimachus corresponding to this section.

15–26. 'Do brides really hate love? or are the tears that spoil the happiness of parents crocodile tears?'

15. *estne . . . odio Venus?*: cf. 63. 17 *Veneris nimio odio.*

16. *lacrimulis*: note the diminutive; cf. 63 *uuidulam.*

17. *intra limina*: = 'on the threshold' (as they go in); the scene is that evoked in 61. 224–8.

18. *ita me diui . . . iuerint*: = 61. 189–90 *ita me iuuent | caelites*; for the perfect subjunctive cf. 61. 195–6 *bona te Venus | iuuerit*; *iuerint*, a syncopation of *iuuerint*, is an optative form like 28 *ausit*; cf. the common forms *faxim* and *ausim*; for the order (hyperbaton) see on 44. 9 *dedit.*

19–20. The *coma* contrasts the crocodile tears of brides with the real tears shed by Berenice when her husband set out for the wars.

19. *querellis*: 'lamentations'.

20. *inuisente*: 'off to see', i.e. 'on his way to'; cf. 64. 384 *domos inuisere castas.*

    torua: the stock epithet of Mars.

21–32. Addressed to Berenice.

21–5. The question anticipates Berenice's protest that her grief, though real, was for a brother not a husband. To which the speaker's reply (23–5) is, 'That was love all right!' (The Egyptian king's consort was officially styled his sister; Berenice was in fact the cousin of Ptolemy.)

21. *at tu*: [*et* O; *at* is a correction found in G. C. perhaps wrote *an*.]

    luxti: = *luxisti*; cf. 30 *tristi*, 14. 14 *misti*, 91. 9 *duxti*, etc.

22. *flebile*: 'worthy of tears'.

23. *exedit cura medullas*: cf. 35. 15 *ignes interiorem edunt medullam*, Virgil, *A.* 4. 66 *est mollis flamma medullas*; *exedit* is perfect; *cura*, 'grief', often of the unhappiness of love.

24–5. *ut . . . excidit!*: = 'how distraught you were!'; cf. 51. 5–7:

misero quod omnis
eripit sensus mihi: nam simul te,
Lesbia, aspexi, nihil est super mi. . . .

24. *sollicitae*: with *tibi* (dative of the person interested).

25–6. *at te . . . magnanimam*: = 'and yet you were never lacking
in courage'.

26–8. The reference is to Berenice's share in the assassination
of her previous husband Demetrius, as a result of which she
became queen of Egypt; Demetrius had been the lover of
Berenice's mother, hence his assassination is described as a
bonum facinus.

28. *quod*: the antecedent is *facinus*, not *coniugium*.

alis: a by-form of *alius*; cf. 29. 15 *alid*.

29–30. Pick up 19–20.

29. *mittens*: = *demittens*.

30. *tristi*: see on 21 *luxti*.

31. *quis te mutauit tantus deus?*: 'who was the god so powerful
that he changed you?' The answer is Cupid.

31–2. *an quod amantes | non . . . abesse uolunt?*: 'or is it that lovers
are unwilling . . .?'

33. *cunctis . . . diuis*: see on 9 *multis . . . dearum*.

35. *si reditum tetulisset*: 'if he should return'; see on 63. 47
tetulit.

35–6. *is haut in tempore longo | . . . addiderat*: = 'in no time he
had added . . .'.

37. *quis*: = *quibus*; see on 64. 145.

reddita: = 'duly accorded my place'.

coetu: dative; cf. 64. 385.

38. *pristina uota nouo munere dissoluo*: An epigram, to conclude
this section of the poem: the vow discharged is an old-fashioned
one, but the manner of its discharge is novel. The reference is
probably to the hair of Achilles, promised by his father to the
river god Spercheios if Achilles returned home from Troy, *Il.*
23. 141–51 (see on 8 *caesariem*); *nouo munere* is both 'a new func-
tion' (the *coma*'s previous function was to adorn the head of

Berenice) and 'an unprecedented function' (no previous case of tress into star); *dissolŭo* counts as 4 syllables.

39–76. The *coma* laments its fate. Most of the surviving lines of the Callimachean original come from the section corresponding to these lines.

39. A line made famous by Virgil's recasting, *A*. 6. 460 (Aeneas to Dido in the Underworld) *inuitus, regina, tuo de litore cessi*. The Callimachean model, if there was one, has not survived.

40. *adiuro teque tuumque caput*: Callimachus had σήν τε κάρην ὤμοσα σόν τε βίον. It was not uncommon to swear by the head of the person addressed, the idea being that one would not put a friend in danger by perjury; but of course Berenice's *caput* has a special *locus standi* as the possessor of the *caesaries*.

41. *quod*: with *adiurarit*; 'and may anyone who idly invokes that (your head) suffer appropriately'. The spondaic 5th foot heightens the mock solemnity.

42. Mock heroic: 'But who would seek to be matched against steel?'; *ferro*, the epic word for sword, can also denote implements of less heroic stature; cf. 47 *ferro* and 50 *ferri*. For *qui = quis* before a word beginning with s, see on 17. 22.

43–6. The rhetorical question of 42 is now backed up by a suitably impressive precedent from history: Mt Athos could not withstand the steel of Xerxes. (He dug a canal across the isthmus connecting Athos to the Macedonian mainland. See Herodotus 7. 24.)

43–4. *quem maximum in oris ... superuehitur*: 'the greatest mountain on earth that the sun journeys over'. The qualifying phrase *maximum in oris* is incorporated in the relative clause according to the normal Latin idiom, instead of being, as in English, attached to the antecedent; Athos (just over 6000 ft) is not remarkable as mountains go, but C. hardly means his rhetoric seriously (the Callimachean original of line 43 has not survived).

44. *progenies Thiae clara*: 'the bright progeny of Thia' is Helios, the sun; Thia was his mother, his father was Hyperion

(Hesiod, *Theog.* 371–4). Pfeiffer argues that the (badly mutilated) Callimachean original refers to Boreas, the North Wind, grandson of Thia; C.'s *superuehitur* fits the sun better, however, and provides a better play on *clara* ('famous' and 'brightly shining').

45. *peperere nouum mare*: by turning a peninsula into an island.

46. *per medium . . . Athon*: actually, across the isthmus behind Athos.

nauit: see on 64. 2 *nasse*.

47. A general reflection, in the high style; for *ferro* see on line 42.

48–50. Denunciations of inventions which have done more harm than good, and of progress in general, are common clichés in Roman poetry. For references see Fordyce.

48. *Chalybon*: Greek genitive plural in long o. The Chalybes, a race of miners and workers with iron, lived in the area of the Black Sea.

50. *ferri stringere duritiem*: i.e. to draw molten iron into cast-iron bars; cast iron is much harder than wrought iron; *stringere* is the technical term for the process; cf. Virgil, *A.* 8. 420–1 (of the workshop of the Cyclopes) *striduntque cauernis | stricturae* ('moulds') *Chalybum*.

51. The line seems constructed to suggest a variety of grammatical relationships, among which *abiunctae paulo ante comae sorores*, 'the sisters of the recently severed tress', predominates without wholly excluding other relationships (*abiunctae comae* with *fata*, or nominative plural with *sorores*; *paulo ante* with *lugebant*).

52–8. A piece of Alexandrian ingenuity. The 'twin brother of Memnon the Ethiopian' is the West Wind (Zephyrus), here imagined as a winged horse (cf. Pegasus). Arsinoe, the consort of Ptolemy II (the previous king of Egypt), was identified after death with Aphrodite, and known as *Aphrodite Zephyritis*, from the temple dedicated to her at Zephyrium near Alexandria. Zephyrus and Arsinoe are linked by a pun on *Zephyritis*. The title means of course 'having power over Zephyrium'; C., following Callimachus, pretends it means 'having power over Zephyrus', i.e. able to send the West Wind on errands.

52–4. *cum se . . . obtulit*: inverted *cum*-clause; characteristic of the high style.

52. *Aethiopis*: Greek genitive singular.

53. *unigena*: see on 64. 300.

    nutantibus . . . pennis: 'on nodding wings'; a nice phrase (Callimachus has 'twisting his dappled wings').

54. *Arsinoes Locridos ales equos*: 'winged horse of Arsinoe the Locrian'; *Arsinoes* and *Locridos* are both Greek genitive singulars; *equos* = *equus*. Arsinoe's connexion with either the Greek or the southern Italian Locris is obscure. [*elocridicos* V, *Locridos* Bentley, confirmed by the discovery of the Callimachean original Λοκρίδος.]

55–6. The West Wind snatches up the tress and carries it off to the temple of Aphrodite Zephyritis (alias Arsinoe), and lays it on the goddess's lap; i.e. a magic wind wafted the tress off to the temple of Aphrodite (naturally interested, as goddess of love, in the vow of a loving wife). In fact, it appears, the tress disappeared from a Pantheon in Alexandria.

55. *per aetherias . . . umbras*: the theft naturally took place at night.

57–8. 'The goddess herself had despatched her retainer upon this errand (*eo*), she who was a Greek though she dwelt upon the shores of Canopus'. The 8-line sentence ends with a suitable flourish — a 5th-foot spondee in the hexameter followed by a 4-word pentameter.

58. *Canopeis incola litoribus*: cf. 64. 300 *cultricem montibus Idri*. Canopus was near Alexandria, the site of the famous temple of Serapis [*Canopicis* V; *Canopitis* Estaço.]

59–64. The tress becomes a star.

59. *inde Venus*: No convincing restoration of the opening words has been suggested; Postgate's *inde Venus* provides a stopgap, but 64 *diua* then reads awkwardly. The sense is plain: Ariadne's crown was not to be left alone (i.e. the only case of promotion

from mortal's head to the heavens); *solum* is probably adverbial.

uario . . . in limine caeli: 'in the spangled threshold of the sky'; cf. on 7 *caelesti in limine*; with *uario* cf. 61. 87–8 *in uario hortulo*.

60–1. *ex Ariadnaeis aurea temporibus / . . . corona*: 'the golden crown from the brows of Ariadne'. The story of Ariadne and her crown is told by Ovid, *Fast.* 3. 459–516 and *Met.* 8. 174–82; cf. 8 *e Bereniceo uertice caesariem* (like line 60 a 4-word pentameter).

61. The second final clause follows as though *ut* and not *ne* had preceded.

62. 'The dedicated spoils of a flaxen head'. A fine 4-word pentameter. Callimachus had simply καλὸς πλόκαμος; see on 8 *caesariem*.

63. = 'A little wet by spray from my journey to the dwelling place of the gods (i.e. the heavens)'. The temple of Aphrodite Zephyritis overlooked the sea. With *templa deum* cf. Ennius, Epic Fragment 46W *ad caeli caerula templa*, Lucretius 1. 1014 *caeli lucida templa*, etc. [Some change *a fluctu*, 'from the sea', needlessly to *a fletu*, 'from tears' (Berenice was no longer weeping when she discharged her vow).]

64. With the antithesis cf. 38 *pristina uota nouo munere dissoluo*.

65–70. The tress's present position fixed: she lies between Virgo, Leo, the Bear and Bootes. The *coma Berenices* is actually a star cluster, like the Hyades and the Pleiades.

65. *namque*: for the word order cf. Virgil, *Ecl.* 1. 14 *hic inter densas corylos modo namque gemellos. . . .*

66. *Callisto*: Greek dative singular, with *Lycaoniae*. Callisto, daughter of King Lycaon of Arcadia, became first a bear, then the constellation of that name.

67–8. 'I wheel to my setting in advance of slow Bootes (the Wagoner), who only just sinks into the deep Ocean'; i.e. he only just manages to set before day breaks.

68. *uix sero*: cf. 62. 2 *uix tandem*.

69–76. = 'Though I keep company with the gods, I pine for my former way of life'.

69. 'But though the gods trample me by night ...'. The gods dwell beyond the stars and in their journeyings to earth and back naturally cross the *limen caeli*.

70. 'whereas dawn restores me to white-haired Tethys ...'; *autem* opposes two parallel clauses, like Greek μέν and δέ. For Tethys, the wife of Oceanus, see 64. 29–30; *Tethyi* is a Greek dative in short i.

71. *Ramnusia uirgo*: Nemesis. See on 64. 395.

73. *nec si me ... discerpent sidera*: 'not even if the stars pull me to pieces (i.e. criticize bitterly)'.

74. With 72 *non ullo uera timore tegam*; 'and so not unfold the things pent up in a truthful breast'. For Lucretius the *pectus* is the site of the intellect as well as the feelings; *euoluam* scans as 4 syllables.

75–6. The construction is *non tam laetor quam discrucior*; note the chiasmus *me afore semper* | *afore me*.

76. *discrucior*: +accusative and infinitive also in Cicero, *Att.* 14. 6. 1 *discrucior Sextili fundum a uerberone Curtilio possideri*; see on 85. 2 *excrucior*.

77–94. Mainly about scent.

77–8. 'So long as I was with my mistress, I imbibed huge quantities of scent (*quicum ego ... una milia multa* [*unguentorum*] *bibi*) — though till then deprived completely, so long as she was unmarried (*dum uirgo quondam fuit, omnibus expers unguentis*)'; i.e 'Berenice, once married, lavished scent upon me'. (For Berenice's extravagance in the matter of cosmetics see Athenaeus 15. 689a [in Kroll].)

In the corresponding lines in Callimachus, the speaker contrasts the lavish perfumes used by Alexandrian ladies with the simple dressings used by unmarried girls: though she had plenty of the latter (πολλὰ πέπωκα λιτά) the tress was denied all taste of the former (γυναικείων δ᾽οὐκ ἀπέλαυσα μύρων) — by being separated from her mistress so soon after marriage; hence her dissatisfaction (ἀσχάλλω) with her present elevated status. C. seems to have contented himself with the rhetorically more effective point: 'no *unguenta* before marriage, no shortage after marriage'. It makes an effective basis for the appeal for libations which follows; no difficulty in supposing mistress and tress together long enough after marriage for the latter to acquire a taste for *unguenta*.

quicum . . . una: cf. 68. 22, 23, 94 and 95 *tecum una*.

77. *expers*: with *ego*.

78. *milia multa*: also 5. 10; cf. 61. 203 *multa milia*, 68. 45–6 *multis milibus*. [Lobel's *uilia* for *milia* (='with whom I had many cheap drinks while she was unmarried, though denied all *unguenta*') is an attempt to bring C. into line with Callimachus.]

79–94. A general appeal (79–88), addressed to all (respectable) brides, for gifts of scent (in the form of libations), followed by a particular appeal (89–94) to Berenice. Nothing corresponds in the papyrus of the Callimachus to C.'s 79–88, though the papyrus preserves the opening letters of the couplets corresponding to C.'s 89–94.

79. *optato . . . lumine*: (1) 'on the longed-for day'; cf. 64. 31 *optatae luces*; (2) 'with its longed-for light' (i.e. that of the marriage-torch); for *optato* see on 64. 22.

80–1. *non prius . . . tradite*: = *ne prius tradite*, *non prius* forming a kind of compound; a negative present imperative is a feature of the high style; cf. 61. 193 *ne remorare*, 62. 59 *ne pugna*, 67. 18 *ne dubita*.

80. *unanimis*: cf. 9. 4 *fratresque unanimos*, 30. 1 *unanimis false sodalibus*.

81. *reiecta ueste*: cf. 88. 2 *abiectis tunicis*.

82. *quam*: with 80 *non prius*.

onyx: i.e. an onyx scent-pot, from which a libation is to be poured to the *coma Berenices*, as though to a divinity; cf. Horace, *Carm.* 4. 12. 17 *nardi paruus onyx*.

83. '*Your* scent-pot, I mean, you who keep the laws (of marriage) in an unpolluted bed'; in Latin a pronominal adjective can provide the antecedent for a relative pronoun.

85. *bibat irrita*: 'absorb and render ineffective'; prolepsis.

87. *sed magis*: 'but instead' (of indulgence in adultery).

89–94. Final appeal to Berenice.

89. *tuens . . . sidera*: i.e. looking up as she makes her sacrifice.

90. *festis luminibus*: 'on holy days'.

91. 'do not allow her, who am yours, to go without my share of scent'; *unguinis* from *unguen*, an archaic by-form of *unguentum*; *expertem* more often with the genitive (as here) than with the ablative (as in line 77). [*sanguinis* V, *unguinis* Bentley.]

92–3. 'But rather ply with gifts, so that the stars say repeatedly, "Would I could become a royal tress!"' With this use of *cur* cf. 10. 9–11 *nihil . . . esse . . . cur referret*, Ovid, *Am.* 1. 3. 2 *aut amet aut faciat cur ego semper amem.* [*effice . . . cur iterent* V; most print *largis affice muneribus. sidera corruerint utinam! coma regia fiam!*, 'let the stars crash down, I want to become a royal tress'. See on line 94.]

94. A crowning conceit, to round off a clever poem? It seems so, though the remnants of a further couplet follow the corresponding line in Callimachus (fragmentary, but Hydrochoos and Oarion can be identified). Probably *fulgeret* (present subjunctive of the by-form *fulgerare*) is a further exclamation parallel to *coma regia fiam*: 'Let Aquarius' neighbour Orion shine!', i.e. 'I don't care how bright Orion is, I only want to be a *coma regia*!' In their anxiety to have similar gifts lavished upon themselves, the other stars are imagined by the *coma Berenices* as dismissing Orion (the most brilliant of the constellations) as 'the next-door neighbour of Aquarius (for the ancients, a bringer of storms)'; for this sense of *proximus* cf. Virgil, *A.* 2. 311–12 *iam proximus ardet/Vcaligon*; *Hydrochoi* is probably genitive, *proximus* being treated as a noun like Greek γείτων.

[Those who read *affice* in 92 and accept Lachmann's *corruerint* in 93 take 94 as an example of the celestial cataclysm which the speaker is prepared to accept provided she can return to her old way of life and become once more a tress on Berenice's head; in fact Orion and Aquarius, though 100 degrees apart, occupy much the same region of the sky; for other objections see Fordyce. KIDD takes 94 as parallel to *cur iterent*: 'give Orion beside Aquarius cause to flash [in anger]'.]

See:

R. Avallone, 'Il carme 66 di Catullo e la *Chioma di Berenice* di Callimaco', *Euphrosyne* 4 (1961), 23–48.

W. Clausen, *HSPh* 74 (1970) 85–94.

D. A. Kidd, 'Some problems in Catullus LXVI', *Antichthon* 4 (1970).

D. N. Levin, 'Ambiguities of expression in Catullus 66 and 67', *CPh* 54 (1959), 109–11.

M. C. J. Putnam, 'Catullus 66. 75–88', *CPh* 55 (1960), 223–8.

D. E. W. Wormell, 'Catullus as translator', *The Classical Tradition* ed. L. Wallach (1967).

67

In form, a dramatic duologue. In theme, close to some of the elegiac fragments — e.g. the Gellius epigrams (Poem 74, etc.). The main speaker is the street door of a house in Verona. After some prompting, the door recounts the scandals with which the house has been associated.

No doubt there was an ancient audience in Verona for whom all was 'as clear as it is obscure today' (Lenchantin); but we need not doubt either that the audience for whom the poem was eventually published was expected, like us, to piece together the data provided into a coherent whole. The story is admittedly somewhat complicated, and it is not made simpler by the door's flair for sardonic innuendo. It remains a legitimate assumption that only one hypothesis will fit the clues provided. And in fact, though there is room for debate about details, the main facts are clear enough. The door is that of a house in Verona (34), now the property of a certain Caecilius (9) — perhaps the poet of Poem 35. Formerly it had been the establishment of an elderly widower (4 + 6) named Balbus (3). On Balbus' death his son married (6). His wife, though married before (21), passed for a virgin (19); in Brixia where she came from she had been the subject of more than one scandal (23–6). After she came to live in it the house in Verona got a bad name. Asked to explain its neglect of duty (7–8), the door goes into some details about the adventures of the former mistress.

The street door plays an important role in Greek and Roman love poetry, usually as the recipient of the lover's tearful reproaches — it bars him entry to his mistress; see F. O. Copley, *Exclusus Amator* (1956). C. turns the door into a garrulous, gossip-loving slave (cf. Poems 4 and 31). Propertius also wrote an elegy (1. 16) in which a street door tells its story.

1. The opening line introduces two of the main characters in the story: a 'beloved husband' and his father — the former owner and his father: the street door was the symbol of a house for which they felt affection. With *dulci* cf. 66. 33 *pro dulci coniuge*. The formal greeting is impregnated of course with sardonic overtones.

2. 'May Jove vouchsafe prosperity to you.'

3–4. Further information: report has it that once upon a time the door proved a willing retainer to Balbus *père*, an old man when he came to live here; the door, i.e., kept his house safe and free from scandal. With the personification implicit in *seruisse benigne* cf. Poem 31, especially 12–14.

5–6. 'But they say you let the son down after the old man's funeral, when you got yourself a wife'; *es . . . marita* sounds an odd way to put it, but the meaning seems clear: Balbus *père* was a widower; Balbus *fils* by marrying gave the house a mistress once again. [*uoto* V (*nato* Froehlich); *maligno* X; *est* V.]

7–8. 'Please explain why you have this reputation for abandoning your old loyalty to your master.' Rhythmically *ueterem* goes more closely with *fidem* than with *dominum*; in sense it belongs to both.

9–14. The door's disclaimer.

9–10. *non . . . culpa mea est*: 'I'm not to blame'.

9. *ita Caecilio placeam*: 'so may I win favour with Caecilius'; for *ita* see on 97. 1.

   cui tradita nunc sum: i.e. the house now has a new master, in whose service the door is anxious to redeem itself.

11. 'no one can say it was anything I did wrong'; for *pote* = *potest* see on 17. 24.

12. The meaning seems to be 'you can't blame a door for local ways', but no satisfactory restoration of the line has been proposed. Munro's *uerum est ius populi: ianua quicque facit* ('it's true what they say: blame the door for everything') is as good as any.

13–14. = 'Everybody blames me for everything.'

13. *quacumque aliquid reperitur non bene factum*: 'whenever (lit. wherever) anything nasty comes to light'.

15–18. A short interchange, in which the first speaker demands a more detailed explanation.

15. *uno . . . uerbo*: = 'flat denial isn't enough'. Cf. Terence, *An.* 45 *quin tu uno uerbo dic*.

    istuc: = *istud* (cf. 37 *istaec*).

18. *ne dubita*: the common form of a prohibition in the high style; cf. 61. 193 *ne remorare*, 62. 59 *ne pugna*.

19–28. The door's detailed account begins: 'First, there was that father of her previous husband. . . .'

19–20. *uirgo quod fertur . . . falsum est*: 'as for the story that I was given a virgin to look after, it's a lie'; for this use of *quod* see on 68. 1–10.

20. *non illam uir prior attigerat*: i.e. Balbus *fils* was not her first husband, but the previous husband had been impotent — no doubt the reason for the story that she had come to the house a virgin. [*attigerat*, a Renaissance conjecture, seems a necessary correction of *attigerit* V (perfect subjunctive and pluperfect indicative are often confused). The subjunctive can be explained as concessive, but the tense is wrong: 'admittedly her previous husband hasn't laid hands on her' implies he is still around; 'admittedly her husband hasn't been the first to lay hands on her' should imply she is married to Caecilius. Either way we are faced with a datum which is hard to integrate into a plausible hypothesis.]

21–8. The door, like a garrulous slave, indulges in some picturesque elaboration of the bald statement of the previous line; its authority is allegedly the lady herself — see 37–42.

21. *tenera . . . beta*: ablative of comparison.

sicula: a diminutive, found only here in Classical Latin, of *sica*, the name for a curved dagger. (Not to be confused with *secula*, 'sickle'.)

23. The principal caesura separates *illius*, genitive dependent on *pater*, (put in to make it clear that it is the father of the *uir prior* who is meant) from *gnati*, genitive dependent on *cubile* (put in to emphasize the unnaturalness of the crime).

illīus: elsewhere in C. this i is short; cf. e.g. 17. 10 *totĭus*. [Baehrens' *illusi* is tempting.]

24. *miseram . . . domum*: = 'the unhappy family'.

26. *natus*: 'the son'; i.e. the *uir prior*.

27. [*querendus unde* V; *quaerendum unde unde* Estaço.]

neruosius: 'more sinewy'.

29–30. = 'A fine father he was!'

30. *minxerit in gremium*: no doubt a colloquial euphemism; cf. 78b. 2 *comminxit*, 99. 10 *commictae*.

31–6. The door resumes. It now turns out that the lady and her previous husband lived in Brixia (about as far west of Sirmio as Verona is east).

32. 'Brixia that lies below Cycnus' watch-tower'. For the 4-word pentameter see on 66. 8. Cycnus was the Ligurian prince who was turned into a swan while grieving for his friend Phaethon; cf. Virgil, *A.* 10. 189–93, Ovid, *Met.* 2. 367–80. [*chinea suppositum specula* V; *Cycneae speculae* Vossius.]

supposita: the final a counts as long before the double consonant following; see on 17. 24.

34. = 'Brixia whom I love as the mother of my own Verona'. Makes it clear that the house of Caecilius and the dramatic setting of Poem 67 are in Verona. Brixia is not elsewhere referred to as the mother city of Verona. It may simply have been the larger town.

35–6. i.e. local gossip says there were a couple of lovers too.

35. *de Postumio et Corneli narrat amore*: more colloquial and more

agreeable to the ear than *de Postumi et Corneli narrat amore*;
Cornelius is hardly Cornelius Nepos (see on Poem 1); possibly
the Cornelius of Poem 102 — he at any rate had a secret to
keep.

37-40. ='I expect you wonder how a stay-at-home like me
knows all this.' The door personified has words attributed to it
which are of course literally true of doors, but satirize at the same
time the sort of picturesque exaggeration we can easily imagine
on the lips of a real janitor.

37. *dixerit hic aliquis*: 'suppose somebody says at this point'.

istaec: accusative plural.

39. *hic suffixa tigillo*: 'stuck here beneath this lintel'. The
ancient street door turned on two vertical pivots, one lodged in the
sill, the other in a socket in the underside of the lintel.

40. *tantum . . . soles*: ='you never do anything except'.

41-4. We may imagine that the new mistress would often talk
about the old days in Brixia with the *ancillae* she had brought
with her to Verona.

41. *furtiua uoce*: in hushed tones, like a thief.

44. *speraret*: 'expect'. [*speret* V; see on 76. 10.]

45-8. The 'tall chap with the red eyebrows' is referred to more
circumspectly, presumably because he is a citizen of Verona, and
still around to punish indiscretion.

46. *nomine*: picks up 43 *nomine*.

ne tollat rubra supercilia: according to the scholiast on
Aristophanes, *Wasps* 655, a sign of anger; perhaps here rather of
feigned indignation.

47-8. ='He got into awful trouble that time with the law — a
trumped-up story that there was going to be a baby.' A nice
juicy piece of gossip to end with, though the concluding 4-word
pentameter is aimed more at giving rhetorical status to savoury
gossip than at getting the facts straight. No doubt, while purport-
ing to identify the 'tall chap', the door's concluding remark
leaves us to infer that it was he and the court case that got the
house (and the door) a bad name; did the former mistress try to

get the last of the lovers to marry her by pretending she was with child by him? (Cf. Phronesium in Plautus' *Truc.*)

See:

F. O. Copley, 'The "riddle" of Catullus 67', *TAPhA* 80 (1949), 245–53.

D. N. Levin, 'Ambiguities of expression in Catullus 66 and 67', *CPh* 54 (1959), 109–11.

L. Richardson Jr, *AJPh* 88 (1967) 423–33.

68

Two poems, or one? The answer seems to be that Poem 68 affects the form of an open letter, which becomes a poem, without ever quite ceasing to be a letter; the relationship between lines 1–40 and 41–160 is more subtle than that between Poem 65 and Poem 66; like Poem 64, Poem 68 is an experiment in complex structure.

The result is an extremely interesting poem, and a tantalizing fragment of autobiography. Themes blend into one another, to form a sequence in which the unity is psychological rather than logical: Allius — Lesbia — Laodamia — Troy — the grave — Troy — Laodamia — Lesbia — Allius. Lines 89–100 are the nucleus of this structure: they might stand on their own as a short elegiac poem. Lines 101–60 follow in reverse order the thought-sequence of 41–88. Lines 1–40 are a kind of prelude, introducing the two dominant themes: grief for a brother wholly lost, love for a mistress upon whom C.'s claim is precarious. But however interesting the formal structure, Poem 68 reads clumsily. Whatever the genesis of the poem, the transitions in this early experiment in stream of consciousness technique are too obviously contrived. Nor can the quite exceptional richness of the imagery disguise a good deal of shoddy craftsmanship.

Most assume that 67–72, 131–48 and 156–60, if not 27–30, refer to Lesbia. WILAMOWITZ remarked that no man capable of distinguishing the accents of the heart from commonplaces ('der

o

Herzenstöne von Gemeinplätzen unterscheiden kann') could
doubt it. The most likely date is 59 B.C. — or perhaps 58 B.C., the
year preceding C.'s journey to Bithynia, undoubtedly motivated
(at least in part) by the desire to visit his brother's grave (see
Poem 101). Lesbia's husband (assuming Lesbia was Clodia
Metelli), though still living at the time spoken of in lines 67-72
(as appears from lines 145-6), was dead in that case when
C. wrote Poem 68 (he died about March 59 B.C.); the liaison
could thus be spoken of more openly, perhaps. See on 29
deserto.

Among the problems of interpretation are: (1) Is the Mallius of
1-40 the Allius of 41-160? (see on 41 *Allius*) (2) The meaning of
line 10. (3) The meaning of 27-40. (4) The reference of the simile
in 57-62. (5) The text of 155-8.

1-40. C. has received a tearful letter (2 *conscriptum . . . lacrimis
. . . epistolium*) from his friend Mallius: Mallius is dejected and
cannot sleep — a love affair, it seems, is not going well; he asks
C. for a poem to console him (1-10). C. answers that the death of
his brother has left him in no mood for love and love poetry
(11-30); Mallius must excuse him (31 *ignosces igitur*) if grief and
the limited material he has at hand in Verona prevent full
compliance with his request (31-40).

1-10. These lines pick up, with more than a hint of sad irony,
the extravagant language used by Mallius to describe his plight:
contrast the sombre eloquence with which C. sets out his own
misfortune in 19-26, and the wry rejection in 27-30 of what
Mallius seems to have intended as a friendly hint, wittily
expressed.

Mallius is spending his sleepless nights alone *in lecto caelibe*
because, unlike Flavius in Poem 6, he is forced *uiduas iacere
noctes* (6. 6). Cf. 5-6 with Propertius 1. 1. 33-4: *in me nostra Venus
noctes exercet amaras, | et nullo uacuus tempore defit amor*. The *nox
uigilanda* (Propertius 3. 15. 2 *nec ueniat sine te nox uigilanda mihi*) is
one of the commonplaces of love poetry — it goes back perhaps
to the lines once attributed to Sappho (*LGS* 468):

δέδυκε μὲν ἀ σελάνα
καὶ Πληϊάδες, μέσαι δὲ
νύκτες, παρὰ δ'ἔρχεθ' ὥρα,
ἐγὼ δὲ μόνα καθεύδω.

C. exploits the commonplace in 50. 9–17. For Mallius' idea that
poetry can console in such circumstances see on Poem 38.

The construction is *quod mittis epistolium . . . id gratum est mihi*
etc.; the two phrases are separated by a summary of Mallius' own
words. Cicero often uses *quod* in this way in going through the
points in a letter to which he is replying; see, e.g., *Fam.* 5. 2. 3
quod autem ita scribis . . .; ibid. 5 *quod scribis . . .*; ibid. 6 *quod
scribis. . . .* C. uses the formula again in 27 *quare quod scribis . . .*;
cf. 67. 19–20 *quod . . . falsum est.*

1. *mihi*: A letter is usually written *ad aliquem*, but the dative
also occurs, especially perhaps when, as here, what is written
amounts to an instruction; cf. Livy 10. 27 *consules Fuluio, ut ex
Falisco, Postumio, ut ex Vaticano exercitum ad Clusium admoueant . . .
scribunt.* See on 116. 1 *tibi.*

2. *epistolium*: Greek diminutive; not found again till Apuleius.

3–4. The rhetorical language ('asking me to rescue the ship-
wrecked sailor from death's door') has caused some to suppose real
tragedy. Contrast 76. 17–22. Cf. the nautical imagery, of C.'s
own requited passion, 63–6; for the rejected lover as shipwrecked
sailor see Horace, *Carm.* 1. 5.

4. *a mortis limine*: cf. 76. 18 *iam ipsa in morte.*

5–6. See on 1–10.

6. *desertum*: the most natural assumption is that Mallius'
mistress has walked out on him; so 64. 57 *desertam* (of Ariadne);
cf. Ovid, *Ep.* 1. 7 (Penelope, 'deserted' by Ulysses) *non ego deserto
iacuissem frigida lecto.* See on 29 *deserto.* Cf. Ovid, *Am.* 3. 5. 42
frigidus in uiduo destituere toro.

7–8. Mallius attempts to combat insomnia by reading the
classical poets, but they do not appeal to him. (He turns, therefore,
to C., hoping modern poetry will prove more effective.) In 50.
10–17 C. deals with insomnia by *writing* a poem.

8. *cum . . . peruigilat*: temporal; *peruigilat* also 88. 2.

9. *id gratum est mihi*: cf. Cicero, *Att.* 1. 8. 1 *quod tu scribis, id ego Tadio et gratum esse intellexi. . . .*

10. *muneraque et Musarum hinc petis et Veneris*: Hard; most likely = 'and you ask me to do something for you: to send you some poems as a present; about love'; *munera* both of the task imposed and the gifts expected; *et . . . et* to separate two requirements, 'poetry inspired not only by the Muses, but by the goddess of love', i.e. 'not just poetry, but love poetry'. C. is going to tell Mallius in 39–40 that he is unable to meet both requirements; *munera* need not imply more than one poem, but the insistence on *copia* in 33, 39 and 40 suggests that Mallius expected a sheaf of poems. The 'gifts of the Muses' and the 'gifts of Aphrodite' are frequently referred to in Greek poetry; Anacreon combines the phrases, Fragment 96D, praising the man who unites Μουσέων τε καὶ ἀγλαὰ δῶρ' Ἀφροδίτης.

11–14. C. excuses himself.

11. *incommoda*: 'misfortunes'.

    Malli: [V, here and in line 30, had *mali*, i.e. *Malli*; in R the name is altered to *Manli*, which some print. Lachmann's *Mani*, adopted by Mynors, attempts to reconcile the name of C.'s friend here and in line 30 with the Alli of 41 etc., on the assumption that Manius was his *praenomen* and Allius his *nomen*. See on 41 *Alli*.]

12. *odisse*: 'despise' and hence 'avoid', as often.

    hospitis officium: Either 'my obligation to my host', in anticipation of line 68; or 'my obligation to my *hospes*', *hospes* being used, like the Greek ξένος of one who looks after a visitor from another city or country; the reference in that case is presumably to Mallius' protection of C. when he came to Rome from Verona.

13. *quis merser fortunae fluctibus ipse*: the same imagery as was used of Mallius (line 3); *fortunae* picks up 1 *fortuna*. For *quis* see on 64. 145.

14. *dona beata*: i.e. the sort of gift a man needs to be happy to give.

15–20. The obvious meaning of 17 *multa satis lusi*, 'I had my full share of the fun', is underpinned by the following words, 'I am not unknown to the goddess who concocts the bitter-sweet anguish of love'; cf. 156 *et domus in qua nos lusimus et domina*; for this sense of *ludere* see on 17. 1. But C. also uses *ludere* of writing *uersiculi* (50. 2 and 5; cf. Horace, *Ep.* 1. 1. 10 *uersus et cetera ludicra pono*), and that meaning should not be excluded here: for C. and his set, making love and making poetry went together — as a substantial part of the Catullan *corpus* demonstrates (see also 6. 15–17). It was natural for Mallius to turn to C. for a love poem, but his brother's death has cut C. off from all that (19 *totum hoc studium*, 26 *haec studia*, i.e. both love and love poetry). He can only half comply with Mallius' request: he can send him a poem, but not a love poem: cf., for C.'s abandonment of love poetry, 65. 12–14 *semper maesta tua carmina morte canam* etc.

15. *tempore quo*: = 'ever since'; cf. 35. 13.

   uestis . . . pura: i.e. the plain white *toga uirilis*, which replaced the *toga praetexta* at age 15–16. Cf. Propertius 3. 15. 3–4 *ut mihi praetexti pudor est ablatus amictus/et data libertas noscere amoris iter*.

17–18. = 'love has not exactly passed me by: I know the pleasure and the anguish too'; *non . . . nescia* is studied understatement (litotes). Cf. 64. 95 *sancte puer, curis hominum qui gaudia misces*. The concept of love as bitter-sweet goes back to Sappho; cf. Plautus, *Ps.* 63 *dulce amarumque una nunc misces mihi*.

19. *fraterna mihi mors*: the rhythm is deliberately jerky (cf. 64. 315); for *fraterna* = *fratris* see on 64. 1; cf. 64. 181 *fraterna caede* and 399 *fraterno sanguine*. See on 100. 4.

20–4. The sense flows over from line 19, then C. breaks off in a long aside; cf. 92–100 and 65. 10–14. Note the repetitions 19 *fraterna*, 20 *frater*, 21 *frater* and also the repetitions of *tu* and *tecum*. For the brother see also Poem 101.

20. *o misero frater adempte mihi*: The words recur (with one small change) at line 92. Cf. 101. 6 *heu miser indigne frater adempte mihi*.

21. = 'your death ruined everything for me'; *commoda* picks up 11 *incommoda*.

22–4. = 94–6.

24. *tuus . . . dulcis . . . amor*: cf. 117 *tuus altus amor*. C. seems to mean that his brother's affectionate approval encouraged C. in the way of life (scandalous by conventional standards) which he had chosen.

25. *tota de mente fugaui*: cf. 64. 398 *cupida de mente fugarunt* and 76. 22 *expulit ex omni pectore laetitias*.

26. *haec studia*: i.e. love and love poetry.

delicias animi: almost = 'intellectual self-indulgence'; for *deliciae* = 'any display of over-fastidiousness or self-indulgence' see the quotations from Cicero on 2. 1; C. adds *animi* to exclude the meaning 'making love'; he means writing love poetry, or rather the frame of mind that finds pleasure in that. Cf. 2. 10 *animi curas*, 102. 2 *fides animi*. (In 64. 372 *animi amores*, sometimes quoted as a parallel, *animi* is better taken as locative with *optatos*.)

27–30. Hard. The text is corrupt and much emended. Did Mallius' letter contain a hint (to which C. now attempts an answer) that Lesbia was finding many only too ready to console her for the loss of her husband — or perhaps just for the absence from Rome of her lover (see on 29 *deserto*)? This gives good sense, but will really only work if we assume that C. transcribes Mallius' words verbatim. In a normal letter quotations are modified according to the conventions of *oratio obliqua* (see, e.g., Cicero's quotations from Metellus' letter, *Fam.* 5. 2 and Metellus' actual words in 5. 1). But a verse letter is not a normal letter. And if Mallius had written *his* letter in verse (as seems likely from the sound of 1–8), his words, if recast in *oratio obliquâ*, might no longer scan. It could be both easier and more natural to quote the words verbatim; lines 5–8 look rather like a verbatim quotation. If this can be granted, we have an interpretation that keeps to the MSS and fits in well with 135–48 (see on these lines). The alternative, to suppose that Mallius wrote in effect, 'Verona's no place for you, Catullus, all the best people there bed alone' (Mallius' urbane version of a common view of provincial life), creates more difficulties than it solves: see on 28 *hic*.

27–8. '*Veronae turpe, Catulle, | esse*'; i.e. *Veronae esse turpe* [*est*],

Catulle; *est* (or whatever the verb was that went with *turpe*) is dropped, perhaps because it could not conveniently be incorporated in the quotation. The MSS have *Catulle*, which most change to the dative *Catullo*; but the vocative is perhaps C.'s warning to the reader that Mallius' words were being given verbatim.

28. *quod*: with the double *quod* cf. 37–9 *quod . . . quod. . . .* The style of 1–40 (apart from the echoes here and in 1–10 of Mallius' words and the aside in 20–4) is almost studiously prosaic.

hic: i.e. *Romae*. This is the word around which discussion of these lines chiefly turns. If we regard Mallius' words as reported in the normal way, *hic* must refer to Verona (cf. 36 *huc*); if Rome were meant, the normal conventions of *oratio obliqua* would require *illic* (cf. 35 *illic mea carpitur aetas*) or some equivalent word. But to suppose Verona is meant involves difficulties with 29 *deserto*; and to take the words as *oratio obliqua* involves turning *tepefactat* into the subjunctive *tepefactet*, and probably turning *Catulle* into *Catullo*. It also presents Mallius with a weak joke, instead of allowing him to drop a timely hint.

quisquis de meliore nota: = 'all the best people'; cf. Cicero, *Fam.* 7. 29. 1 *Sulpici successori nos de meliore nota commenda* ('give me a high-class introduction to Sulpicius' successor').

29. *deserto*: It is tempting to see a reference to the death of Metellus Celer (about March 59 B.C.) and the beginning of Clodia's career as a merry widow. But Mallius need only mean the absence from Rome of C. — Clodia's *amant en titre*. Cf. 6 *desertum*. (Those who assume Verona is meant are more or less forced to take *deserto* as 'empty'; if the normal meaning 'deserted' is kept, it is hard to extract a condemnation of the *mores* of Verona that can be plausibly attributed to Mallius.)

tepefactat: a frequentative not found elsewhere; cf. 64. 360 *tepefaciet*. The original long e in such compounds (cf. *tepēfaciet*) was shortened in ordinary speech, as here (*tepĕfactat*). [*tepefactat* is found as a correction in R; *tepefacit* V, which is unmetrical.]

30. *magis*: 'rather'.

miserum: i.e. a misfortune to be endured.

31. *luctus ademit*: picks up 19–20 *luctu . . . mors abstulit*.

32. *munera*: picks up 10 *munera*.

33–4. *quod . . . hoc fit, quod . . .*: = 'the fact is I *haven't* a whole stock of stuff on hand, because . . .'. It is usually assumed that *scriptorum* is from *scriptores* (cf. 7 *ueterum . . . scriptorum*), not from *scripta*, and that C. means he hasn't his library with him. 'The excuse is revealing evidence of the methods and ideals of the *doctus poeta*; what is expected of him is Alexandrian poetry, translated from, or modelled on Greek, and for that he needs his library' (Fordyce). (Cf., however, Horace, *Ep.* 2. 1. 112–13 *prius orto/sole uigil calamum et chartas et scrinia posco*.) It seems more likely that C. is rejecting Mallius' assumption that he must have lots of material on hand (just completed or nearing completion) which he can send, even if he isn't in the mood for writing fresh poetry (*scriptorum* in that case from *scripta*); this is after all how poets work. Mallius perhaps used the phrase *scriptorum magna copia*, 'a whole stock of stuff that you've written' (*scriptorum* from *scripta*), and C. picks it up: C.'s insistence on *copia* in 39 and 40 rather suggests this.

35. *carpitur aetas*: cf. Virgil, *A.* 4. 32 *perpetua maerens carpere iuuenta?*

36. *una . . . capsula*: Did the 'single box' contain the material (including standard authors whom C. might want to consult) which C. had brought from Rome with a view to working on an elegy on his brother's death, as suggested by 65. 12 — including, i.e., a draft of what became Poem 68?

37–40. = 'Don't take it amiss, therefore, if I send you a poem that doesn't meet your requirements — it's all I can manage'; cf. 149–50 *hoc tibi, quod potui, confectum carmine munus | pro multis, Alli, redditur officiis.*

38. *animo*: repeats *mente*, for emphasis. See on 63. 44–7.

non satis ingenuo: i.e. as a meanish trick (dodging the obligation to give a friend what he asks).

39–40. 'I haven't provided stock of each of your requirements (i.e. both poems in general and love poems in particular). I'd deliver the goods if there were any stock.' The reference is to 10 *munera . . . Musarum . . . et Veneris*, while the repeated *copia* picks up 33 *non magna est copia apud me*. The language seems deliberately non-poetic — C. perhaps permits himself a hint of wry irony: poets are always expected to deliver the goods.

39. *posta*: =*posita*.

41–160. The letter now becomes the poem — the *munera Musarum* if not the *munera Veneris*. The chief difficulty, apart from the discrepancy in the names (see on 41 *Allius*), lies in reconciling 155 with 5–6 (see on 155).

If we set C.'s claim in 149 that his poem is the best he can manage alongside 31–40, it seems a reasonable inference that the poem was put together (149 *confectum*) from existing material (perhaps the *una capsula* of 36). The core was perhaps a draft of an elegy on his brother's death, which provided 89–100. Whether C. had had in mind to connect the theme of his brother's death with the Laodamia theme, or whether the desire to comply with Mallius' request led him to combine drafts of two separate poems, adding a long introduction and a shorter conclusion as a more direct compliment to his friend, the role of Mallius' request in the finished composition is to provide a formal excuse for an experimental poem.

41–4. = 'My sense of obligation to Allius compels me to put on record the extent of his services to me and the circumstances.'

41. *deae*: the Muses. The reason why C. addresses them becomes clear in 45 ff.; no doubt a reference to 10 *munera . . . Musarum* is also intended.

Allius: The name *Allius* occurs in the Oxford MS at line 66 with *manllius* as an alternative (*manlius* X) and occurs (in the form *Alli* or *Ali*) in all the principal MSS at line 50; it was restored here [*quam fallius* V] and in 150 [*aliis* V] by Scaliger. [Allius is really the only name that can be got out of the combined MS readings at 41, 50, 66 and 150 (only a name beginning with a vowel will work metrically in line 50); on the other hand, a name beginning with a consonant seems needed in 11 and 30.]

20

It is hard to imagine that anybody other than the addressee of 1–40 is meant; Allius, i.e., must somehow be Mallius. If Allius were a pseudonym (for Mallius or Manlius), it ought to be possible, if C. were following the normal conventions, to substitute the real name each time; but this is not possible in line 50. Lachmann's suggestion that the name of C.'s friend was Manius Allius, addressed by his *praenomen* in 1–40 and his *nomen* in 41–160, merits consideration, though no parallel exists. Another solution (originally put forward by Schöll) is to substitute *mi Alli* for *Malli*, though *mi Alli* gives a very odd rhythm in line 11; to suppose that C. wrote *Malli* (meaning *mi Alli* to be understood) involves supposing that he disguised his friend's name in 1–40, but not in 41–160: we should rather expect the reverse.

43–50. Picked up by 151–2.

43. *fugiens . . . aetas*: = 'the flight of time through ages of forgetfulness' (Merrill).

45–50. A poem, i.e., will ensure that the matter is known to all and not forgotten. A commonplace — elaborated, e.g., by Horace, *Carm.* 4. 9.

45. *porro*: 'in time to come'; cf. 45. 3.

46. *carta . . . anus*: cf. 78b. 4 *fama loquetur anus*; 95. 6 *cana diu saecula peruoluent*.

47. A hexameter is needed.

49–50. Another commonplace — cf. Homer, *Od.* 16. 34 (of the bed of Odysseus), Propertius 2. 6. 35–6 and 3. 6. 33 (the latter a reminiscence of Homer). A sign, perhaps, of C.'s determination to strike an appropriately literary tone; cf. the high style of 51–66.

49. *sublimis*: 'high up'.

50. *deserto*: The Muses, i.e., can ensure (by inspiring C.) that the name of Allius does not lie forgotten in a copy of C.'s poem thrown by its owner into a neglected corner. An echo also, perhaps, of 6 *desertum* and 29 *deserto*.

51–6. An exercise in the high style; in essence, a conventional portrait of the victim of unrequited love, beset by *cura*, on fire with love, weeping tears of anguish; cf. Horace, *Carm.* 1. 13. 1–8;

briefly evoked by Propertius 1. 9. 7 *me dolor et lacrimae merito fecere peritum*. We may suspect from 3–8 that this is the style which (M)allius appreciates.

51. *duplex*: no doubt a reference to 17–18: Venus is the goddess who brings misery as well as joy.

Amathusia: = Venus; cf. 36. 14.

curam: 'torture'; see on 2. 10.

52. *scitis*: C. continues to address the Muses.

torruerit: cf. 100. 7. [*corruerit* V, which some retain.]

53. *Trinacria rupes*: Etna. Horace used the same image in an early poem (*Ep.* 17. 30–3).

54. *lympha . . . Malia*: i.e. the hot spring which gave the pass its name (*Thermopylae* = 'hot gates'). From Malia, the name of the district.

Oetaeis: from Mt Oeta.

55–6. The traditional paradox of unrequited love — where there's fire, there's water.

55. Cf. 64. 242 *anxia in assiduos absumens lumina fletus*.

57–66. Some hold that both similes — 57–62 as well as 63–5 — refer forward to 66: Allius' intervention, i.e., brought instant relief, as a mountain stream brings relief to a sweating traveller on a hot summer's day. The resultant complex structure will really only work if we depart from the MSS in line 63, to read *ac* for *hic* (O has *hec*, i.e. *haec*) with Schuster and Mynors (1961 reprint), following F. Skutsch, *RhM* 47 (1886), 141, an interpretation rejected by Friedrich and others, and regarded as improbable by Fordyce. It seems simpler to separate the similes; moreover, the structure of 57–62 is in favour of taking the first simile with what precedes: 57–9 illustrate admirably tears welling up and rolling down the cheeks; 60–2 can readily be felt as a Homeric expansion.

59. *prona*: 'downward-sloping'; cf. 65. 23 *prono praeceps decursu*.

61. *lasso*: Idiom links *lasso* with *in sudore*, however much the pull of the sense and the rhythm of the first half of the line draw *lasso* to *uiatori* (transferred epithet). Or did C. write *salso*?

63–72. By putting a meeting place at the disposal of the lovers,
Allius saved C. from the tortures of unrequited passion. We
learn from 146 that C.'s mistress was married; from 135 ff. that
C. had to accept that he was not her only lover. With the nautical
imagery in 63–6 cf. that used of Mallius' unrequited passion in
line 3.

63. *hic*: temporal, 'at this juncture', as in 64. 269.

nigro: in poetry, not uncommonly of storms. See *L & S*.

65. Fifth foot spondaic. Also 87, 89, 109; see on 64. 3.

iam . . . iam . . . implorata: = *iam dudum implorata*; *implorata*
nominative with *aura*.

Pollucis . . . Castoris: the *Dioscuri*, traditionally the protectors
of those in peril at sea; see on 4. 27.

66. = *tale fuit nobis Allii auxilium*, or *tali fuit nobis Allius auxilio*.

67. = 'he opened a broad path to an enclosed field'; i.e. made
available a private place, readily accessible, where they could
meet; *lato . . . limite* with *patefecit* (so Benoist-Thomas; Baehrens
with *campum*: 'quo commode possemus ambulare iter amoris');
cf. Virgil, *A*. 9. 323 *lato te limite ducam*.

68. *isque . . . isque*: repeats 67: *is* for emphasis.

domum: 'a house', rather than 'his house' (see next note).

dominae: Allius provided, i.e., a house for C. and the
woman who thus became its mistress; cf. 61. 31 *domum dominam
uoca* and 61. 149–51. Perhaps also the first allusion to the concept,
constant in Augustan elegy, of the lover as his mistress's slave;
see *Cat. Rev.* 81–2 and F. O. Copley, 'Seruitium amoris in the
Roman elegists', *TAPhA* 78 (1947), 295–300. [*dominam* V;
dominae Froehlich. Fordyce attempts to justify *dominam*.] Cf. 156
domina and 136 *erae*.

70. *candida diua*: develops the imagery implicit in 68 *dominae*.
C., like Attis in Poem 63, is the *famula* (63. 90) — not of a mortal
mistress, but of a goddess (cf. 76 *eros*, 78 *eris*, 63. 13 *Dindymenae
dominae uaga pecora*, and 63. 91 *dea domina Dindymi*); with *candida*
('resplendent') cf. 134 *candidus*.

71–2. The image captures Lesbia (if it is Lesbia) at the

moment before she took the fatal step (cf. 145–6 *furtiua dedit mira munuscula nocte,* | *ipsius ex ipso dempta uiri gremio*): she paused (*constituit*), resting her foot, clad in its shining sandal, (*fulgentem ... plantam ... innixa*) upon the well-worn threshold (*trito ... in limine*). At the same time the image picks out a familiar detail of the traditional marriage ceremony, dwelt on by C. also in 61. 159–61:

> transfer omine cum bono
> limen aureolos pedes,
> rasilemque subi forem.

Cf. 61. 9–10. It is clear from 67–9 that both parties regarded the visit of 70–2 as the first step towards a liaison; cf. the wedding imagery 133–4. If the reference is to Lesbia-Clodia, the liaison can hardly have begun later than 60 B.C. — a year or more earlier than the composition of Poem 68. (BAKER argues that, by *resting* her foot on the threshold, Lesbia commits an unlucky act; 'Unlike the bride, ducking her head and lifting her feet carefully over the threshold to avoid bad luck, Lesbia places her foot on the threshold of the borrowed, sensuous, and unsanctified house.')

71. *fulgentem*: resplendent like the divinity herself.

72. *arguta ... solea*: instrumental with *innixa*; C. is clearly trying to record the moment in all its individuality. But did the sandal squeak, or did Lesbia tap the threshold with it (impatiently, or as a signal)? (*argutus* denotes any sharp, clear sound); *constituit* (and C.'s concentration on the significance of the instant) are in favour of the former.

73–88. A further long simile (cf. 57–62 and 63–6), developing into a planned digression. Protesilaus was doomed, as the first who jumped ashore (whence his name), to be the first Greek to die in the Trojan War. Homer (*Il.* 2. 695–710) tells us that he left behind in Phylace his grieving wife Laodamia and a house half built. Later writers, captivated by the evident pathos of Homer's data, embroidered the tale (Euripides wrote a play around the story); according to a version used by Propertius (1. 19. 7–10), Protesilaus was allowed to return briefly from the dead to his grieving bride. 'In the use to which he puts the story of Laodamia Catullus anticipates an important feature of Augustan elegy. He makes of the myth an illustration of his own love. . . . The Greeks . . . had begun this use of myth, but they had not developed it in the same way. In Augustan elegy however and especially in Propertius the phenomenon is so common as to require no illustration.' (Wheeler 173)

73–6. C. sets out from Homer's data (the loving bride, the house half-finished), but shifts the emphasis from Protesilaus to Laodamia, to apply the legend to 67–72; he adds a detail (taken over from some Alexandrian version, or perhaps invented): the sacrifice which had not been carried out. Though the common element is not specifically disentangled, the legend becomes the symbol of his affair with Lesbia.

74. A 3-word pentameter, of which *Prōtĕsĭlāĕām* forms the first half; *Lāŭdămīā* again in 80 and 105; cf. 112. For the adjectival form of a proper name see on 64. 1.

76. *pacificasset*: i.e. the *pax deorum* (the gods' agreement not to frustrate a course of action embarked on by a mortal) had not been obtained. If C. means that Laodamia did not wait for the ceremony seeking divine approval of her union with Protesilaus, this would fit C.'s own case most neatly; cf. Dido's attempt to obtain *pax* from the gods for her union with Aeneas, Virgil, *A*. 4. 56–67; *inceptam frustra* in that case = 'begun to no purpose' (because the marriage was doomed); it is not necessary to suppose, i.e., that what they did wrong was to begin the construction of the house without divine approval.

77–8. Translated into non-heroic terms, this means that C. prays that he will never, to gain gratification of desire, embark precipitately upon a course of action which is doomed to disaster. Though put in general terms, the specific reference is obvious.

77. *Ramnusia uirgo*: Nemesis; see on 64. 395.

79. *quam*: 'how much'.

pium: the blood is *pium* because it is shed in doing reverence to the gods.

81–8. Somewhat diffusely expressed. Helen had already been stolen; the Greek force was already being mustered; Laodamia was parted from her husband before they had been man and wife long enough to enable her to endure — not temporary separation (like that imposed on Berenice in Poem 66), but the permanent separation which was fated.

81. i.e. the separation was painful for they were still very much in love.

83. *saturasset*: for the pluperfect subjunctive with *antequam* cf. e.g. Cicero, *Ver.* 2. 171.

84. *abrupto*: i.e. broken off for ever; cf. 106–7 *ereptum coniugium*.

85. *quod*: i.e. *abruptum coniugium*.

  scibant: archaic = *sciebant*; cf. 64. 319 *custodibant*; 84. 8 *audibant*.

  non longo tempore abesse: = 'to be close at hand'.

86. *si ... isset*: = 'once he went to fight at Troy'; the *oratio obliqua* version of *si iuerit*; for *si* = 'as soon as' see on 14. 17 *si luxerit*.

87. *Helenae raptu*: 'in view of Helen's rape'; cf. 14. 2 *munere isto*.

88. The idea that Troy summoned men to their death, though appropriate to the Trojan War, is introduced in preparation for the transition to C.'s brother.

89–100. Emotionally and structurally the core of the poem, though formally an aside, like 20–4 and 65. 10–14.

89. (*nefas!*): Virgil's parenthetical *nefas!* of Cleopatra (*A.* 8. 688 *sequiturque* (*nefas!*) *Aegyptia coniunx*) is perhaps an echo of C.; cf. also *A.* 7. 73.

90. *uirtutum*: echoes *uirum* (as in Virgil, *A.* 1. 566; cf. *A.* 4. 3 *uiri uirtus*); for C.'s use of *uirtutes* see on 64. 51. Three elisions in this line; see on 73.6.

  cinis: feminine, as in 101. 4 (see note there, and the fragments of Calvus quoted); masculine (the normal gender) in line 98 *cognatos ... cineres*. Troy can be regarded as covered with the ash of the dead buried there; but the equation *Troia ... acerba cinis* is an example of tensioned statement.

91–2. The transition to his brother's death is achieved by an indignant, or incredulous, question, a not uncommon idiom. [*quaene* is Heinsius' solution to the corrupt reading of the MSS; for an interrogative particle attached to a relative pronoun cf. 64. 180 and 183 and Horace, *S.* 1. 10. 21–2

92. *ei misero frater adempte mihi*: an echo of 20 *o misero frater adempte mihi*; cf. 101. 6 *heu miser indigne frater adempte mihi*.

93. *misero*: this time with *fratri* instead of *mihi*: 'alas for the light of day, from my unhappy brother snatched away'.

94–6. Repeat 22–4; *domus* in both places, apparently, in the transferred sense ('household', 'family'); no connexion, i.e., with the *domus* of line 68, though the insistence on the idea of 'house' in this poem is remarkable.

97–100. Contrive the transition back to Troy. An echo in Propertius 3. 7. 10 *nec pote cognatos inter humare rogos*.

97. *longe*: with 98 *compositum*.

98. *cognatos . . . cineres*: =*cognatorum cineres*.
    compositum: 'laid to rest'.

99. *Troia obscena, Troia infelice*: all ablative; with *infelice* (=*infelici*) cf. 43. 4 *elegante*.

100. 'foreign land, in ground remote, keeps'.

101–30. C. returns via Troy to Laodamia, to emphasize her exceptional love for her husband. A rather disjointed exploration of a somewhat far-fetched sequence of images (especially 109–16 and 119–24).

101–2. Some of the ideas in these lines occur in more fully developed form in 64. 1–7.

101. *lecta undique pubes*: [Many prefer *simul*, a conjecture of Renaissance editors, to complete the hexameter.] Cf. 64. 4 *lecti iuuenes, Argiuae robora pubis*.

102. *penetralis . . . focos*: the sacred hearths which formed the centre of the home.

103–4. *libera . . . otia*: 'time in plenty, without interference'.

104. *pacato*: the participle is commonly used adjectively = 'peaceful', 'tranquil'.

105. *tibi*: Laodamia is addressed; cf. 117 *tuus . . . amor*, and 129 *tu*.

    casu: 'misfortune'. Cf. 1 *casu . . . acerbo*.

106–7. *ereptum . . . coniugium*: picks up 84 *abrupto . . . coniugio*; for *ereptum* see on 82. 3.

106. *uita dulcius atque anima*: cf. 64. 215 *longa iucundior uita*.

107–8. An echo of 107–8 occurs in Virgil, *A*. 3. 421–2 (of Charybdis) *imo barathri ter gurgite uastos | sorbet in abruptum fluctus*.

107. *uertice*: any swirling rush of water, a 'whirlpool' etc.

108. *aestus*: the meaning here is close to that of 107 *uertice* — a swirling rush of water; but primarily *aestus* denotes the swirl of extreme heat and thus the swirl of boiling water, whence it is applied as a metaphor to the swirl of the sea etc., and to the swirl of the passions (such as love); most take 107 *amoris* with *aestus*, instead of with *uertice*, but as *aestus* and *uertice* mean much the same, *amoris* is better regarded as belonging to both, if rhythmically closer to *aestus*.

108–10. Primarily, *barathrum* denotes a deep pit or 'abyss'; but the word is also a technical term applied to the underground drainage shafts, used to drain floodwaters from the low-lying plain near the town of Pheneus (by Mt Cyllene) in Arcadia (said to have been the work of Hercules; see, e.g., Pausanias 8. 14. 1, quoted by Kroll). The linking of the two meanings here and the excursus on Hercules which follows smell of the lamp.

109. Fifth foot spondaic.

110. *emulsa . . . palude*: 'the marsh having been drained away'; *emulgere* (rare) is possibly a technical term (also 80. 8).

111. *quod*: i.e. the *barathrum*. C. apparently thought of the drainage system as a single deep pit; Pausanias speaks of βάραθρα (plural).

    montis: Mt Cyllene.

112. A 3-word pentameter, the second half a single word (cf. 74). Presumably a *tour de force* of Alexandrianism metrically, as well as in ingenuity of statement: *Amphitryoniades* = Hercules, but the patronymic involves a false attribution of parentage, since

Amphitryon was not his father, but Jove; hence *falsiparens*. Virgil borrows *Amphitryoniades*, *A*. 8. 103.

    audit: =*dicitur*; a Graecism.

113–14. A reference to the fifth labour of Hercules, the killing of the man-eating birds by Lake Stymphalus in Arcadia, performed while Hercules was the slave of Eurystheus; see on 116.

114. *deterioris eri*: picks up Hercules' own description of Eurystheus in Homer (*Od*. 11. 621).

115. i.e. in order that Hercules might swell the number of the immortals who frequent the palace of Jove (the *tecta bipatentia* of Virgil, *A*. 10. 5).

    ianua: 'doorway'; *tereretur ianua* picks up 71 *trito . . . in limine*, rather as 114 *eri* picks up 68 *dominae*, 76 *eros*, and 78 *eris* (cf. 136 *erae*); the recurrence of a series of themes and symbols in different contexts (the master-slave relationship, thresholds crossed, people and places deserted, loved ones gained and lost) seems intended to hold the poem together. See also on 133–4.

116. Hebe, i.e., became the bride of Hercules in Olympus; in *Od*. 11. 601–8 Odysseus sees Hercules still alert to ward off the Stymphalian birds.

117–18. An attempt to weld the two senses of *barathrum* together.

117. *tuus altus amor*: Laodamia is addressed; cf. 24 *tuus . . . dulcis . . . amor*.

118. *qui*: the antecedent is 117 *amor* (*barathro* is neuter).

    indomitam: revives the metaphor latent in *ferre iugum*; cf. 63. 33. Horace exploits the idea in *Carm*. 2. 5. 1–9.

119–28. The imagery illustrates the intensity of Laodamia's love, asserted in 117–18. The structure is *nec tam carum caput nepotis nata alit*; *nec tantum gauisa est ulla compar*.

119–24. Laodamia's love exceeds the love an old man has for his only daughter's long-awaited baby son — an heir to frustrate the hopes of a greedy relative waiting for the old man to die to get his hands on his money. The image is oddly detailed; C. seems to be trying to isolate affection from sexual attraction, as in 72. 3–4.

(The legacy hunter is a common Roman phenomenon, of course.)

119–20. *carum . . . caput*: high style, an echo perhaps of the opening line of Sophocles' *Antigone*; cf. Horace, *Carm.* 1. 24. 2 [*desiderium*] *tam cari capitis*; *carum* with *parenti*.

119. *confecto aetate parenti*: Aeneas uses the phrase of Anchises, Virgil, *A.* 4. 599.

120. *una*: emphatic; the old man has no sons, only a daughter.

121–4. The expansion is somewhat unfortunate, since it appears to rationalize (and therefore degrade) the old man's affection for his grandson.

121. *diuitiis uix tandem inuentus auitis*: 'found for his grandfather's fortune (i.e. as a male heir), only just in time'; *uix tandem* also 62. 2.

122. = 'has his name entered in a duly witnessed will'.

123. *derisi*: = 'made a laughing-stock' (i.e. for cultivating a rich old man who now has a male heir).

124. The relative, i.e., has been circling round the old man's head like a vulture round its prey; the image illustrates the relative's assiduous attentions and at the same time reveals the true nature of his *impia gaudia*.

  capiti: primarily, 'head'; but the other sense, 'life' (as in 120), though inappropriate to the image, is appropriate to the intentions of the relative; *capiti* is an archaic ablative in -i.

125–8. A contrasting image? Doves are cited in both poetry and prose as models of conjugal fidelity, rather than (as here) of passion; see, e.g., Pliny, *Nat.* 10. 104 [*columbae*] *coniugii fidem non uiolant communemque seruant domum*.

126. *improbius*: 'more wantonly'.

128. *multiuola*: apparently = *multos uolens*; the female dove, i.e., gives more evidence of passion with one mate than the most flirtatious woman (with all and sundry). The compound is found only here in Classical Latin; cf. 140 *omniuoli*. Does it foreshadow the return to Lesbia in 131 ff.?

129–30. A bridge passage, the counterpart of 73–4.

129. *sed tu*: as in 117 *sed tuus* etc., C. returns to Laodamia, to assert her exceptional love for her husband.

horum . . . furores: the love of the dove and her mate for one another; 'but you are the only one to have exceeded their great passion'.

130. *ut semel*: = *cum semel* (5. 5), 'just as soon as'.

flauo: see on 64. 63.

conciliata: 'joined in marriage'; not a reference to Protesilaus' return from the dead.

131–48. Back to Lesbia. The bridge passage 131–2 picks up the narrative of Lesbia's first visit to him at the point where C. left it in line 72.

131. *aut nihil aut paulo*: = *aut nihil aut paulum*. Note that C. lets Lesbia rank second to Laodamia.

tum: i.e. 'that day'.

concedere digna: = *digna quae concedat*; the infinitive with *dignus* becomes common in the Augustan poets.

132. *lux mea*: colloquial, 'my precious one' (cf. Cicero, *Fam.* 14. 2. 2, of his wife: *mea lux, meum desiderium*), revivified by context. Again in line 160.

gremium: cf. 146 *ex ipso . . . gremio*.

133–4. The image is both vivid and fanciful, though the fancy is underpinned by traditional elements. For the attendance of Cupid upon (happy) lovers see 45. 8–9 and 17–18. Cupid's presence here, however, seems more in the role of an attendant upon a bride (like the *pueri* of 61. 114 ff.); he wears, e.g., a saffron tunic — the colour traditionally associated with a Roman marriage ceremony (see on 61. 8). Cupid is normally represented naked, though Sappho, Fragment 54 LP = *LGS* 210, has him coming from the sky in a purple mantle. Lesbia is of course C.'s *candida diua* (line 70), and it is appropriate that a divinity should have a divine attendant.

134. *fulgebat*: picks up 71 *fulgentem*.

candidus: ('resplendent') picks up 70 *mea . . . candida diua*.

135–48. The switch from illusion to an attempt to face facts is very moving. The transition seems abrupt, however, unless it somehow corresponds to the associational structure of 101–60, which follow the sequence, in reverse order, of 1–88. The most natural assumption is that 135–48 are C.'s answer to Mallius' hint in 27–30 (see on these lines).

135–7. C.'s answer is in effect, 'Yes I know there are others, but she keeps within reasonable bounds; I'll just have to put up with it — I'd only look a fool if I made a fuss.' C.'s attitude here is far from the ideal expressed in Poem 109. Did the hope of *aeternum sanctae foedus amicitiae* come later? or is the ideal crumbling? Does *uerecundae* express a hope for the future, or betray self-deception about the present? Cf. the Lesbia of Poems 11 and 58.

136. *furta*: cf. 140 *furta*, 145 *furtiua . . . munuscula*, and 7. 8 *furtiuos amores*.

    erae: see on 68 *dominae*.

137. *molesti*: cf. 10. 33 *molesta*.

138–40. Best taken as conscious irony — C. demonstrates his ability to keep things in perspective by a comparison which is whimsically far-fetched; the heroic tone, i.e., is part of the process of detachment from overcommitment. At the same time, Juno is spoken of in terms that are ironically realistic (cf. the treatment of Ariadne in Poem 64).

139. *culpa*: see on 75. 1 *tua culpa*.

    concoquit: = 'swallowed' (*L & S* II B 1).

140. *omniuoli*: = *omnes uolens*; cf. 128 *multiuola*.

    furta: picks up 136 *furta*.

141–6. Most editors mark a lacuna after 141, assuming that the point of 142 is lost. (Cf. the demonstrable lacunae after line 46, and after 51. 7 and 65. 8, and the gaps in Poem 61). But the lines, though abrupt, are intelligible as they stand: C. breaks off to develop two arguments, linked by 141 *nec* and 143 *nec*, for shutting his eyes to Lesbia's infidelities. The first is that human partners cannot expect stricter standards than the gods themselves observe. The second is that Jove and Juno are after all husband and wife: C.'s mistress was the wife of another man; he cannot expect even the fidelity that husbands receive. Line 141 *atqui nec diuis homines componier aequum est* is surely a wry echo of 51. 1–2 *ille mi par esse deo uidetur,* | *ille, si fas est, superare diuos.* . . .

141. *componier*: the archaic form of the passive infinitive is restored on the analogy of 61. 42 etc. (see on that line). [*componere* V.]

142. Probably = 'stop assuming the responsibilities of an elderly father — it will bring you no thanks' (C.'s answer to the hint referred to in 27–30; or perhaps a warning to himself). With *tolle . . . onus* cf. Virgil, *A.* 10. 451 *tolle minas*, 'stop threatening', and Horace, *Ep.* 1. 12. 3 *tolle querelas*, 'stop complaining'; *tolle onus* might equally well mean 'take up the burden', but this provides no intelligible meaning here. For *tremuli* see on 17. 13 *tremula*.

143. Probably opposed to 142: '*her* father didn't bring her to me . . .'. In other words, theirs was not a formal marriage, approved of by the bride's father. (As far as we know, a bride's father played no part in the actual ceremony of the *deductio*.) Cf. 62. 60 *non aequom est pugnare, pater cui tradidit ipse*.

144. *Assyrio . . . odore*: cf. 6. 8.

145. The reference is again to 70–2. Many boggle needlessly at *mira*. Cf. 7. 7–8. Also Propertius 2. 15. 1 *o nox mihi candida!*

furtiua dedit . . . munuscula: 'made her poor little stolen gift'; the diminutive cuts the occasion down to size, not C.'s feelings for Lesbia.

146. Develops the imagery latent in 145 — as though the poor little gift were an actual object stolen from her husband's lap while he slept; but the phrase suggests, ironically, a second meaning (cf. 132 *se nostrum contulit in gremium*); *ipsius ex ipso* for emphasis.

147–8. = 'It is enough if only the days reserved for me are reckoned by her as red-letter days'; *nobis . . . unis*, 'to me alone'. The ancient commentator Porphyrio on Horace, *Carm.* 1. 36. 10 tells us that the Cretans used to drop a white pebble into their quivers to mark a happy day (and a black pebble to mark an unhappy day). Cf. 107. 6 (of Lesbia's return) *o lucem candidiore nota*.

148. *dies*: if right, an example of hyperbaton (dislocated word order). Many read *diem* (i.e. agreeing with *quem*).

149-60. The letter to (M)allius has now become the poem which C. sends to his friend as a present, and C. begins to sum up in a series of allusions to 1-50.

149. *quod potui*: = 'such as it is'; cf. 37-40.

  confectum carmine munus: 'a gift made out of poetry'; i.e. 'a poem composed as a gift'; cf. 10 *munera . . . et Musarum . . . et Veneris*.

150. *pro multis . . . officiis*: i.e. not only that recalled in 63 ff. Cf. 42 *quantis . . . officiis*.

151-2. Pick up 43-50.

151. *uestrum . . . nomen*: 'the name you bear' (which is the common property of the Allii); cf. 39. 20 *iste uester dens*.

152. *haec atque illa dies atque alia atque alia*: = 'a few brief days'; cf. 64. 16 *illa atque haud alia luce*; poetry confers immortality, the Allii would otherwise be quickly forgotten; cf. 43-50. For the idea see Horace, *Carm.* 4. 9.

153. *Themis*: i.e. *Iustitia*; cf. 64. 397 ff.

155-8. On the text of these lines ('perhaps the most baffling passage in Catullus') see G. P. Goold, *Phoenix* 12 (1958), 108.

155. *tua uita*: Allius' wife, or, more likely, his mistress. See on 45. 13. If Allius and Mallius are the same person, the most reasonable assumption is that C. takes it for granted that his friend will not be long exposed to the anguish of unrequited love of which Mallius had complained to C. (1-6).

156. Picks up 68 *isque domum nobis isque dedit dominae*; for *lusimus* see on 15-20.

157. Corrupt. No satisfactory suggestion has been put forward, even as to the meaning of the line.

158. 'from which blessing all my blessings were originally derived'. But until 157 is corrected, both the meaning and the text of this line must be regarded as uncertain. For the hiatus following *primo* see on 10. 27.

159–60. The poem concludes with a couplet expressing C.'s devotion to his mistress.

159. *quae me carior ipso est*: cf. 82. 3–4 *multo quod carius illi | est oculis*.

160. *qua uiua uiuere*: The poem ends with an implicit contrast: 'my brother is dead, but so long as my mistress lives, living is sweet'; cf. 5. 1 *uiuamus, mea Lesbia, atque amemus*.

See:

Sheridan Baker, 'Lesbia's foot', *CPh* 55 (1960), 171–3.

F. O. Copley, 'The unity of Catullus 68: a further view', *CPh* 52 (1957), 29–32.

Eduard Fraenkel, *Gnomon* 34 (1962) 261–3.

Robert Godel, 'Catulle, poème 68', *MH* 22 (1965), 53–65.

T. E. Kinsey, 'Some problems in Catullus 68', *Latomus* 26 (1967), 35–53.

Godo Lieberg, *Puella Divina* (1962) 152–263.

Henry W. Prescott, 'The unity of Catullus LXVIII', *TAPhA* 71 (1940), 473–500.

Karl Vretska, 'Das Problem der Einheit von Catull c. 68', *WS* 79 (1966), 313–30.

U. von Wilamowitz-Moellendorff, 'Catulls Liebe' in *Hellenistische Dichtung* (1924) ii 305–10.

L. P. Wilkinson, *CR* 84 (1970) 290.

Gordon Williams, *Tradition and Originality in Roman Poetry* (1968), 229–33 etc.

C. Witke (see above, under Poem 30).

J. Wohlberg, 'The structure of the Laodamia simile in Catullus 68', *CPh* 50 (1955), 42–6.

69

Rufus' lack of success with the ladies, a mystery to himself, is easily explained. The contrast between tone (grave, urbane) and subject is heightened by the somewhat ambiguous imagery of lines 5–9: C. is less concerned with helping Rufus than with exposing him to (good-natured?) ridicule.

Rufus appears to crop up again in Poem 71. We meet him also in Poem 77, under very different circumstances. Is he the Caelius Rufus whom Cicero defended, the man who succeeded C. as Clodia's lover? And is he the Caelius of Poem 58, and/or Poem 100? See Introduction.

With Poem 69 compare Poem 71.

1. *femina nulla*: *femina* makes the statement as general as possible, as in 64. 143 *nunc iam nulla uiro iuranti femina credat*; cf. 61. 84 *ne qua femina*.

2. *supposuisse*: practically = *supponere*. The only instance in C. of an archaism which is somewhat overworked in Augustan elegy when the form of the perfect infinitive is metrically convenient.

3. *non si illam rarae*: A plausible tidying up by Renaissance editors of the meaningless *nos illa mare* of V; *rarae*, 'thin' (and therefore expensive).

   labefactes: 'corrupt' (literally 'cause to totter'); said by *L & S* to be a favourite word with Cicero.

4. *perluciduli*: the diminutive forms a learned polysyllable found only here.

5. *quaedam mala fabula, qua . . . fertur . . .*: 'a particular unfortunate rumour, according to which . . .'.

6. *ualle*: the word is chosen for its appropriateness to *habitare*, rather than as the accepted anatomical term.

7. *hunc metuunt omnes*: goats stank of course (cf. Horace, *Carm.* 1. 17. 7); they were also proverbially lusty (Horace, *Ep.* 10. 23 *libidinosus caper*; cf. *Carm.* 3. 13. 3–5) — a fact which may contribute ironical overtones to the imagery here. Cf. 37. 5.

8. *quicum*: rare as feminine (also 66. 77).

   bella puella cubet: the phrase recurs at 78. 4.

9. *nasorum interfice pestem*: preserves the imagery of lines 6–8, 'despatch this destroyer of noses'; *pestis* of persons, is not uncommon, e.g. Cicero, *Sest.* 33 (of Clodius) *ab illa peste patriae*.

10. *cur fugiunt*: the indicative in indirect questions is archaic and colloquial; the subject is 7 *omnes*.

70

A poem deeply rooted in literary tradition (an epigram of
Callimachus provides the starting-point, the poem concludes with
a reminiscence of Sophocles; for other possible echoes see
LAURENS) and yet poignantly simple and direct in its statement
of personal feeling.

Poem 70 is the first of a series of fragments in which we see C.
struggling to win more complete awareness of what went wrong
between him and Lesbia by repeated, increasingly precise
formulation in verse; cf. Poems 72, 75 and 85. The fragments
form, as it were, snatches of conversation in a dramatic con-
tinuum — the circumstances, the order, sometimes even the
person addressed all beyond our recovery. Poem 73 begins a
fresh series. Compare the way in which the journey to Bithynia
forms a recurrent theme in Poems 1-60.

Is the juxtaposition of 69 and 70 fortuitous?

1-3. *dicit . . . dicit*: the repetition helps to evoke Callimachus,
Epigram XXV:

ὤμοσε Καλλίγνωτος Ἰωνίδι μήποτ' ἐκείνης
    ἕξειν μήτε φίλον κρέσσονα μήτε φίλην.
ὤμοσεν· ἀλλὰ λέγουσιν ἀληθέα τοὺς ἐν ἔρωτι
    ὅρκους μὴ δύνειν οὔατ' ἐς ἀθανάτων.
νῦν δ' ὁ μὲν ἀρσενικῷ θέρεται πυρὶ τῆς δὲ ταλαίνης
    νύμφης ὡς Μεγαρέων οὐ λόγος οὐδ' ἀριθμός.

But whereas Callimachus treats a conventional theme with a
light and ironic detachment, C. offers us a serious statement of his
own disillusionment in which every word, practically, hits home.
Note, too, that Callimachus' anecdote is set in the past; C. describes
a state of affairs which exists in the present: 'she keeps saying . . .'.

1. *nulli se . . . nubere malle*: 'there's nobody she wants to marry
more'; *nubere*: = 'to be married to', i.e. 'to *become* the wife of' — not
'to be the wife of'; the action of getting married, not the state of
marriage. If Lesbia was Clodia, the possibility of her marrying C.

after the death of Metellus early in 59 B.C. may well have been
raised by C. — and evaded by Clodia. The fact that *nubere* occurs
in colloquial or euphemistic contexts should not cause us to
suppose that C.'s tone is other than sober and serious.

mulier mea: Both the word *mulier* and the order (*mulier mea*,
rather than C.'s more usual *mea puella*) reinforce the impression
produced by the simple, unadorned diction and the measured
rhythm (a 3rd-foot caesura before *mulier*, a 4th-foot caesura
before *mea*) that C. is choosing his words with care; *mulier* also
prepares the way for *mulier* in line 3. Cf. 87. 1.

2. *Iuppiter*: cf. 72. 2 *nec prae me uelle tenere Iouem*.

3–4. An echo, probably, of Sophocles, Fragment 741 N (=811
Pearson): ὅρκον δ' ἐγὼ γυναικὸς εἰς ὕδωρ γράφω. Both the
sentiment and the image were no doubt proverbial; for the image
cf. Plato, *Phaedrus* 276c. C.'s language remains dignified and
restrained, the style almost elevated.

3. *dicit*: *sed mulier . . . quod dicit . . .*: 'that's what she says; but
what woman says . . .'. The repeated *dicit* picks up 1 *dicit*; *mulier*
picks up 1 *mulier*.

cupido: cf. 64. 374 and 107. 1, 4 and 5; the word is isolated
between a 3rd-foot and a 4th-foot caesura.

4. *uento*: see on 30. 10.

rapida: cf. 63. 16 *rapidum salum*.

See:

P. Laurens, 'A propos d'une image catullienne (c. 70. 4)',
    Latomus 24 (1965), 545–50.

Godo Lieberg, *Puella Divina* (1962) 264–75 (especially for
    parallels in Propertius, etc.).

Brooks Otis, *Virgil* (1963) 102–4 (on the 'dramatic continuum',
    and on metre and syntax).

71

An epigram, picking up the theme of 69, so that 3 *aemulus iste tuus* is presumably a rival of Rufus; he can hardly be a rival of C., since both rival and addressee are being got at. However, the final couplet cannot easily be felt to crown the preceding double hypothesis with the logical precision which the closely-reasoned structure of 1–4 appears to invite; 4 *a te* is often regarded as suspect, but no acceptable repair has been suggested.

1–3. i.e. 'that rival of yours suffers from both these disabilities, if anybody does!'

1. *iure bono*: = 2 *merito*; a remodelling, apparently, of the common *iure optimo*. [*uiro* V.]

sacer alarum . . . hircus: cf. 14. 12 *horribilem et sacrum libellum* (where *sacrum* = something like 'awful'). [The MSS have *sacrorum* and *sacratorum*, *sacer alarum* is due to the Renaissance editor Calfurnio, after 69. 6 *ualle sub alarum trux habitare caper*.]

obstitit: 'has spoiled his chances'.

2. *podagra*: the penultimate syllable counts as long here, but in line 6 it is short.

3. *qui uestrum exercet amorem*: 'who busies himself with your affair'; cf. 68. 69 *communes exerceremus amores*; *uestrum* = apparently *tuum et tuae puellae*.

4. 'It's extraordinary how he's caught *both* complaints from you.' The adverb *mirifice* occurs some 30 times in Cicero's letters; cf., e.g., *Fam*. 3. 1. 2 *mirifice ipse suo sermone subsecutus est humanitatem litterarum tuarum*; cf. 53. 2 and 84. 3. If the text is right, the rival's plight is spoken of as a twofold *malum* which he has caught from the addressee, as one catches a disease.

6. *affligit . . . perit*: possibly both words have erotic overtones.

72

C., with the restraint that is one form of contempt, tells his mistress that he despises her — but still cannot tear himself free. These four patiently argued couplets are remarkable no less for their clarity of insight than for their precise formulation of a lost ideal.

1–2. Did Lesbia say *solus me nouit Catullus*, or *solum ego noui Catullum*? Or are Baehrens, Benoist-Thomas and Kroll right in maintaining that *uelle* is to be 'supplied' from line 2, so that what Lesbia said was either *solum ego nosse Catullum uolo*, or *solum Catullum me nosse uolo*?

The matter is settled by the pentameter, which requires us to supply both *dicebas* and *te* from line 1. So that line 2 expanded becomes: *nec dicebas* [i.e. *negabas*] *te prae me uelle tenere Iouem*, where *te* is the accusative of the accusative and infinitive construction, not the object of *tenere*. It follows that *te*, since it is supplied from line 1, should have the same grammatical function there as in line 2. What Lesbia said, therefore, was *solum ego Catullum nosse uolo, nec prae Catullo tenere Iouem*. Hexameter and pentameter are interwoven: each depends on the other, neither line stands alone.

Poem 72, in other words, picks up Poem 70 (as the echo in the pentameter suggests); except that this time Lesbia is made to say, not merely that there's nobody she'd rather marry than C., but that she wanted only one man in her life (an allusion to the virtuous wife's traditional ambition to die *uniuira*, referred to in 111. 1–2). It is clear from 5 *nunc te cognoui* that the words represent her attempt, at an earlier stage in the liaison, to reassure C.: what was for C. an analysable ideal became on her lips a cliché.

1. *dicebas*: cf. 70. 1 and 3 (twice) *dicit*; what was present in Poem 70 is past in Poem 72; disillusionment has become resignation.

quondam: reinforces the notion of pastness; cf. 8. 1–8.

nosse: COPLEY holds that both *nosse* and *tenere* in line 2 are phrases which lie wholly in the physical sphere, but the parallels quoted by editors for a sexual meaning of *nosse* are all examples of the compound *cognoscere*.

2. *tenere*: cf. 64. 28–9 *tene Thetis tenuit pulcerrima Nereine? | tene suam Tethys concessit ducere neptem?*

3–4. An echo of 58. 2–3 *quam Catullus unam | plus quam se atque suos amauit omnes?*

3. *dilexi*: 'Catullus does not mean that he felt as a father feels,

qua father. He means only that his love had the same spiritual,
non-physical quality that a father's love possesses.' (COPLEY)
With *dilexi* cf. 6. 5 *diligis*, 76. 23 *diligat*, and 81. 2 *diligere*. See
also on 68. 119–24.

4. *generos*: at first sight, oddly specific. Does C. wish to exclude
the attraction of one sex for another in all its forms — *gnatos* in
common usage can include daughters, *generos* can scarcely include
daughters-in-law?

5–6. The couplet expresses in more fully analysed form the
thought of 85. 1 *odi et amo*.

5. *nunc te cognoui*: Again the expression one might use of a
respectable marriage (=almost 'now we are man and wife'):
cf. 61. 179–80 *bonae senibus uiris | cognitae bene feminae*, Ovid, *Her.*
6. 133, etc. But plainly a quite different emphasis falls this time on
te and the words are bitterly ambiguous, the context drawing out
equally the sense 'now I have found you out'; cf. 91. 3 *quod te
cognossem*; *nunc* picks up 1 *quondam*.

impensius: 'more earnestly'; cf. Cicero, *Fam.* 13. 64. 1 *nunc eo
facio id impensius, quod eius causam Nero suscepit.*

7. *qui potis est, inquis?*: cf. 85. 1 *quare id faciam, fortasse requiris?*
With *qui* cf. 24. 7 *qui?* and expressions such as *qui fit ut*; for *potis*
see on 65. 3.

amantem iniuria talis . . .: Note the collocation. Though
iniuria can of course be used of the infidelity of a mistress (so, e.g.,
Propertius 2. 24. 39), in this carefully phrased context it clearly
refers to the legally assertable right to redress of a husband. But
while normally husbands seek redress through divorce — they
only want to get rid of a wife who has proved unfaithful — a man
who is in love (*amantem*) feels differently.

8. *bene uelle*: 'be fond of'; cf. Plautus, *Truc.* 441 *egone illam ut non
amem? egone illi ut non bene uelim?*, *Trin.* 437–8 *quid agit filius? | bene
uolt tibi.* COPLEY, arguing that 'in the end, the expression is fumb-
ling', maintains that *bene uelle* 'expresses nothing more than a
rather vague feeling of good will, a sort of warm friendliness'. But
a conventional expression is often the most effective form of

understatement. Unlike Poem 85, which ends with the passionate *excrucior*, Poem 72 ends, as it began, on a note of dispassionate logical analysis, yet leaves us in no doubt about the effort it costs C. to preserve his pose of icy detachment.

See:

F. O. Copley, 'Emotional conflict and its significance in the Lesbia-poems of Catullus', *AJPh* 70 (1949), esp. 27–31.

J. T. Davis, *AJPh* 92 (1971) 196–201.

H. Akbar Khan, 'A note on the expression *solum . . . nosse* in Catullus', *CPh* 62 (1967), 34–6.

73

The first of a series of fragments (Poems 73, 76, 77) in a further dramatic continuum: 73 and 76 are linked by the leitmotive *ingratus* (73. 3, 76. 6 and 9); 73 and 77 by the theme of friendship betrayed. See also Poem 91. Is the faithless friend of 73. 5–6 Caelius Rufus, the addressee of 77? Or Gellius (see Poem 91)?

1. The feeling that we are entitled to be treated decently by those whom we have treated decently is very characteristic of Roman thinking: cf. Virgil, *A.* 4. 317 (Dido appeals to Aeneas) *si bene quid de te merui. . . .*

uelle: emphatic: 'stop *wanting* people to be grateful for things'.

2. ='stop thinking people can be made *pii*'; *pietas* = a man's recognition of his responsibilities to gods, relatives, friends, etc. — a less shallow concept than gratitude.

3. *omnia sunt ingrata*: i.e. one mustn't expect *any* recognition for right action. The concept which lies behind *gratus* and *ingratus* is wider than our gratitude: e.g. 64. 103 *non ingrata . . . munuscula diuis* (one wouldn't expect the gods to be grateful, in our sense of the word); cf. 68. 142. For *gratus* in C. see 2. 11, 68. 9, 96. 1, and especially 107. 2 and 3. Cf. Seneca, *Ben.* 2. 31 *beneficium qui dat uult excipi grate.*

4. *prodest*: [The conjecture of the Aldine editor Avanzi; the

MSS have *immo etiam taedet obestque magisque magis*, where *magisque* is a fairly obvious intruder.]

5. *mihi*: with 4 *obest*.

6. Many have criticized this heavily elided line. It is true that lines can be quoted from early Roman poets where heavy elision seems a symptom of slovenly or incompetent writing: e.g. the line of Caecilius Statius quoted by Cicero, *Sen.* 25 *sentire ea aetate eumpse esse odiosum alteri*; cf. Lucilius 728W *frigore inluuie inbalnitie inperfunditie incuria*. C., however, not uncommonly resorts to heavy elision when expressing intense personal feeling; e.g. 11. 19–20 *nullum amans uere, sed identidem omnium | ilia rumpens* (including the elision of the last syllable of *omnium*). The effect aimed at seems to be a harsh, slurred rush of words. See LEE.

See:

M. Owen Lee, 'Illustrative elisions in Catullus', *TAPhA* 93 (1962), 144–52.

74

The first appearance of Gellius. The charge is amplified and embroidered in Poems 88–90, and repeated in passing in Poem 91 (from which it appears that Gellius was also one of Lesbia's lovers); the theme of Poem 80 is somewhat different; Poem 116 claims that Gellius has not responded to C.'s efforts to bring about a reconciliation. He is usually identified as L. Gellius Poplicola (son of the consul of 72 B.C.), about whom, according to Valerius Maximus 5. 9. 1, there had been rumours of *in nouercam commissum stuprum*. There is some evidence that he belonged to the Clodian circle and was connected with the prosecution of Caelius in 56 B.C. through his mother (or stepmother) Polla; see Neudling 75–6. The uncle was perhaps the Gellius attacked by Cicero, *Sest.* 110–12, in 56 B.C. Cf. Poem 78.

1–2. A general proposition ('one's uncle is apt to make a fuss . . .'), ironically offered as the motive for Gellius' action.

Roman uncles are traditionally stern upholders of morality; see, e.g., Cicero, *Cael.* 25.

2. *delicias . . . faceret*: = 'talked about, or indulged in funny business'; see on 2. 1 *deliciae meae puellae*.

3. *perdepsuit*: Cicero, discussing indecent words and expressions, *Fam.* 9. 22. 4, links *depsit* with *battuit*, remarking that the former is *multo impudentius*: *atqui neutrum est obscenum* (i.e. both are euphemisms); *perdepsuit* (only here) implies Gellius made a proper job of it.

4. *Arpocratem*: an Egyptian sun-god, represented as a boy with a finger in his mouth; again 102. 4.

5. *irrumet*: = 'show his contempt for' but no doubt a hairraising pun is intended (see on 16. 1); *quamuis*, 'however much', rather than 'although'.

75

A striking example of epigram put to a serious purpose: instead of giving an ingenious twist to something essentially straightforward, the lines analyse a complex situation not easily sorted out into words. A single sentence, spread over 4 hard-hitting, ruthlessly clear-sighted lines, bitter rather than vindictive.

1–2. *tua . . . culpa . . . officio . . . suo*: Syntactical parallelism and chiasmus achieve a perfect formulation of the opening 'you let me down, I played my part properly', in preparation for the tightly packed, hard-hitting antithesis of 3–4.

1. *mea*: with *mens* (as here printed), rather than with *Lesbia* (despite 87. 2 *Lesbia mea*).

tua . . . culpa: almost = 'by your infidelity'; *culpa* often serves as a euphemism for *furtiuus amor*, as in 68. 138–9 *saepe etiam Iuno, | maxima caelicolum, | coniugis in culpa flagrantem concoquit iram*; cf. Virgil, *A.* 4. 19 *huic uni forsan potui succumbere culpae*, and *A.* 4. 172 *hoc praetexit nomine culpam*. Here, no doubt, the sense is less specific. None the less (as in 11. 22, probably) C. is less concerned with pinning the blame on Lesbia, or claiming it was 'all her fault',

P

than with stating the consequences for himself of her faithlessness. See on 2 *ipsa suo*.

2. *perdidit*: 'destroyed' — a strong word.

ipsa suo: emphasizes that C. does not really blame Lesbia; his present anguish is the result of his own attitude of mind to her; it is almost an admission in retrospect that he should have known better.

3–4. *optima fias | . . . omnia . . . facias*: a bitter jingle, like 85. 1–2 *faciam . . . fieri*.

3. *bene uelle*: see on 72. 8.

See:

F. O. Copley, 'Emotional conflict and its significance in the Lesbia-poems of Catullus', *AJPh* 70 (1949), 31–3.

76

Apart from 65–8 the longest of the elegiac poems (next comes Poem 99 — 16 lines), and regarded by many as the prototype of Latin love elegy. The doggedly rational tone, the self-centred melancholy certainly foreshadow one of the characteristic moods of love elegy.

Poem 76 is not a final dismissal like 11 — there is too much indignant protest, too much talk of shattered illusions; the thing still rankles too much for dismissal, even for clear analysis.

Structure: 8 + 8 + 6 + 4. In the first and third sections, feeling is kept under control, the syntax is flowing and elaborate; in the second and last sections, feeling threatens to get out of control and the syntax becomes jerky.

1–8 — C. reassures himself: you will have the consolation that you did all you could. 9–16 — if it has been in vain, you must come to grips with reality, and shake yourself free. 17–22 — prayer to the gods for help. 23–6 — the prayer made explicit: all I want is to be free.

Close comparison with Poem 8 is instructive (see on 11–12);

note too the verbal echoes of Poems 51 (see on 19–22), 72 (see
on 23 *contra me ut diligat illa*), 73 (see on 1 *benefacta*, 2 *pium*, 6
ingrato, and 7–8), 77 (see on 20 *eripite* and *pestem perniciemque*, and
21 *subrepens*), 85 (see on 10 *excrucies* and 16 *facias*), 87 and 109 (see
on 3 *foedere* and 17–26). (Cf. also Poems 70, 104 and 107.) If at
each echo we ask, 'Does this sound like a conscious echo (a cross-
reference)?', usually we feel we want to answer, 'Yes'; if we ask,
'Which in that case must come first?', nearly always we feel we
must answer, 'Not Poem 76'.

1–8. Structure: lines 1–2, basic hypothesis; 3–4, the hypothesis
re-phrased in negative form; 5–6, conclusion; 7–8, reason for
reaching this conclusion. Lines 1–6 form a slow deliberate
prelude to the theme of 7–8 ('you have done all you could'),
upon which the remainder of the poem is built. The tone of 1–6
seems one of bitter self-righteousness — C., i.e., pins his hopes,
not without a hint of conscious irony (in 5–6), on a belief in an
ultimately just world (contrast the flat contradiction of Poem 73).

1. *benefacta*: contrast 73. 3–4 *nihil fecisse benigne | prodest*.

2. *pium*: cf. 26 *pro pietate mea*; contrast 73. 1–2 *desine aliquem
fieri posse putare pium*.

3–4. C. overstates his case — this is no way for a man to talk
because the course of *furtiuus amor* has not run smooth, however
high his hopes. But the poem is, like Poem 8, an interior mono-
logue (or a work of art purporting to be that), not the poet's
apologia to the reader: we are *intended* to feel that C. has lost his
sense of proportion.

3. *fidem . . . foedere*: cf. 87. 3 *nulla fides ullo fuit umquam foedere
tanta*; 109. 6 *aeternum hoc sanctae foedus amicitiae*. The key words
have here a more general sense, but they are perhaps chosen all
the same with an eye to the echoes of other poems which they will
evoke. For *foedus*, of the marriage-bond, see 64. 335 and 373. For
the double negative *nec foedere nullo* (a colloquialism) cf. 48. 4.
With the idea contrast Poem 70. [Some read *nec foedere in ullo*.]

5. *in longa aetate*: 'in the long years to come'.

Catulle: for the device of self-address see on 8. 1.

6. *ingrato*: cf. 9 *omnia quae ingratae perierunt credita menti*. Note the echoes of 73. 3 *omnia sunt ingrata*.

gaudia: alongside *amore*, the word suggests undercurrents of irony.

7–8. Almost pedantically precise in its wording (*dicta* picks up *dicere*, *facta* picks up *facere*). An echo of the theme of Poem 73, but addressed by C. to himself.

7. *cuiquam*: 'anyone at all'.

9. *omnia quae*: also 64. 66.

credita: not, e.g., *data* or *impertita*: C. expected some response to his affection, but got none — his mistress was not the kind of person who could respond. C. expresses this difficult concept in terms of a bad investment (*credita* — the characteristic Roman *do ut des*) which has proved a total loss (*perierunt*); the words perhaps also suggest a crop sown on unfertile ground (Martial 10. 47. 4 speaks of *non ingratus ager*); cf. 65. 17 *nequiquam credita uentis* ('entrusted to', 'placed in the care of').

10. *cur te iam amplius*: Many regard the hiatus after *iam* as intolerable, especially as *iam* is elided in lines 18 and 23. The traditional repair is *quare iam te cur*. But given the staccato rhythm of the first half of the line, the hiatus is perhaps better taken as deliberate. (Hiatus at the principal caesura in the pentameter is usually eliminated by editors at 67. 44, 97. 2 and 99. 8, and only left at 68. 158 because of the corrupt state of the preceding hexameter.) [Baehrens suggested *tete* (cf. 101. 5).]

excrucies: cf. 85. 2 *excrucior*.

11–12. Cf. 8. 10–11 *nec miser uiue, obdura* (also 8. 12 *obdurat* and 19 *obdura*); *offirmas*, like *obdura*, is intransitive.

11. *atque . . . teque*: clumsy, even if *istinc teque reducis* (=*istincque te reducis*) can be regarded as correlative with 12 *et . . . miser*; see on 57. 2. [Ellis's *te ipse* is tempting.]

12. *dis inuitis*: the gods, i.e., cannot wish such unhappiness.

miser: see on 8. 1; cf. 19 *miserum*.

13. Better taken as a question.

longum subito: an emphatic collocation.

14. *hoc qualubet efficias*: 'this you must somehow manage'; with *qualubet* cf. 40. 6; notice the anaphora 14 *hoc* . . . 15 *haec* . . . *hoc* . . . 16 *hoc*.

15. *una salus haec est*: the usual attraction of the demonstrative; cf. Virgil, *A.* 4. 347 *hic amor, haec patria est*.

peruincendum: The polysyllable and spondaic ending stress the effort that must be made. For the spondaic 5th foot see on 64. 3.

16. *facias*: picks up 14 *efficias* (see on 10. 20); cf. 85. 1 *quare id aciam* .

pote: see on 17. 24; cf. 24 *potis*. Note the order.

17–26. A more solemn prayer than in 109. 3–4.

17–20. Structure: 17–18 *si*-clauses; 19 imperative *aspicite*; 19 *si*-clause; 20 imperative *eripite*. As in line 1, no real doubt is implied by *si* (= 'if, as is the case').

18. Should assert that C. is himself at the extremity of despair, though the reading is doubtful. [*extremo* V, corrected to *extrema* and *extremam*.]

19–21. Note the reminiscences in these lines of 51. 5–10:

misero quod omnis

eripit sensus mihi: nam simul te,

Lesbia, *aspexi*, nihil est super mi

.   .   .

lingua sed *torpet*, tenuis *sub artus*

flamma demanat. . . .

19. *miserum*: cf. 12 *miser*.

puriter: archaic, as in 39. 14. C. claims strict adherence to a personal ideal, though it could hardly be said that by the standards of the conventional morality of his time his life had been *puriter acta*. The self-righteous note troubles the modern reader. Is C. still too close to things to have regained his sense of proportion? Or does he draw too uncritically upon the clichés of tragic rhetoric?

20. *eripite*: An echo of 77. 4 *eripuisti* (as well as 51. 6 *eripit* and 82. 3 *eripere ei noli*)? The word may be used quite generally of

saving a person from danger, the danger usually expressed by an ablatival phrase — *eripere aliquem e periculo*, etc.; but also of such actions as tearing out a person's eyes (Terence, *Ad.* 318 *adulescenti ipsi eriperes oculos*). Perhaps some idea of surgical intervention is present here, as in Propertius 1. 1. 26–7 *quaerite non sani pectoris auxilia: | fortiter et ferrum saeuos patiemur et ignis.*

pestem perniciemque: The repetition for the sake of alliteration, but also a hendiadys, 'destructive disease' (25 *morbum*); C. means of course his infatuation, as 21–2 make clear. Contrast 77. 6 *nostrae pestis amicitiae.*

21–2. By speaking of his infatuation as a disease which has pervaded his body, C. is able to suggest that the disease has in fact driven all happiness from his *pectus*; the statement is helped by the ambiguity of *pectore*: (1) the trunk; (2) the site of the *animus*, and the seat of the emotions.

21. *subrepens*: cf. 77. 3 *subrepsti.*

22. *laetitias*: = 'all forms of happiness'.

23. *contra me ut diligat illa*: 'that *she* should feel affection for *me*'. An echo perhaps of 72. 3–4 *dilexi tum te | pater ut gnatos diligit et generos.*

24. *quod non potis est*: impersonal, rather than personal; cf. 16 *siue id non pote siue pote*. For the form *potis* see on 65. 3.

pudica: did C. ever expect this?

26. *pietate*: picks up 2 *pium.*

See:

Steele Commager, 'Notes on some poems of Catullus', *HSPh* 70 (1965), 95–8.

R. Fries, *Agon* 1 (1968) 39–58.

H. A. Kahn, *Athenaeum* 46 (1968) 54–71.

L. A. Moritz, *G & R* 15 (1968) 53–8.

77

These lines are remarkable in two ways: First, for their tortured violence of expression. C.'s outbursts are usually more firmly controlled, or more assured in their contempt; cf. Poems 58 and 73;

yet the style of 77 seems more consciously literary than that of 73;
even in Poem 76 the mood is closer to cynicism and disillusion-
ment than to anguish; cf. Poems 30 and 60. Second, for the verbal
echoes in lines 3–6 of 76. 20–5 — the more remarkable if, as most
assume, similar imagery expresses a different idea.

For Rufus see on Poem 69. Of the four poems possibly ad-
dressed to Clodia's lover (not counting, i.e., Poem 71), this is the
only one in which C. speaks of betrayal.

1. *mihi . . . credite amice*: Possibly 'believed my friend', as in
Ovid, *Fast.* 2. 176 *quae fuerat uirgo credita, mater erat*; in that case,
mihi attaches itself primarily to *amice*. Possibly 'the friend whom I
believed', as in Virgil, *A.* 2. 247 *non umquam credita Teucris*; in that
case, *mihi* attaches itself primarily to *credite* (dative of agent). But
analysis is artificial — both ideas are implicit in C.'s words. The
appositional expansion of a vocative (instead e.g. of a relative
clause) belongs to the high style; cf. 64. 215–17, 68. 92, 101. 6.

frustra ac nequiquam: the repetition mainly for emphasis and
weight; *nequiquam* is the more 'poetic' word (Virgil is fond of it);
frustra is much commoner in Cicero's letters.

2. *immo*: cf. Cicero, *Catil.* 1. 1. 2 *hic tamen uiuit. uiuit? immo uero
etiam in Senatum uenit*, etc.

3. *sicine*: also 64. 132 and 134.

subrepsti: echoes 76. 21 *subrepens*; an uncommon, 'poetic'
word (Horace, *S.* 2. 6. 100, is a pastiche of epic style); for the
contracted perfect see on 14. 14.

intestina perurens: These words make it clear that *subrepsti* (like
subrepens in 76. 21) is used to suggest the insidious onset of a
slowly debilitating disease. It is still not clear how a false friend
can be said *intestina perurere*, if C. is, as most assume, accusing
Rufus of the theft of his mistress. The words make better sense if
they can be taken to mean that Rufus somehow misused his influ-
ence over C. to destroy his friend's happiness (cf. 5–6 *nostrae
crudele uenenum* | *uitae*) by reducing him to inert despair.

4. *ei misero*: cf. 68. 92–3 *ei misero frater adempte mihi*, | *ei misero
fratri iucundum lumen ademptum*.

eripuisti omnia nostra bona: Usually taken to mean 'you have stolen Lesbia from me' (*omnia nostra bona*, 'all I possess', in the sense of 'all I treasure'). But the meaning of *eripuisti* may be closer to 76. 20 *eripite* and (probably) 82. 3 *eripere ei noli*; cf. 51. 5–6 *misero quod omnis | eripit sensus mihi*. In that case, something like 'you have deprived me of everything I had in life'. See on Poem 82.

5. *eripuisti*: the repetition for pathetic effect.

5–6. *nostrae crudele uenenum | uitae*: = probably 'you have cruelly poisoned my life', continuing the imagery of 3 *intestina perurens*. But we should perhaps remember that for C. *uita* becomes synonymous with Lesbia (in 104. 1 and 109. 1 *mea uita* = Lesbia).

6. *nostrae pestis amicitiae*: (1) continues the imagery of *intestina perurens* and *uenenum* (cf. 76. 20 *pestem*); (2) but *pestis* can denote anything that destroys (cf. 69. 9 *nasorum interfice pestem*) — it is used by Virgil, e.g., of the fire which destroyed part of the Trojan fleet, *A.* 5. 699; its use of persons is not uncommon. One is tempted to accord *amicitiae* the meaning it has in 109. 6, despite the echo of 1 *amice*.

                                   78

Three syntactically self-contained couplets, each beginning with a simple positive proposition in which the victim's name forms the opening word (1 *Gallus habet fratres*; 3 *Gallus homo est bellus*; 5 *Gallus homo est stultus*).

The first couplet provides the basic data. The second and third couplets state and prove contradictory assessments of this would-be smart Alec. Gallus is unidentifiable, except perhaps as the brother of Gellius' unfortunate uncle in Poem 74.

1. *lepidissima*: *lepidus* = 'smart', with all the connotations of that word. Cf. 10. 4 *non sane illepidum* (of Varus' girl-friend); 6. 2 *illepidae* (Flavius' girl-friend can't be that); 6. 17 *lepido uersu* (of a poem C. proposes to write); 1. 1 *lepidum nouum libellum* (of C.'s new book of poems); 36. 10 *lepide* (of Lesbia's vow); 36. 17 *illepidum* (of C.'s counter-proposal).

2. *alterius . . . alterius*: a pentameter beginning and ending with what would normally be a throw-away word.

3. *homo . . . bellus*: see on 3. 14 and 22. 9.

   dulces iungit amores: 'arranges a pleasant love-match'. Cf. 64. 372 *optatos animi coniungite amores*; Tibullus 1. 1. 69 *dum fata sinunt, iungamus amores*.

4. *cum puero ut bello bella puella cubet*: = 'sends pretty girl to bed with pretty boy'; cf. 69. 8 — Rufus is not the sort of man, *quicum bella puella cubet*. An improvement on Plautus, *Bacch.* 81 *ut lepidus cum lepida accubet*. Note the elegant chiastic arrangement round the caesura. Note too how 3 *Gallus homo est bellus* implies that all three enter into the spirit of what they regard as an elegant demonstration of their independence of conventional morality.

5. *Gallus homo est stultus*: The final word in what is otherwise a repetition of the first half of line 3 pricks the bubble: Gallus is a fool — one doesn't put a nephew up to such pranks when one has a wife oneself. Cf. 17. 12 *insulsissimus est homo*.

6. *patruus patrui*: The fact that uncles figure in Roman literature as stern upholders of morality (see on 74. 1) adds of course to the fun.

78b

An isolated fragment? Or do these lines belong after 80. 8, as Bergk suggested? [As usual the MSS are no help: in O, e.g., 77–9 are run together.] The poem perhaps began with an unreal condition. Cf. 21. 9–10, where the hypothesis *atque id si faceres satur, tacerem* is followed by *nunc ipsum id doleo, quod. . . .* Attempts have also been made to attach the lines to Poems 77, 91 etc.

2. *suauia*: 'lips' (*L & S* I).

   comminxit: [*connuxit* O; *coniunxit* X; *comminxit* Scaliger, on the basis of 99. 10 *commictae spurca saliua lupae*; cf. 67. 30 *minxerit*.]

3. *uerum id non impune feres*: cf. 99. 3 *uerum id non impune tuli*.

4. *fama loquetur anus*: cf. 68. 46 *haec carta loquatur anus*; 95. 6 *cana diu saecula peruoluent*.

79

The pun in line 1 makes it tolerably certain that the victim of this lampoon is Clodia's infamous brother, P. Clodius Pulcer, for whom, if Cicero's repeated insinuations are to be taken seriously, she had a more than sisterly affection (*Cael.* 32, 36 and 78; *Pis.* 28; *Sest.* 16, etc.).

Was the identity, then, of Lesbia no longer a secret? Or was the purpose of these lines to put the pseudonym in a context that left no doubt who Lesbia was?

1. *Lesbius est pulcer. quid ni?*: cf. 89. 1 *Gellius est tenuis: quid ni?* A pun on Clodius' *cognomen* (traditional in the Claudian *gens*): 'Lesbius is handsome' and 'Lesbius is a Pulcer'; the following relative clause is offered as a proof of either statement. The same pun in Cicero, *Att.* 1. 16. 10 *surgit pulchellus puer*, 'up gets Pretty boy'; cf. *Att.* 2. 1. 4. *quid ni?* = 'of course'; equivalent to *quippe*.

quem . . . malit: best taken as potential: 'she'd rather have him . . .'.

2. *cum tota gente . . . tua*: picks up the opening pun, suggesting (ironically) that Lesbia's preference is based (*quid ni?*) on grounds of family.

3–4. If the opening couplet ironically compliments Lesbia (she puts her brother first), the point of the second couplet seems to be that her brother is a man who would stop at nothing.

3. *sed tamen hic pulcer*: the pun repeated.

uendat: apparently 'would put up for sale as slaves'—i.e. sell what was not his to sell, in order to get what he wanted.

cum gente Catullum: C. is fond of reiteration (the repetition of a whole phrase) for rhythmical or incantatory effect: the object seems more often to contribute to the intensity of feeling in a statement, than to support a logical argument; cf. 8. 3 and 8, 103. 2 and 4, and especially Poem 82.

4. *tria notorum suauia*: *tria* indicates a trivial number (*L & S* II); *tria notorum suauia*, isn't anything particularly worth having — close

friends commonly greeted one another with a kiss (cf. 9. 9 *iucundum os oculosque suauiabor*). But Lesbius is the man to commit a major crime, just to get a few friendly greetings. It is not hard to feel all sorts of *innuendo* implied. [*notorum* O; some adopt *natorum*, the reading of G, supposing a reference to the *ius trium liberorum* and an implication that Lesbius was impotent.]

80

Gellius again (see on Poem 74), in a mock-lyric, obscene version of the theme of Poem 6.

1–2. The sham lyricism of the opening couplet is undercut by the concluding line of the poem.

3–4. *quiete e molli*: i.e. after your siesta; cf. 32. 3 and 61. 110–12, and Ovid's famous siesta poem, *Am*. 1. 5. The turn of phrase, however, belongs to the high style: cf. 63. 38 *in quiete molli*, 63. 44 *de quiete molli*.

4. *longo . . . die*: i.e. in summer, when the daylight hours are longer.

5–6. *an uere . . . uiri?*: sham high style. For *nesciŏ* see on 6. 16.

7. *clamant*: cf. 6. 7.

Victoris: unidentifiable; the diminutive *miselli* is ironic.

7–8. *rupta . . . ilia*: cf. 11. 20 *ilia rumpens*.

8. *emulso*: cf. 68. 110 *emulsa palude*.

labra: contrast the diminutive *labella* in line 1. Do 78b. 1–4 belong here, as Bergk suggested?

81

Like Poem 24, a protest addressed to Juventius: does it have to be a man like that? For Juventius (also Poems 48 and 99) see on Poem 24.

2. *bellus homo*: cf. 24. 7 *homo bellus*; for the phrase see on 22. 9.

diligere inciperes: 'form an attachment'; for *diligere*, see on 72. 3.

3. *praeter quam*: for the construction cf. Cicero, *Att.* 5. 21. 5 *nec in quemquam meorum praeter quam in L. Tullium legatum.*

iste tuus: for the combination, see on 17. 21; cf. 71. 3 *aemulus iste tuus.*

moribunda ab sede Pisauri: The periphrasis, which suggests the high style (cf. Virgil, *A.* 3. 687 *angusta ab sede Pelori*), is undercut by its 'stock' epithet: Pisaurum (an Umbrian town on the Adriatic) has had its day.

4. *hospes*: a visitor to Rome, apparently, not a resident.

inaurata pallidior statua: again ostensibly the high style, but hardly complimentary to Juventius' friend from the country.

5. *cordi est*: cf. 44. 2–3, 64. 158, 95b. 1.

praeponere: cf. 47. 4 *praeposuit.*

6. *nescis quod facinus facias*: 'you know not what you do'; the echo of some such colloquialism as *nescio quid mali facis*, 'there is something not nice about what you are doing', is probably intentional, to take the edge off C.'s reproach. [The reading of V was *quid*.]

82

Two interpretations are possible. If we take 3 *eripere* like 77. 4 and 5 *eripuisti*, we have, probably, a poem entreating Quintius not to steal Lesbia (presuming it is Lesbia who is meant) from C. If we give *eripere* the sense 'extirpate', as in 76. 20 *eripite*, we have, probably, a poem entreating Quintius not to interfere between C. and Lesbia. Quintius also in Poem 100; he is perhaps the brother of the Quintia of Poem 86.

1. *tibi oculos debere*: = 'owe life itself to you'; cf. 3. 5, 14. 1, 104. 2. The colloquialism forms the basis of the epigram.

2. *aut aliud si quid*: = *aut si quid aliud*; cf. 13. 10, 22. 13, 23. 13, 42. 14.

3. *eripere*: perhaps 'snatch away', i.e. 'steal'; but the context favours the sense 'extirpate', i.e. 'free from'; C. pleads in other words with Quintius not to intervene to free him from a mistress whom Quintius considers harmful to his friend—a thing to be wrenched away like a diseased growth. But C. would rather have his eyes gouged out than have Lesbia torn from him. For *eripere* in C. see on 77. 4.

ei: one syllable. The forms *eius* (84. 5) and *ei* are uncommon in verse.

illi: like *ei*, = *Catullo*. The change from *is* in the principal clause to *ille* in a subordinate clause is not uncommon.

4. *seu quid*: = *uel si quid*, as in 13. 10. The effect of the repetition is as though C. has asked himself if he really meant what he had said, had decided he did, and repeated the statement. One feels the second pentameter should be read more deliberately than the first.

See:

Cat. Rev. 41–2.

83

For some reason, Lesbia is annoyed with C., and takes it out on him in front of her husband. If Lesbia was Clodia, these lines should date from some time earlier than the death of Metellus Celer (died about March 59 B.C.). Has the affair begun and is this a lovers' tiff? Or are the two sparring with one another before taking the irrevocable step? For the theme that Lesbia's abuse of C. means she loves him, cf. Poem 92. The structure resembles that of Poem 78: succinct statement of the basic data, followed by assessment of the situation. Interesting echoes of Poem 17.

1. *mi ... mala plurima dicit*: 'roundly abuses me'. The way in which she does it is defined in line 4.

praesente uiro: i.e., all three actors are present in this little drama—Lesbia isn't just abusing C. behind his back.

2. *laetitia*: the husband, i.e., finds Lesbia's abuse of C. re-assuring, as well as a great joke.

3. *mule*: cf. 17. 26.

nihil sentis?: 'have you no perception?'; cf. 17. 20 *tantundem omnia sentiens quam si nulla sit usquam*.

nostri oblita: 'with no thought for what's between us'; geni-tive of respect; less likely that *nostri* is plural for singular.

4. *sana*: i.e., unwounded by love; cf. Virgil, *A.* 4. 8 *male sana*, and contrast 41. 7.

quod gannit: 'as for her snarling'; with this use of *quod*, cf. 68. 1 etc.

obloquitur: 'interrupt', rather than 'abuse'; *gannit* and *obloquitur* taken together mean that Lesbia (1) keeps biting C.'s head off; (2) won't let him get a word in edgeways.

5. *meminit*: sc. *nostri*: i.e., 'she can't keep us out of her thoughts'.

acrior: i.e., what sharpens her tongue more than the incident itself is that she's angry about it.

6. *hoc est*: = 'which shows'.

uritur et loquitur: Those who take *obloquitur* to mean 'abuse' find the repetition *loquitur* weak. But C. means that Lesbia, in-stead of brooding or letting the men talk, keeps talking herself; for the idiomatic repetition of a compound verb in its simple form, see on 10. 20. [Many (including Kroll) have been tempted to read *coquitur*, but this simply repeats *uritur*.] The parataxis *uritur et loquitur* represents a common way of formulating a logically drawn conclusion: 'she burns ... and (therefore) she talks'. Propertius devotes an elegy (3. 8) to the theme that an angry tongue is a proof of love.

See:

J. W. Zarker, *CJ* 64 (1969) 172–7.

84

Arrius and his aitches have given rise to much speculation. Is Arrius a kind of Roman Cockney who has mastered the aitch-sound, but isn't sure where it is called for, and takes no chances?

Or are his mispronunciations, as some maintain, a dialectal peculiarity—Etruscan or Venetic? Those who seek support for the latter view in lines 5–6 are on precarious ground: *credo* is just as likely to be ironical. On the whole, the text offers better support for the former view: (1) Arrius' aitches cost him conscious effort (line 4); (2) he is obviously (even fatuously) pleased with the result (line 3). But, to be worthy of an epigram, Arrius should be more than an innocent, if over-zealous, semi-literate. He might of course be a personal enemy, but the lines offer no evidence of that.

The mispronunciations quoted seem to provide a valid clue: *commoda* and *insidiae* are common words, but hardly words one would pick out from a man's ordinary conversation to make the point C. is making; on the other hand, both are words that naturally come to the lips of an orator (both occur frequently, e.g., in the speeches of Cicero). The suspicion that Arrius' forensic style is being got at seems supported by lines 3–4, and perhaps by 7 *requierant omnibus aures* also. Moreover, a suitable candidate is available, the self-made orator Q. Arrius, referred to by Cicero, *Brut.* 242–3, as a stooge (*secundarius*) of Crassus (see Neudling for details and the view that there were two Q. Arrii). Rather less likely is Cicero's boring neighbour at Formiae (*Att.* 2. 14. 2 and 2. 15. 3). Whoever the man, he was not in Rome when Poem 84 was written, having been sent some time previously to Syria (line 7)—perhaps with Crassus in 55 B.C.

For a full discussion of the aitch-question, see Fordyce.

Structure: Arrius' mispronunciations provide the first and the last words in the poem, and the last word of the first and second couplets.

1–4. Note the stress laid on the fact that Arrius, though once a familiar feature of the Roman scene (imperfects *dicebat*, *sperabat*; frequentatives *si quando . . . uellet*, *cum . . . dixerat*), is so no longer; cf. 7 *requierant omnibus aures*.

1. *chommoda*: For the contemporary fashion for aspirating consonants in the Greek manner, even in words of Latin origin

(*lachrimae*, *sepulchrum*, *pulcher* etc., also words like *triumphus* and *Otho*), see Cicero, *Orat.* 160, and Quintilian 1. 5. 20 (who refers to *Catulli nobile epigramma*).

si quando . . . uellet: the subjunctive in frequentative clauses, normal in Silver Age Latin, is occasionally found in Republican Latin; cf. 63. 67 *linquendum ubi esset*; contrast 4 *cum . . . dixerat*.

3. *mirifice*: see on 71. 4.

5–6. Note that only Arrius' mother and her family (her brother and parents) are mentioned. Apart from the obvious inferences to be drawn about Arrius' father, C. may have in mind that women tend to preserve older and purer ways of speaking. Cicero remarked on the fact about this time (*de Orat.* 3. 45, published about 55 B.C.): *facilius enim mulieres incorruptam antiquitatem conseruant, quod multorum sermonis expertes ea tenent semper quae prima didicerunt*. The joke lies (unless we take 5–6 seriously—see introductory note) in pretending that Arrius' family (or such of it as could be pointed to) had always spoken in this eccentric fashion.

5. *liber*: Arrius' maternal uncle apparently passed for free-born —hardly likely unless his sister was also free and their parents at any rate *libertini*. Which is presumably the point C. wishes to make (though many have held that the text is corrupt).

eius: the forms *eius* and *ei* (82. 3) are uncommon in verse.

8. *audibant*: =*audiebant*; cf. 64. 319 *custodibant*, 68. 85 *scibant*. The subject is *omnes*, understood from the dative *omnibus*.

eadem haec: the words *commoda* and *insidiae*.

leuiter: the Greek symbol which denoted an absence of an initial aitch was called *spiritus leuis* by the Romans (opposite: *spiritus asper*).

10. *cum subito affertur nuntius horribilis*: The inverted *cum* construction helps the climax and reinforces the mock-heroic tone (cf. the messengers' speeches in Greek tragedy); *horribilis* = simply 'fearful', 'dreadful', but the sound of the word and the connexion with *horreo* suggest in this context the overtones 'rough', 'bristly'—a sort of transference from Arrius' pronunciation of *Ionios* to the news of it; *affertur* is historic present.

12. *Hionios*: It would be pleasant if a suitably hair-raising pun could be discovered in the final word of the epigram. For some attempts see Fordyce. The most convincing is that *Hionios* = χιονέους — i.e. Arrius' blast of aspirates has inflicted a chill upon the Ionian. See EINARSON.

See:

B. Einarson, 'On Catullus 84', *CPh* 61 (1966), 187–8.
E. S. Ramage, 'Note on Catullus' Arrius', *CPh* 54 (1959), 44–5.

85

A couplet which is justly famous. It easily stands on its own feet as a 2-line fragment. But in the context of the persistent, probing analysis which began with Poem 70, to be doggedly resumed again and again till Poem 109, the impact of Poem 85 is even greater, for it represents the poet's admission that there is a point beyond which logical analysis cannot advance, or help. How can one both love and loathe? It is not something you do; it is something that happens to you. And it hurts.

That love can turn to hate is common knowledge. That one can both loathe a woman and still be drawn to her is a commonplace of literature (see, e.g., the parallels in Kroll and WEINREICH 49–70), though no poet before C. brought to bear on it the acuity of introspective analysis we find in Poems 72 and 75. Kroll remarks, 'die Kraft und Prägnanz des Ausdrucks zeigen, dass seine Stimmung echt ist'. Perhaps we should do better to say what we can see to be genuine is C.'s talent as a poet, rather than the emotion which produced the poem. We must not make C. too childlike and innocent. The *donna fatale* was certainly a familiar phenomenon. Likely enough C. entered into his liaison with Clodia with his eyes open. It hurt when she threw him over, but he must have expected it. The problem, however, of stating how he felt in simple, telling, poetic language with a convincing, personal ring was fresh enough to become obsessive.

1. *odi et amo*: It is the emotions and the fact that he feels both together that matter; a direct object is irrelevant. Note how word order and elision transfer the emphasis to *amo*: the hating is taken for granted, what motivates the poem is that C. cannot resist the attraction of the woman he despises.

   quare id faciam, fortasse requiris?: A question put as simply as it could be put. But (1) asking a question gets the poem going (see on 7. 1); (2) *faciam*, while it stands for *oderim et amem*, prepares the way for *fieri sentio* and the distinction between doing and feeling the thing happen to you (as if love were independent of the will; cf. 8. 6 *fiebant*). The question and answer perhaps owe something to Philodemus, *AP* 5. 131; cf. 104. 1–2.

2. *nescio*: the final o is short. See on 6. 16.

   fieri sentio: cf. 75. 3–4 *optima fias . . . omnia facias*.

   excrucior: The word is common in prose and verse from Plautus onwards. C.'s procedure seems the opposite here to that in Poem 46: not the unusual, precise word, but the well-worn dramatic word, revitalized by the prominent place given to it. Cf. 76. 10 *excrucies* and 99. 12 *excruciare*; 66. 76 *discrucior*.

See:

J. D. Bishop, *Latomus* 30 (1971) 633–42.

Steele Commager, 'Notes on some poems of Catullus', *HSPh* 70 (1965), esp. 92–4.

Otto Weinreich, *Die Distichen des Catull* (1926) 32–83.

86

What does a woman need before you can call her 'beautiful'? More than good looks, as a comparison of Quintia with Lesbia makes plain.

C. and his friends had little use for dumb blondes: they expected their *scortilla* to appreciate and match their own *urbanitas*, as Poem 10 shows; Lesbia, if she was Clodia, can have had little difficulty in measuring up to the standard imposed — Poems 5, 7 and 51 must otherwise be regarded as exercises in self-deception.

This was not the common view, however. These elegant, lucid lines give succinct, cogent expression to a *prise de position*. Quintia is unidentifiable, unless perhaps as the sister of the Quintius of Poems 82 and 100.

Structure: Three couplets, each complete in itself, each containing the key word *formosa* (cf. the repetition of *puella* in Poem 41, of *Gallus* in Poem 78, of *nulla* in Poem 87).

1. *formosa*: C. uses the word only in this poem, and in line 3 he places it, as it were, in quotation marks. Though *formosus* originally meant no more than 'shapely' and is applied by C.'s contemporaries to such mundane objects as farm animals and geometrical shapes, it becomes after C. one of the hard-worked words in the love poet's vocabulary, normally implying warm approval. The word occurs only once in Plautus (*Merc.* 229), of a (symbolic) goat, and only once (*Eun.* 730) in Terence, of a man. See Varro, *Men.* 432, quoted on 1–2 *candida, longa, recta*.

multis: 'in the eyes of many'; dative of the person interested.

1–2. *candida, longa, recta*: 'fair-complexioned, tall, holds herself straight'. For *candida* see on 13. 4; with *recta* cf. 10. 20. For the ideal implied (the Junoesque blonde) see *Latin Explorations* 66–7 — was Clodia called βοῶπις because she was the Juno type? Cf. Varro, *Men.* 432 *amiculam . . . proceram, candidam, teneram, formosam*, and Horace, *S.* 1. 2. 123–4 (an ironical echo of C.?) *candida rectaque sit, munda hactenus ut neque longa / nec magis alba uelit quam dat natura uideri*. Perhaps Cicero, *Cael.* 36 (*uicinum adulescentulum aspexisti: candor huius te et proceritas pepulerunt*), is also an ironical echo. Cf. also Philodemus, *AP* 5. 121, Propertius 2. 34. 46, Ovid, *Am.* 2. 4. 33 and 3. 3. 8; contrast *Ars* 3. 263.

2. *sic*: 'listed like this'.

singula: 'individual points', 'details'.

3. *formosa*: the word stands outside the grammatical construction, as if in quotation marks.

uenustas: the word embraces all the connotations of *uenustus*; see on line 6.

4. *in tam magno . . . corpore*: That Quintia is a large woman is conceded as a point in her favour, not the contrary. For parallels from Greek literature see Fordyce.

mica salis: cf. the pun on *sal* in 13. 5; 'naughtiness' or 'sauciness' seem to be among the connotations of the word, as well as 'wit', 'fun', 'sparkle' — see 16. 6–8; cf. 10. 33 (Varus' girl-friend is *insulsa male*), 17. 12 *insulsissimus est homo*, 37. 6 (Egnatius and his companions are *insulsi*), and Cicero, *Att.* 9. 10. 2 ἐν τοῖς ἐρωτικοῖς *alienant immundae, insulsae, indecorae*. C. also uses the adjective *salsus* (12. 4 and 14. 16).

5. *cum*: correlative with 6 *tum*.

pulcerrima: C. uses the superlative of Thetis, 64. 28, and Laodamia, 68. 105; *pulcer* is the ordinary literary word for 'beautiful', or 'handsome'. (For the idiomatic use of the adverb *pulcre* see on 23. 5.)

6. The primary meaning in C.'s intention was probably 'one woman though she is, she has purloined a *uenus* (some kind of grace or charm) from every woman possessing this quality'; the plural because there are many *ueneres*, though only one is stolen from each person. Quintia, i.e., has no form of *uenus* (*nulla uenustas*), Lesbia has every *uenus* that there is. As usually printed (*Veneres* with a capital V) the meaning becomes, 'one woman though she is, she has purloined a Venus (an embodiment of Venus, or even a statue of Venus) from everybody'. Lesbia, i.e., combines in herself all embodiments of Venus. No doubt this meaning is intended as well. But zeal for analysis must not make us lose sight of the main function of the line, which is to suggest, suddenly and unexpectedly, a whole complex of meanings, presented as though the statement were a self-evident truth. For the plural see on 3. 1; for *uenustus* etc. see on 3. 2. Cf. Plautus *St.* 278 *amoenitates omnium uenerum et uenustatum adfero*.

surripuit: cf. Horace, *Carm.* 4. 13. 20 *quae me surpuerat mihi* (a reminiscence?).

See:

Latin Explorations 66–73.

87

Two couplets, each aimed at consciously matter-of-fact statement of something about which there should be no argument; each begins with *nulla*, and ends with *mea est*. But the echoes of the first couplet in the second underline the change of key. 'As in 76 and again in 109, Catullus turns, not in self-righteousness but in despair, to the obsessing thought of his own loyalty.' (Fordyce)

1–2. A recurring theme: cf. 8. 5 *amata nobis quantum amabitur nulla*, 58. 2–3 *quam Catullus unam | plus quam se atque suos amauit omnes*.

3–4. The simple assertion of the first couplet is now rephrased in terms which stress what was really unique in the affair — C.'s concept of absolute, lasting fidelity. Note how much more emphatic (*nulla . . . ullo . . . umquam*) the second couplet is than the first.

3. *foedere*: cf. 109. 6 *aeternum hoc sanctae foedus amicitiae*, and see on 76. 3. [Some avoid the simple ablative by reading *ullo fuit umquam in foedere*.]

4. *in amore tuo*: 'in my love for you'. Note the switch to direct address. For the phrase cf. 64. 253 *tuoque incensus amore*. Three elisions in this line; see on 73. 6.

    ex parte . . . mea: 'on my part'.

See:

F. O. Copley, 'Emotional conflict and its significance in the Lesbia-poems of Catullus', *AJPh* 70 (1949), 26–7.

88

There are a few instances in the collection of a pair of poems (e.g. 2–3 or 110–11), and rather more of a pair separated by an unrelated poem (e.g. 5 and 7, or 41 and 43): four in a row is unparalleled. Yet Poems 88–91 pretty clearly form four separate epigrams. For Gellius see on Poem 74.

1–2. A fresh charge of incest.

1. *matre*: actually, it seems, his stepmother (*nouerca*) — see on Poem 74.

2. *abiectis . . . tunicis*: cf. 66. 81 *reiecta ueste*.

peruigilat: also 68. 8.

3. A reiteration of the charge levelled in Poem 74.

5–6. High style.

5. *ultima Tethys*: the wife of Oceanus; she is called *ultima* because she lived (like her husband) on the edge of the world; cf. 29. 4 *ultima Britannia*.

6. *Nympharum*: The daughters of Tethys and Oceanus, the Oceanids, not to be confused with the Nereids (also called *nymphae*, 64. 17). That the waters of the ocean will (or will not) wash away crime is a familiar cliché, from Euripides (*IT* 1193) to *Macbeth*.

7–8. The pastiche of high style in 5–6 now gives way to blunt statement.

7. *nihil est quicquam*: a colloquial tautology, not infrequent in comedy.

quo prodeat ultra: 'to which he can advance further'.

89

Gellius again (see on Poems 74 and 88). Like Poem 80 (also Gellius), a variation on the theme of Poem 6; Gellius' *latera ecfututa* (6. 13), however, have been earned strictly within the family.

1. *Gellius est tenuis*: *quid ni?*: cf. 79. 1 *Lesbius est pulcer. quid ni?*; *quid ni?* = 'naturally'.

cui: the antecedent is 4 *is*.

tam: the word occurs 5 times in 3 lines.

bona: 'obliging', as in 110. 1 *bonae amicae*; cf. 3 *bonus*.

2. *ualens*: cf. 61. 227–8 *ualentem / exercete iuuentam*.

3. *patruus*: for the uncle see Poem 74 and 88. 3.

omnia plena: idiomatic; cf. Cicero, *Att.* 2. 24. 4 *ita sunt omnia omnium miseriarum plenissima*; 3. 18. 2 *omnia mittit spei plena*.

5–6. i.e. even though he sticks to forbidden relationships, Gellius' family connexions readily account for his appearance.

5. *ut*: concessive.

tangere: for a simple verb following a compound see on 10. 20.

6. *quantumuis quare sit macer*: 'all the excuse you could wish for being thin'; for *quare* cf. 80. 1.

90

Gellius again (see on Poems 74 and 88). This time an old Persian custom contributes a touch of fantasy.

1. *nascatur*: a wish: may Gellius and his mother be blessed with a very special son.

magus: There are a number of allusions to the practice of incest among Persian *magi*; see scholia on Euripides, *Andromache* 173 ff. and the references in Kroll, including Nachträge on S. 262.

3–4. Not to be taken too seriously (despite Kroll).

4. *religio*: the first syllable counts as long, as in Lucretius.

5. *gnatus*: repetition for the sake of emphasis is characteristic of C.; the *gnatus* of line 5 is not the same person of course as the *gnato* of line 3 but the son referred to in the opening word of the epigram. [*gnatus* V; *gratus* Müller.]

accepto: 'favourably received'.

6. *omentum*: the membrane enclosing the intestines; it appears from Strabo 732 that the Persians did not offer flesh to the gods, only the surrounding skin.

liquefaciens: second syllable long. The polysyllabic ending is mock-solemn, like 2 *aruspicium*.

91

New light on Gellius (see on Poems 74 and 88): he has betrayed C.'s trust, by stealing (or attempting to steal) his mistress (6 *hanc*).

Cf. Poems 73 and 77. Gellius makes a final appearance in Poem 116.

1–6. 'Gellius, I thought I could trust you: she wasn't in your line.' Bitter irony dictates the heavy, measured syntax of these lines.

2. *in misero hoc nostro, hoc perdito amore*: cf. 76. 6 *ex hoc ingrato amore*; *perdito*, 'desperate', is a reinforcement of *misero* (the usual term for unrequited love — see on 8. 1; cf. 45. 3 *perdite amo* and 104. 3 *tam perdite amarem*); for *nostro* = *meo* see Fordyce on 107. 3 f.

3. *quod te cognossem bene*: 'because I had come to know you well' (he did know Gellius, as line 7 indicates, but that wasn't C.'s reason for trusting Gellius); the subjunctive is used both of a possible reason but not the one meant, and of a false reason, as in *constantemue putarem* etc.; for the expression cf. 72. 5 *nunc te cognoui*.

constantemue putarem: 'or thought you reliable' (as he did not).

5. *neque quod*: = *quod neque*.

6. *cuius me*: three long syllables.

edebat: 'was consuming'; cf. 35. 15 *ignes interiorem edunt me dullam*.

7–8. = 'Admittedly you and I were friends, but I didn't suppose you'd think that reason enough (to betray my trust in you)'.

7. *quamuis . . . usu*: 'however long our acquaintance'; the words seem chosen to exclude the idea of close friendship.

9. *duxti*: = *duxisti*; see on 14. 14 *misti*.

9–10. *tantum . . . sceleris*: 'you get real pleasure out of a liaison when there's something criminal about it'; for this sense of *culpa* see on 75. 1 *tua culpa*.

10. *aliquid sceleris*: even a limited opportunity for villainy was enough.

92

A justification of the premise of Poem 83 that disparaging words are a sign of love. How does C. know? He knows from observing himself. But he is far from exultant in these lines; instead, there is a hint of pathos.

1–2. The two propositions form a paradox (which 3–4 will justify) — the second is *not* offered as a self-evident deduction from the first.

1. *mi dicit semper male*: = *mi maledicit*, 'is constantly abusing me'; the word does not necessarily imply that the person ill spoken of is addressed (cf. *nec tacet . . . de me*). Contrast 104. 1 *credis me potuisse meae maledicere uitae*.

nec tacet: cf. 6. 3 *dicere nec tacere*.

2. *me dispeream nisi amat*: = 'damned if she doesn't love me'; see on 45. 5. C., as we say, is prepared to swear she loves him. With *dispeream* cf. 106. 2 *discupere*.

3. *quo signo*: *dispeream* implies conviction, not proof, and conviction in the face, apparently, of the evidence of line 1. What has C. got to go on? (*quo signo?*)

sunt totidem mea: = probably something like 'it adds up to the same with me'; i.e. 'I'm in the same position', or perhaps 'I'm just as bad (equally irrational in the way I behave)'.

deprecor: literally 'entreat relief from'; C., i.e., keeps wishing (aloud) that he could be rid of Lesbia. But *deprecor* is used in an unusual way (see 44. 18 for a more normal use), and Aulus Gellius, in rejecting criticism of this poem, felt obliged to explain the word by a whole string of near-synonyms (7. 16. 2): *sic enim 'deprecor' a Catullo dictum est quasi 'detestor', uel 'exsecror', uel 'depello' uel 'abominor'.*

4. *uerum dispeream nisi amo*: as though even one's own feelings were a matter for conviction, rather than certainty.

93

The relationship of these lines to the other three poems in which Caesar is attacked (Poems 29, 54 and 57) cannot be determined, however much we should like to know in what connexion C.

chose to tell Caesar that he had no particular desire to be in his good books, and didn't in fact give a damn about him.

1. Conversational idioms, in Latin as in English, often verge on pleonasm, to put the speaker's meaning beyond doubt. The point C. wishes to make is that he is 'not especially keen (*nil nimium studeo*) to want to be liked (*uelle placere*)' by Caesar; so lukewarm an attitude (more insulting than positive dislike) needs careful definition. Cf. Cicero, *Fam.* 12. 30. 7 *illud non nimium probo*; *nil* practically = *non*, like *nihil* in 16. 6 *nihil necesse est*.

2. Apparently proverbial — cf. Cicero, *Phil.* 2. 41 *uide quam te amarit is qui albus aterne fuerit ignoras*. But the coolly-worded context revitalizes the idiom: 'nor am I especially keen to know you from Adam'.

Quintilian has an odd comment on this line (11. 1. 38): *negat se magni facere aliquis poetarum utrum Caesar ater an albus homo sit — insania: uerte ut idem Caesar de illo dixerit, arrogantia est.*

94

The first of four epigrams directed at Mentula: in Poem 105 his literary pretensions are ridiculed, in Poems 114 and 115 his pretensions as a landed proprietor. The name Mentula is usually assumed to be the *nom de guerre* of Caesar's henchman Mamurra (described in 29. 13 as *diffututa mentula*) rather than a pseudonym designed to conceal Mamurra's identity; see Neudling 114–15. Poem 94 is a play upon this name. For Mamurra see on Poem 29 and cf. Poems 41, 43 and 57.

2. *hoc est quod dicunt*: 'as the saying goes'; cf. 98. 2 *id quod dicitur*.

ipsa olera olla legit: 'the pot itself (*ipsa olla*) gathers the vegetables (*olera*)'; i.e. Mentula seeks what a *mentula* needs. If a proverb (and not a jingle made up by C.), it is not found elsewhere.

95

Cinna's *Zmyrna*, an epyllion like C.'s *Peleus and Thetis* (Poem 64), has at last seen the light of day; Cinna is a more careful craftsman than Hortensius and his poem is assured of a less ignominious fate than the *Annales* of Volusius. Gaius Cinna (also 10. 30 and 113. 1) is usually identified with the tribune of 44 B.C., C. Helvius Cinna, who was lynched (in mistake for L. Cornelius Cinna) following the funeral of Julius Caesar.

The subject of the *Zmyrna* was the incestuous passion of Zmyrna for her father Cinyras, her metamorphosis into a tree and the birth from her trunk of Adonis. Two fragments survive (*FPL* p. 88), one two lines in length, the other a single line, as well as a number of fragments of other poems. For Ovid's version (in which Zmyrna is called Myrrha) see *Met.* 10. 298–528.

Structure: 'The art of this poem is minute. There are, or rather were, eight verses, divided into two sections of four verses, each section beginning with the title of Cinna's poem. . . . Two rivers are named, the Satrachus and the Po: *Satrachi* stands immediately before the caesura in the first hexameter, *Paduam* immediately after the caesura in the second; and both hexameters conclude with similar phrases: *mittetur ad undas, morientur ad ipsam.* . . . A polemical poem in the Callimachean style was not meant to be merely a confutation; it was meant to be simultaneously a demonstration of how poetry ought to be written.' (CLAUSEN 189)

On 95b see below.

1. *nonam post denique messem*: An appropriately urbane opening: behind the words actually used we catch the echo of words that might be employed to describe a more usual gestatory period, *nonum post denique mensem*; the echo is supported by 2 *edita*. For the accusative cf. Cicero, *Fam.* 16. 21. 1 *uenerunt post diem quadragesimum et sextum quam a uobis discesserant.*

2. *est*: unless a main verb has been lost with the missing line 4, *est* has to do double service with *coepta* and *edita*.

3. *Hortensius*: Doubtless the orator Q. Hortensius Hortalus and presumably the Hortalus of Poem 65, who seems indeed to have been something of a poetaster; perhaps he also wrote a long poem, as implied here. Cf. Horace's disparagement of the over-productiveness of Lucilius, *S*. 1. 4. 9–10 *in hora saepe ducentos, | ut magnum, uersus dictabat stans pede in uno*.

4. Froehlich's *uersiculorum anno quolibet ediderit* satisfactorily completes the sense, if rather prosaically; one suspects some continuation of the *double entendre* of the opening couplet.

5–8. The Satrachus is a river in Cyprus, linked by Nonnus (13. 459) with the Adonis legend. Clearly C. is paying his friend an elegant compliment: his *Zmyrna* will be read by the banks of the river which it celebrates.

5. *cauas*: 'deep-channelled'; Lucan, 2. 421–4, applies the word to the Rutuba, a tributary of the Tiber, where it flows swiftly down from the Apennines.

6. *cana . . . saecula*: 'the grey-haired generations to come'. For *saeculum* see on 1. 10; cf. 68. 46 and 78b. 4; Cinna's poem, unlike Volusius', will go on being read.

peruoluent: 4 syllables (the second u is vocalic).

7. *Volusi annales*: the *cacata carta* of Poem 36.

Paduam . . . ad ipsam: A branch of the Po; Volusius' *Annales* will end up in the region where they originated, or with which their author was somehow connected, and even their fate will be an inglorious one. Very possibly, there is also a jibe at Volusius' rusticity — cf. the charge of *Patauinitas* (*Patauia* = the modern Padua) levelled at Livy by Asinius Pollio.

8. *laxas . . . tunicas*: Perhaps only wrapping paper for fish, which Volusius' *Annales* might well provide in abundance. THOMSON argues the reference is to a method of cooking fish in a loose-fitting paper jacket.

See:

Wendell Clausen, 'Callimachus and Latin poetry', *GRBS* 5 (1964), 188–91.

D. F. S. Thomson, 'Catullus 95. 8', *Phoenix* 18 (1964), 30–6.

95b

Some complete the hexameter with *sodalis*, in which case *mei* . . . *monimenta sodalis* = *Zmyrna mei Cinnae*, the opening words of Poem 95. Those who take the lines as a separate fragment supply a proper name — usually a Greek poet (to match Antimachus), but Leo suggested *Catonis* (the poet and critic of Poem 56, author of a poem on Diana, the *Dictynna*; cf. Cinna's line: *saecula permaneat nostri Dictynna Catonis*).

2. *Antimacho*: The author of the famous *Lyde*, a collection of myths linked by the theme of unhappy love in elegiacs, condemned by Callimachus for its verbosity (Fragment 398 Pf.; cf. C.'s *tumido*).

96

To C.'s friend Licinius Calvus (see on Poem 50), on the death of his young wife Quintilia: 'even in the grave she perhaps feels your grief, and rejoices that you love her still'.

We gather from Propertius (a passage listing the Roman elegiac poets who wrote of love) that Calvus wrote a poem on the death of Quintilia (2. 34. 89–90): *haec etiam docti confessa est pagina Calui, | cum caneret miserae funera Quintiliae*, where *haec* = something like 'such themes' (i.e. those of love elegy). If we set Propertius' words alongside a remark by Ovid in the *Tristia* (2. 431–2) *par fuit exigui similisque licentia Calui | detexit uariis qui sua furta modis*, it seems a reasonable inference that Calvus' lines on the death of Quintilia formed an introduction, or perhaps an epilogue, to a collection of love poetry comparable to that of C. Two lines, probably, survive (*FPL* p. 86): *cum iam fulua cinis fuero* . . . and *forsitan hoc etiam gaudeat ipsa cinis*. FRAENKEL argues that the first represents a reproach addressed to Calvus by Quintilia (? after her death), while the second represents a hope expressed by Calvus. Poem 96 very possibly picks up the key lines of Calvus' elegy, as a compliment from C. to his friend. The 6 lines form a carefully constructed, strangely impressive periodic sentence. Poem 101 likewise implies that the dead and the living can communicate. Cf. Sulpicius' words of consolation to Cicero on the death of his daughter Tullia in 45 B.C., *Fam.* 4. 5. 6: *quod si quis etiam inferis sensus est, qui illius in te amor fuit pietasque in omnes suos, hoc certe illa te facere non uult.*

1. *si quicquam*: 'if anything at all' (stronger than *si quid*). Also 102. 1 and 107. 1.

mutis: cf. 101. 4 *mutam cinerem.*

gratum acceptumue: a not uncommon combination, used here to cope with the uncertainty of what is being discussed rather than for emphasis; with *acceptum* cf. 36. 16 *acceptum* and 90. 5 *accepto.*

3. *quo desiderio*: cf. the common use of *quo tempore* (=*eo tempore quo*); the noun antecedent, i.e., is transferred from the demonstrative phrase to the relative clause; cf. Cicero, *Div. Caec.* 2 *si quod tempus accidisset, quo tempore aliquid a me requirerent.* . . . Here, however, the noun in the relative clause is a near-synonym of an expressed antecedent (2 *dolore*); cf. 64. 73 *illa tempestate, ferox quo ex tempore Theseus.* The idiom is not literally translatable; we have to say something like, 'with that sense of longing with which . . .'.

4. Most take *missas* as =*amissas*, 'lost'; but FRAENKEL argues that the meaning is 'abandoned' or 'thrown away', the reference being to Calvus' (self-confessed) neglect of the affection (*amicitias*) shown him by Quintilia; cf. 109. 6 *amicitiae.*

5-6. *tanto . . . dolori . . . quantum gaudet*: the combination of adjectival *tantus* with adverbial *quantum* is uncommon.

See:

J. T. Davis, *Hermes* 99 (1971) 297–302.

Eduard Fraenkel, 'Catulls Trostgedicht für Calvus', *WS* 69 (1956), 278–88.

97

A savage, if genially exuberant, attack on an unknown Don Juan (9 *hic futuit multas et se facit esse uenustum*).

A fragment of a Greek epigram (*AP* 11. 241) by Nearchos (? age of Nero) closely resembles 97. 1–4 and is perhaps an imitation of C.'s lines.

Structure: 1–4 — hypothesis. 5–8 — explanation (with details of the assertion in line 4). 9–12 — paradoxical success of Aemilius.

1. *ita me di ament*: cf. 61. 189–90 *ita me iuuent | caelites*, 66. 18 *non, ita me diui, uera gemunt, iuerint*, 67. 9 *ita Caecilio placeam*. The i of *di* is shortened in hiatus, instead of being elided; see on 55. 4 *te in omnibus* and on 10. 27.

putaui: i.e. this is what C. thought, but he has been proved wrong as line 9 concedes.

2. *utrumne*: [*utrum* V; *utrumne* Avanzi, to avoid hiatus after *culum* (see on 76. 10).]

3. *hoc . . . illud*: the *os* and the *culus* respectively; cf. 100. 3, and see *L & S* s.v. *hic* I D2. Both neuter for symmetry.

4. *mundior et melior*: alliteration for the sake of emphasis.

5–8. A series of images forming an increasing triad, each more breathtaking than the previous one in its merciless fantasy; the crudity of 7–8 is intended of course to prepare for the surprise in line 9. Cf. Poem 39.

5. *os*: [*hic* V; many read *hoc* (i.e. =*os*, as in line 3); Froehlich's *os* is very plausible.]

6. *ploxeni*: According to Quintilian, a word C. picked up in the Po valley (1. 5. 8 *Catullus 'ploxenum' circa Padum inuenit*); explained by Festus as a wagon-box (260 Lindsay: *ploxinum (sic) appellari ait Catullus capsum in cisio capsamue, cum dixit 'gingiuas* etc.'); i.e., probably, large, clumsy, battered, covered in dirt.

9. *se facit*: 'pretends'; cf. Cicero, *Fam.* 15. 18. 1 *itaque facio me alias res agere*.

10. *pistrino . . . asino*: Probably to be taken together; why, i.e., is Aemilius not given the slave's job of driving the ass that turns the mill? Cf. Cicero, *de Orat.* 2. 144 *tibi mecum in eodem est pistrino, Crasse, uiuendum*.

11. *attingit*: cf. 67. 20 and 89. 5.

12. *lingere*: cf. 98. 4 *culos lingere*.

See:

Cat. Rev. 36.

98

Victius (if that is his name) has a foul tongue.

Victius, or Viccius, or Vittius (all variant spellings of the same name) is unknown; a possible candidate is L. Vettius, a contemporary perjurer. See Neudling.

1. *si in quemquam*: 'if against anyone at all'; cf. 96. 1 *si quicquam*.

pote: =*potest*; see on 17. 24.

putide: A term of abuse, as in 42. 11–12 and 19–20, but especially appropriate to Victius — he really does stink; for the trick of using a word in a context that suggests a meaning later rejected or expanded see on 39. 9–16.

2. *id quod . . . dicitur*: 'as the saying goes'. Cf. 94. 2 *hoc est quod dicunt*.

uerbosis . . . et fatuis: dative.

3. *ista cum lingua*: *cum* with the instrumental is an archaism.

si usus ueniat tibi: 'if you should have occasion'.

4. *carpatinas*: adjectival; καρβάτιναι were cheap leather shoes, apparently used by peasants.

5–6. 'If you want to be the undoing of us all . . . open your mouth'; *hiscas*, i.e., remakes the point made by 1 *putide* — Victius has a foul tongue in more senses than one. [*discas* V, adopted by G. L. Hendrickson, *RhM* 59 (1904), 478, as a contraction of *deiscas* (=*dehiscas*, 'yawn').]

99

The last, longest and most elegantly worded of the Juventius poems, and one of the few elegiac poems apart from those addressed to Lesbia to take the form of a personal statement to an addressee; a little like an English sixteenth-century lyric (cf., e.g., Wyatt's 'Alas! madame, for stelyng of a kysse'), especially lines 11–16. For Juventius see on Poem 24 (also Poems 48 and 81).

Apart from Poem 76, Poem 99 is the longest in the group 69–116.

Structure: 1–6 — the stolen kiss. 7–10 — Juventius' gesture of disgust. 11–16 — C. reduced to despair.

The 16 lines form a neat pattern of five sentences: (2 +4) +4 + (4 +2).

1. *surripui*: cf. 86. 6 *surripuit Veneres*.

dum ludis: a present indicative in the *dum*-clause when the principal clause is past (usually perfect) is common; cf. line 5; *ludis* perhaps 'teasing me'; for *ludere* see on 17. 17.

mellite: cf. 3. 6 *mellitus erat* (Lesbia's sparrow) and 48. 1 *mellitos oculos tuos* (of Juventius).

2. The first of four 4-word pentameters in this poem. See on 66. 8.

suauiolum: the diminutive, picked up in line 14, is not found elsewhere.

dulci dulcius: cf. 22. 14 *infaceto infacetior*, 27. 4 *ebrioso acino ebriosioris*. Pun on *dulcis* = *suauis*.

3. *uerum id non impune tuli*: cf. 78. 9 *uerum id non impune feres*.

amplius horam: *amplius, plus* etc. are often used appositionally (without *quam*) with an accusative of extent in time or space.

4. *suffixum . . . cruce*: cf., for similar words (used literally), Cicero, *Pis.* 42 *si et te et Gabinium cruci suffixos uiderem, maiore afficerer laetitia?* Cf. 12 *excruciare*.

memini esse: i.e. the incident took place some time ago. Both the present and perfect infinitive are common with *memini*, the former expressing a fresher or more vivid recollection.

5. *dum . . . me purgo*: see on 1 *dum ludis*.

6. *uestrae*: Sometimes quoted as one of the very few clear instances of *uester* = *tuus*; the idiom, if it exists, is much rarer than

Q

noster = *meus*; see Fordyce on 39. 20. It seems safer to assume that by *uestrae* C. means 'that *saeuitia* which is characteristic of young men like you'; cf. 39. 20 *uester dens*.

7. *simul*: = *simul atque*; cf. 22. 15, 51. 6 etc.

8. *guttis*: sc. *aquae*.

abstersti mollibus: [*abstersti omnibus* O; *mollibus* unpublished conjecture by A. G. Lee; most eliminate the hiatus after *abstersti* by printing *abstersisti*; with *mollibus* cf. Quintilian 11. 1. 70 *quam molli articulo tractauit Catonem*.] For the form *abstersti* see on 14. 14 *misti*; cf. 12 *cessasti*.

articulis: = *digitis* (*L & S* I B).

9. *contractum*: the word used of a contagious disease.

10. *commictae . . . lupae*: cf. 78b. 2 *suauia comminxit spurca saliua tua*; *lupae*, 'whore'.

11. *miserum*: see on 8. 1. Again in line 15.

Amori: better taken as the god, who becomes C.'s torturer; contrast 15 *misero . . . amori*.

12. *excruciare*: picks up 4 *in summa . . . cruce*. See on 85. 2 *fieri sentio et excrucior*.

13. *ambrosia*: picks up 2 *ambrosia*.

14. *suauiolum*: picks up 2 *suauiolum*.

tristi tristius: picks up 2 *dulci dulcius*.

15. *misero*: cf. 11 *miserum* and 91. 2 *in misero amore*.

See:

H. A. Kahn, *Latomus* 26 (1967) 609–18.

J. C. D. Marshall, *CW* 65 (1971) 57–8.

L. Richardson Jr., '*Furi et Aureli* . . .', *CPh* 58 (1963), 95–6.

100

Caelius and Quintius are united in the pursuit of love. C. backs Caelius. Poem 100 raises a number of interesting questions. Does C. mean what he says in lines 5–7? The words sound as if they were meant to be taken seriously; if they aren't, what do we make of the wish in line 8? If they are meant seriously, do they then refer to the Lesbia affair? If so, how did Caelius prove a true friend to C., and how can C. bring himself to draw together within the same epigram mention of his love for Lesbia and the prospective *ménage à quatre* which forms the subject of Poem 100? If lines 5–7 do not refer to the Lesbia affair but to some (earlier?) adventure, must we not be a little careful, always, in giving full weight to what sounds like the talk of a man desperately in love?

Quintius looks like the Quintius of Poem 82 (he is perhaps the brother of the Quintia of Poem 86); Caelius looks like the Caelius of Poem 58; if he is Caelius Rufus (whom nothing except this poem connects with Verona), he is likely to be the Rufus of Poem 77 (which might help us with lines 5–8) and Poem 69. Aufillena crops up again in Poems 110 and 111, her brother only here.

2. *flos*: cf. 63. 64 *gymnasi fui flos*, 24. 1 *flosculus Iuuentiorum*.

Veronensum . . . iuuenum: = *Veronensium . . . iuuenum*; the phrase offers no valid clue to the setting of the epigram, since it can = 'the boys from Verona' just as easily as 'the boys of Verona'.

depereunt: cf. 35. 12 *illum deperit impotente amore*; see also on 45. 5.

3. *hic fratrem, ille sororem*: cf. the situation in Poem 78.

4. *fraternum . . . sodalicium*: The joke lies in applying a popular saying in which *fraternum* = the subjective genitive *fratrum* to a situation in which *fraternum* has to stand for the objective genitive *fratrum*; normal Latin idiom allows the application of the collective *fratres* to brother(s) and sister(s).

5. *faueam*: 'support', 'back', as if Caelius and Quintius, as yet, it seems, the victims of unrequited love, were competitors in a race. For the pattern cf. 1. 1–3.

6. *perspecta est igni tum*: if right, 'was then tried by fire'; picked up by 7 *cum*. [*perfecta* V, *est igitur* O; variously restored by editors. The version printed here is due to Palmer.]

7. *uesana*: cf. 7. 10 *uesano*.

101

C. at the grave of his brother, after a long journey; a dramatic monologue, based on the formal rites of a traditional ceremony.

The poem's strength is due in great part to the delicate balance between the sad, resigned irony with which C. both accepts and detaches himself from the formal valediction it is his obligation to pronounce (*aduenio . . . ut . . . mutam nequiquam alloquerer cinerem*, 'I am come to make an idle speech to ashes mute'), and the confident assumption of an understanding between the brothers transcending the inadequacies of the ceremony. Cf. 68. 89–100 (for the echo here see on line 6).

For the idea of a bond between living and dead see on Poem 96. For the common convention of grave-epigrams by which the dead speak to the living, see on Poem 4. Cf. the funeral ceremonies in Virgil, *A*. 6. 214–35 and 11. 182–202.

1. The opening line (1) provides essential data—one isn't normally separated from a brother's grave by a long and complicated journey; (2) establishes, through rhythm and repetition as much as diction, an appropriate emotional level (though any notion of a 'pilgrimage' should probably be resisted as a modern intrusion). Virgil puts an echo of C.'s words on Anchises' lips in welcoming Aeneas, *A*. 6. 692–3: *quas ego te terras et quanta per aequora uectum | accipio!*; cf. *A*. 5. 627–9 for a quite different formulation of a similar idea.

2. *aduenio*: An echo perhaps of Orestes' opening words (at his father's tomb, on return from exile) in Aeschylus' *Choephori* (line 3: ἥκω γὰρ ἐς γῆν τήνδε καὶ κατέρχομαι).

miseras: The stock epithet, sharpened by a special appropriateness—the ceremony which follows, because of the place, because C. is alone, etc., is more pathetically inadequate than normally.

frater: the vocative is repeated in lines 6 and 10.

inferias: Strictly, the ritual offering to the *Di manes*, referred to in lines 3 and 7–9; again line 8.

3. *postremo . . . munere mortis*: = 'that final gift which the dead receive'. For *munus* see on 17. 7 and 68. 10.

donarem: imperfect, despite the present *aduenio*, because, though C.'s arrival belongs to the present, the purpose that brought him lies in the past.

4. Irony, rather than emotional incitement; *alloqui* is used of any formal speech, including the speech made by one character to another in high-style poetry, e.g. Virgil, *A.* 4. 8 *adloquitur sororem*; *mutam*, the obvious word, perhaps suggests the actors who play mute roles in a tragic performance. The heavy elision of the final syllable of *nequiquam* and the sequence of k- and kw-sounds seem intended to undercut the solemn m-sounds in *mutam* and the previous line; *cinis* is more commonly masculine (also feminine in 68. 90 and in two fragments of Calvus, *FPL* p. 86: *cum iam fulua cinis fuero . . .* and *forsitan hoc etiam gaudeat ipsa cinis*; the latter perhaps echoed here).

5–10. Psychologically effective: fate has deprived C. of actual contact with his brother (they were destined, as we say, never to see one another again); but the impulse to make contact, to do *something*, remains; all that can be done to satisfy it is to go through the forms of the ritual: to do so brings comfort, and perhaps achieves more; cf. 96. 1–2 *si quicquam mutis gratum acceptumue sepulcris | accidere a nostro dolore potest*.

(ROBINSON argues that 5–6 should be taken with 1–4, not with 7–10. But this structure, though more obviously logical, is flat; in 64. 218 (a similar context) *quandoquidem fortuna* introduces a subordinate clause that precedes its principal clause.)

6. A line full of echoes—68. 20 *o misero frater adempte mihi*, recalled at 68. 92 and followed by 93 *ei misero fratri iucundum lumen ademptum . . .* ; cf. 68. 31 *quae mihi luctus ademit*. For the appositional expansion of the vocative *frater* see on 77. 1; *indigne* is the adverb.

7. *nunc tamen interea haec*: The force of *interea* resembles that in 14. 21 *uos hinc interea ualete* and 36. 18 *at uos interea uenite*—something approaching 'anyhow', 'at any rate', rather than 'meanwhile'; the idiom suggests the best made of a bad job.

prisco: a distancing epithet; cf. 64. 50 *priscis figuris* and 64. 159 *prisci praecepta parentis*.

parentum: 'ancestors'.

8. *tradita sunt*: (1) 'handed down'; (2) 'handed over' to form the funeral offering (*ad inferias*).

tristi munere: Combines the idea of 'gift' (as in line 3) with the idea of 'duty', 'obligation'; the gift offered (the traditional wine, milk, honey and flowers) is also a rite to be carried out; cf. Virgil, *A.* 6. 223 *triste ministerium*. With the ablative cf. 65. 19 *furtiuo munere*.

9. *fraterno multum manantia fletu*: 'all wet with a brother's tears'.

10. The words *aue atque uale* possibly formed part of the traditional ceremony; cf. Virgil, *A.* 11. 97–8 (Aeneas to Pallas) *salue aeternum mihi . . . | aeternumque uale.*

See:

C. E. Robinson, '*Multas per gentes,*' *G&R* 12 (1965), 62–3. *Latin Explorations* 80–3.

102

'Don't worry, Cornelius, I can keep a secret.' Whether C.'s friend is Cornelius Nepos (Poem 1) or the Cornelius of 67. 35 (who had a secret to keep)—or another Cornelius altogether, and what the secret was, are equally unknown.

1. *si quicquam*: 'if anything at all' (stronger than *si quid*). Also 96. 1 and 107. 1.

tacito: used as a noun; cf. 64. 110 *saeuum.* The dative is somewhat awkward in view of the ablatives following.

2. *cuius*: the antecedent is 1 *tacito.*

3. *meque*: probably correlative with 4 *et*, a variation on the high-style *-que . . . -que* (see on 64. 201); cf. 28. 5 *frigoraque et famem,* 44. 15 *otioque et urtica*; several examples in Virgil's *Aeneid* (see Williams on *A.* 5. 467). The effect is to emphasize that the future indicative *inuenies* counts as parallel to the imperative *puta.*

illorum iure sacratum: 'bound by the code that binds such people'; *illorum* because 1–2, though formally singular, imply a group of people.

4. *Arpocratem*: an Egyptian sun-god, represented as a boy with a finger to his mouth. Also 74. 4.

103

A note of complaint to Silo, a pimp who has turned nasty. C. offers him an alternative; money back, or some courtesy in business, please. Cf. Poem 110.

1–3. *aut . . . aut*: either the one or the other; Silo must choose; cf. 12. 10–11.

1. *sodes*: 'please' (from *si audes*); ironically polite. See *L & S*.

decem sestertia: = 10,000 sesterces — the price quoted, apparently, by Ameana in Poem 41; a tidy, if not a large, sum. Silo, i.e., has not kept his part of the bargain and cuts up rough when asked to do so.

2. 'then you can be as savage and as uncontrollable as you like'.

3. *desine quaeso*: i.e., 'if you want to go on being a *leno*, you must stop . . .'; again ironically polite.

4. *idem*: = 'at the same time'; cf. 22. 3.

saeuus et indomitus: for the reiteration, see on 79. 3 *cum gente Catullum*.

See:

W. de Grummond, *CPh* 66 (1971) 188–9.

F. W. Lenz, 'Catulliana', *RCCM* 5 (1963), 67–70.

104

A sequence of recurring themes. One cannot, however, with any confidence extract a precise statement from these tantalizing lines.

1. *credis*: as in 85. 1, we cannot be sure whether Lesbia or an imaginary interlocutor (the reader) is meant.

potuisse: 'could bring myself to' (a common force of the perfect of *possum*); as in 3 *potui* some specific occasion now past seems intended.

meae . . . uitae: cf. 109. 1 *mea uita* and 68. 155 *tua uita*, and see on 45. 13.

maledicere: contrast 92. 1 *Lesbia mi dicit semper male*.

2. *ambobus . . . carior . . . oculis*: cf. 82. 3–4 *eripere ei noli, multo quod carius illi | est oculis.*

3. *non potui*: Does C. mean that he has been wrongly suspected of saying nasty things about Lesbia, or that he tried to say nasty things about her (in his verse) and couldn't? The latter seems more likely.

nec, si possem . . . amarem: The imperfect subjunctives can refer to present or past time. (The imperfect, of the past, whether in protasis or apodosis, or both, is fairly common down to the end of the classical period.) C. perhaps intends past and present equally, meaning in retrospect that his love for Lesbia might not have been so disastrous for him if he had been able to release his pent-up feelings when she betrayed him, and meaning too that this is still the position. (Cf. the way in which past and present are viewed as one in idioms of the type *undecimum iam annum regnat*.)

In either case, it is clear that C. is not talking about the kind of cutting remark that reveals the attempt to conceal passion (as in Poems 83 and 92): he means the kind of attack that relieves passion, violently abusive lampoon, perhaps—something more than the sudden, brief flaring sally of Poem 58 or 11. 17–20.

perdite amarem: cf. 45. 3 *ni te perdite amo* and 91. 2 *in hoc perdito amore*. Elision of a long vowel before a short in the 5th foot is rare.

4. Best taken as pathetic understatement—the nearest C. can bring himself to *maledictio* where Lesbia is concerned. Walde-Hofmann, *Lateinisches Etymologisches Wörterbuch*, take *Tappo* as the name of a stock character in Italian farce. In that case the words perhaps = something like 'while you stop at no enormity with a clown'. But it seems possible, from a comment in Festus (496. 30 Lindsay) on a line of Lucilius, *Tappulam rident legem, conterunt ϲpimi*, that the name was used as a conventional pseudonym: *Tappulam legem conuiuialem ficto nomine conscripsit iocoso carmine Valerius Valentinus, cuius meminit Lucilius hoc modo, 'Tappulam rident* etc.' (See Marx on Lucilius 1307.)

omnia monstra facis: cf. Cicero, *Att.* 4. 7. 1 *mera monstra nuntiarat*.

105

For Mentula (=Mamurra), see on Poem 94. For Mamurra's
literary pretensions, cf. 57. 7, where he and Caesar are described
as *uno in lecticulo erudituli ambo*.

1. *Pipleium scandere montem*: 'to scale the mountain of the
Muses'; from Pipla, the name of a spring on the northern slopes of
Mt Olympus.

2. A proverbial expression for expelling an intruder; cf. Cicero,
Att. 16. 2. 4 *quoniam furcilla extrudimur, Brundisium cogito*, Horace,
Ep. 1. 10. 24 *naturam expelles furca, tamen usque recurret*. The 4-word
pentameter undercuts the mock-heroic hexameter: the *doctae
uirgines* (65. 2) will have nothing to do with Mentula; a pun on
the name is of course intended.

106

A reasonable inference.

2. *quid credat . . .*: i.e., *nisi puerum se uendere discupere*. An echo,
perhaps, of Calvus, *FPL* p. 86, *quid credas hunc sibi uelle?*

discupere: 'to be *very* keen'; cf. 92. 2 *dispeream*.

107

Lesbia has come back! After one of the *rara furta* of 68. 136? Or a
reconciliation after Bithynia? C.'s extravagant reaction seems
devoid of irony (contrast Poem 109), but the text of this little
poem is in a sorry state.

1–2. Put as generally as possible: any man who gets what he
wanted badly but wasn't hoping to get is pleased. But note the
almost legalistic determination to be precise.

1. *si quicquam*: [*quicquid* X; *quid quid* O.] For *si quicquam* as an
opening phrase, see Poems 96 and 102.

cupido optantique: very emphatic. The *-que* was added by the Aldine editor, to remove a hiatus; there is already a hiatus after *cupido* at the principal caesura; some print *cupidoque*. See on 27. 10.

optigit: the perfect in a frequentative statement.

2. *insperanti*: has its true participial force (though there is not of course a finite verb *inspero*): 'when he was not hoping for it'. For the antithesis (it was perhaps a cliché), see Cicero, *de Orat.* 1. 96 *insperanti mihi sed ualde optanti cecidit*.

proprie: with *gratum*, 'in the true sense of the word'.

3–4. The general statement of 1–2 is applied to the present case, and the key words *gratum* and *cupido* are repeated to emphasize that this is what C. wants and that he accepts his good fortune unreservedly.

3. *nobis quoque, carius auro*: The text can just be translated as it stands by taking *carius auro* as an appositional expansion of *gratum* and by giving *nobis quoque* the sense 'to me as well' (i.e., the general statement holds good in my case too). The result is a jerky line, but none of the emendations suggested is convincing.

For the plural *nobis*, cf. 68. 132 *lux mea se nostrum contulit in gremium*; for the (common) shift from singular to plural or plural to singular (3 *nobis* . . . 4 *mi* . . . 6 *nobis* . . . 7 *me*), see Fordyce.

5–8. An almost lyrical expansion of 3–4.

5. *ipsa*: Lesbia, i.e., is returning of her own accord.

6. *lucem candidiore nota*: 'day with a whiter mark'; cf. 68. 147–8 *quare illud satis est, si nobis is datur unis | quem lapide illa dies candidiore notat*.

7. *me uno*: emphatic, as in 10. 17. For the pattern, cf., e.g., Cicero, *Att.* 11. 2. 3 *quis me miserior uno iam fuit?*

7–8. *aut magis . . . poterit?*: The words do not make sense, though the general drift is plain. The suggested emendations— e.g. Lachmann's *hac res optandas uita* ('who can mention things more desirable than this life?')—though palaeographically innocuous, are implausibly pedestrian. In view of line 6, it seems reasonable to suspect an echo of 68. 159–60.

108

A sticky end is imagined for Cominius, perhaps one of two brothers from Spoletum mentioned by Cicero, *Clu.* 100–2, etc., for their prosecution in 66 B.C. of a certain C. Cornelius; C.'s lines, however, must have been written 5–10 years later than that; otherwise, one might be tempted to identify the Cornelius of Poem 102 as the victim of their attentions.

Resemblances between Poem 108 and lines of Ovid's *Ibis* (165–72) suggest that C., like Ovid, may have drawn on the lost *Ibis* of Callimachus.

1–2. *populi arbitrio . . . intereat*: i.e., 'if the people were to decide to lynch you' (e.g., by stoning Cominius to death).

1. *tua cana senectus*: possibly 'when you are old and grey', but 'now that you are old and grey' accords better with line 2 and also fits better the supposition that the addressee is one of the brothers from Spoletum. With the phrase cf. 61. 155 *cana anilitas*.

2. *impuris moribus*: need imply no more than that Cominius was a scoundrel.

4. *lingua exsecta*: cf. Cicero, *Clu.* 187 *Stratonem in crucem esse actum exsecta scitote lingua*; Cicero met a similar fate himself at the hands of Fulvia.

sit data: Present subjunctives (including present perfect) are often used of future events; cf. the present subjunctive *uoret* in line 5. The perfect here probably has an aoristic force, emphasizing the rapidity with which the action would be over and done with.

5. *effossos oculos uoret*: = *oculos effodiat et uoret*.

6. *lupi*: cf. Horace, *Ep.* 5. 99–100 *post insepulta membra different lupi / et Esquilinae alites*.

109

Once again (cf. Poems 70 and 72) C.'s mistress is all promises of lasting love, but her promises are received by C. with doubts and reservations, if not with bitter irony. Contrast Poem 107.

1–2. Instead of the vague assurances of Poems 70 and 72 we have a specific proposal: their love is to be mutual (*nostrum inter nos*) and lasting (*perpetuum*). The words *iucundum . . . amorem hunc nostrum inter nos perpetuumque fore* are usually regarded as accusative + infinitive dependent on *proponis*. But *iucundum*, though a word C. is fond of, sounds odd on Lesbia's lips in this context, and rather an inadequate partner for *perpetuum*. Perhaps we should take *iucundum . . . amorem* as the direct object of *proponis* (*iucundum* then expressing C.'s—ironic—appraisal, not hers) and *hunc nostrum inter nos* as an appositional expansion (cf. Metellus to Cicero, *Fam.* 5. 1. 1 *pro mutuo inter nos animo*) and *perpetuumque fore* as a further expansion ('and it will last for ever, you say'); *propono* + accusative and infinitive commonly has a preparatory direct object; cf. Cicero, *de Orat.* 2. 33 *nunc hoc propono, quod mihi persuasi, nihil esse perfecto oratore praeclarius.*

1. *mea uita*: see on 104. 1.

3–4. An outburst expressed as a prayer; *di magni* very much, therefore, as in 14. 12 and 53. 5. The couplet catches up the promise implicit in *perpetuumque fore*, to hammer at the idea 'if only she could mean what she says!': note the repetition *uere . . . sincere . . . ex animo*; nor is *possit* otiose—C. suspects his mistress is incapable of a serious promise. Cf. the piling up of synonyms in 63. 45–7. With *uere promittere possit* cf., 87. 1–2 *potest . . . dicere . . . uere.*

5–6. The second *ut* is better regarded as consecutive: C. now spells out (*tota uita . . . perducere . . . aeternum*) what *perpetuum* (used, he suspects, by Lesbia as a vague assurance) would have to mean. Cf. 63. 90 *semper omne uitae spatium.*

5. *nobis*: plural, as in 2 *nostrum inter nos.*

tota . . . uita: =*per totam uitam*; the ablative is occasionally found instead of the accusative, even in Classical Latin, in expressions involving *totus.*

6. *aeternum hoc sanctae foedus amicitiae*: The words make explicit

what is implicit in Lesbia's promise (*hoc . . . foedus* = 'the pact you are proposing'): they express an ideal which C. doubts his mistress's ability to live up to, rather than C.'s concept of anything that exists, or has existed, between them. Contrast 87. 3–4 *nulla fides ullo fuit umquam foedere tanta,* | *quanta in amore tuo ex parte reperta mea est.* For *foedus,* see on 76. 3. For *amicitia,* 'affection', see on 96. 4.

See:

F. O. Copley, 'Emotional conflict and its significance in the Lesbia-poems of Catullus', *AJPh* 70 (1949), 24–6.

Gordon Williams, 'Some Aspects of Roman marriage ceremonies and ideals', *JRS* 48 (1958), 25.

Cat. Rev. 81.

Critical Essays 48–9.

110

Aufillena, like Silo, the *leno* of Poem 103, does not stick to a bargain, which arouses C.'s indignation. We first meet Aufillena as the girl-friend of Quintius in Poem 100; she makes a last appearance in Poem 111.

1. *bonae*: 'obliging', 'co-operative'; cf. 89. 1 *tam bona mater.*

2. *pretium quae facere instituunt*: = *pretium eorum quae facere instituunt*; *quae* is accusative plural. Omission of an antecedent in a case other than the nominative or accusative, though rare in Classical Latin, is not uncommon in Plautus, e.g. *Curc.* 581 *ego illam reddidi qui argentum a te attulit* (= *ei qui*).

instituunt: 'undertake' (*L & S* II E).

3–4. The three *quod*'s read rather awkwardly; it seems best to take the first and the last as causal, the second as a relative pronoun, object of *mentita . . . es*: 'you do me wrong, in making a promise, which you have broken—no way for a girl-friend to act —and in repeatedly collecting but never giving'.

3. *promisti*: = *promisisti*; see on 14. 14 *misti.*

4. *nec das et fers*: [*nec das nec fers* V; *et* Guarino.]

5. *ingenuae*: i.e., a girl-friend who is not a *meretrix* should keep a bargain—or not make it.

6. *data*: accusative plural.

7. *fraudando officiis*: 'by withholding your services'; the instrumental notion can be felt to follow loosely out of *data corripere*: Aufillena, i.e., reaps a harvest by cheating; if she didn't cheat, she'd rake in less. [*efficit* V; the text is far from certain—*officiis* is Bergk's conjecture.]

plus quam meretricis: *plus quam* ('something worse than') does not affect the construction of *meretricis auarae*.

est: [Added by Calfurnio.]

8. *toto corpore*: = 'with no holds barred'; an improvement on such expressions as *corpore quaestum facere*.

III

To Aufillena, a final insult: to the accusation of not delivering the goods though she collected the fee (Poem 110) is now added the charge of incestuous relations with an uncle. We seem to be a far cry from the Aufillena to whom Quintius paid court in Poem 100. It is tempting to link her exploits here with those of uncle Gallus in Poem 78 and/or those of nephew Gellius in Poems 74, 88 and 89.

1–2. It was the Roman matron's ideal to live and die *uniuira*; see on 72. 1–2.

3–4. Possibly *quamuis* = *quantum uis* (cf. 24. 9 *quam lubet*); but better, probably, to take *quamuis* as feminine singular: 'but it's fair enough for any girl to go to bed with anyone at all, so long as a mother draws the line at getting cousins via an uncle'.

4. *fratres*: i.e., *fratres patrueles*, 'cousins'.

Three syllables are missing, either before or after *ex patruo*
See:
A. C. Bush, *CW* 65 (1972) 148–51.
W. de Grummond, *CW* 64 (1970) 120–1.

112

Apparently a pun on two (or more) meanings of *multus*. Naso is unknown.

1. *multus homo es*: Perhaps 'you're an eager beaver'; cf. Cicero's definition of the bore, *de Orat.* 2. 17 *qui aut tempus quid postulet non uidet aut plura loquitur aut se ostentat aut eorum quibuscum est uel dignitatis uel commodi rationem non habet, aut denique in aliquo genere aut inconcinnus aut multus est, is ineptus esse dicitur*; ibid. 358 *ne in re nota et peruolgata multus et insolens sim*. This sense goes well with 2 *descendit*. But 2 *multus es et pathicus* seems to require the sense 'you're a lot of man' (i.e. a large man), which is perhaps equally present, at any rate while the pattern of meanings is falling into shape: cf. Ovid, *Am.* 2. 4. 34 *potes in toto multa iacere toro*.

neque . . . multus homo est qui: 'but there's not a lot of men who . . .'; apparently this time the high-style use of the singular of *multus* in place of the plural; cf. e.g. Lucan 3. 707–8 *multus sua uolnera puppi | adfixit moriens*. [The line is a syllable short in the MSS; *est qui* Scaliger.]

2. *descendit*: Probably 'goes to the Forum'; cf. Cicero, *Phil.* 2. 15 *hodie non descendit Antonius*. But the possibility of obscene overtones (drawn out by the second half of the line) cannot be ruled out.

multus es et pathicus: perhaps 'you're a lot of man—and a queer', or perhaps simply 'you're an eager beaver and a queer'. For *pathicus*, see on 16. 2.

See:
H. A. Kahn, *Hommages Marcel Renard* (1969) i 3–11.

113

Fifteen years separate the first and second consulships of Pompey; so that, in addition to the mock-solemnity achieved by using the official formula for dating events, the hint is dextrously, because obliquely, conveyed that Maecilia is past her prime. The original *ménage à trois* has survived, but Maecilia has widened the circle of her activities considerably. Looked at through C.'s eyes, the facts (or C.'s inflation of them) acquire a sublime absurdity: two such faithful lovers, so wholly unfaithful a mistress.

Maecilia is unidentifiable; likewise, therefore, her two unnamed lovers. If the name were not old and well-attested, the temptation would be strong to accept Pleitner's *Mucillam* — a diminutive of Mucia, the name of the third wife of Pompey, whom he married about 80 B.C. and divorced in 62 on returning from the East, alleging an affair with Caesar: we might then be tempted to identify the *duo* of lines 1 and 3 as Pompey and Caesar, though Caesar had been out of Rome, of course, since early in 58 B.C. while these lines cannot be earlier than the consular elections for 55. See Poem 29.

1. *consule Pompeio primum*: 'in Pompey's first consulship', the usual formula. Pompey's first consulship was in 70 B.C., his second in 55; his colleague each time was Crassus.

solebant: An appropriate infinitive is left to the imagination — no doubt a colloquialism (cf. Horace, *Ep.* 12. 15 *Inachiam ter nocte potes*). But the emphasis falls on the tense and sense of *solebant*: already fifteen years ago the situation was well established.

2. *facto consule nunc iterum*: the turn of phrase implies Pompey had not yet entered on his second term; the date of these lines is presumably early in 55 B.C., therefore — the consular elections were held late, in January 55 B.C.

3. *manserunt duo*: Note that *duo* is emphasized each time by its position in the line — before a bucolic diaeresis in line 1, before a break at the end of the second foot in line 3 (permitted when accompanied by a 2nd-foot caesura). To assume that C. means anything other than that the original two have remained weakens the irony and neglects the tense-contrast *solebant . . . manserunt* (true perfect).

3–4. *creuerunt milia in unum | singula*: i.e., each veteran lover has now to contend with a host of younger men. For the sense of *creuerunt* ('grown to manhood') cf. Horace, *Carm.* 2. 8. 17–18 *adde quod pubes tibi crescit omnis, | seruitus crescit noua*; *Carm.* 4. 4. 46

Romana pubes creuit; *in*, not uncommon in distributive expressions
(e.g., Livy 9. 41. 7 *binae tunicae in militem exactae*), here expands
creuerunt with the meaning 'against', 'as opponents of', as in
Horace, *Carm.* 4. 4. 61–2 *non Hydra secto corpore firmior* / *uinci dolen-*
tem creuit in Herculem; at the same time the words *milia in unum*
singula (= *milia in utrumque singula*) form a single phrase, 'a thous-
and against each'.

4. *fecundum semen adulterio*: An outrageous mock-proverb, to
sum up the situation and clinch the epigram. The phrase sug-
gests a whole range of new meanings for *creuerunt* and *semen*: if some
of the combinations are wildly improbable, that is part of the fun.

See:

H. A. Kahn, *Hommages Marcel Renard* (1969) i 3–11.

114

For Mentula (= Mamurra) see on Poem 94. A description of his
estate at Firmum.

1. *Firmano saltu*: [The Aldine editor's correction of *firmanus*
saluis; some print *Firmanus saltus*, making Mentula the addressee
of the epigram.] Firmum, now Fermo, is south of Ancona, on the
Adriatic.

1–2. *non falso . . . diues* / *fertur*: 'is rightly reckoned rich'.

3. *aucupium omne genus*: 'fowl of all description'; with the
accusative *omne genus* cf. *hoc genus* and *id genus*.

prata, arua: 'pastures, arable land'.

4. = 'but it's no good: he always spends more than the estate
brings in'; *fructus* is accusative plural. For Mamurra's capacity for
spending money see 29. 13–22.

5. 'And so I don't mind his being rich, so long as he's short of
everything'.

6. 'Let's praise the estate, so long as the owner is broke'.

modo: For a final vowel shortened in hiatus see on 10. 27.
[As the final o of adverbial *modo* is normally short anyway, the
hiatus here is suspect; Lenchantin's *dum modo et ipse egeat* is as good
as any of the repairs suggested.]

ipse: 'the owner'; see on 2. 9 *ipsa*; cf. 115. 7.

See:

H. A. Kahn, *Hommages Marcel Renard* (1969) i 3–11.

115

For Mentula (= Mamurra) see on Poem 94. As in Poem 114, the subject is his estate at Firmum.

1. *habet*: the second syllable must count as long ('lengthening in arsis', cf. 62. 4, 64. 20, 66. 11), if the text is sound (some suspect *instar*).

instar: 'approximately' (*L & S* I B 2); normally followed by the genitive; *triginta* is of course indeclinable (cf. Cicero, *Att.* 16. 5. 5 *mearum epistularum nulla est synagoge, sed habet Tiro instar septua-ginta*); we should expect *iugerum*, however, not *iugera*, but apparently *instar* is to be taken only with the numeral, *iugera* being accusative after *habet* — a rare construction (editors quote Columella 4. 8. 2 and 12. 28. 1), perhaps necessitated by the following genitives *prati* and *arui*.

1–2. *triginta iugera prati, quadraginta arui*: = '20 acres of pasture land, 27 of arable land'; not much of course.

2. *maria*: i.e., probably, 'swamp'; cf. 5 *paludes*.

3. *potis*: for the form see on 65. 3.

5. *altasque paludes*: [*saltusque paludesque* V, which requires an awkward repetition of 4 *saltu* (where the meaning was 'estate', whereas here only the meaning 'glades' will work) and a hyper-metric *-que*, an artifice of high style (cf. 64. 298) which may have crept in here after the corruption of *altas* to *saltus*; *altasque paludes* is an old conjecture revived by Fordyce.]

7. *ipsest*: *ipse* = 'the owner', as in 114. 6.

ultro: 'actually'.

8. *non homo, sed*: idiomatic; cf. Cicero, *Att.* 7. 13a. 2 *non hominem sed scopas solutas*. The final syllable of *homo* is short ('iambic shortening'); see on 6. 16.

sed uero: 'but in truth'.

See:

H. A. Kahn, *Hommages Marcel Renard* (1969) i 3–11.

116

Poem 116 informs us, rather to our surprise, that C. had once hoped to patch up his quarrel with Gellius (the monster of incest, the man who thought it fun to steal C.'s mistress from him) by sending him some poems of Callimachus, but now sees it was a waste of time; well, Gellius will smart for his attacks upon C. Despite its position at the end of our texts of C., the traces of archaism (see on 3 *qui*, 8 *dabi'*), the metrically clumsy line 3, and a general stylistic gaucheness suggest early work: is Poem 116 a prelude to the savage attacks in Poems 74 and 88–91, rather than a last word?

For Gellius, see on Poem 74.

1. *tibi*: With the dative (instead of the more normal *ad te*) cf. 14. 7 *tantum tibi misit impiorum*, and 65. 15–16 *mitto tibi carmina Battiadae*; see also on 68. 1 *mihi*.

studioso animo uenante requirens: If right, 'casting around with my eager (or studious) mind hunting about'; an oddly artificial turn of phrase; unlikely, however, that *studioso* should be taken as dative with *tibi*.

2. Presumably a translation of Callimachus, as in 65. 15–16 *mitto | haec expressa tibi carmina Battiadae*; cf. 68. 149–50 *hoc tibi, quod potui, confectum carmine munus | redditur*.

3. *qui*: =*ut*; the old instrumental form, common in final clauses in Plautus.

nobis: presumably =*mihi*; cf. 6 *nostras*.

conarere: The only entirely spondaic hexameter outside Ennius; only two other 5th-foot spondees in Poems 69–116 (76. 15 and 100. 1); see on 64. 3.

4. A patched-up line. [*telis* V; *tela* Muret, who also added *meum*.]
mittere: 'hurl'; *L & S* II K.

in usque caput: cf. 4. 24 *hunc ad usque limpidum lacum*.

5. *mihi*: dative of agent.
nunc: with *uideo*.

6. *Gelli*: The name of the addressee is not normally delayed beyond the second line, and is often the opening word of the poem.

nostras: presumably =*meas*; cf. 3 *nobis*.

7. Another patched-up line. Baehrens's *acta* provides the neatest repair. [*euitabimus amitha* V, which is meaningless; many read *euitamus amictu*, 'parry with my clothing'; *contra* has then to be taken as adverbial and *nos* as nominative.]

contra nos: with *acta*.

8. *nostris*: i.e. *telis*.

dabi': =*dabis*; the dropped final s (common in the older Latin poets) occurs only here and (probably) in 44. 8 (a poem containing several archaic touches) in C.

Index

The following examples show the system which has been adopted.

10. 2 = See Commentary on Poem 10, line 2.
I 35 = See introductory note on Poem 35.
P 41 = The person etc. named in this entry figures prominently in Poem 41.
T 58. 3 = See the Latin text of Poem 58 at line 3.

Where a topic is fully cross-referenced in a Commentary main entry, the Index normally refers only to this entry.

Metrical and syntactical points are gathered under 'Metre' and 'Syntax'.

457